Vernon Blackwood

A History of the Western Educational Experience

A History of the Western Educational Experience

Gerald L. Gutek

Loyola University

For information about this book, write or call:

Waveland Press, Inc.
P.O. Box 400
Prospect Heights, Illinois 60070
(312) 634-0081

To
Jennifer Ann
my daughter

Preface

My work on this book has reaffirmed my belief that the history of education is a valuable cultural and professional component in teacher preparation. As the prospectus for the book grew into a manuscript, I renewed my commitment to work for humanistic interpretations of our educational experience. I believe that history, philosophy, literature, politics, and even poetry are as relevant to the educational profession as are mechanical innovations, empirical investigation, and lists of behavioral objectives. The educational historian is true to his discipline when he uses the historical method to illuminate the past and to find therein educational alternatives for the present.

The writing of this book was a long, often fatiguing, but rewarding labor. The preparation of the manuscript was facilitated by assistance from many individuals. The training in the historical method that I received from Professor J. Leonard Bates and Professor Norman Graebner has always helped me in my research. Lawrence McCaffrey's lectures on the history of Western civilization helped me to establish some of the interpretations that can be found in the book.

I was fortunate to have been a student of such dedicated educators as Harry S. Broudy, William O. Stanley, and Joe R. Burnett of the Department of History and Philosophy of Education at the University of Illinois. The memory of my adviser, the late Archibald W. Anderson, has continued to provide me with a model of the exemplary historian of education.

I am also grateful for the interest and support given by John Wozniak, Dean of Loyola University's School of Education, and by my colleagues in the Department of Foundations of Education. A grant from the Research Committee of Loyola University assisted in the early stages of research. My graduate students in the Foundations of Education have always been a source of stimulation.

I wish to express my appreciation to Robert Weiss, who encouraged my work, and to David Bartlett, my editor at Random House, for his continued interest in the book's progress. Paul Nash's comments and suggestions were valuable in helping me to gain perspective into my own writing and into the problems of historical interpretation.

I am grateful to Beatrice Van Cleave who patiently typed the manuscript.

Most of all, I am grateful to my wife, Patricia, who has always created an atmosphere that is conducive to my work. Her understanding helped me to write, especially during days of difficulty.

GERALD LEE GUTEK

Preface, 1987

I am very pleased that Waveland Press is making *A History of the Western Educational Experience* available once again. The book, a product of my teaching of the history of education at Loyola University of Chicago, should be useful to students in teacher education, educational policies, and foundations of education programs as well as to those in the history of education. My general perspective is that educational history is an integral part of the broad sweep of the major historical movements that have shaped western civilization. Each significant epoch such as Graeco-Roman classicalism, Medieval scholasticism, Renaissance humanism, Christian reformation and counter-reformation and the Enlightenment have contributed significant cultural dimensions to our continuing educational experience.

The book also reveals my emphasis on the roles that key persons have exercised in contributing to and shaping our educational experience. The biographies of theorists such as Plato, Quintilian, Aquinas, Comenius, Pestalozzi, Froebel, Spencer and others are used to illustrate the development of educational thought and practice. These biographical sections illustrate the educator's role in being an agent of cultural continuity or change.

The book rests on the premise that the history of education should illuminate the past in order to provide the required perspective in time and place that we need to make reflective decisions on the educational choices that face us today. With the exception of being guided by this premise, I have resisted the framing of large sweeping ideological generalizations that often torture historical evidence to fit preconceived patterns. The generalizations in the book are limited ones that arise from their cultural and historical contexts. To me, these generalizations are part of a continuing dialogue between the educators of the past and those of the present. I hope that the readers of *A History of the Western Educational Experience* will join in that dialogue.

Gerald Lee Gutek
Loyola University of Chicago
April 1987

Contents

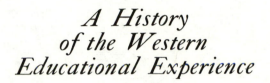

A History
of the Western
Educational Experience

CHAPTER 1

An Overview and Perspective

My purpose in writing this first chapter is to indicate to the reader my conception of the history of education and to provide an overview into the book's pattern of organization. In the past, some historians of education have sought to explain historical events by weaving very large and often unwieldy generalizations. At times, the interpretation of historical events became a rather tortured attempt to follow pre-conceived patterns and to prove preconceived theses. In contrast, this book relies on the use of limited generalizations derived from the context of particular historical situations. Although sweeping generalizations have been studiously avoided, I believe it possible to identify and to explore threads of historical continuity within the context of the Western educational experience. In addition to relying on the use of the limited historical generalization, this book will also seek to avoid two other trends that have frequently accompanied the writing of educational history: (1) equating schooling and education as synonymous terms; (2) analyzing education solely from the context of a pragmatist-progressive point of view.

Early historians of education in the United States, such as Ellwood P. Cubberley and Paul Monroe, had distinguished careers as professional educators and administrators before turning to historical writing.[1] These early writers regarded history as a means of inspiring prospective teachers and introducing them to their professions. Their uncritical blending of moral preachment and inspirational homily with historical data often produced a propagandistic treatment of the rise of the American public school system and the development of the

[1] Representative historical writings of the early American educational historians that deal with Western educational history are Ellwood P. Cubberley, *The History of Education: Educational Practice and Progress Considered as a Phase of the Development and Spread of Western Civilization* (Boston: Houghton Mifflin, 1920), and Paul Monroe, *A Brief Course in the History of Education* (New York: Macmillan, 1934).

3

American educational ladder. These accounts often glossed over the weaknesses of the system and ignored the socioeconomic forces that impeded the realization of genuine equality of educational opportunity.

Moreover, these early historians of education generally had a restricted conception of their field that limited the history of education to an analysis of the formal aspects of schooling. They wrote solid accounts of the rise of the school, of instructional methods, and of teacher preparation. But although the history of the school is certainly a necessary part of the history of education, it is only one aspect of it. These writers unfortunately neglected the broader context of informal, or milieu, education, which acquired more sophisticated and extensive forms in the mass societies of both the democratic and totalitarian nations of the modern world. This same limited conception of educational historiography could also be found in many of the early histories of Western education that appeared in the United States.

In the 1960s, American educational historians reacted strongly against this "Cubberley approach" to educational historiography.[2] They reexamined the state of their discipline under the stimulus of what was referred to as the "Bailyn thesis." Bernard Bailyn, an American historian, had commented that the development of American educational historiography had taken place:

> . . . in a special atmosphere of professional purpose. It grew in almost total isolation from the major influences and shaping minds of twentieth-century historiography; and its isolation proved to be self-intensifying: the more parochial the subject became, the less capable it was of attracting the kinds of scholars who could give it broad relevance and bring it back into the public domain. It soon displayed the exaggeration of weakness and extravagance of emphasis that are the typical results of sustained inbreeding.[3]

Although Bailyn's criticism of the state of educational historiography stimulated a searching examination of the discipline, he was not the first to have urged a broadened context for the writing of educational history. Archibald W. Anderson, William E. Drake, Adolphe E. Meyer, Robert Ulich, R. Freeman Butts, Lawrence Cremin, Carl Gross, and a number of other historians of education had been working to enlarge the scope of educational history to include an examination of the sociocultural context of education. It was the sustained efforts of this group of educational historians and Bailyn's telling comments that stimulated a new wave of scholarship in the history of education.

[2] For a critical examination of the Cubberley interpretation of the rise of American education, see Lawrence A. Cremin, *The Wonderful World of Ellwood Paterson Cubberley: An Essay on the Historiography of American Education* (New York: Teachers College, Columbia University, 1965).

[3] Bernard Bailyn, *Education in the Forming of American Society* (New York: Vintage Books, 1960), pp. 8–9.

Educational historians enlarged the scope of their researches to include broadened perspectives into the social, political, economic, religious, and intellectual context in which educational developments occurred.

While sharing the view of many of my colleagues that the history of educational institutions should be written within its broad cultural context, I still am indebted to Cubberley and Monroe for their belief that the history of education is not only desirable but indispensable in the professional preparation of teachers. The acceptance of the view that educational history encompasses more than the accounts of the development of formal schooling should not detract from the work of the early historians of education, which remains a valuable contribution to both general and professional literature.

American professional educators have labored under the misconception that the development of American education was a unique experience that was isolated from events occurring elsewhere in the world. It was not only Cubberley and Monroe who may have contributed to this view. Individuals associated with philosophical pragmatism and educational progressivism often subscribed to a form of cultural relativism that asserted that education was always unique to a particular cultural situation at a given time and place. This stress on cultural relativism de-emphasized transcultural and transnational commonalities and emphasized unique and particular aspects of cultural and educational development. Thus, both the older history of education and the newer progressive conception exalted the development of American educational institutions as a unique phenomenon. Not only educators but many historians, influenced by Frederick Jackson Turner's frontier thesis, supported this view of American institutional development.

The history of Western education clearly reveals, however, that American educational developments were not isolated culturally from events occurring elsewhere.[4] There was a continuous interaction between American and European educators from the first days of colonial settlement. Franklin and Jefferson shared the general orientation of the Enlightenment's concepts of science and progress. A score of American educators visited Europe and returned with ideas of European educational developments. This was especially true in the nineteenth century, when Horace Mann and Henry Barnard visited Pestalozzian and Prussian schools. During the same era, William Mac-

---

[4] Paul Nash (ed.), *History and Education: The Educational Uses of the Past* (New York: Random House, 1970), brings together a collection of essays on various aspects of recent educational historiography that examine the relevance of the history of education to teacher preparation. The essays, written by leading American and English educational historians, seek to overcome the older forms of cultural isolation that limited the scope of educational history on both sides of the Atlantic.

lure introduced Pestalozzian educational ideas and teachers into the United States. The English utopian socialist Robert Owen conducted a communitarian experiment at New Harmony, Indiana, which was designed to be the prototype of a new society in the United States. Although Maclure and Owen failed to achieve their major goals, their social and educational activities were part of a transatlantic sequence of events.

The major intellectual, political, and social movements that swept Europe also had an impact on the United States. Liberalism, conservatism, and socialism influenced both European and American educational developments. The years of the American common school crusade, the late 1830s, 1840s, and 1850s, also saw the creation of state and national systems in many of the European nations. What Arthur M. Schlesinger, Jr., called the "Age of Jackson" was part of a larger movement of political ascendency.[5] Although liberals acted with varying degrees of enthusiasm on matters of school establishment and educational expenditure, the various liberal parties in both Europe and the United States did generally extend the possibilities of greater popular education. This is not to deny, however, that the American common school developed in a particular environmental and historical context that had the effect of distinguishing it from its European counterparts.

American secondary and higher education was also influenced by the educational traditions of the Middle Ages, the Renaissance, and the Reformation. Like their European counterparts, the American Latin grammar schools and academies were selective institutions designed to prepare youth for higher education. Even the high school of the late nineteenth and early twentieth centuries continued to perform a selective function by preparing youth for college admission. The colleges and universities of both Europe and the United States evolved from the foundations that had been established in the medieval universities of the twelfth and thirteenth centuries. In the nineteenth century, the concentration on specialized scholarship and scientific research in the German universities was imitated in American higher education.

Charles Darwin's theory of evolution exerted a profound influence on both European and American intellectual outlooks. Traditional conceptions of man's origin on this planet were questioned. The social Darwinism of men like Herbert Spencer influenced American and European social, political, and educational development. Darwinism exerted a shaping influence and stimulated the stream of "reformed Darwinism" in the United States. It was this variety of reformed Dar-

---

[5] Arthur M. Schlesinger, Jr., *The Age of Jackson* (New York: Little, Brown, 1945).

winism that came to influence John Dewey, William Kilpatrick, George Counts, and other advocates of the "new education."

The preceding recital of events recounts only a few of the educational ideas and movements that were in constant interchange between Europe and the United States. An understanding of this interchange should be useful to the professional educator by providing a perspective into the forces of educational continuity and change that were at work throughout the Western world.

History of Education and Teacher Preparation

One of the shibboleths that has been hurled back and forth in various educational controversies has been that of "relevance" or more accurately "irrelevance." The charge of irrelevance has been used as an all-embracing term to attack those positions opposed to one's particular world view, personal philosophy, or brand of political ideology. The demand for relevance in education is not a new one. It was the initial impetus to many educational reforms in the past and remains a meaningful plea of many today. Unfortunately, some have naively used relevance as a slogan to justify unexamined whims. A few have made the demand for relevance into a new dogmatic absolute that is used to destroy alternative positions and possibilities that may challenge their own particular point of view.

The charge that certain aspects of human experience or that certain learned disciplines are educationally irrelevant has contributed to an anti-historical attitude that denigrates the past. The history of education, in particular, has been challenged as being irrelevant to the task of teacher preparation. Since I disagree with this view, some explanation of the role of educational history is needed. The dictionary defines relevant as bearing upon the matter at hand or implying a traceable and significant connection or appropriateness to a situation. In this light, the history of education is not only appropriate but necessary to the professional preparation of teachers. The criteria for judging the relevance or irrelevance of a particular subject, person, idea, or practice are relative to the experience of the person who develops the criteria. One who has had only limited or parochial experiences will necessarily hold restricted criteria of relevance and will find more things to be irrelevant. On the other hand, if his experience is broadened and heightened, then the scope of relevance will be enriched to include more possibilities of human experience and enable him to frame more alternatives of action. If education is truly liberating and genuinely makes men free, then it must provide a variety of alternatives of action so that each man can make choices about his life and destiny. If professional education is to prepare teachers who can explore and critically examine alternative educational theories and practices, then it must deliberately seek to expand the possibilities for personal and professional action. The history of education can contribute to strengthening both the personal and professional competence of the teacher by encouraging him or her: (1) to examine, evaluate, accept, reject, or modify the cultural inheritance; (2) to become an educational critic and an agent of responsible cultural transmission and change rather than to blindly accept either the status quo or unchallenged claims for panacea-like innovation.

By studying the motivations and behavior of other human beings who were caught up in the social, economic, religious, moral, and educational aspects of concrete historical situations, the educator can discern the various choices that were instrumental in shaping human purposes in the past. He can also discern the successes or miscarriages of these purposes. Through a critical examination of past action, the educator can illuminate the possibilities and alternatives of decision-making in the present. In other words, an examination of educational theories and practices in their historical context may encourage teachers to take a critical look at contemporary theories and practices.

Believing that the intelligent study of educational history can affect the conduct of the teacher's personal and professional activities, the educational historian Paul Nash holds that the study of the past has crucial relevance in improving the quality of present action. In examining the need for balance between scholarly detachment and relevance on the part of the educational historian, Nash has also provided a useful perspective for the educator who seeks to use the past as a professional instrument:

> Unless the historian of education meets the demands of the criterion of detachment, his work will lack power because of its vulnerability to distortion. But unless he meets the equally stringent demands of the criterion of relevance, his work will lack power because it will be ignored by those through whose lives and work its implications could be manifested. Thus he must work in the light of a threefold demand: he must be past-minded (in being able to see with the eyes of people in the past); he must be present-concerned (in speaking to real issues of his day); and he must be future-oriented (in being alive to the probable consequences of his work).[6]

As one who is engaged in preparing teachers in the foundations of education, I am concerned about what appears to be an overemphasis on the empirical and statistical aspects of teacher education. To be sure, statistical and empirical techniques are necessary and useful instruments for the teacher. However, the humanistic purposes of edu-

---

[6] Paul Nash, "History and Education: The Dialectics of Enquiry," in Nash (ed.), *History and Education, op. cit.*, p. 15.

cation must receive renewed emphasis and not be forgotten in the rush to develop new empirical or behavioral techniques and mechanical innovations. Even some of those who are devotees of the "new history of education" have sacrificed the humanistic moorings of their discipline in the race to develop scientific, empirical, statistical, and behaviorialistic bases for the history of education. While the processes of measurement and quantification are useful in checking tendencies to exaggerate or to overgeneralize, they can also be exaggerated themselves when they are used as ends rather than as instruments of research. When this occurs, the broad theoretical and humanistic possibilities of the history of education are neglected. I believe that philosophy, political theory, theology, literature, and art are the sources from which are derived the purposes of education.[7] When these sources are used to their fullest, then professional education receives the benefits of a heightened perspective into its humanistic foundations.

The history of education properly includes the description, elaboration, and analysis of both the formal and informal aspects of education. The informal aspects refer to the total cultural context in which persons are born, nurtured, and brought to maturity. Through the process of enculturation, they acquire the symbolic, linguistic, and value patterns of their culture. The informal educational agencies of the family, church, media, state, and peer group introduce the immature person to the roles that are accepted in his particular society. Included in informal, or *milieu*, education are the philosophical, intellectual, theological, political, aesthetic, and economic patterns that constitute the cultural experience of a given people. By living in a society, within a given culture, the person acquires these patterns to some degree of competency.

The history of education should properly include definitions, descriptions, and interpretations of the formal aspects of education as found in institutional form, in the school. Educational institutions of varying degrees of refinement are the agencies that societies establish for the specific purpose of transmitting skills, knowledge, and values. Although the informal agencies previously mentioned also introduce the immature to their cultural heritage, the school was specifically created to do so. Those who staff schools or are otherwise entrusted with formal education seek to develop ways of performing their special function.

Education, in both the broad and formal senses of the term, is also related to the major intellectual, social, political, economic, and theological movements that were significant forces in the Western experience. For example, medieval scholasticism was firmly grounded in both

[7] An example of the humanistic orientation to the history of education is Maxine Greene's, *The Public School and the Private Vision: A Search for America in Education and Literature* (New York: Random House, 1967).

Aristotelian logic and Christian theology. Although based on classical scholarship, Renaissance humanism, as expressed by da Feltre and Erasmus, was an intellectual force that anticipated the coming of the modern area. In the eighteenth century, the rationalistic philosophies of the Enlightenment introduced the ideas of science, natural rights, and progress, which came to exercise a profound scientific, political, and educational impact. The nineteenth-century romantic reaction to the Age of Reason reasserted the mystical and the aesthetic modes of life and expression. The educational theories of Rousseau and Pestalozzi curiously blended both these rational and romantic impulses. Each of these movements added ideas, modes of inquiry, and patterns of values to the Western conception of life and education. The history of education can function as a humanistic discipline that illuminates the contributions made by these various significant movements that shaped the Western heritage.

In the nineteenth and twentieth centuries, in particular, the modern ideologies of conservatism, liberalism, socialism, Marxism, social Darwinism, and nationalism became the bases of political parties and programs. Each of these modern ideologies had particular educational consequences. The various conservative, liberal, or socialist parties of the Western nations either advanced or retarded the extension of programs of popular or mass education.

In the modern era, the force of nationalism cutting across the neat ideological lines of political theory swept the Western world. School systems became national systems and expressed national sentiments and loyalties. At times, the impact of nationalism reduced both formal and informal education to a kind of strident chauvinistic indoctrination. Once the fires of nationalism were kindled by press, school, publicist, and teacher, they soon got out of control. In World War I, the intensity of nationalism had reached such a point that the diplomats and politicians could no longer control the force that they had created as a political weapon. It was World War I that radically transformed the course of Western civilization and paved the way for the rise of the modern totalitarian states, Nazi Germany and Soviet Russia.

Each major cultural period in the Western experience can be characterized by an ideal type who might be considered that era's concept of the educated man.[8] It is he who personifies the values of the society,

---

[8] Works that have analyzed the various models found in the Western educational experience are Harry S. Broudy and John R. Palmer, *Exemplars of Teaching Method* (Chicago: Rand McNally, 1965); Paul Nash, Andreas Kazamias, and Henry Perkinson (eds.), *The Educated Man: Studies in the History of Educational Thought* (New York: Wiley, 1965). Selections from the writings of leading Western educational theorists are available in Paul Nash, *Models of Man: Explorations in the Western Educational Tradition* (New York: Wiley, 1968). A thorough historical analysis of leading educators can be found in Edward J. Power, *Evolution of Educational Doc-*

and his training reflects its needs. A study of educational history can therefore tell us much about the political, cultural, and economic currents that prevailed in a particular age. Among the models of the educated man in past eras are Homer's warrior, Plato's philosopher king, Isocrates' rhetorician, Aquinas' rational Christian, da Feltre's classical humanist gentleman, Erasmus' cosmopolitan Christian, Loyola's Catholic gentleman, Comenius' pansophist, Chernyshevsky's new man and woman, Spencer's rugged individual, Rousseau's natural man, Hitler's Nazi, Lenin's dedicated Communist, and many others. Such a study of the past conceptions of the educated man can put present educational trends into clearer perspective and even offer alternatives to them.

History is also an account of man's transitions from one stage of development to another as well as the elements of cultural stability or continuity. The rate of change may vary. Usually, man's material world changes more rapidly than his social and intellectual outlook. The more rapid the rate of change the greater are the possibilities that the cultural elements that make up man's life will be in disarray. For example, the early stages of the Industrial Revolution, which introduced mass production techniques, made more products available to more people than ever before in history. Unfortunately, the same industrial processes caused psychic and social upheavals that debased man's dignity. The records of the Sadler Report in nineteenth-century England give clear evidence of the imbalance between material and social advances in the early stages of English industrialism.

Education is a process that attempts to ensure the cultural continuation of the group, race, or nation. As previously mentioned, it transmits skills, knowledge, modes of inquiry, and values from the mature to the immature, either informally through the milieu or formally through the school. In highly integrated cultures, the school's task is to transmit the dominant aspects of the cultural heritage by emphasis on cultural continuity. When cultural discontinuity occurs in times of rapid social change, formal education either grows increasingly formalized and remote from the realities of life or appears to be confused as new educational patterns compete for supremacy.

The history of Western education supplies a number of clear examples of the problems of education during periods of acute cultural transition. When Athenian life underwent rapid economic and social changes in the fifth century B.C., the sophists appeared with a new form of education. Plato also came forth, in opposition to the sophists, with his Republic designed to create a perfect social order in which change was unwanted and unneeded.

---

trine: Major Educational Theorists of the Western World (New York: Appleton-Century-Crofts, 1969).

Since the time of Plato, other social theorists have designed plans of education to fulfill the purposes of either conserving the old order of life or reconstructing society into new forms. The nineteenth-century English utopian Robert Owen gave a major role to education in bringing about the new moral society. Thomas Jefferson relied on republican education to prepare both intelligent leaders and followers. Napoleon, Hitler, Lenin, and Stalin politicized education to the point that it became a method of indoctrinating the young to accept and to advance the totalitarian regime's policies.

Conclusion

I view the history of Western education as a humanistic discipline that illuminates the development of both formal and informal educational agencies, movements, and trends. It is also an instrument for examining alternative conceptions of the educated man in a historical perspective. By examining the prevailing thought of an age, one can discover its patterns of education. Finally, I believe that the study of educational history is a worthwhile and valuable enterprise in its own right since it explains a part of the human experience.

Suggested Readings

Bailyn, Bernard. *Education in the Forming of American Society.* New York: Random House, 1960.

Barzun, Jacques, and Henry F. Graff. *The Modern Researcher.* New York: Harcourt Brace Jovanovich, 1957.

Brickman, William W. "Revisionism and the Study of the History of Education," *History of Education Quarterly,* IV, No. 4 (December 1964), 209–223.

Broudy, Harry S., and John R. Palmer. *Exemplars of Teaching Method.* Chicago: Rand McNally, 1965.

Cantor, Norman F., and Richard I. Schneider. *How to Study History.* New York: Thomas Y. Crowell, 1967.

Cremin, Lawrence A. *The Wonderful World of Ellwood Paterson Cubberley: An Essay on the Historiography of American Education.* New York: Teachers College, Columbia University, 1965.

Drake, William E. *Intellectual Foundations of Modern Education.* Columbus, Ohio: Charles E. Merrill Books, 1967.

Greene, Maxine. "The Professional Significance of History of Education," *History of Education Quarterly,* VII, No. 2 (Summer 1967), 182–190.

Krug, Mark M. *History and Social Sciences.* Waltham, Mass.: Blaisdell Publishing Co., 1967.

Nash, Paul. *History and Education: The Educational Uses of the Past.* New York: Random House, 1970.

————. "History of Education," *Review of Educational Research,* XXXIV, No. 1 (February 1964), 5–21.

————. *Models of Man: Explorations in the Western Educational Tradition.* New York: Wiley, 1968.

————, Andreas M. Kazamias, and Henry J. Perkinson (eds.). *The Educated Man: Studies in the History of Educational Thought.* New York: Wiley, 1965.

Power, Edward J. *Evolution of Educational Doctrine: Major Educational Theorists of the Western World.* New York: Appleton-Century-Crofts, 1969.

Simon, Brian. "The History of Education." In J. W. Tibble (ed.), *The Study of Education.* London: Routledge & Kegan Paul, 1966.

Smith, Wilson. "The New Historian of American Education," *Harvard Educational Review,* 31 (Spring 1961), 136–143.

CHAPTER 2

Greek Education

Historians of Western civilization and education frequently refer to ancient Greece with its city-states as the place of origin of Western culture. The Greek Aegean region, part of the larger Mediterranean world, exhibited great topographic and climatic diversities. The rough topography of the Peloponnesus and surrounding islands denied an easy agricultural living to the Greeks, who, surrounded by water, readily developed a brisk fishing and maritime trade. Until the Macedonian conquest, the Greeks were never united into one nation or empire but lived in small independent and sovereign city-states, or *poleis*. Most of these city-states possessed a fertile plain, upland pastures, forested mountain slopes, and high mountain summits. With its inhabitants variously pursuing agriculture, fishing, or seaborne commerce, the economically self-sufficient Greek city-states enjoyed a balanced communal life.

Greek fishing and trading vessels visited the islands and coastal areas of Asia Minor. The Ionian island chain, stretching from the Peloponnesus to the Turkish coast, bridged the older Oriental civilizations of Egypt and Persia with that of Greece. In contrast to the autocratic and hierarchical political structures of the Oriental empires, the citizens of the Greek city-states evolved a set of well-defined civil rights and responsibilities. While such Oriental cultures as that of Egypt were conservative, traditional, and static, the Greeks, especially the Athenians, emphasized the humane, the dynamic, and the rational modes of life. Basically humanistic in temperament, the Greeks concentrated on earthly achievements rather than life after death. Despite a basically humanistic world view, however, Greek culture bore some signs of Oriental influence. The Spartan caste system bore a slight resemblance to that of India. Athenian women lived in seclusion as did some of their Oriental counterparts. When it depicted the human form, archaic Greek sculpture tended to follow the rather stiff Egyptian stance.

Although Hellenic origins are obscure, Greek culture probably began at Knossos, first spreading to Crete and the Aegean islands, and then coming to the southern and central areas of the Peloponnesus. The Minoan civilization of Crete, flourishing from 2100 to 1400 B.C., and known for its creative builders, engineers, and artists, undoubtedly influenced Greek cultural development. It was the Mycenaeans, speaking an Indo-European language, who migrated to and dominated Greece from 1400 B.C. until the Dorian invasions of 1200 B.C. Mycenaean society was hierarchically organized, with landholding nobles at the top, warriors, courtiers, and merchants in the middle, and slaves at the bottom. By the thirteenth century, the legendary Agamemnon, leader of the famed expedition against Troy, was the acknowledged overlord of Mycenae. In the eighth century, the famous poet Homer recalled the Mycenaean siege of Troy in his epic work the *Iliad* and then told of Odysseus, or Ulysses, King of Ithaca, who wandered for a decade after the destruction of Troy before returning to his native land and his wife, Penelope.

Homeric Education: The Iliad and the Odyssey

Homer's *Iliad* and *Odyssey*, appearing about 850 B.C., were the first significant historical works in Greek culture. Recounting the early episodes of Greek history, the Homeric epics embodied the wisdom and crystallized the traditions, beliefs, and values that constituted the ancient Greek life style. Educationally, Homer's poems were instruments of enculturation which introduced the young Greek to the ethos, manners, and aspirations of his cultural group. Resembling the chivalric literature of the Middle Ages, the *Iliad* and *Odyssey* told the youth of his heroic ancestors. Through the songs and stories of this inspirational literature, the young boy became familiar with those heroic exemplars, or cultural models, after which he could pattern his own values. As significant poetical, aesthetic, historical, and pedagogical works, the *Iliad* and *Odyssey* told Greek generations of that moral climate in which heroes, by combining wisdom and action, sought and won glory.

Mycenaean society, as represented by Agamemnon's court, was headed by the king, who was surrounded by a council of elders and knights and presided over a chivalric culture dominated by an aristocracy of warriors. Within the milieu of soldierly camaraderie, Homer's knights served their king as warriors and orators. The dominant events in courtly life were athletic contests and the preparation and actual waging of war. The young man who successfully imitated the ideal of the Homeric hero, as exemplified by Agamemnon, Ulysses, and Achilles, was the knight who behaved courteously in court, spoke elegantly and poetically, performed the warrior's arts of hunting, riding, and fencing, and observed the required religious proprieties and rituals. The young Greek noble learned the warrior's role, skills, and ethics by participating in courtly life and by hearing literature rather than by attending formal educational institutions. By imitating heroic models, he was inducted into a life of courtesy, correct etiquette, and proper behavior.

The Homeric hero was moved by a sense of duty to himself, his friends, his king, and his gods. As he pursued *arete,* or excellence, through all the varieties of human experience, this hero was buffeted by obstacles put in his path by a seemingly capricious and irresponsible fate. Designed to test the mettle of man, these trials were overcome by the man of truly heroic dimensions. Homer's stories, the *Iliad* and *Odyssey*, were also ethical lessons. When Homer told of the clash of Agamemnon and Achilles over a slave girl, he developed the theme of personal argument between two friends within the broader context of the Trojan War. Internal bickering among their leaders jeopardized the Greek cause. Since this animosity threatened the well-being of their compatriots, Homer made the point that individuals were often required to sacrifice personal interests for the common good. Ulysses, as an example of the hero, personified the Homeric ethic by combining wisdom and action. Although motivated by the hero's quest for glory and honor, Ulysses was not foolhardy but exercised discretion and cunning to extricate himself from awkward and dangerous situations. Often by retreating at strategic times, Homer's heroes lived to fight another day.

Even after the passing of the Greek feudal age, the Homeric virtues, associated with an aristocratic fighting and ruling elite, continued to influence Greek cultural and educational developments. Foremost among Homer's values was the ethical principle that held that a man, to be truly human, was to participate fully in his *polis,* or community. Even when it became more formal and literary, Greek education was devoted to Homeric epic poetry, which portrayed life's heroic dimension and inculcated an ideal of glory.

Invasion and Colonization

From 1200 to 1050 B.C., the cultivated Greek kingdoms such as Mycenae were overrun by the more primitive Greek tribes, the Dorians, who entered the peninsula from the Balkans. The Dorian invasions ushered in the so-called "dark ages," which saw the fabled city-states of Homer's epics reduced to isolated and unprosperous petty states.

Although it took more than two centuries to recover from the Dorian invasions, the Greek city-states were prosperous enough, by 800 B.C., to begin to send forth colonizing expeditions. From 800 until 550 B.C., Greek colonists extended Hellenic culture throughout the Aegean, from the Peloponnesus to the Ionic Islands, to Sicily, and even to southern Italy. Spurred on by such varying motives as overpopulation, political and social unrest, and economic adventurism, colonization was a safety valve for the land-hungry Greeks. Although living space was often their first objective, the colonists soon developed prosperous commercial and trading centers. Greek colonies were not mere extensions or dependencies of the mother city but rather independent foundations which went their own political way. The period of colonization had two major effects on Greek civilization: (1) it led to conflict with Persia; (2) increased wealth and the rise of commercial classes produced significant social changes. For educational historians, the latter effect had greater consequence. The *nouveaux riches,* or rising commercial classes, acquired sufficient economic power to challenge the privileged political position of the older landed aristocrats. The first professional educators, the sophists, came into existence to satisfy the educational needs of these rising classes by preparing them for political leadership. The rise of the sophists and the Platonic reaction against them will be treated in Chapter 3.

In 550 B.C., the Persians conquered Ionia, one of the Greek colonies. Fifty years later the Ionian Greeks revolted against their Persian masters. In sympathy with the struggle of their Ionian kinsmen, the Greek city-states joined in temporary alliance against the Persians. In 490, Darius, the Persian emperor, sent a small expeditionary force to take punitive action against Athens, which had aided the Ionian rebels. The Athenian army defeated the Persian invaders at the Battle of Marathon. In 480, Darius' heir, Xerxes, assembled a large army and fleet to crush the Greeks. Again the Greeks combined against the Persian invaders. The Athenian navy defeated and destroyed the Persian fleet at Salamis in 480; the united Greek forces, led by the Spartans, crushed the Persian army at Plataea in 479 to end the Persian threat. Although they had succeeded against the common Persian enemy, the unity of the Greek city-states was only temporary. The Athenians organized an alliance of city-states, the Delian Confederation, which soon became the Athenian empire, and the Spartans organized a counterforce, the Peloponnesian League. Hostility between these rival alliances eventually led to open warfare and the weakening of Hellenic civilization. Before turning to an examination of the rival states, Athens and Sparta, certain common features of Greek civilization and education will be examined.

Greek Cultural Patterns

Greek religion was a polytheistic fusion of two kinds of religious experience, one relating to nature and the other to the social group. The Greeks deified external natural forces, such as climate and weather, and constructed an elaborate mythology to explain the universe. The various gods were not conceived of as remote supernatural beings but were rather superhuman projections of forces and objects in nature. Giving bent to their dramatic and plastic sense, the Greeks endowed their gods with human forms and inclinations. The Greek desire for unity and logic was exhibited in the creation of a theological Olympiad presided over by Zeus, the father of both gods and men.

The social element in Greek religion was as strong as the natural one. While doctrinal theology was minimized, formal rituals which integrated social and religious experiences were evident. Greek religious interpretations of sociological phenomena were decidedly humanistic and not based on the conception of a supernatural afterlife. The religious rituals, holidays, and festivals heightened and illuminated the events of political and social life. Everyday pursuits and occupations were regulated closely by the deities, who were believed to have jurisdiction over individual and group affairs. Religious mythology and ritual performed educational roles when the young Greek, through his participation in public festivals and ceremonies, was introduced to patterns of civic loyalties and responsibilities.

Performed at festivals and civic events, Greek drama combined civic splendor with religious ritual to touch the deepest centers of man's personal and corporate consciousness. The philosopher Aristotle asserted that tragedy effected a catharsis in the spectator by purging his emotions through pity and terror. Since dramatic performances were major public affairs, the tragedies were approved by a selection committee for performance at certain annual festivals. The acceptance of a tragedy gave great distinction to its author. In the fifth century B.C., Greek tragedy reached its height when the works of such playwrights as Aeschylus (525–456), Sophocles (c. 495–c. 406), and Euripides (c. 480–c. 406) were publicly acclaimed. The aesthetic skills of these famous dramatists rested on their powers of using narration and impersonation. By employing ritualistic expression, they interpreted for their audiences the workings of natural forces and the rhythms of birth, life, and death. The chorus, functioning as a corporate actor and commentator, combined song and dance in a manner that reflected the religious and ritualistic origins of the dramatic festivals. Since they dealt with familiar themes from the legendary or heroic past, Greek tragedies integrated the past with the present and the future. Since the audience already knew the major events of the story, the dramatist could move swiftly to the particular situation which he had chosen to develop the theme. The central figure was a man of heroic proportions who was also a tragic figure, tried by fate and found wanting because of some character flaw. This impediment to perfection, or tragic flaw, prevented the hero from achieving that integration, harmony, and balance that were so much desired as part of the Greek way of life.

Greek theater reflected the experiences and values of the culture from which it drew sustenance and support. By crystallizing the major events of the Greek experience in dramatic form, it was a major agency of informal education. The authors of award-winning tragedies were publicly acclaimed, and their works were recognized as valuable aesthetic contributions to life. The young boy who witnessed the dramas received an aesthetic education through the portrayal of the concerns and dilemmas of man's search for personal and social harmony.

In some ways, Greek drama reflected the Hellenic belief in the existence of a universal design which explained even the most complex and fortuitous combinations of events. As humanists, the Greeks firmly believed that human reason was powerful enough to find and extract the meaning of existence and nature. Driven by their curiosity, Greek philosophers speculated about man and hoped to find the universal patterns that governed reality. Socrates, Plato, Aristotle, and Isocrates, each in his own way, sought to discover universal truths and to make them known to their fellow men so that they might follow them and thereby live the good life. The Greek emphasis on design, order, and structure was also reflected in their language, which expressed with great accuracy the relationships between ideas and the fine shades of meaning and emotions. The Greeks regarded those who spoke their language as civilized while all non-Greek-speaking people were considered barbarians.

The emphasis placed on design, harmony, and balance in the universe had a personal implication for the Greek, whose art and philosophy exemplified the quest for *arete,* or excellence. Embracing all varieties of human excellence, *arete* was different from the technical skill needed in performing a specialized activity. *Arete* expressed the mode of life of the man who had attained harmony and balance by exercising rationality in his affairs and who pursued a mean of moderation between the excesses of extreme self-repression and extreme exhibition.

Greek life focused in the *polis,* a community of shared religious, civic, economic, social, political, and aesthetic endeavor in which the individual lived his personal and corporate life. The Greek emphasis on harmony and balance found expression in this institution, which had both private and public ramifications.

The Polis

The key to understanding Greek civilization was the *polis*, or city-state, an association of citizens designed to promote the common welfare and security. The city-states generally grew up at the base of a defensible high point, or acropolis, which became the religious, social, and political center of the community. Politically, the polis was a sovereign and independent state, whose particular form of government varied from place to place. It might be a monarchy, a diarchy (as in Sparta), an oligarchy, or a democracy (as in Athens). However, the polis was more than a government or a political agency. As a total community, it served to focus and integrate every dimension of the citizen's life. As the center of human loyalties and commitments, the polis objectified the values of Greek life. Although the life styles of particular poleis might exhibit radical contrasts, as those between Spartan fascism and Athenian democracy, all Greeks saw a reciprocal relationship between the good man and the good society. No matter how virtue was defined, the good man could be such only in a society which permitted and encouraged excellence. As the integrative focus of community life, the healthy polis required citizens who were generally competent in the economic, political, social, military, and religious concerns of the community. This meant that the Greeks placed a priority on cultivating virtues common to all citizens rather than specialized or technical skills. As long as such a community of generalists was tenable, the polis was an effective unit of social and personal integration.[1]

As the source of group norms, values, and behavior, the polis served as an informal educational agency and exercised a strong formative effect on the shaping of human conduct and character. Since all citizens were expected to participate in the community, the polis stimulated each man to develop his potentialities. In the courts or assemblies the Greek was educated politically; as a citizen-soldier, he received military training; by participating in religious rituals, he experienced a religious education. As a producer or critic of art, he developed aesthetically. In all these common human concerns, the Greek citizen received the education which was felt to be appropriate to free men.

Although the polis integrated life in the individual Greek city-states, the Greeks never extended the concept of community beyond the borders of their own city-states. Loyalty of the citizens to their own communities produced a variety of disunited and sharply antagonistic rival states, which, jealous of their sovereignty, had difficulty in organizing to ward off threats to mutual security. Although they had

[1] H. D. F. Kitto, *The Greeks* (Baltimore: Penguin Books, 1962), pp. 64–79.

rallied to defeat the Persian enemy, internecine warfare between the city-states, especially Sparta and Athens, exhausted Greece both materially and spiritually. After wasting their energies in the Peloponnesian war, the Greeks fell victim to the Macedonian invaders who, like the earlier Dorian conquerors, came from the Balkans. Despite the pleas of some of their leaders, the Greeks were incapable of transforming the polis into an instrument of Panhellenic unity.

In the fourth century B.C., an accelerated rate of commercial growth caused major socioeconomic changes which altered Greek life. Although most of the states experienced some degree of socioeconomic change, Athens was most profoundly affected. Commerce was conducted on such a large scale that more specialized production and trading arrangements were needed. Citizens grew more interested in their private affairs and fortunes than in the public good. As indicated earlier, the polis was designed for the amateur, or generalist, who could be all things and who could perform all functions well. The polis itself rested on a community of interest which was sustained through face-to-face functioning relationships. If these functions were to be performed by all citizens, they had to be simple enough for the ordinary man to learn and perform. With the flow of new wealth into the Greek city-states, the interests of the rising commercial classes and of the older landowning aristocracy diverged so sharply that the polis was weakened as a socially integrated community. In Athens, the rise of special interest groups weakened the political restraint and wisdom needed in a direct democracy. The old Greek concept of the well-rounded man was made obsolete by the rise of a class devoted primarily to commerce. The decline of commonly shared core values produced social and political disintegration which induced a cultural crisis. Much of the philosophical speculation, especially that of Plato, attempted to formulate a political theory which was adequate to reconstruct Greek cultural life. Education became a major instrument of those theorists who sought to devise a method of cultural reintegration.

Although it was the focus of personal and community life in all of the Greek city-states, sharp contrasts existed between the various poleis. Since the rival city-states of Sparta and Athens had divergent conceptions of the meaning of human life and education, they not only provide perspective into Greek culture but also are valuable for furnishing insights into fascism and democracy as alternative modes of political and educational organizations.

Spartan Education

Sparta presents a classic example of a state which deliberately rejected humanistic education in favor of exclusively practical and military training.[2] Like many of the other tribes occupying Greece, the Spartans were descendants of the Dorian invaders; but unlike the other tribes, they refused amalgamation with the conquered people, whom they enslaved as agricultural serfs. Although experiencing a brief period of literary and aesthetic achievement, Sparta became an anti-intellectual and reactionary totalitarian state around 550 B.C., when the Code of Lycurgus was promulgated. The Code restricted the Spartans to soldiering and prohibited their occupation in agriculture and commerce. Spartan society was organized according to a caste system based on racial origins and distinctions. The three basic classes were: one, the *Spartiates,* or ruling military elite, who descended from the Dorian conquerors and numbered only about 10 percent of the total population; two, the *Perioikoi,* or commercial class, who possessed economic but not political rights; three, the slave class, or *Helots,* who greatly outnumbered the Spartiates but were brutally subjugated. Sparta's government, a diarchy, consisted of two kings, each with veto power over the other, an executive council of five *Ephors,* and an assembly, composed of all the Spartiates.

Resting on a racist, authoritarian, and totalitarian rationale, Spartan society and education were, in many ways, prophetic of the modern twentieth-century Fascist and Nazi dictatorships which sought to integrate the energies of their citizenry into a corporate military life for the advancement of state interests. In the Fascist and Nazi pattern, membership in the ruling Spartan military elite was determined racially. As is usually the case in societies where a small ruling elite subjugates a larger mass, the education of the elite emphasized military training. In contrast to the imperialistic expansionism of Fascist Italy and Nazi Germany, the nonadventuring Spartan isolationists were more interested in protecting their privileged domestic status against internal subversion and external threat than with extending their boundaries. Spartan conservatives combated any changes which jeopardized the status quo which ensured them a favored position. Trade was discouraged with foreign nations, and aliens were admitted only grudgingly.

Sparta retained many of the educational activities associated with earlier Homeric knightly training such as riding, athletics, and gymnastics, which contributed to individual physical fitness and state military preparedness. With the emergence of the infantry, the ideal of

[2] For a thorough examination of Greek education, see H. I. Marrou, *A History of Education in Antiquity* (New York: Sheed and Ward, 1956).

devotion to the state developed as the exclusive focus of human activity and energy. Concentrating on the warlike arts, Spartan educators sought to train an entire city of heroes, who, as one man, would readily surrender their lives to defend their polis. While it professed ties to the archaic Homeric definition of virtue, the Spartan model of collective courage perverted Homeric heroism into a deliberately planned and executed savagery. As a political and educational policy, Spartan educators used their skills to transform young men into disciplined savages.

Spartan education sought to promote and secure the national interest by building a totalitarian morale that rested on an ideal of absolute patriotic devotion to the state. Sparta represented the classical example of the totalitarian ideal, which made the state the focus of human life and endeavor. To serve this ideal, education was designed to produce a collective hero rather than an individual who did great deeds for his own glory. Sparta's hero obeyed commands and followed orders without question. Public morality emphasized devotion to the laws of the state. By keeping students isolated from foreign ideas and by purging internal dissent, Spartan educators inculcated unchanging values and achieved a high degree of community consensus and social stability.

The Ephors, the five ruling magistrates who controlled political and social life, also controlled the state-dominated educational system. They appointed the state educational commissioner, or *paidonomos,* who supervised all educational activities. Since every Spartan was actually the state's property, each Spartan infant was brought at birth to the Ephors, who decided if he was physically strong and healthy enough for a rigorous military life. Deformed or physically weak children were exposed and left either to die or to be taken by the Helots who raised them as workers. Until age seven, the healthy boy was raised by his family and taken by his father on occasional visits to the soldiers' clubs where the men gathered at their leisure. These visits familiarized the boy with the soldier's life which was his destiny. At seven, he entered the military school barracks which would be his home for the next eleven years. There he was subjected to a rigorous course of physical training and patriotic indoctrination. The boys were organized into large companies, headed by older youths of eighteen. The companies were subdivided into smaller patrols or squads of six, headed by the smartest, strongest, wiliest, and toughest boys. At age eighteen, the Spartan youth received two additional years of strenuous and intensive military training. From twenty to thirty, he was on active duty in the army. Upon reaching thirty, he took a healthy wife and began to raise a family of future soldiers.

As a result of spending his boyhood and youth in the company of his male peers first as a member of a pack and then as a soldier in the army, the Spartan was conditioned to function as a part of the regimented garrison state. This continued emphasis on group life built within him a strong sense of collective loyalty and discipline. Since he was obliged to obey any adult citizen, the child soon learned that obedience was a fundamental requisite to a life of military courage, which was every Spartan's highest goal.

Spartan boys were taught to endure pain and deprivation without complaint. Poorly dressed, they were often naked in the cold, went barefoot, and slept on reeds. They were given little food to eat, to encourage stealth as they raided Helot farms and foraged for food. Beatings and other forms of corporal punishment were administered liberally to induce manliness and the Spartan conception of a fighting spirit.

The Spartan curriculum, designed to produce physically active and able-bodied soldiers, emphasized physical and military training. Drill, tactical formations, and weaponry were practiced. Intellectual content was minimized, and only the rudiments of reading and writing were taught. The meager military songs and stories which told of heroic exploits were designed to arouse sentiments of courage.

Although they were educated at home, girls also received some military training. At age seven, they were organized into packs to practice military tactics, athletics, racing, and riding. From their mothers they received domestic training and learned to supervise household slaves. While given more freedom than her secluded Athenian counterpart, the young Spartan maiden was raised primarily for the purpose of producing future Spartan soldiers.

Athenian Education

Historians have often delighted in contrasting repressive and authoritarian Sparta with liberal and democratic Athens. Although some of these contrasts have been simplistic, Athens and Sparta did represent a clear clash of cultural, political, and educational conceptions. Their rivalry resulted in the Peloponnesian War, 431–404 B.C., which weakened the Greek city-states and led to their subsequent conquest by the Macedonians. Since Athens and Sparta present divergent cultural and educational patterns, these rival poleis can be used as models by the educational historian who wishes to highlight the distinctions between totalitarian and democratic life and education. Indeed, the famous Athenian statesman Pericles (461–429 B.C.) contrasted Sparta and Athens in his oration commemorating the Athenian dead of the first year of the Peloponnesian War:

Our form of government does not enter into rivalry with the institutions of others. We do not copy our neighbors, but are an example

to them. It is true that we are called a democracy, for the administration is in the hands of the many and not of the few.

*   *   *

. . . our military training is in many respects superior to that of our
adversaries. Our city is thrown open to the world, and we never ex-
pel a foreigner or prevent him from seeing or learning anything of
which the secret if revealed to an enemy might profit him. We rely
not upon management or trickery, but upon our own hearts and
hands.

*   *   *

. . . in the matter of education, whereas they from early youth are
always undergoing laborious exercises which are to make them
brave, we live at ease, and yet are equally ready to face the perils
which they face.[3]

During its history, Athens experimented with a variety of governmental forms ranging from oligarchy, to tyranny, to direct democracy.
At first, Athens had been governed by *archons,* or aristocratic rulers,
selected by the landholding noble oligarchy. In 594 B.C., the lawgiver
Solon widened Athenian citizenship by basing suffrage on property
qualifications rather than birth. This gradual process of democratization improved the status of the lower classes and included them within
the framework of citizenship. From 546 until 527 B.C., Athens was
ruled by the tyrant Pisistratus, who had seized power as a result of
political unrest. Pisistratus was followed by Cleisthenes, who, often
referred to as the true founder of Athenian democracy, introduced
sweeping constitutional and administrative reforms. In 502 B.C., the
Constitution of Cleisthenes made Athens a direct democracy and in-
vested legislative power in a Popular Assembly composed of all the
citizens. Executive power was entrusted to the Council of Five Hundred, chosen by lot and subdivided into ten ruling committees of fifty
members each. Each of these executive committees was responsible
for guiding the civic course of the Athenian polis for one-tenth of the
year. Judicial proceedings took place in the elected law courts. With
the exception of the ten admirals and generals, or *strategoi,* who commanded the army and navy, political life was carried on by the ordinary
citizens rather than by a ruling oligarchy or an aristocratic elite. According to the Athenian theory of direct participatory democracy, all
citizens were to share voluntarily in public discussion and decision-
making. In contrast to Sparta's model of the collective military hero,
the Athenian ideal was the well-rounded, liberally educated individual,
who while not a specialist, was capable in politics, military affairs, and
in general community life.

[3] *Thucydides,* B. Jowett (tr.), 2nd ed. (Oxford, England: Oxford University
Press, 1900), pp. 167–177.

The zenith of Athenian democracy was reached in the Periclean Golden Age of the fifth century B.C. According to Pericles, Athens did not seek to suppress or to rival other states but rather, as the "School of Hellas," to set an example for them. Stressing the citizen's obligation to participate in the public affairs of the polis, Pericles referred to majority rule as the basis of Athenian government. The Athenian citizen's pursuit of culture, literature, art, and philosophy did not mean a loss of manliness or courage but rather cultivated free individuals who were suited to live in a free city.

In following the Periclean concepts of participatory democracy, much of Athenian education resulted informally from the experience of living in Athens. The plays of the dramatists, the dialogues of the philosophers, the orations of the sophists, and participation in the daily life of the polis contributed to shape the Athenian citizen. Both the formal and informal aspects of Athenian education aimed to produce a cultivated and many-sided person who was both an excellent man and a contributor to the general welfare. The Athenian educational goal was to produce the man of broad culture, liberally educated in all those activities which were distinctively humane.

Since its way of life was broader and more democratic than that of Sparta, a greater variety of formal educational patterns and institutions existed in Athens. Since the Athenians let more of their educational matters rest in the hands of private teachers, a greater individualism was apparent in Athenian educational institutions. Although attendance was voluntary, most Athenians spent some time in formal school. State patterns of educational control were minimal and emerged very slowly. For example, the polis paid tuitions of boys whose fathers had died in the national defense. The state had only the minimal requirement that parents see that their children learn to read and to swim. Eventually, the Popular Assembly appointed a public official to supervise the teaching of letters, music, and gymnastics. By the third and second centuries B.C., Athenian education grew more systematic, as clear patterns of elementary, secondary, and higher education appeared. Public support and control over education increased as the state exercised a role in selecting school administrators, appointing teachers, and contributing to the salaries of educators.

In the early history of Athenian education, formal schools were rather primitive and were conducted by teachers who were supported by tuition payments. By the sixth and fifth centuries B.C., three types of schools had appeared in Athens: that of the *grammatist,* or teacher of reading, writing, and letters; that of the *citharist,* or music, literature, and poetry teacher; that of the *paedotribe,* or teacher of physical education, gymnastics, and athletics. Little state supervision was exercised over these private venture schools. In the course of time, the schools of the grammatist and the citharist merged into one institution for literary education. The gymnastic schools, known as the *palaestra,* continued their separate existence. The Athenian boy was tutored by a slave, or *pedagogue,* until he reached age seven, when he began to attend the various schools. The basic curriculum pursued by the Athenian boy consisted of reading, writing, arithmetic, and music. The teaching of letters and of reading was highly mechanical and depended on the student's ability to memorize. The teacher first taught the letters of the alphabet, then syllables, and finally words and sentences. Reading was essentially a matter of reciting the words and passages called out by the teacher. Writing was taught as the students copied the teacher's letters and words by imprinting them on a wax tablet with a stylus. After the student had attained copying skill and was able to form the letters correctly, the teacher dictated passages from poetry or literature, which the boy wrote down and memorized. Arithmetic was mainly a matter of counting, either on the fingers or with the abacus.

Music, which included singing and playing the lyre, the national instrument, was closely related to the interpretation of lyric poetry. Music was further believed to generate orderly habits and was considered indispensable to the proper understanding of the lyric poets. Dancing combined music, poetical recitations, and rhythmic movements. The presentation of drama united poetry, dancing, and singing in what was both a civic and religious experience.

The Athenians, like all Greeks, were concerned with cultivating a healthy and well-formed body. This became a crucial component of the basic curriculum followed by Greek boys, with gymnastics, athletics, and physical education aimed at increasing health, strength, and dexterity. Gymnastic training was also believed to foster courage and manliness.

Although they originated the idea of a functioning participatory democracy, the Athenians did not extend the concept of democratic equality to women. While Spartan women were involved in social life, Athenian women were kept in an almost Oriental seclusion. Restricted to the jobs of domestic management and child rearing, the Athenian wife was not a social or intellectual companion to her husband. For intelligent female companionship, the Athenian male turned to the *hetaerae,* a class of well-educated foreign courtesans. The women of Athens were not enfranchised, could not attend the Assembly, and did not have property rights. The education of the Athenian girl reflected her sheltered and restricted role. There were no schools for girls, who learned to read at home and were instructed by their mothers in the household arts.

By the fourth century B.C., Athens experienced the cultural changes that resulted from the acquisition of a commercial empire. Commercial expansion brought into existence a rising class of businessmen which threatened the cultural supremacy of the older landed aristocracy. Economic growth and specialization also wrought havoc with the simple patterns of face-to-face democracy, which were slowly disintegrating. Educational patterns responded to the impact of cultural change by becoming increasingly specialized and divergent. In 335 B.C., military tactics had grown specialized enough to require the Popular Assembly to enact compulsory military training for all Athenian males between the ages of eighteen and twenty. These young men entered the Ephebic College, a military training school, to study tactics, formations, and strategy and to participate in armed exercises. At age twenty, after two years as a cadet, the Athenian youth was admitted to full citizenship.

As a result of the impact of social change on Athenian life, the young man who wished to be successful in business and politics needed to continue his education by pursuing higher studies. Like elementary education, Athenian higher education was neither systematic nor well-defined. The young man had to choose among competing philosophical and rhetorical schools. The various schools of higher education and the educational theories upon which they were based will be examined in Chapter 3.

The Peloponnesian War

Although the two city-states of Athens and Sparta had different conceptions of the ideally educated man, they both recognized the relationship between the individual and his community. It was the polis that furnished educational aims. While Athenian education was conceived of in terms that blended personal culture with state service, Spartan education was rigorously prescribed to fit the military needs of a totalitarian state.

After the defeat of their common Persian enemy, the Greek city-states divided into two antagonistic compacts, the Athenian-dominated Delian Confederation and the Spartan-dominated Peloponnesian League. While Athens favored democratic constitutions among her allies, Sparta favored reactionary oligarchies. Athens and her allies had dominant naval power, and Sparta and her allies were strong on land. The hostility of the rival alliances led to the Peloponnesian War (431–404), which was a turning point in the history of the Greek city-states. The war saw the demise of the polis as a creative force in fashioning and fulfilling the lives of its members. The inconclusive Spartan victory and the general undermining of Greek morale contributed to the conquest of the Greek city-states, initiated by the Macedonian King Philip II and completed by his son Alexander.

Conclusion

Greek educational ideas had originated in the Homeric epics, which emphasized the man of heroic and knightly bearing. Homer's *Iliad* and *Odyssey* supplied Greek education with a model that furnished guiding objectives that influenced the course of ancient Greek culture. Greek culture and education were also characterized by the dominating and integrative influence of the community, or *polis*. Although it took a variety of political forms, the Greek polis was sustained by the concept of a total community which integrated the lives of its citizens. Foremost among the many Greek city-states were the rival poleis of Athens and Sparta. While Athens represented a model of a democratic life and educational pattern, Sparta was a totalitarian and fascist state.

Greek philosophers and educators were also concerned with developing an educational theory which could integrate and order their lives. The philosophical and educational theories of Socrates, Plato, Aristotle, and Isocrates formed a rich theoretical heritage that had a lasting influence on Western thought. Chapter 3 will examine the contributions of these ancient Greek theorists.

Suggested Readings

Botsford, George W., and Charles A. Robinson, Jr. *Hellenic History*. New York: Macmillan, 1956.

Bowra, Cecil M. *The Greek Experience*. New York: New American Library, 1958.

Burn, A. R. *Pericles and Athens*. New York: Macmillan, 1949.

Chambliss, J. J. (ed.). *Nobility, Tragedy, and Naturalism: Education in Ancient Greece*. Minneapolis: Burgess, 1971.

Dobson, John F. *Ancient Education and Its Meaning to Us*. London: Longmans, Green, 1932.

Forbes, Clarence A. *Greek Physical Education*. New York: Century, 1929.

Freeman, Kenneth J. *Schools of Hellas*. New York: Macmillan, 1922.

Hadas, Moses. *A History of Greek Literature*. New York: Columbia University Press, 1950.

Homer. *The Iliad*. R. Lattimore (tr.). Chicago: University of Chicago Press, 1951.

Jaeger, Werner. *Paideia: The Ideals of Greek Culture*. 3 vols. Gilbert Highet (tr.). New York: Oxford University Press, 1945.

Kitto, H. D. F. *The Greeks*. Baltimore: Penguin Books, 1962.

Klein, Anita E. *Child Life in Greek Art*. New York: Columbia University Press, 1932.

Marrou, H. I. *A History of Education in Antiquity*. New York: Sheed and Ward, 1956.

Muller, Herbert J. *Freedom in the Ancient World*. New York: Harper & Row, 1961.

Smith, Morton. *The Ancient Greeks*. Ithaca, New York: Cornell University Press, 1960.

Starr, Chester G. *The Awakening of the Greek Historical Spirit*. New York: Alfred A. Knopf, 1968.

Whitman, C. H. *Homer and the Heroic Tradition*. Cambridge, Mass.: Harvard University Press, 1958.

Woody, Thomas. *Life and Education in Early Societies*. New York: Macmillan, 1959.

Zimmern, Alfred. *The Greek Commonwealth*. Oxford, England: Oxford University Press, 1931.

CHAPTER 3

Greek Educational Theory

In the foregoing chapter, Greek education was treated as a reflection of Greek historical experience. From this experience came the Hellenic world view, which saw man as a rational inhabitant of a purposeful and orderly universe. Although the early Greeks relied on myths to explain the mysteries of the universe, such later speculative philosophers as Socrates, Plato, and Aristotle sought to explain the universe in rational terms. True to their intense individualism, these philosophers did not provide a single metaphysical system but rather offered various explanations of reality. They also constructed educational theories that were based on their metaphysical outlooks. In contrast to these speculative philosophers, the sophists, who were more practical, sought to formulate an educational methodology that would bring success to their students. This chapter will explore the educational theories formulated by those Greek philosophers and educators who are still major figures in the history of Western thought.

Sophists

The sophists flourished from 470 to 370 B.C., a time in which Athens rose to leadership in the Aegean commercial world. The Persian threat had been eliminated, and Athens had benefited from the resulting expansion of trade. Athenian commercial success had made the attainment of material wealth a goal for many citizens and had brought into being a new class of entrepreneurs and traders who rivaled the older aristocracy based on birth. As the *nouveaux riches* gained economic power, they sought an education that would enable them to exercise political power. The instruction offered by the sophists generally appealed to the new monied class, which needed to acquire intellectual and rhetorical skills to consolidate its economic, social, and political position. Through rhetoric, the art of persuasion, the new class sought to manipulate the democratized political and juridical institutions of the polis.[1]

The sophists, a poorly defined assortment of itinerant teachers, never constituted a single body of educators. They disagreed on philosophical and pedagogical specifics and thus did not develop a systematic and coherent educational theory, nor did they establish schools in the institutional sense. Although primarily rhetoricians, certain sophists claimed the ability to teach any subject or skill to any student. This exaggerated claim caused them to be accused of preaching opportunism and expediency. On the positive side, they extended educational opportunities to more people, contributed to class mobility, and furthered the processes of Athenian democratization.

Aristophanes, a conservative writer of comedy, satirized the teaching abilities and the educational claims of the sophists in his play *The Clouds*. Aristophanes charged that the sophists failed to prepare young men for the virtuous life and alleged that their educational method encouraged students to cheat and to lie. Further, their predilection for social change was subversive to morals and detrimental to Athenian social stability. Plato, a conservative philosopher, was also antagonistic to the sophists, who he felt miseducated Athenian youth.

Since their major educational aim was to teach the art of practical politics, the sophists were concerned with developing persuasive techniques rather than with examining more philosophic and speculative issues. Through their specialization in grammar, logic, and rhetoric, they developed what came to be the trivium of the later Roman and medieval education. Logic was to aid the individual in clarifying his own thinking; grammar was a means of expressing ideas clearly; rhetoric, the most important of the three, was the power of persuading others through speech. Through the teaching of these three basic subjects, the sophists closely integrated thought and language. In pursuing the practical aim of training their students as successful advocates and legislators, the sophists were greatly concerned with developing communications skills. As practical educators, they tried to develop the methodological insights and operational techniques needed to transmit knowledge to their students.

On an individual basis, the sophists ranged from excellent scholars who sought to devise a well-grounded theoretical base for rhetorical instruction to charlatans who promised their students instant success through the mastery of a few tricks of the trade. Protagoras (c. 480–410 B.C.), among the most popular of the sophists, was one of the most effective rhetoricians. He collected large fees from his students. His method of teaching was to present a sample lecture or declamation

---

[1] For a treatment of the rhetorical education offered by the sophists, see Harry S. Broudy and John R. Palmer, *Exemplars of Teaching Method* (Chicago: Rand McNally, 1965), pp. 15–30.

on a topic suggested by the audience. This model lecture, which might consist of the presentation of proofs in an argument or the interpretation of a myth or legend, was designed to demonstrate to potential students the oratorical powers that would come to them if they enrolled in the course. The student's course of study consisted of an analysis of great orations that could be used as models of speech and included the theory of rhetoric and exercises in grammar and logic. The culminating experiences for the fledgling orator were practice orations presented under the critical eye of their peers and the teacher and, finally, a public oration. Like the modern teacher of debate, Protagoras claimed that it was possible to argue persuasively for or against any proposition, for the effective orator had to learn to win any kind of argument. Protagoras is alleged to have asserted that "man is the measure of all things." As a relativist, he, and other sophists, held that values are subjectively determined by each individual. Truth and morality are relative and depend on contingencies of time, place, and circumstances.

Gorgias of Leontini, another popular sophist, asserted that the particular skills of rhetoric, grammar, and disputation could be developed through a carefully structured teaching method. He formulated the general rules, which grew into a body of methodological skills for a systematic training in the art of public speaking. Callicles and Antiphon boldly asserted the validity of socioeconomic class interests and saw education as an instrument designed to serve these special interests. Men should free themselves from the inhibitions placed upon them by custom and tradition and learn to recognize, define, and assert their own interests.

The emphasis the sophists placed on asserting special interests rather than on the concept of the public good, as traditionally expressed in the polis, reflected the shift that had occurred in Athenian social and economic life. Although they were often accused of undermining the traditional values of Athenian life, the education offered by the sophists reflected the deep-seated changes that had occurred as Athens went from a self-contained polis to the seat of a major commercial empire. Traditional morality had rested on the values of courage, justice, and self-restraint, which were rooted in and integrated by the polis. In the period when the sophists were at their height, these values were being challenged by others that were more individualistic, subjective, and hedonistic.

As practical educators, the sophists consciously sought to adapt their teaching to the realities of social and economic change. Recognizing the personal element in all thought and knowledge, they tended to deny universal and objective standards of morality and behavior and grounded their educational goals in social utility. Unfortunately, like many educators who claim to be completely practical and utilitarian, they often failed to formulate a coherent educational theory. Their frequently exaggerated claims sometimes reduced learning to verbal formulas or mechanical tricks of the oratorical trade. Despite its negative features, the education espoused by the sophists, with its concentration on language, grammar, rhetoric, and logic, exercised a continued influence on Western educational development. It contributed to the formulation of the liberal arts and the oratorical education that dominated the Roman education of Cicero and Quintilian.

In the last half of the fifth century, the Athenian philosopher Socrates (c. 469–399 B.C.) sought to discover the universal principles of truth, beauty, and justice. In contrast to Protagorean relativism, he sought to demonstrate a generalized morality that governed all men. Since none of Socrates' writings have been preserved, it is necessary to rely on secondary sources, especially Plato's dialogues, for information regarding this famous Athenian theorist. In many respects, Socratic philosophy was a simple ethic that held that man's only reason for being is to experience moral excellence. The morally excellent man lives a life of wisdom and his actions are governed by rationality. Accordingly, Socrates believed that moral education is the only defensible educational objective for any society.

According to Plato's accounts, Socrates felt that the sophists had performed a disservice to Athenian education by confusing such practical skills as oratory and rhetoric with generalized human excellence. In asserting that oratory is only one kind of human excellence, Socrates held that the virtue of being excellent as a human being is above technical expertise of any kind. The man who is excellent as a human being is one whose actions are governed by reason. In denying that knowledge can be poured into an individual from external sources or by teachers, Socrates asserted that genuine knowledge exists within each man and needs to be brought to consciousness. A proper education would be the kind that stimulates the learner to recall, or to bring to consciousness, that truth that is latently present in all men.

Socrates sought to stimulate men to define themselves. Through self-examination and analysis, each man should look inward to seek that truth that is universally present in all men. In the Socratic method, a skillful teacher asked leading questions to stimulate the students to ponder basic human concerns about the meaning of life and truth. As a result, definitions were constructed, criticized, and reconstructed. The process continued until both teacher and learner were satisfied.

The Socratic method has been described as a kind of "shock treatment" that jolts the learner into anxiety about his own condition as a human being. Once the learner sees and admits the consequences of his ignorance, he is in a stage of readiness for learning. Discipleship, an intense personal relationship between teacher and student, was related closely to Socratic education. Education and healing were also closely related in that the healthy soul has order and form. The goal of education, an intense personal relationship, is to build in the soul a set of value preferences or moral predispositions. In the healthy soul, rationality dominates and governs the man. Such a man subordinates appetite to reason.

In pursuing his self-proclaimed vocation as an intellectual "gadfly" and "midwife of ideas," Socrates frequented the Athenian marketplace, where he discussed political, aesthetic, moral, and philosophical issues. His method of rigorously examining other people's ideas made him some influential enemies. In 399 B.C., he was brought to trial on the charge of being disrespectful to the gods and corrupting Athenian youth. Found guilty of impiety, he was executed by his fellow Athenians.

Plato

Socrates' work did not die with him but was elaborated and extended by his pupil Plato (c. 427–347 B.C.). A speculative philosopher, Plato founded the higher philosophical school known as the Academy in 387 B.C. and was the author of such works as *Protagoras,* a discourse on the nature of virtue; *Phaedo,* an argument in favor of man's immortality; and the *Republic* and the *Laws,* treatises on political, legal, and educational theory. As a scion of an old aristocratic Athenian family that had suffered reverses at the hands of the newer and more democratic leadership, Plato was antagonistic to the course of democratization, which he believed had contributed to the disintegration of Athenian cultural stability. He faced the problem of social change and solved it by denying any kind of change. His metaphysical system construed an ideal world of perfect forms, or ideas, such as the universal forms of truth, goodness, justice, and beauty. As they appear to the human senses, individual actions were conceived to be imperfect approximations or representations of these universal and eternal ideas. Plato rejected Protagoras' relativistic assertion that "man is the measure of all things." He also challenged the sophists' emphasis on change and sense experience as the basis of educational methodology. In contrast, he asserted that men are good and just only as they participate in the ideal forms, or concepts, of justice and goodness. To fulfill his human character as a rational being, each man must try to reach perfection by recognizing the good, the true, and the beautiful and by seeking to participate fully in the ideal and universal system of truth and value.

Plato's theory of knowledge, or epistemology, was based on the doctrine of "reminiscence," by which man recalls the truths, or ideas, that are present within his mind and within the minds of all men. This doctrine implied that man possesses a soul that existed prior to its encasement in a physical body. Before its temporal imprisonment, man's soul inhabited a spiritual world in proximity to the pure forms, or ideas, that are the source of all truth and knowledge. With the shock of birth—actually an imprisoning of the psyche—man forgot, or repressed within his subconscious mind, his knowledge of truth. Nevertheless, knowledge—the ideas of the perfect forms—remains present latently in the mind. Learning, the rediscovery of truth, is the recollection of this latent knowledge, bringing it once again to consciousness through philosophic reflection, or introspection.

In his "Allegory of the Cave," Plato made it clear that the world revealed to us by our senses is not the real world but only an imperfect copy of it. Sense impressions therefore give man nothing that he can truly believe. Knowledge comes only to those men whose intellect has penetrated beyond the confusing shadows of sense perception, experience, and opinion. True knowledge, as contrasted with sensory experience, is eternal and changeless, since the forms, or ideas, upon which it rests are likewise eternal and enduring. Since there is a universal truth from which all lesser truths derive, there is also one idea of perfection common to all men. Truth is attained through the direct vision of reason and its confirmation in man's consciousness. Since truth is universal, proper education should also be universal and unchanging. Since reality can be apprehended only intellectually, education should direct the student's mind toward reality.

Plato's Republic

As a defender of the older conception of the polis as a functioning community, Plato opposed the rising opportunism and relativism that were endemic with economic expansion and the growth of specialized interests. In *The Republic*, Plato fashioned a theoretical design for a perfect state, which bore an idealized and intellectualized resemblance to Sparta. However, Plato's Republic was to be ruled by an intellectual elite of philosopher kings rather than by a military caste.

Plato's conceptions of the ideal state and ideal system of education were intimately related to his metaphysical and epistemological systems. Since both truth and value are derived from unchanging forms, he asserted that knowledge is eternally valid and that values are unchanging. To escape the discord and social disintegration induced by social change, Plato proposed an eternal city, a perfect polis based on the concept of eternal and unchanging truth. Change was thus reduced to a sensory illusion. Individuals like the sophists who tried to benefit from social change or who sought to induce change were misguided. Plato's Republic, an organic community existing for the purpose of cultivating truth and virtue in its inhabitants, rested on two major assumptions: (1) only knowledgeable men should govern the state; (2) all men should contribute to the general welfare according to their particular aptitude. The harmonious state, like the harmonious individual, was to be both a functional and an aesthetic unity. Education was to be one of the major means of determining the relations of the inhabitants in this utopian Republic.

In the social blueprint enunciated in the *Republic*, Plato divided the inhabitants into three major classes or castes: the intellectual ruling elite of philosopher kings; the auxiliaries, the military group of defenders and soldiers who protected the polis; and the providers—the working proletariat, peasants, artisans, and laborers—who sustained the economic life of the community. Membership in the various classes depended upon the capacity or constitution of the person. What a child became as an adult was determined partly by heredity and partly by environment, an important component of which was education. The crucial component in determining class was intellectual capacity, or the ability to grasp and use abstractions.

Plato assigned to the Republic's educators the task of evaluating individuals and selecting those who were intellectually able. This type of selective function is usually assigned to the formal educational system in elitist societies that are either totalitarian or hierarchical. Schools in these societies perform the task of sorting out people according to some criterion. Although Plato's criterion was intellectual, other totalitarians or elitists have used nonrational determinants, such as race. Once individuals have been sorted out according to the criterion, they are given an education that is appropriate to the role they are expected to perform in the society.

The highest class in the Platonic hierarchy was that of the guardians, or philosopher kings, who guided the destiny of the polis. Because of their intellectual propensity, the philosopher kings were judged capable of obtaining a clearer view of the good, true, and beautiful. Virtuous and intelligent men, they governed the polis because they were highly endowed with the capacity for leadership. The auxiliaries, or warriors, were second in the hierarchy. Their capacity for intellectual abstraction was inferior to that of the philosopher kings. More inclined to follow will than intellect, the warriors functioned as the defenders of the polis. Those who were intellectually inferior, having low abstractive competency, were relegated to the lowest class as providers or workers. These individuals were governed by their appetites rather than their reason or will. For each of these three homogeneous classes, there was an appropriate educational track designed to prepare them to perform their functions.

Although his societal model is elitist, Plato did not conceive of the Republic as a fascist, dictatorial, or otherwise coercive state. He assumed that each component class in the polis would fulfill a necessary socioeconomic function by contributing to the life and harmony of the community and did not conceive of a situation developing in which the ruling elite would coerce the masses or a spirit of rebellion would be present in a seething proletariat. In contrast, he believed that the integrated society was a just one and that justice would emerge from the harmonious relationships of all classes. The Republic was to be integrated in the same way that the rational, volitional, and appetitive elements in human nature are integrated in the properly balanced individual. *The Republic* was a scheme designed to achieve a socially integrated polity at a time of acute social disequilibrium.

Plato's Educational System

Plato's coherent and systematic educational philosophy carefully integrated metaphysical, epistemological, pedagogical, sociological, and political elements.[2] His educational system, a highly idealized and intellectualized version of that of Sparta, rested on the concepts of "reminiscence" and the "organic state." Education, in the Platonic sense, is not to be confused with merely imparting information or cultivating a skill. It is instead a conversion, or a redirecting of personality, a turning of the eyes of the soul to genuine reality. Each man's cognitive power should be turned away from the contingencies and images of the sensory world and focused on the unchanging reality of the perfect forms. The teacher's task is to prepare an environment that will aid the student in his quest for truth by redirecting him from appearance to reality.

Plato held that man's soul, or psyche, is a living and developing entity. In the infant and child, this self-active principle is reached through imagination and emotions. In the early stages of education, the task is to stimulate the love of the good, the true, and the beautiful by cultivating correct habits or dispositions. At a later stage of greater intellectual maturity, the soul's object is the recognition of truth.

In the Republic, children were separated from their parents and placed in state nurseries to be reared until age six. Plato believed that parents were often a corruptive influence on children in that they passed on their own prejudices and ignorance. Man's search for virtue began as an initial predisposition that was properly cultivated by exposure to virtuous teachers within the context of a deliberately prepared educational environment. From the nurseries were purged all

[2] For systematic analyses of Plato's educational theory, see Robert S. Brumbaugh and Nathaniel M. Lawrence, *Philosophers on Education: Six Essays on the Foundations of Western Thought* (Boston: Houghton Mifflin, 1963), pp. 10–48; J. J. Chambliss, "The Guardian: Plato," in Paul Nash, Andreas M. Kazamias, and Henry J. Perkinson (eds.), *The Educated Man: Studies in the History of Educational Thought* (New York: Wiley, 1965), pp. 29–52.

those habits, ideas, and practices that could be injurious to the child's proper development.

From ages six to eighteen, the students studied music and gymnastics. Music, a subject broadly conceived, included exercises in letters, reading, writing, choral singing, and dancing. After mastering the basic literary skills of reading and writing, the students read the approved classics. Plato deliberately excluded the traditional poets and the Homeric epics, which, he felt, distracted the mind from its proper pursuit, the cultivation of rationality. Such literary censorship was to prevent students from forming false or harmful impressions. In selecting literature, he said, it was most important to choose stories or poems that portrayed persons who were worthy of emulation by the young. Such exemplary men were always truthful, temperate, and obedient to legitimate authorities; they were in control of bodily appetites and passions and avoided the vices of pride and insolence. In stressing an ethical rather than an aesthetic criterion for selecting literature, Plato considered literature to be a subject that was potent for forming character. After he had mastered the basic arithmetical processes, the student was to concentrate on geometry and astronomy. Plato believed that mathematics was of supreme educational value in awakening the mind's abstractive powers.

He reserved gymnastics for the last two years of adolescence. More than just physical exercises, gymnastics was to promote character formation and to develop the skill and strength of the body. By promoting the qualities of spirit and courage, gymnastics was to produce a well-balanced and harmonious character. Plato was critical of the athletic competitions that were popular among the Greeks because he felt that such spectator-oriented performances failed to promote proper emotional dispositions. The competitive spirit fostered an unhealthy individualism rather than a cooperative spirit. Gymnastics was to be restored to its original purpose of military preparation and defense and was to consist of such functional exercises as fencing, archery, javelin-throwing, slinging, and riding. Since gymnastics related directly to the building of a strong and healthy body, Plato included the rules of diet and hygiene in his curriculum.

From eighteen to twenty, the students pursued more intensive physical and military training. At twenty, the future philosopher kings were selected for additional higher education. For ten more years, those destined for membership in the ruling intellectual elite studied mathematics, geometry, astronomy, music, and science. When they reached thirty, these students were again divided into two groups: the less capable intellectually were assigned to civil service positions; the more capable continued their higher studies by concentrating on dialectics and metaphysics. At age thirty-five, the formal education of the philosopher kings was completed, and they went out to direct the military and political affairs of the Republic. When they reached age fifty, they joined the inner decision-making circle and assumed the role of elder statesmen.

Plato's conception of education was not restricted to formal schooling but was conditioned by the cultural context. Devoting major interest to broad educational issues, he believed that formal education, in the sense of schooling, was intimately related to, and conditioned by, informal educational processes, or enculturation. Within the reformed polis portrayed in the utopian Republic, both formal and informal educational agencies would function cooperatively to form the kind of character that was appropriate to an ideal society. Plato's system was not directed to mass education but was intended to educate an elite ruling class. As is generally true of formal education in elitist societies, Platonic schools would have been organized into various tracks in which homogeneous groups of students pursued the education appropriate to them.

Plato's educational system was closely tied to his view of the utopian society and state. Formal education was to be a state concern, with the teachers and schools carefully supervised by the ruling elite of philosopher kings. The fulfillment of the Platonic educational idea depended on a fundamental reordering of the state, or polis, into a functional and organic social and political system.

Aristotle

Aristotle (384–322 B.C.) was born at Stagerios in Thrace, the son of the court physician of King Amyntas II. After studying with Plato, Aristotle went to Macedonia as the tutor of Alexander, who was destined to be historically famous as "the Great." In 334, he returned to Athens and founded a philosophical school, the Lyceum, which as one of the most prestigious institutions of higher learning of its time, rivaled Plato's Academy. He was the author of treatises on physics, astronomy, zoology, biology, botany, psychology, logics, ethics, and metaphysics. His *Nicomachean Ethics* reflected the highest ideals of Hellenic life by emphasizing reason, moderation, and harmony. In *Politics*, he examined man's social nature, the purpose of government, and the most desirable kind of social order.

Following the general interests of their teacher, Aristotle's students at the Lyceum studied a variety of subjects which included the natural sciences, the various constitutions of the Greek city-states, the organs and habits of animals, and the characteristics and distribution of plants. Coming close to a theory of evolution, Aristotle's natural science described an order of natural progression. First, there are lifeless things, inanimate objects such as stones and minerals. Upward in the scale of being come plants, which, while alive when compared with inanimate objects, are relatively lifeless in comparison to animals. In the animal kingdom, there is a continuous scale of ascent upward to man himself. Unlike his fellow animals, man is endowed with a power of rationality.

Aristotle's Philosophy

Frequently cited as the founder of Western philosophical realism, Aristotle asserted the existence of an objective order of reality.[3] All objects are composed of form, or design, and matter and exist independently of man's knowledge of them. Man, endowed with the defining human quality of rationality, is capable of knowing these objects. He can observe the patterns of regularity that govern the interaction of these natural objects. This theoretical knowledge, derived from careful and systematic observation, is man's surest guide to conduct. Underlying Aristotle's philosophy was the implicit belief that man, a rational being, inhabits a rational and purposeful universe.

Subject to the essential dualism that pervades the universe, man is endowed with form, defined as soul or mind, and with matter, the corporal body. As a physical being like the animals with whom he shares the powers of locomotion, nutrition, and reproduction, man is appetitive and has a number of physical needs or drives that he must fulfill in order to survive. Man is unlike the animals, however, in that his defining quality—soul, mind, or intellect—endows him with a potential for rationality. The good or virtuous man is one who activates this rational potentiality to its fullest extent. Such a man is purposefully reflective and rational in his behavior. He is capable of exercising a practical reason that can guide his ethical behavior and political decision-making. When carried to its highest and most general level, rationality can be exerted in pursuit of that pervasive and eternal truth that is the design of the universe.

Aristotelian epistemology asserts that cognition, like the universe, comprises two component phases: sensation and abstraction. All cognitive activity begins with man's sensation of objects that are external to him. The perceptions of the qualities of sensible objects, such as size, shape, hardness, and softness, are conveyed by the sense organs to the mind, the common sense, as the raw materials needed for conceptualization. Man arrives at concepts by abstracting the form of these objects from the material content that conveys them to the

[3] See Brumbaugh and Lawrence, op. cit., pp. 49–75, for an excellent essay, "Aristotle: Education as Self-Realization."

senses. While Plato held that knowing is a matter of recognizing ideas already lodged in consciousness, Aristotle asserted that knowledge begins with objects that are external to man.

Aristotle's ethical theory was related to his conception of reality and to his view of man as a rational being. The universe, in general, and man, in particular, are moving to a prescribed end or goal. For man, the universal quest is happiness—the "summum bonum," or the "good at which all things aim." For Aristotle, all things are led by a universal natural law to realize some good end or purpose. There is thus an end involved in every form of moral action or physical movement.

Although Aristotle believed that each man defines happiness according to the tenor and inclinations of his own life, he identified three general modes of life: the life of pleasure, the life of sociality, and the life of contemplation. His value theory recommended moderation, a mean between habits of extreme repression and extreme exhibition.

Aristotle, a student of Plato, tested his mentor's metaphysics in a public common-sense world rather than in pure speculation. In Book VIII of *Politics,* he propounded his educational theory. Like Plato, Aristotle called attention to the relationship that exists between the good individual and the good state. If the legislator neglects education, then the constitution suffers. Aristotle defined "happiness" as the virtuous life and gave to education a major role in developing *arete,* or virtue, that generalized and encompassing excellence or perfection. Education, in the broad sense, refers to the cultivation and perfection of human potentialities.

Aristotle and the Liberal Arts

Following the conventional Greek distinction between "free men" and "servile men," or slaves, Aristotle designated the liberal arts as those studies that liberate man by enlarging and expanding his choices. Other occupational and vocational pursuits, such as trade, commerce, and farming, he claimed, distort the body and reduce the time available for leisurely cultivating intellectual excellence.

Like Plato, Aristotle recognized that education directly related to both the healthy individual and the harmoniously integrated society, or polis, and recommended compulsory public schools. Infants were to be given opportunities for play, physical activity, and proper stories. For children aged seven to fourteen, Aristotle emphasized moral and physical education to develop proper habits and predispositions. At this stage of human development, he said, it is important to cultivate proper inclinations in the young rather than to concentrate on matters that are essentially intellectual. Children were to have gymnastic training, or physical education. Music, again broadly conceived, was to bring about proper emotional dispositions. Reading and writing skills were to be cultivated as essential prerequisites to liberal education.

During the period from fifteen to twenty-one, or adolescence and youth, Aristotle's proposed curriculum emphasized intellectual pursuits. Mathematics—encompassing arithmetic, geometry, and astronomy—was to be studied for its practical and theoretical consequences. To enlarge their view of the world, students were to study such humanistic subjects as grammar, literature, poetry, rhetoric, ethics, and politics. Upon reaching twenty-one, the student was to pursue the more theoretical and speculative studies such as physics, cosmology, biology, and psychology. He would also engage in further philosophical pursuits such as logic and metaphysics.

Aristotle's Significance

In the twelfth and thirteenth centuries, Aristotle's philosophy was introduced to Western intellectuals by way of Mohammedan scholars. Scholastics such as Thomas Aquinas accepted the premises of Aristotelian philosophy and used them as an intellectual rationale for Christian theology. Making a great impact on Western scholastic education, Aristotle's philosophy became a basic study in the medieval universities, especially at Paris. His metaphysics has remained an integral part of Catholic Christianity's philosophic rationale. In addition, such modern Aristotelians as Robert Hutchins, Mortimer Adler, and Harry Broudy have made his realism an important cornerstone in their philosophies of education.

Isocrates

During the life of Isocrates (436–338 B.C.), Greece experienced great political, social, economic, and educational changes. Such internal struggles as the Peloponnesian War had undermined the vitality of the polis. Many Greeks had deserted the older value core based on civic duty and sought personal advancement. Educational theory, not immune to these cultural dislocations, reflected the broader conflicts that beset the social order. While some educators continued to emphasize civic virtue and wisdom, others sought fame and fortune by promising their students personal success. Isocrates reacted strongly against this educational confusion. In *Against the Sophists*, he attacked teachers who claimed to be able to teach virtue and also opposed those who taught rhetoric as a mechanical formula based on the mastery of a few tricks of the trade. In *Antidosis*, Isocrates wrote in defense of his own program of educational reform. Conscious of the need for moral and political regeneration of Greek life, he believed that reform could be brought about only by educating virtuous leaders who themselves would be worthy of imitation by their fellow citizens.[4]

Isocrates, like Aristotle, conceived of human nature as a duality of the mental and the physical. Although both mind and body require appropriate exercises for their development, man's mental agency should be given priority since it determines what is useful to the whole being, the body being the agent that carries out the decisions of the mind. Although he emphasized the intellectual side of human nature, Isocrates should not be confused with speculative philosophers such as Plato. He did not believe that man can ever formulate absolute truths. In his view, knowledge is useful only as it improves character and prepares one for life. Believing that conjecture about useful things is preferable to idle speculation, Isocrates tried to stimulate his students to develop a working theory of politics.

He wanted to educate men who could function effectively in the realities of fourth-century Greece. He realized that the internecine warfare between the city-states had weakened Greek life. Believing that Greece had a civilizing role to play in the world, Isocrates stressed the need for a Panhellenic confederation of all the Greek city-states. Such a confederation would be practical, however, only if educated men managed their daily life well, were honorable in their associations, and were rational in outlook and temperament. To educate such men, Isocrates recommended the study of broad, liberal, and useful culture. Each man should approach the cultivated life through the liberal studies appropriate to free men. Of these studies, rhetoric, the rational expression of thought, is most important. Rhetorical studies, he believed, cultivate morality and contribute to practical politics.

Isocrates was critical of those sophists who, lacking a theoretical rationale for their discipline, taught rhetoric as a set of "practical" gimmicks. In contrast, he believed that man's power of discourse raises him above the animal level. The teaching of rhetoric should be based on a complete humanistic education that includes the learning of the tools and techniques of speech. The worthy orator should be able to discern and choose great and honorable causes, be devoted to human welfare, and advance the common good. To persuade his listeners, the orator should be trustworthy because of his exemplary personal life and conduct.

Isocrates' students enrolled in his school for a period of from three to four years, during which they studied rhetorical theory, heard model orations and sample discourses, and practiced intensive declamation. To develop men of broad and liberal outlook, Isocrates also included the study of politics, ethics, and history. Ethical and political

---

[4] See Costas M. Proussis, "The Orator: Isocrates," in Nash *et al., op. cit.,* pp. 55–76.

studies were intimately related and referred to the practical application of the codes of right conduct toward the gods, parents, children,
friends, enemies, and society. History was both an ethical and practical subject in that it was the source of examples to be used as evidence in support of argument. Above all, the teacher was of crucial
importance in Isocrates' method of rhetorical education. As a model,
the teacher had to be capable of influencing his pupils through his
knowledge, skill, manners, and ethical conduct.

In assessing Isocrates' educational contribution, it can be said that
he was probably not one of the great theorists of the Western world.
But as an effective and well-organized educator, he contributed to the
rhetorical tradition in education and influenced the Roman theorists
Cicero and Quintilian. By recognizing that rhetoric carried with it a
civic responsibility, Isocrates also contributed to the ideal of the liberally educated man.

Stoics and Epicureans

By the fourth century, the conquests of Alexander the Great had
ushered in the Hellenistic Age, which extended roughly from 323 to
30 B.C., or until the rise of the Roman Empire in the West under the
Emperor Augustus. The Hellenistic Age saw the extension of Greek
culture to much of the eastern Mediterranean, to Asia Minor, and to
northern Africa by the conquering armies of Alexander. This period
also served as the background for both the Roman Empire and the
coming of Christianity. It was not a remarkably creative period intellectually but rather a time of consolidation. Although Alexander may
have planned to effect a political, cultural, and economic merger of
the East and West, he emphasized Greek civilization. The resulting
Hellenistic culture was essentially a new phase of Greek thought. The
great Hellenistic philosophies, Stoicism and Epicureanism, drew heavily upon their philosophic antecedents, Platonism and Aristotelianism.
Epicurus (c. 342–270 B.C.), the founder of Epicureanism, based his
view of nature on a primitive atomic theory. He conceived the world
to be the product of units of matter—atoms—coming together almost
accidentally to form man and his environment. In this materialistic
context, man has no immortal soul and his only object in life is to
secure pleasure and to avoid pain. Pleasure is not to be identified with
sensuality or hedonism since overindulgence eventuates in pain. The
good Epicurean was to lead a simple life by cutting down his wants
and desires and subsequently his fears.

The philosophic rival to Epicureanism was Stoicism, founded by
Zeno (c. 340–265 B.C.), a contemporary of Epicurus. The name of
the philosophy derived from Zeno's use of the Stoa, the colonnade of

the Athenian marketplace, for his philosophic discussions. The Stoics held the universe to be guided by Divine Reason, a spark of which is present in every man. The purpose of man's existence is to lead a virtuous life based on temperance, judgment, bravery, courage, and justice. What happens to the body is really unimportant as long as man preserves his inner independence and hence his freedom. Each man is to fulfill his practical social duties and also preserve his independence.

When the Romans conquered Greece, they encountered Epicureanism and Stoicism, the Hellenistic philosophies, and imported them to Rome. Both of these philosophies attracted adherents among the Roman literati and politicians. The Roman poet Lucretius, for example, expounded on Epicurean themes in his *On the Nature of Things*. The Roman senator Cicero was a loyal disciple of Stoicism.

Conclusion

Socrates, Plato, Aristotle, Isocrates, Epicurus, Zeno, and their colleagues pondered the questions that have persistently faced man. Rejecting a reliance on simplistic superstition, the Greek theorists sought rational answers for man's basic questions about truth, beauty, and justice. Contemporary educational theorists still find that many of the concerns of Plato and Aristotle are at the core of current controversies. The issue of vocational versus liberal education debated by the sophists and their more speculative adversaries is still a point of contention among modern educators. Isocrates' concept of rhetorical education influenced the Roman orators, Cicero and Quintilian, and the humanist educators of the Renaissance. Greek education had a decided impact on the Roman educational experience. Chapter 4 will deal with the rise of Roman civilization and the educational system that was developed to transmit Roman culture.

Suggested Readings

Bailey, Cyril. *Epicurus*. New York: Russell and Russell, 1964.

Bosanquet, Bernard. *The Education of the Young in the Republic of Plato*. Cambridge, Mass.: Harvard University Press, 1901.

Broudy, Harry S., and John R. Palmer. *Exemplars of Teaching Method*. Chicago: Rand McNally, 1965.

Brumbaugh, Robert S., and Nathaniel M. Lawrence. *Philosophers on Education: Six Essays on the Foundations of Western Thought*. Boston: Houghton Mifflin, 1963.

Burnet, John. *Aristotle on Education*. Cambridge, Mass.: Harvard University Press, 1928.

Davidson, Thomas. *Aristotle and Ancient Educational Ideals*. New York: Franklin Burt, 1969.

Eckstein, Jerome. *The Platonic Method*. New York: Greenwood Publishing, 1968.

Frankena, William K. *Three Historical Philosophies of Education: Aristotle, Kant, and Dewey*. Chicago: Scott, Foresman, 1965.

Hadas, Moses. *Humanism: The Greek Ideal and Its Survival*. New York: Harper, 1960.

Kennedy, George. *The Art of Persuasion in Greece*. Princeton: Princeton University Press, 1963.

Livingstone, Richard. *Plato and Modern Education*. London. Cambridge University Press, 1944.

Moberly, Walter. *Plato's Conception of Education and Its Meaning Today*. New York: Oxford University Press, 1944.

Nettleship, Richard L. *The Theory of Education in the Republic of Plato*. London: Oxford University Press, 1939.

Norlin, George. *Isocrates*. Cambridge, Mass.: Harvard University Press, 1966.

Plato. *The Republic of Plato*. A. D. Lindsay (tr.). New York: Dutton, 1950.

Shorey, Paul. *What Plato Said*. Chicago: University of Chicago Press, 1957.

CHAPTER 4

Roman Education

In the fifth century B.C., Rome was but one of several small Latin city-states that existed on the Italian peninsula. From 509 until 250 B.C., the rural, landowning patricians who had deposed Tarquin, the last Etruscan ruler, and established an oligarchic republic dominated Rome. They elected the 300-member Senate, which made the policies. These policies were enforced by two elected consuls, who served one-year terms during which they exercised executive civil, military, and religious powers. Since each consul could veto the other's decisions, neither could assume an exclusive executive control.

In contrast to the powers of the patricians, the plebeians, who were of lower socioeconomic status, were second-class citizens. Although they were rewarded with land grants for military service during Rome's wars with its Latin neighbors, the plebeians became dissatisfied with their virtual disenfranchisement and threatened to secede from Rome and establish their own city-state. Faced with this threat, the patricians conceded more political rights to the plebeians, permitting them to elect their own representative assembly and ten tribunes to represent and safeguard their interests. Although the two classes were rigidly separated during Rome's early history, the social barriers were gradually weakened as some plebeians acquired commercial fortunes, and some patricians intermarried with the wealthy plebeians.

Education in the Early Republic

The educational patterns that developed in early Rome were those of the patrician family.[1] As the distinctions between the two classes fell, the plebeian also shared the patrician concept of education. Until

---

[1] For a thorough treatment of Roman educational patterns and developments, see H. I. Marrou, *A History of Education in Antiquity* (New York: Sheed and Ward, 1956).

the entry of large numbers of Greek slaves into Rome, however, the slave population was uneducated and illiterate.

As is true of most agricultural societies, life in early Rome was supported by religious, social, economic, and political rituals that stressed traditional belief and value patterns. It was the function of education to transmit these traditions to the young. Through participation in the rituals of his society, the young Roman learned to respect the body of valued traditions—or *mos maiorum,* the ways of the ancestors—that was the cultural core of Roman life. Deriving from a civic morality that embraced tradition, established institutions, religious ritual, and an exalted reverence for ancestral ways, Roman education sought to continue the status quo and avoid departure from established modes of conduct. To the Roman of the early republic, these proven skills and values were the surest guarantee to a secure and stable future.

During the early republic traditional roles and values were clearly defined. The boy of patrician ancestry quickly learned what was expected of him. He would become a landowner, a dutiful citizen, and a guardian of Rome's cultural heritage. As in other primitive societies, the child learned his role through direct association with his parents, who served as models of Roman life. Because formal educational institutions, or schools, did not exist in the early republic, the family thus became the agency by which the traditional values were transmitted to Roman children. The child's direct participation in the routines of family, political, and religious life reinforced the transmission of those values.

Essentially, it was the father, as both head of household and family priest, to whom the state entrusted the process of inducting the young Roman boy into citizenship. Nevertheless, the mother was the first educational influence on the child, as she was and is in most societies. Unlike her Athenian counterpart, the Roman mother held a respected position in her family. She served as a model of Roman womanhood to her daughters as she taught them the domestic skills that they would need as adults. When the boy reached age seven, the father assumed the role of chief teacher. Education was the deliberate association of father and sons, with the former serving as the personification of Roman tradition and values. As a sacred obligation, the father's authority over his household was reinforced by his religious role as the family priest. Roman children learned religious duties by participating in family prayers and rituals, which centered devotion on Vesta, the goddess of the hearth; the *penates,* or household gods; and the *lares,* the spirits of the family. Like most Roman activities, religious observance was more utilitarian than aesthetic. It sanctified patriotism, responsibility, and duty and enforced these values by encasing them in religious and emotional commitments.

Throughout its existence, Roman civilization was devoted to law. Originating as a society of individual landowners, Roman citizens were keenly conscious of rights and duties relating to property, possession, and inheritance. The Laws of the Twelve Tables, adopted in 450 B.C., codified the basic legal regulations governing Roman life. The rights and duties of a Roman citizen were clearly defined by legal specifications such as that of *patria potestas*, the right of the father over his family; *manus*, the right of the husband over his wife; *potestas dominica*, the right of the master over slaves; and *dominium*, the right of possession over property. The Roman boy had to memorize the legal prescriptions of the Tables. As he accompanied his father, the boy learned his lessons in law, politics, and customs.

The Roman style of life itself was basic to the religion, politics, and law that the Roman was expected to practice. Early Roman education sought to form the learner's character by inculcating a rigid system of moral values. The product of this education was to be a tradition-oriented person who knew and did his duty to the gods, the family, and the republic by maintaining a well-ordered estate and contributing to the public welfare. At the summit of the Roman value hierarchy were *pietas*, complete submission to parental authority, and *pudor*, reverence for family tradition. The good Roman life embodied the values of duty, self-control, fear of the gods, temperance, frugality, courage, patriotism, and self-sacrifice. These values were to be exemplified by the father and accepted and imitated by the son.

The formal aspects of education were minimal, the Roman boy learning only rudimentary reading, writing and arithmetic. Physical training, strictly utilitarian, included fencing, javelin-throwing, swordplay, riding, and weaponry. The father continued to educate his son until he reached age sixteen, when the youth put on the *toga virilis* and assumed his adult role. For wealthy youth, there was an extra year of education, or *tirocinium fori*, during which the young man was placed under the tutelage of a trusted family friend.

The successful product of early republican education was the highly practical man who made his property pay by knowing how to manage his land and superintend his slaves. He was a patriot and citizen soldier who was always ready to defend Rome against her adversaries. Above all, the good Roman knew his traditions and laws, loved them, and lived them.

Cultural Change and Roman Education

Roman educational patterns were altered by the cultural dynamics unleashed as Rome changed from a relatively isolated, small agricultural city-state to a vast empire with overseas colonies. Through a series of defensive wars, Rome conquered the neighboring Latin tribes. By 265 B.C., the city-state dominated the Italian peninsula and had become a major Mediterranean power. Rome's movement into the Mediterranean Sea, however, brought her into conflict with Carthage, a North African rival. Three long wars between Rome and Carthage profoundly affected both Roman life and education. As a result of the First Punic War (264–241), Carthage was forced to cede Sicily to Rome. Coming into contact with the Greek city-states of Sicily, Rome began a long courtship with Greek culture. During the Second Punic War (218–201), Hannibal's armies invaded Italy and seriously threatened Roman survival. As the Carthaginian armies poured over the Alps, the Latin farmers fled before them and sought safety in the city of Rome. Although the Carthaginians were again defeated, the Roman social structure was profoundly altered. Rome's population was swollen by the mass of dispossessed farmers, who existed at a level of near poverty. An equestrian elite emerged as the old patrician aristocracy merged with the upper-class plebeians. With the complete destruction of Carthage in the Third Punic War (149–146), Rome dominated the western Mediterranean and took possession of Corsica, Sardinia, and Spain.

Rome also moved eastward. In 201 B.C., Macedonia was defeated; in 188, the Seleucid Empire fell; by 146 B.C., Rome controlled all of Greece. These victories in the eastern Mediterranean gave Rome possession of the quarreling Greek city-states, and Roman administrators found themselves in charge of a predominantly Greek-speaking empire. This extension of Roman hegemony profoundly affected Roman education patterns. Faced with the necessity of governing an empire, Roman diplomats, generals, and civil servants were forced to rely on Greek as an international language. Therefore, Greek teachers and rhetoricians entered Rome to meet the demands of those Romans who wanted to learn Greek. As the contacts between Greeks and Romans increased, the Roman ruling elite grew conscious of their intellectual deficiencies and set out to capture Greek culture as they had captured Greek lands. It was to be Greek culture that mastered the Romans, however. As Horace stated: "Captive Greece took captive her savage conqueror and brought civilization to barbarous Latium."

The transition from city-state to world empire affected the quality of Roman life as Rome began to experience the complex political, social, religious, and economic transformations that characterized her later history. The simple, direct, and traditional values of piety, duty, and obedience, which had integrated Roman life in the early republic, proved inadequate in equipping Romans to manage, control, and exploit a great empire. Since they were primarily a political and legal people, the symptoms of cultural crisis were most evident in Roman politics and government. Although most Romans continued to revere the Laws of the Twelve Tables as did the statesman Cicero, the managing of overseas colonies required more sophisticated political and managerial competencies.

The booty expropriated from conquered peoples and the economic exploitation of the newly acquired colonies resulted in the rise of a new equestrian class of wealthy men—generals, governors, and commercial and agricultural magnates. This new class was so named because its members had enough wealth to equip themselves to serve as *equites* or knights in the cavalry, which was the most costly branch in the Roman army. The landless Latin peasantry, dislocated by the Carthaginian forays into the Italian peninsula, remained at the bottom of the Roman socioeconomic structure. Recognizing that extreme economic disparities between the equestrian elite and the landless poor boded ill for Rome, the Gracchi brothers, Gaius and Tiberius, attempted to inaugurate a reform program in the period from 133 to 121 B.C., which involved a relief system for the poor and a limitation on the size of the estates of the agricultural magnates. The stillborn reforms of the Gracchi resulted in a deadlock between reformers and conservatives.

Although Rome won a vast empire, her politicians were unable to establish processes for peaceful political change. A series of political intrigues, cabals, and outright civil wars attested to Rome's chronic inability to effect nonviolent domestic political change. This political conflict was not a matter of popular uprising but rather a series of struggles between various elite factions for control of power. The clash of conflicting interests filled the pages of Roman history with accounts of the intrigues and violence of the rivals Marius and Sulla, then Caesar and Pompey, and finally Octavian and Anthony.

After the assassination of Julius Caesar in 44 B.C., his nephew Octavian proclaimed himself successor to Caesar and consolidated power. Tired of domestic intrigue and civil war, most Romans welcomed their first emperor, Augustus, whose reign from 27 B.C. to A.D. 14 marked the transition from republic to empire. With the advent of Augustus, Roman life was profoundly changed. Although he appeared to preserve the old republican forms, he actually inaugurated a centralized administration that depended increasingly on the emperor's person. Gradually, Augustus and his successors came to control the army, treasury, and bureaucracy. Inherited institutions such as the Senate lost actual power and became fossilized formal vestiges of Rome's republican past.

After the reigns of Augustus and his more capable successors, the empire slowly but steadily declined. As the decline continued, the army gained the preponderance of power in proclaiming the emperors. Although historians have sought to explain Rome's decline, no one generalization adequately explains the complex processes of political, economic, and social dislocation and disintegration. Among the historical post-mortems that have been offered are the following: (1) a steady decrease in rainfall reduced agricultural productivity and resulted in periods of famine; (2) there was a crisis of political authority since Rome never really developed a clearly defined process of transferring power; (3) financial crisis occurred as the currency was debased to maintain an overextended army and officialdom; (4) the rise of Eastern mystery cults and Christianity weakened the indigenous Roman religion's emphasis on service to the state; (5) a psychological weariness pervaded Rome as its citizens, tired of the problems of empire, sought to escape reality by turning either to immediate pleasure or to a supernatural afterlife.

Institutional Patterns of Roman Education

The foregoing brief outline of the transition of Rome from city-state to empire was presented to illustrate the changing patterns of Roman life. In the republic's early years, the family, especially the father, had served as the major educational agency. Roman life had been integrated upon the core of tradition, and the father's role, as head of the family, was to transmit that tradition—its values, obligations, and rituals—to the child. However, in the later republican period, political and economic expansion had changed the basic patterns of Roman life. The father might now be a general, bureaucrat, or commercial magnate rather than a landowning aristocrat. Roman life had grown more complicated, more sophisticated, and less primitive. In a more advanced society, exclusive reliance on informal educational agencies such as the family is inadequate. As educational patterns become more formal, they are entrusted to specialized institutions, or schools.

In the course of establishing and administering an empire, the Romans came under the influence of Greek culture, which provided a model for a formal educational system. They therefore patterned their own educational institutions on the Greek school, curriculum, and teacher.

By the end of the fourth century B.C., an elementary school, or *ludus*, had appeared in Rome, presided over by a teacher, the *ludi magister*, or *literator*. Although ludus means play as well as place of practice in Latin, the routine of the Roman ludus emphasized strenuous discipline and corporal punishment. An institution for developing the skills of reading, writing, and arithmetic, the ludus was attended by children from the ages of seven through twelve. At first, it merely supplemented the home in matters of formal education. As in the case of other elementary institutions, either ancient or modern, the emphasis was on acquiring literacy. Instruction in reading consisted of memorizing the letters of the alphabet, constructing syllables, learning the meaning of words, and studying sentence structure. Writing instruction was simply a matter of copying down statements dictated by the teacher, and in arithmetic the students merely learned to count. As education grew more formal, the actual memorizing of the Twelve Tables was replaced by the reading of Homer's *Odyssey*, translated into Latin by Livius Andronicus (c. 284–c. 204 B.C.). The boy who attended the ludus was accompanied by a slave, or pedagogue, preferably Greek, who could act as tutor. The appearance of the pedagogue revealed a weakening of the idea that education should be directly supervised by the father. These elementary schools were completely private and without state supervision.

In the middle of the third century B.C., a Greek grammar school appeared as an institution of secondary education. Under the direction of a grammar teacher, *grammaticus,* Roman boys from ages ten to sixteen studied Greek grammar, composition, poetry, and history. The school routine involved a careful examination of all aspects of grammar—words, phonetics, conjugations, and declensions. A Latin grammar school, which taught the grammar of the Roman vernacular, appeared in the first century B.C. By the reign of Augustus, the Latin grammar school was a recognized part of Roman education, and the educated Roman was expected to be thoroughly familiar with the works of Vergil and other Roman poets. The Greek and Latin grammar schools were parallel rather than rival institutions, and the educated Roman boy of the late republic and the empire was expected to have attended both institutions. As the school of the grammaticus became more formal, its curriculum came to embrace all of the liberal arts and included elements of grammar, rhetoric, dialectic, arithmetic, geometry, music, and astronomy.

For higher studies, the Roman youth at ages sixteen through eighteen attended the rhetorical schools, which appeared in the first century B.C. Concerned with the education of the orator, rhetorical studies combined both the Greek conception of the liberally educated man and the Roman emphasis on practicality. Rhetorical studies were immensely practical for the Roman in that speaking abilities helped the politician to gain control of the crowd, influence voting in the Senate, and inspire troops. The study of rhetoric led the Roman to other aspects of Greek culture.

During the republican period, education was primarily a private matter in which the state exercised little or no direct control. During the empire, however, the emperors gradually exerted their authority over education by subsidizing teachers and schools. Emperor Vespasian (A.D. 69–79) was notable for his patronage and support of educational institutions. He introduced taxation benefits and exemptions in order to attract Greek teachers, established library facilities, and provided endowments for distinguished rhetoricians. Emperor Antoninus Pius (A.D. 138–161) required the major cities of the empire to support grammarians and rhetoricians.

With the advent of Christianity, church schools came to have greater significance. Catechumenal schools were established to provide instruction in the Christian religion to those who were candidates for baptism. These schools were attended by adults who took two or three years of instruction in Christian doctrine provided by the elders of the Christian community. During the various persecutions of Nero, Decius, and Diocletian, the Christian schools were conducted secretly. In 313, Constantine accorded the Christians full legal rights, and in 325 Christianity was recognized as the official state religion.

Rome's Educational Ideal: The Orator

The Roman conception of education is best exemplified in the person of the orator, who served as a model of the educated man during most of Rome's history. By examining the general Roman conception of the orator and the education that was designed to produce him, it is possible to achieve an understanding of Rome's educational ideal.

The Roman conception of the orator as a model of the educated man had Greek roots. Isocrates, one of the most prominent of the Greek rhetoricians, had an impact on Roman educational theory and practice through his program of rhetorical education, which conceived of the orator as a liberally educated participant in public affairs. This concept was not restricted to politicians or lawyers but included teachers and civil servants as well. In sum, the Roman orator was the educated man who demonstrated an interest in the affairs of the republic.

In discussing the Roman conception of oratorical or rhetorical education, two major theorists are significant: Cicero and Quintilian, each of whom represents the art of rhetoric at a particular stage of development. Like any educational theory, their conceptions of the educated man rested upon the broad framework of social, political, religious, and economic life. In other words, their theories reflected the cultural demands of the period in which they were developed.

Cicero's Conception of the Orator

Although Cicero (106–43 B.C.) is probably best known historically as a major spokesman of the conservative faction in the Roman Senate, he is significant in Western educational history for his writings on the preparation of an orator that appeared as *De oratore* in 55 B.C.[2] Cicero himself experienced both the old Roman and the Hellenized styles of education. He studied Greek grammar and literature and Latin literature and history and concentrated on rhetoric as a higher study. As the scion of a wealthy family, he toured Greece and Asia Minor and was familiar with both Stoic and Epicurean philosophies.

Cicero's life coincided with the period of cultural and educational transition in which Rome was faced with what seemed to be two conflicting ways of life: the older Roman and the newer Greek. But he appreciated both the old Roman values of practicality and utility and the Greek emphasis on humanistic culture. When he wrote *De oratore*, Cicero was ostensibly concerned with the education of his son Marcus. However, his book served a wider purpose in that it represented a synthesis of both the Roman republican and the Greek conceptions of the educated man. He presented the Roman view that oratory had practical consequences such as the winning of debates in the Forum and the Greek view that the orator should be educated as a man of broad culture, or *humanitas*. After contrasting these apparently divergent conceptions of the orator, Cicero effected a compromise that retained the best of both: (1) the orator as a rational man should be broadly educated in the liberal arts; (2) because oratory should affect the public interest, the humanely educated orator should use his education for the public good. Thus, Cicero sought to reconcile the Roman values based on traditional authority with the humanistic and liberalizing influences emanating from Greek culture.

Concerned only with Roman higher education, or rhetoric, Cicero did not develop a systematic plan for education at the elementary and secondary levels. He did, however, comment on the work of the grammaticus, the secondary school teacher, insofar as it affected preparation for rhetorical study. The grammaticus was to comment on the poets, teach history, correct accent and delivery, and explain the meaning and nuances of language. Although Greek was to be the major language of instruction, the young Roman was also to be skilled in using his own Latin vernacular.

After the prospective student of rhetoric had been adequately prepared in grammar, he embarked on the higher studies that were needed for oratory. He was to be thoroughly prepared for the liberal arts, the chief instruments in forming the truly humane person.

Although Cicero recommended that the orator acquire a general knowledge of ethics, psychology, military science, medicine, natural

---

[2] For a comprehensive study of Roman education, which includes a discussion of Cicero, see Aubrey Gwynn, *Roman Education from Cicero to Quintilian* (Oxford, England: Clarendon Press, 1926). Gwynn's book has been reprinted in a recent edition of the Classics in Education series of Teachers College Press, Columbia University.

science, geography, and astronomy, the most important subjects were history, law, and philosophy.

History was to provide the young Roman with perspective into his own tradition, into the lives of his ancestors, and into the memory of past deeds of Roman greatness. It would give him a rich stock of rhetorical illustrations, and an awareness of great men, public morality, and human psychology.

A true Roman, Cicero was devoted to and emphasized the study of law. He felt that the Laws of the Twelve Tables were the basis of Roman jurisprudence and had aided Rome in maintaining a vast empire. As he put it:

> When due attention is paid to the origins and principles of our laws, a single copy of the Twelve Tables has greater weight and authority than all the libraries of all the philosophers in the world.[3]

Cicero also believed that great oratory was impossible without a philosophical perspective. But like most Romans, he regarded philosophy as practical ethics rather than abstract speculation. Statesmen such as Isocrates, Themistocles, and Pericles were to be studied rather than Plato and Aristotle and other speculative philosophers. The Ciceronian conception of philosophy included psychology, ethics, politics, and logic.

Having completed this broad framework of liberal study, the orator was then to pursue the study of rhetoric. Since he was to be above all a public man and a public speaker, he had to learn how to choose his words carefully and structure his arguments in the most persuasive manner. He also needed to develop keen psychological insight in order to excite the emotions of his audience and influence the conduct and affairs of men. A man of grace and wit, he had to be quick to reply and to attack and be competent in using a variety of speaking styles.

The Ciceronian oratorical ideal is best expressed by the concept *humanitas*, which signifies all that is worthy in man—that is, to be a man in all that is human and to be humane in human relationships. He believed that oratory could be dynamic in that it could influence public opinion and state policy and thus be an instrument of power. Cicero's death in 43 B.C. marked the end of the republican conception of oratory. With the coming of the empire, the external forms related to oratorical education remained intact, but the dynamic quality disappeared. Although the educated man was still an orator, the emperor and the army exerted actual power over decision-making.

[3] *Ibid.*, p. 109.

The Quintilian Oratorical Model

Quintilian (A.D. c. 35–c. 95) was born in the Spanish provinces of the Roman Empire. After working in Rome as an assistant to the lawyer Domitius Afer, he spent some time in Spain as a teacher of rhetoric. Returing to Rome, he occupied the first public chair of Latin rhetoric for a period of over twenty years. As the valued retainer of five Roman emperors ranging from Galba to Domitian, he headed the Roman teaching profession. Although he worked in the sophisticated capital of the empire, Quintilian's outlook and values remained provincial. He was still devoted to the older system of Roman values, which rested on the authority of tradition and emphasized basic loyalties to family, duty, and nation. Although it suggested a program of oratorical education designed to revitalize the commitments of Roman life, Quintilian's oratorical conception nevertheless reflected the continuing transition that was taking place in Roman culture. Under the emperors, imperial decrees were a more potent instrument of public policy than persuasive speech. Although oratory remained the dominant educational pattern, it had become more ornamental and less dynamic.

Unlike Cicero, who was actively engaged in Roman politics, Quintilian was primarily a teacher of rhetoric. Directly concerned with educating orators, he was more involved with elaborating a systematic educational theory than was Cicero.[4] Despite these differences in orientation to the problems of rhetorical education, both men shared a conviction that the orator should be a person of humanitas, or liberal culture. For Quintilian the perfect orator was not only an excellent speaker but was also a worthy human being.

Quintilian's Institutio oratoria, a plan for the proper education of the orator, appeared in A.D. 94. As a systematic educational work, it dealt with the education of a boy prior to the study of rhetoric, the studies proper to rhetoric, and the theory and practice of rhetoric. Quintilian's work is useful not only as a commentary on oratorical preparation but also as a systematic treatment of education.

Far in advance of the general development of educational theory, Quintilian recognized that there are significant stages of human development that hold important implications for educational practice. Although his identification of these stages is rudimentary by contemporary standards, it does reveal him to be a keen student of educational psychology. According to Quintilian, the child is impulsive from birth

---

[4] William M. Smail, Quintilian on Education (Oxford, England: Clarendon Press, 1938) includes an excellent introduction to Quintilian's Institutio oratoria. Smail's book has been recently reprinted in the Classics in Education series of Teachers College Press, Columbia University.

until age seven in that his actions are directed to the immediate satisfaction of needs and desires. Since the early childhood years are crucial in establishing the right patterns and dispositions for later education, parents should be very careful to select proper nurses, pedagogues, and companions since these persons exercise a shaping influence on the child. Quintilian's comments clearly indicate that the direct influence of the father and mother on the child had weakened by the imperial period in that child care was delegated to slaves. He advised that it was extremely important to have a Greek nurse and pedagogue who used correct speech and pronunciation so that the future orator's speech patterns would be uncorrupted.

Quintilian regarded the period from age seven to fourteen as the one in which the child learns from sense experience, first forms clear ideas, and develops memory. During this stage, the child learns to read and write the languages that he already speaks. The reading and writing teacher, literator, was to be of good character and possess the competency to make learning attractive. Reading and writing were to be taught gradually, and the school was to include games for recreational purposes. Quintilian's conception of elementary schooling was quite different from the conventional ludus, where corporal punishment was an expected part of the daily school routine. He also suggested that the child have a set of ivory letters to aid in learning the alphabet; as he traced the outline of the letters, the child would learn to write. Quintilian's suggestion about ivory letters indicates that he was writing about the education of the upper classes, who could afford such expensive didactic materials.

From fourteen to seventeen, the student was to develop his reasoning power by studying the liberal arts in the school of the grammaticus. Quintilian carefully distinguished between rhetoric and grammar, which he believed should be taught separately. Both Greek and Latin grammars were to be studied concurrently. Grammar involved the study of the literatures of Greece and Rome; historical and mythological allusions were to be explained as texts were critically examined. In addition to grammar, the curriculum preparatory to rhetorical study comprised music, geometry, astronomy, and gymnastics.

After a thorough grounding in grammar and the other liberal arts, the prospective orator was to begin rhetorical studies. As Cicero had done, Quintilian recommended that rhetorical study seek to produce a man of broad culture, or humanitas, humanely educated, and willing to serve his country. The orator was not to specialize in any of the liberal arts but was to have experience with all of them. His continuing studies were to include poetry, drama, prose, history, law, philosophy, and rhetoric.

Among the rhetorical studies, declamation—systematic speaking exercises—was most useful for the orator. The themes of the declamations were to be realistic, and the fictitious was to be avoided. As the student orators delivered their practice orations, it would be seen that certain of them lacked the capacity for oratory. These students were to be dismissed so that the teacher could devote his energies to the most promising orators. As soon as possible, the novice orator was to speak in the Forum before an audience. After doing so, he was to return to the rhetorician for criticism and correction. Although the teacher should be tactful, patient, and kind, he should not hesitate to demonstrate his competence and authority by correcting the student's mistakes. After sufficient practice and correction, the student would become a proficient speaker who could exercise his talents without further benefit of the teacher.

Quintilian's model of the educated man, the orator, was a good man as well as a skilled speaker. Indeed, he believed that speaking and personal excellence were reciprocal and that the development of perfect oratorical delivery depended upon the speaker's own high moral standards. The evil man could never really be the good orator. Since his task was to persuade, the orator had to be worthy of trust.

As mentioned earlier, Quintilian is significant in Western educational history because he addressed himself to many of the theoretical and practical problems of teaching and learning. In anticipating the modern educator's concern for individual differences among learners, Quintilian recommended that learning be made appropriate to the learner's abilities and readiness. He also recommended that the good teacher motivate students by making learning interesting and attractive rather than by resorting to corporal punishment. He preferred group situations to tutorial work since group learning promoted social skills and development. He recognized the importance of early childhood experiences in shaping the character of the young. Since he believed that moral and intellectual learnings are related, he recommended that learning start as early as possible.

When the Greek and Roman literatures were rediscovered by the Renaissance humanist educators, Quintilian's ideas assumed a new currency. His ideas on liberal culture, individual differences, interest, and motivation were rediscovered by Vittorino da Feltre, who used them to educate the Renaissance man.

The Orator and the Empire

As indicated earlier, the orator was the model of the educated man in Rome throughout both the republican and imperial periods. While Rome was a republic, persuasion and argument were relevant to decision-making. Oratory was an instrument of public power, and those who developed and exercised oratorical skill were men who hoped to influence the events of their day. Cicero conceived of oratory in dynamic terms, and his conception of rhetorical education reflected this dynamism.

After decision-making shifted from the oligarchic elites of republican Rome to imperial decree, however, the orator had little actual effect on decision-making, and oratory became increasingly formal. It assumed the artificiality that dominated Roman life during the empire. As a greater concern was given to cultivating an elegant speaking style rather than to determining policy, Quintilian, unlike Cicero, had to caution rhetoricians against becoming too theoretical and losing touch with real life.

Although the portents of cultural disintegration were becoming increasingly apparent to emperors, poets, and educators, Roman education did little to cope with the problems facing the empire. Concerned with style and elegance rather than with service, rhetorical education grew increasingly formalized and ignored the very real issues of political succession, social violence, and economic disparities. As the cultural core disintegrated, Roman political, social, and educational leaders were unable to create values that would command the loyalties of the Roman citizenry. The only alternatives offered were the preachments of emperors, poets, and educators who continued to look backward to tradition and to plead that the old heroic Roman virtues of duty, piety, and obedience be used to revitalize Roman life. Unhappily for Rome, the force of tradition proved inadequate in sustaining an empire that had outgrown these values.

Conclusion

Although the Roman Empire collapsed more than fifteen hundred years ago, the Latin legacy was one that exerted a profound influence on Western culture. The Roman Church adopted Latin as its official ecclesiastical and liturgical language. Although the Latin tradition was weakened during the early medieval period, it reasserted itself strongly during the later Middle Ages. The Renaissance classical humanist, in his zeal to restore Latin to its original purity, impressed it on formal education as the official tongue of the educated man. Until the modern period, Latin dominated secondary and higher curriculums.

Roman practicality and administrative genius created the Roman Empire, a remarkable political achievement which endured for more than a thousand years. Roman education, too, revealed a practicality and utility that contributed to Rome's success until the disintegration of the empire. When Rome fell, Western civilization, too, was on the brink of collapse. Chapter 5 will deal with the long period of the Middle

Ages when Western man attempted to find a substitute for the stability that Rome had offered.

Suggested Readings

Boak, A. E. R. *History of Rome to 565* A.D. New York: Macmillan, 1955.

Butler, H. E. *Quintilian.* Cambridge, Mass.: Harvard University Press, 1963.

Clark, Donald. *Rhetoric in Greco-Roman Education.* New York: Columbia University Press, 1957.

Cowell, Frank R. *Cicero and the Roman Republic.* New York: Chanticleer Press, 1948.

Dill, Samuel. *Roman Society in the Last Century of the Western Empire.* New York: Macmillan, 1921.

Earl, Donald C. *The Moral and Political Tradition of Rome.* Ithaca, New York: Cornell University Press, 1967.

Fowler, W. Warde. *Social Life at Rome in the Age of Cicero.* New York: Macmillan, 1933.

Gwynn, Aubrey. *Roman Education from Cicero to Quintilian.* Oxford, England: Clarendon Press, 1926; New York: Teachers College Press, n.d.

Hadas, Moses. *History of Latin Literature.* New York: Columbia University Press, 1952.

Kenyon, F. G. *Books and Readers in Ancient Greece and Rome.* New York: Oxford University Press, 1932.

Marrou, Henri I. *A History of Education in Antiquity.* New York: Sheed and Ward, 1956.

McDonald, Alexander H. *Republican Rome.* New York: Praeger, 1966.

McMullen, Ramsey. *Soldier and Civilian in the Later Roman Empire.* Cambridge, Mass.: Harvard University Press, 1963.

Nettleship, H. *The Study of Latin Grammar Among the Romans in the First Century* A.D. London: Oxford University Press, 1895.

Parks, E. P. *The Roman Rhetorical Schools as a Preparation for the Courts Under the Early Empire.* Baltimore: Johns Hopkins University Press, 1945.

Rostovtzeff, M. *The Social and Economic History of the Roman Empire.* London: Oxford University Press, 1957.

Smail, William M. *Quintilian on Education.* Oxford: Clarendon Press, 1938; New York: Teachers College Press, n.d.

Starr, Chester G. *Emergence of Rome as Ruler of the Western World.* Ithaca, N.Y.: Cornell University Press, 1953.

Wilkins, A. S. *Roman Education.* New York: Macmillan, 1905.

CHAPTER 5

Medieval Education

The thousand years of history from Rome's fall in the fifth century to America's discovery in the fifteenth century have been widely and variously interpreted. Still bearing the name given by the scholars of the Renaissance and Reformation, the "Middle Ages" are regarded as either bridging or separating the ancient Greco-Roman and modern cultures. Although all histories reveal their authors' biases, the medieval period has suffered from the burden of prejudiced interpretations. While some historians have labeled the medieval period a "dark age" of superstition and ignorance, others have enthusiastically proclaimed it as the pinnacle of Western achievement. Undoubtedly, a balanced assessment of the medieval contribution of Western educational history lies between these two extremes.

Since the predominant cultural influences of the post-Enlightenment era have been empirical, scientific, and technological rather than spiritual, contemporary man may feel a greater empathy for the basically materialistic and humanistic Greek and Roman civilizations than for the otherworldly medieval culture. The medieval theocentric world view with its hierarchical conception of society and its notion of a static universe makes it difficult to use contemporary experience in historically reconstructing the patterns of medieval life and education. In the twentieth century, John Dewey's pragmatic experimentalism, which emphasizes a changing universe and society, the relativity of values, and the use of the scientific method to establish tentative "truths," has influenced the modern educator's propensity to change, innovation, and process. This pragmatic outlook is in sharp contrast to the medieval schoolman's acceptance of religious authority, transcendent and eternal truth, and the existence of permanent values within a stable society.

The Medieval World View

During the Middle Ages, Western Christianity, institutionalized in the structure of the Latin or Roman Catholic Church, sought to integrate and sustain Western civilization. In pursuing this end, the Church operated primarily as a spiritual force, although its policies had strong social, economic, and political implications. Its attempt to integrate medieval life, beliefs, and values, can be examined in terms of those institutional, cognitive, and attitudinal aspects that bear directly on education.

In attempting to unify Western European life, the church sought to weave a synthesis that combined both the content of Christian doctrine and the forms of Roman legalism. Claiming divine sanction, the church traced its foundation to Christ, the Son of God, and asserted that it continued to draw inspiration from the Holy Spirit. As an institution, the church developed a hierarchical government in which authority flowed downward from the highest and most general to the most particular and immediate level. The location of particular offices and persons within the hierarchy was determined on the basis of sanctity. At the summit of the hierarchy, the pope, as bishop of Rome and successor of Peter, exercised general authority over the universal church. The bishops, successors to the apostles, were responsible to papal authority and charged with the episcopal administration of their dioceses. Lower in the hierarchy and responsible to their bishops were the parish priests who administered directly to the individual members of their congregations. It is not difficult to discern the similarities that existed between the Roman Church's hierarchical government and the administrative agencies of the now defunct Roman Empire. Through the hierarchy, the church sought to govern itself and provide some semblance of order to an initially chaotic society.

Medieval Christianity must not be viewed solely within the context of the hierarchical system of the Roman Church but should also be examined in terms of the doctrines, literatures, belief, liturgy, and sacraments that sustained it. The Old and New Testaments, the writings of the church fathers, the councils of the church, and the body of tradition were authoritative sources for Western Christendom. From these sources came the doctrines that were protected, interpreted, and enforced by the hierarchy of the institutional church. As the primary educational agency of the medieval world, the church, through its teachers and in its schools, transmitted the corpus of Christian doctrine to Western man. According to the medieval schoolman, the church's divinely sanctioned teaching authority rested on the sacred Scripture and inspired doctrine.

Although the corpus of medieval religious belief was never as absolutistic nor as monolithic as many interpreters have indicated, certain basic beliefs characterized Christian life. God was omnipotent and perfect, the personal Creator of all existence; man, possessing a spiritual soul and a corporeal body, was created to share in the divine happiness. Endowed with an intellect and will, man had freedom of choice. As a descendant of Adam, man inherited the effects of original sin and was therefore spiritually deprived. God sent his Son, Jesus Christ, to redeem mankind, through His death and resurrection. To aid man in achieving salvation, Christ instituted the church and charged it with administering the grace-giving sacraments to man.

These basic Christian beliefs held great importance for medieval education and continue to have an impact on contemporary Roman Catholic education.[1] First, the believer needed doctrinal instruction so that his belief might be strengthened by knowledge. The church and its schools acted to protect, transmit, and inculcate Christian doctrines. Second, Latin or Roman Christianity was a sacramental system. Of the seven sacraments, the central act of religious worship was the reception of the Eucharist at the celebration of the liturgy of the Mass. Liturgical ceremony and sacramental administration required a specially ordained priesthood. The medieval church devoted much of its energy to educating its priests in Latin, the language of the Western liturgy, in Christian doctrine, and in performing the sacramental duties of the priestly office. In addition to priestly preparation, the medieval church also educated its adherents in the prayers, rubrics, and music that accompanied religious worship and observance.

The effect of the institutional church and the body of doctrinal belief on the psychological and behavioral aspects of medieval life has been noted by Huizinga, who has interpreted the life of medieval man as one of psychological extremes.[2] Never far removed from his primitive and barbaric origins, the medieval Christian was nevertheless intensely pietistical in his religious observance. His psychological tension was exhibited by extreme behaviors that alternated between violent cruelty and romantic gentleness. This uneasy merger of primitive barbarian and gentle Christian produced an underlying tension and a propensity to violence, which the church sought to quiet and harness by codifying and formalizing behavior. The social, economic, and political aspects of many of the events of medieval life, such as feast

[1] For a full treatment of medieval Christian education from a Roman Catholic perspective, see Patrick J. McCormick and Francis P. Cassidy, *History of Education* (Washington: Catholic Education Press, 1953), pp. 167–316. William T. Kane, S.J., *History of Education* (Chicago: Loyola University Press, 1952), pp. 53–129, also presents a very readable account.

[2] J. Huizinga, *The Waning of the Middle Ages* (Garden City, N.Y.: Doubleday, 1954), pp. 9–31.

days, holidays, fairs, and pilgrimages, were given a religious significance. In the code of chivalric education, warfare was formalized into what came to be an ethical system.

Although religious values were well defined, in the early medieval period, political, social, and economic life was fragmented. The one world of Roman law, political administration, and economic production had shattered into thousands of small, local, and semiautonomous political, social, and economic units. Medieval man made his political and economic commitments to his immediate feudal overlord rather than to any larger political unit. This medieval decentralization is in sharp contrast to the post-Renaissance consolidation of people and centralization of power into nation-states. In the twentieth century an even more intensive concentration of power, resources, and people into urban areas has occurred. This contrast is particularly marked when the nationalism, industrialization, urbanization, and economic interdependence of the modern era are compared with medieval localism, agrarianism, and economic self-sufficiency.

The medieval decentralization of political authority and economic power and resources had an impact on the development of formal educational agencies. Until the end of the tenth century, agricultural production remained at the near-subsistence level and required the energies of the bulk of the population. The children of the serfs, a permanently indentured agricultural class, began to work in the field at an early age. Their education was direct and informal as they imitated the skills by which their parents survived. The rather small medieval manors developed no extensive educational institutions but relied instead upon the church's monastic and parish schools. While the feudal lords did educate their own children according to the chivalric code, they left general educational matters to the church, which exercised a virtual monopoly over formal schooling. This is in contrast to the modern era where the nation-state has erected centralized school systems that educate children to be loyal and productive citizens.

Although many other contrasts can be drawn between the modern and medieval modes of life, perhaps none is sharper than the differences in attitudes toward social change. While modern man conceives of the universe and society in dynamic and changing terms, medieval man assumed reality to be permanent, stable, and unchanging. Since the eighteenth-century Enlightenment, modern man has devised and fought for a plethora of economic, social, and political plans designed to reconstruct the social order according to a particular socioeconomic-political design. Such alternative proposals as capitalism, Marxism, anarchism, socialism, syndicalism, utopianism, fascism, and numerous other "isms" represent modern man's search for means to integrate the political, social, economic, and psychological aspects of his life. The bewildering variety of ideologies of the modern era present a particular problem for the educator since each "ism" has an appropriate educational philosophy, content, and method. In contrast to modern man's attempt to engineer the perfect society on earth, medieval man had no such illusion. For him it was possible that the "heavenly city" could ever have a temporal existence. Rather than look for schemes to reconstruct society, medieval man accepted things as they were in the imperfect but temporary existence of this world. He looked toward the perfect world, the other world, promised by his church as the reward for a life devoted to faith and good works. If social and political institutions existed, they were part of the Creator's grand design and were intrinsically good. Corruption was due to man's imperfect nature rather than to institutional imperfection.

When the medieval schoolman rejected the possibility of social change, he also rejected the notion that education might be a strategy for effecting societal reformation. For him, true education was based on the unerring authority of revealed truth. Although doctrines might need clarification, they did not change. The medieval schoolman's task was the transmission of belief, language, doctrine, tradition, and custom rather than social engineering.

As mentioned earlier, the hierarchical conception of authority that governed the church permeated medieval society. Medieval man accepted the existence of hierarchies of authorities, ranks, and estates. According to his conception of an organic society, every individual had an assigned place and performed a needed function. In rejecting social change, the medieval outlook also rejected the notion of socioeconomic mobility. Although there were definite formal political and social distinctions, there was spiritual equality in that all souls—peasant, priest, bishop, knight—were equal before God. The medieval stress on the stasis of social classes contradicts the American conceptions of social mobility and equality of educational opportunity in which the formal school is regarded as an agency of upward mobility.

This rather extended discussion of the medieval world view is intended as an introduction to the various stages of medieval development and to the types of agencies that formed its educational experience. The very early Middle Ages were primarily a time of educational disintegration, with the one bright exception of the Carolingian Renaissance.

The Early Middle Ages: A.D. 500 to 1000

With the exception of the short-lived Carolingian empire, the early Middle Ages was primarily a period of political, cultural, economic, and educational dislocation. The various invasions of the Germanic tribes had weakened the political authority of the Roman Empire.

While the Byzantine emperor at Constantinople maintained the residues of Roman authority in the East, the Western empire completely disintegrated in the fifth century. In what is now present-day France and Western Germany, the kingdom of the Franks arose in the eighth century to fill the power vacuum left in the wake of the demise of Roman political authority. Frankish hegemony was first asserted by the various Merovingian kings and then consolidated by Charles Martel (c. 690–741), the founder of the Carolingian line which produced Charlemagne (768–814), who was crowned by Pope Leo III as the first holy Roman emperor on Christmas Day, 800.[3]

The conversion of the Franks to Christianity by Saint Boniface had represented a cultural as well as a religious transformation. This transition was a difficult one in which the old forms of authority, such as the native Druid nature religion, mythology, and folk customs, came into contact with the Roman church and Greco-Roman culture. The resulting merger of the old "barbarian" and Roman Christian values produced an unwieldy product, the Christian barbarian. The Emperor Charlemagne himself represents such a pattern of often conflicting values. He could be excessively cruel in battle, wreaking vengeance on his defeated enemies, and then remorsefully repent of his barbaric excesses. He was illiterate, yet he valued the Latin language and literature. Although he was the holy emperor, he frequently quarreled with the pope.

Charlemagne's empire included both Franks and non-Frankish peoples, such as the Lombards and Saxons. The administration of this empire raised educational problems that concerned both general culture and practical application. The office of "holy Roman emperor" represented an attempt to revitalize the decayed Roman culture in a Christian and Frankish guise. To secure his empire, Charlemagne allied himself with the Roman Church. Seizing upon Latin Christianity as the cultural cement that would hold this empire together, he involved himself in church affairs and sought to reform the clergy as an instrument of political and cultural as well as religious integration.

Once the empire had been secured militarily, an administrative apparatus was needed to maintain political and juridical control and to collect the needed taxes, fees, tithes, and fines. Charlemagne's own person combined both the offices of monarch and magistrate. He delegated administrative authority to pairs of royal bureaucrats, *missi dominici*, consisting of a bishop and a secular official, who proclaimed decrees, collected taxes, and administered justice. Since these administrators were to maintain records, conduct proceedings, and draw up tax lists, they needed to be literate and have at least some basic

[3] For a biographical study of Charlemagne, see Richard Winston, *Charlemagne from the Hammer to the Cross* (New York: Random House, 1960).

formal education. Concerned with the need for a trained clergy and bureaucracy, Charlemagne sought to discover, reward, and encourage scholars and educators. Alcuin (735–804), an English monk, was foremost among the Carolingian educators who worked to make the Frankish nobles literate. Familiar with the Latin classics and the sixth century writings of Boethius and Cassiodorus on the liberal arts, the scholarly Alcuin organized the Latin literary inheritance into textbooks.

As Charlemagne's chief educational minister, Alcuin conducted the palace school at Aachen, which was attended by the Frankish nobility of the imperial court.[4] In performing the difficult task of teaching Latin to barbarians, Alcuin prepared a number of dialogue textbooks in question-and-answer form. His use of the catechetical method of teaching Latin gave at least a veneer of literacy to his students. He also advised Charlemagne in enacting educational legislation that required every abbey to conduct a school where boys might learn reading, writing, psalm singing, arithmetic, and Latin grammar.

Although Charlemagne's empire provides the best source regarding education in the early Middle Ages, his empire died with him. Under his less competent ninth and tenth century successors, the Carolingian empire disintegrated into a number of independent and semiautonomous local fiefdoms.

Major Educational Agencies

Three major lines of educational institutions developed in the medieval period: (1) those related directly to the church; (2) those concerned with educating the feudal aristocracy; and (3) those related to craft or vocational education. Although all three patterns of educational development bore a religious orientation, the most formal educational institutions, schools, were under church control. Stemming from the church fathers' early concern for a clergy literate in Latin and knowledgeable of doctrine and liturgy, the church schools were most directly concerned with literary education. Chivalric training, the second line of development, was directed to the knightly education of feudal aristocrats, and guild education, the third line, was charged with preparing craftsmen in the use of tools and other productive skills. This three-track system of education was keyed to the class structure of medieval society, providing a distinct education for the cleric, the knight, and the craftsman. Yet the largest class—the mass

[4] Harry S. Broudy and John R. Palmer, "Teaching Courtly Barbarians: Alcuin," in *Exemplars of Teaching Method* (Chicago: Rand McNally, 1965), pp. 47–58.

of serfs, whose labors supported the entire medieval social structure—
was largely uneducated.

The Church and Education

As stated earlier, the medieval world view was decidedly theocentric.
In observing natural phenomena, medieval man was likely to see the
direct intervention of God. Religious and political authorities were not
carefully separated and jurisdictional spheres were often blurred.
These factors led to the various conflicts between ecclesiastical and
political authorities that characterized much of medieval history. Notable among them was the struggle between Pope Gregory VII and the
holy Roman emperor Henry VII over the prerogative of investing
bishops with their authority. Despite these struggles, the Roman
Catholic Church, with the assistance of secular authorities, maintained
a unity of religious belief. According to the medieval synthesis, there
was only one true church, and heretics were regarded as both religious
and political outcasts. They were rigorously and often brutally suppressed, as in the case of the Albigensians in southern France during
the eleventh century. Despite the church's maintenance of a religious
synthesis and unity, it is an oversimplification to assert that medieval
Christendom was a monolithic institution. There were wide differences
of opinion, of theological interpretation, and of organizational forms
within the church. When these differences were internal or communal
conflicts, the medieval church tolerated and assimilated a variety of
viewpoints. When they appeared to go beyond the definitions of the
medieval Christian synthesis, the church vigorously suppressed them.

The medieval church always faced problems of clarifying doctrine
and eliminating corruption within its own ranks. A chronic problem
centered upon control of property. Feudal lords sought to usurp church
wealth; as monasteries became wealthy landowners, some of the
monks lost their zeal for their vows of poverty, chastity, and obedience,
a basic part of monastic life. Periodically, the medieval church experienced waves of internal reformation such as the one that radiated
from the Benedictine monastery at Cluny, founded in 910. The Cluniac
reformation sought to restore simplicity and asceticism to the church,
and it was significant as an educational movement that produced
a number of competent and well-trained scholars.

During the course of the Middle Ages, a growing distinction occurred
in the ranks and kinds of clergy. There were the village and town
priests, or secular clergy, who ministered directly to their congregations and were responsible to bishops. Then there were the monks, or
regular clergy, who lived in communal organizations according to
various *regula*, rules of community life. Monastic life attracted large
numbers in the early Middle Ages. During the breakdown of town life,

the monasteries located in agricultural regions became self-sufficient communities. In addition to fostering agriculture and the various crafts needed to sustain monastic life, the monasteries were literary, artistic, intellectual, and educational centers.

When town life revived in the eleventh century, orders of mendicant friars formed to preach to the city dwellers. Most notable among these were the Franciscans, founded by Saint Francis of Assisi (c. 1182–1226). Believing that certain monastic orders had outgrown their primitive asceticism and were being corrupted by wealth, land, and power, Francis, a Christian mystic, founded a religious order whose members were to exemplify poverty, innocence, and simple devotion. Saint Dominic (1170–1221) founded the Dominican order, which developed a decidedly intellectual bent. Among the Dominicans were a number of famous teachers at the University of Paris, such as Saint Thomas Aquinas.

Church-Related Educational Institutions

During the medieval period, the church exercised a virtual monopoly over formal education either directly or indirectly. Although a formal education was not always directed to religious life, a good part of it was supervised by clerics. Access to education was not universal, but capable boys with a bookish inclination could generally receive some schooling.

Distinctions between elementary and secondary schools were rather vague in the early medieval era. However, it is possible to discern four particular kinds of church-related schools that performed basic, or elementary, educational functions: parish, chantry, monastic, and cathedral schools.

The Council of Rome (853) specified that each parish, as a congregation served by a priest and located in a specifically determined area, should provide elementary education. The instruction in parish schools dealt primarily with the religious ritual and music needed for the celebration of the Mass and secondarily with reading, writing, and music.

The chantry school was supported by an endowment given by a wealthy person to provide for the saying of Masses for his soul. In order to have a choir to chant the responses needed in celebrating the liturgy, the priest might use part of the donation to train boys in music. This involved their learning Latin, the language of the church liturgy.

Associated with monasteries, monastic schools trained monks, either as priests or brothers, in church doctrine and in the particular regula of their communities. Basic instruction was in reading and writing Latin. The monastic schools also provided instruction for those preparing for the secular priesthood and for boys living in the vicinity of the monastery who might be destined for nonreligious occupations and professions. The monastic schools were most important during the early medieval period before the commercial revival.

The monastic schools first appeared in the fourth century. Originally, they had an exclusively religious function—preparing those who were to take monastic vows. In the sixth century, the patterns of monastic life and education were clarified by Saint Benedict (c. 480–c. 583), often cited as the father of Western monasticism. Benedict emphasized literacy as the necessary foundation for revitalizing Christian thought and for maintaining classical culture. He prescribed that the monks spend at least two hours each day in reading. In addition to their literary endeavors, the monks, as members of self-sustaining communities, often became skilled farmers and craftsmen and frequently taught these skills to the people of the surrounding villages. The Benedictine monastery and rule provided a favorable model for the preservation and advancement of learning from the sixth through the twelfth centuries.

Cassiodorus, the "father of literary monasticism," envisioned the monastery as a center of scholarly theological study. For such study, the pursuit of the liberal arts was regarded as necessary. Because of their commitment to preserving scriptural and literary works, many monasteries collected the writings of the early church fathers and served as repositories for the sources of medieval culture. Under the influence of Cassiodorus, the monasteries maintained *scriptoria* and libraries where the ancient manuscripts were copied and preserved.

The monastic schools offered instruction in reading, writing, simple arithmetic, religious doctrine, and the regula of the particular religious community. Reading was taught by having the student memorize the letters of the alphabet and then words. Much attention was given to Latin pronunciation. Since books were scarce, the teacher dictated, explaining the meaning of the passage to the students, who copied it in their own copy books. Writing was practiced by making impressions on wax tablets with a stylus. Arithmetic involved counting and finger-reckoning exercises. Music, used in religious liturgy and chanting, occupied a great deal of instructional time. The general method of instruction was the catechetical use of memorized questions and answers. By the tenth century, the monastic schools offered instruction at a higher level. The curriculum was expanded to encompass a wider range of studies. Frequently, the seven liberal arts were offered and occasionally law, medicine, and the fine and practical arts.

In the eleventh century, political stability and economic prosperity stimulated the revival of cities. As the focus of medieval life moved to the cities, the monastic schools, generally located in rural regions, began to decline as major centers of learning. Although the monasteries continued to house libraries and to provide schooling, the scene of the most vital educational activity shifted to the cathedral schools of such major cities as Paris, Chartres, Laon, Reims, and Liege. In their early stages, cathedral schools offered both elementary and secondary studies. While primarily concerned with general or liberal studies, some of them provided elementary instruction in reading and writing Latin as preparation for the liberal studies. Cathedral schools were flourishing by the twelfth century when the Lateran Council in 1179 recognized that educational change had occurred and required every cathedral, or bishop's church, to maintain a school to educate priests, other clerics, and the poor.

The various types of church-related elementary schools commonly provided Latin instruction, which included lessons in reading and writing the language and the study of Latin literature and grammar. Although some instruction was given in the vernacular languages, they were not really school subjects. Latin, a legacy inherited from the Roman Empire, was the language of religious discourse, liturgical worship, academic and intellectual life, and law and diplomacy. For most of the medieval period, the small compendia, or concise treatments of grammatical rules, were read. Students memorized these Latin texts without necessarily understanding their meaning. As the teacher read from a book or manuscript, the pupil either repeated or copied the words dictated to him. Although corporal punishment was probably used, it was not justified by the medieval Christian theology of learning, which held that the child was spiritually deprived, as an inheritor of Adam's original sin, and that through discipline, effort, and the efficacy of the sacraments, this deprivation could be overcome. Although certain medieval educators might have held notions of human depravity, the medieval Christian educational theory of child nature adhered to the idea of deprivation rather than depravity.

Saint Bede

Although many monks might be cited, the life and works of Saint Bede (c. 673–735) provide a rare insight into the scholarly preparation and writing of an able monk. Bede was born in England in the vicinity of the twin monasteries of Saint Peter at Wearmouth and Saint Paul at Jarrow. He entered the monastery of Saint Peter at the early age of seven, and monastic life was the most important formative influence on his character. A studious and industrious youth, he made extensive use of the monastery's fine library. Bede's intellectual and religious training was directed by the other Benedictine monks of the community. He became a deacon at age nineteen and a priest at thirty. Given an assignment as a teacher in the monastic school, he prepared the younger members of the community in Latin grammar. He also wrote several Latin grammars for his students.

In addition to teaching, Bede devoted himself to scholarship. To develop his interest in history he studied the works of the Jewish historian Josephus, Saint Jerome's translation of Eusebius' *Ecclesiastical History,* and the many local chronicles of Anglo-Saxon England. Although interested in pursuing historical study, Bede as a true medieval monk regarded Scripture as the highest authority.

As a teacher and writer, Bede was most concerned with assimilating and transmitting the scholarship of his predecessors by ordering this material into a form that would be intelligible to less sophisticated students. Possessed by an intense drive to transmit and to preserve knowledge, Bede was always a highly selective teacher and writer. He regarded both learning and history as essentially moral forces. History, he felt, was made by persons acting as individuals rather than by persons caught up in a particular socioeconomic or political trend. His religious background no doubt influenced his desire to persuade people to lead moral lives, and this served as a powerful motive in his writing and teaching. In commenting on the ethical power of history, Bede wrote:

> For if history relates good things of good men, the attentive hearer is excited to imitate that which is good; or if it mentions ill things of wicked persons, nevertheless the religious and pious hearer or reader, shunning that which is hurtful and perverse, is the more excited to perform those things which he knows to be good, and worthy of God.[5]

As a scholar, Bede pursued theological, grammatical, chronological, and historical investigations. These broad interests attest to the high degree of scholarship that existed in some, but not all, of the monasteries. Bede's theological works consisted mainly of commentaries based on the writings of the major Latin fathers of the church, Augustine, Jerome, Ambrose, and Gregory. He also wrote a number of grammars to be used in instructing students in Latin. As a chronologist, Bede attempted to devise a framework into which could be fitted all of the events since the creation of the world. The following chronological sequence, devised by Bede, provides an interesting example of the early medieval conception of the occurrence of major events over time:

1. From the Creation to Noah and the Flood.
2. From Noah to Abraham.

[5] J. A. Giles (ed.), *The Venerable Bede's Ecclesiastical History of England* (London: George Bell and Sons, 1894), p. 1.

3. From Abraham to David.
4. From David to the Captivity of the Jews.
5. From the Captivity to the Birth of Christ.
6. From the Birth of Christ, to an indeterminate date, the end of the world, known to God alone.[6]

Bede's historical writings included *Life of Felix, Life and Martyrdom of Saint Anastasius,* and *Lives of the Abbots of the Monastery of Wearmouth and Jarrow.* His *Book of Martyrs* gathered details from many of the lives of the saints and other ecclesiastical literatures and became a model for the historical martyrologies of the ninth century. Bede's most famous work, the *Ecclesiastical History of the English Nation,* gained him the title of "father of English history." As an historian, Bede showed a remarkable conscientiousness in collecting his information from the best possible sources and in sifting fact from rumor and ill-founded traditional accounts. In commenting on Bede's work, Duckett calls it a "never monotonous" narrative:

> Now it glows with vision and miracle, with the learning and the charity of those called to be saints; now it lowers dark with battle and murder, plague and famine, death and descent to the torment of hell.[7]

This brief commentary on the life of the Venerable Bede, an illustrious monk, indicates the quality of research and scholarship that was carried on in some of the monasteries. The patterns of medieval monastic life and education were never even, however. Some monasteries were corrupted by the acquisition of property, and some housed ignorant men. Nevertheless, some credit for preserving learning is due to the monks who, like Bede, saw themselves as the guardians of culture.

Studium Generale

In the eleventh century, a more distinctive separation of elementary and secondary educational instruction and institutions could be discerned. Although cathedral schools offered preparatory education of an elementary nature, they were chiefly concerned with secondary instruction centering on the liberal arts. The cathedral school taught the trivium and quadrivium, inherited from the educators of Rome's later imperial period. It should be recalled that certain of the early Christian educators, such as Cassiodorus, and theologians, such as

[6] Eleanor S. Duckett, *Anglo-Saxon Saints and Scholars* (New York: Macmillan, 1948), p. 246.
[7] *Ibid.,* p. 319.

Saint Augustine, had argued that the liberal arts were a desirable and necessary preparation for theological study. In the eleventh century, the term *studium generale* was used to designate a location of general learning. The cathedral schools, as centers for the pursuit of liberal studies, were often referred to as studia generalia. Certain of the major cathedral schools, such as Paris, were also the predecessors of the medieval universities. In the eleventh and early twelfth centuries, the terms studium generale, or general school, and *universitas,* or corporation of masters and students, were used synonymously.

The trivium—grammar, rhetoric, and logic—was a most important area of concentration in the studium generale. The study of Latin grammar was indispensable if the non-Latin speaking peoples were to acquire proficiency in the language of liturgy and learning. Rhetorical study had undergone a transformation from the days of Isocrates, Cicero, and Quintilian. Although oratory was no longer primarily conceived of as a means of persuasion, the medieval preachers certainly employed the persuasive arts. Rhetoric contributed to the medieval *ars dictamen,* which emphasized letter writing and correspondence methods useful for economic, political, and legal affairs. Used as an instrument for writing contracts, wills, immunities, and appointments, rhetoric lost its emphasis on speaking and came to be conceived of as writing. Logic was regarded as a separate study rather than an integral part of philosophical systems.

The quadrivium—arithmetic, geometry, astronomy, and music— formed the other liberal studies of the studium generale. Arithmetic involved addition, subtraction, multiplication, and division. Geometry followed Euclid's method and elements derived from the Greeks, Arabs, and Hindus, which had undergone Latin translation.

Astronomy, the most popular subject, dealt with planetary motions and was used to calculate the date of Easter and other movable feasts of the church. Astrology, a pseudo-scientific offshoot of astronomy, concerned itself with the plotting of astrological charts and horoscopes. In the Middle Ages, many state and personal decisions were made according to astrological charts.

Music was studied as both a theoretical discipline and as an intrinsic component of religious liturgy. Musical theory was drawn from the texts of Boethius (470–524) and Isidore (570–636) who had divided it into three major philosophical categories: the music of the spheres, of man, and of instruments. However, the significant developments in medieval music were liturgical rather than strictly theoretical. Drawing upon the Greek choral music of the Byzantine church, the Western church developed a plainchant for its Latin liturgy that was sung without instrumental accompaniment. The plain, or Gregorian, chant, so named because Pope Gregory endorsed it as the official musical style for liturgical celebration, used only a limited scale.

Two significant innovations in the development of medieval music occurred with the introduction of polyphonic technique and Arabic musical measurement. Polyphonic music, introduced in the ninth century, reduced the monotony of plain chanting. New voice parts were added at various intervals, apart from the main melody. As composers experimented, these parallel voice parts were unified and harmonized. After the introduction of Arabic texts on musical measurement, various notes were devised to represent specific lengths of time. By the thirteenth century, medieval composers had mastered the principles of harmony and measurement. Although Boethius had commented on musical instruments in his writing, they were reserved for secular rather than religious use. Harps, lyres, cithers, pipes, and horns were played by medieval musicians. The guitar, probably of Arabic origin, also made its appearance in southern Europe during the Middle Ages.

By the twelfth century, a revitalized form of higher learning appeared as certain of the studia generalia evolved into universities. The cathedral schools' liberal studies were a necessary preparation for university study. The medieval university and scholasticism are an integral development in medieval educational history which will be treated later.

Feudalism and Manorialism

Feudalism and manorialism were related concepts that evolved to meet the needs of a society dependent on a moneyless, agrarian economy, devoid of a strong central government, and constantly threatened by predatory, marauding nobles. In the absence of the imposition of law and justice from a centralized political authority, feudalism and manorialism developed from a system of personal relationships based upon the means of subsistence, or land tenure. While manorialism was a socioeconomic system resting upon the holding of agricultural land, feudalism was the political and military system that protected it. Although primarily social, economic, political, and military, these related concepts were significant for education. Manorialism, originating in food production and the possession of farming land, evolved into a system of well-defined personal relationships that provided the means of sociocultural integration in the period before the rise of strong dynastic and national states. Although the serfs bound to the land as tillers of the soil were largely illiterate, they learned to play their role and to work the land by directly imitating their parents. Feudalism developed an educational system, known as chivalry.

Manorialism described the economic, social, and legal relationships that existed between the proprietorial feudal lord and the tenant serfs who worked the land. The manor, a largely self-sufficient farm community developed from the large estates of the Roman agricultural magnates, was the basis of the medieval society and economy. The manor was a part of a fief, or land grant, given by a more powerful noble or lord in return for the military and other services of a vassal. Feudalism was a political means of maintaining a semblance of order over the territory that had once been governed by the centralized authority of the Roman army and bureaucracy. These property and political arrangements were maintained by rules, procedures, traditions, and the ethical code of chivalry. The feudal pyramid consisted of a weak king at the top, his vassals, their subvassals, and so on, through a complicated process of subinfeudation.

Particular political, social, and economic systems develop appropriate educational contents, methods, and strategies that are designed to bring the immature into participation with institutional life. While the serf's children merely imitated their parents by working along with them in the fields, the son of the feudal lord was exposed to the well-defined patterns of chivalric education. For a warlike aristocracy, knighthood was the ideal form of manly virtue. The essence of chivalric education was, therefore, the imitation and replication of the ideal knight, or hero. As the exclusive concern of a small group of feudal lords, chivalric education was aristocratic, training the prospective knight to master the particular requirements that marked him as a member of a special caste.

The chivalric model demanded that the knight be strong, courageous, honorable, dutiful, and loyal to his feudal lord. Essentially, however, the business of the knight was warfare, battle, and killing, for medieval life was characterized by a violent tension caused by a recently subdued and often resurfacing barbarism. Although the profession of knighthood was battle, the formal precedents and ritualized etiquette of chivalry lessened the barbarism connected with waging war. As education becomes more formal, it becomes increasingly symbolic. Chivalric education involved training in and exposure to the symbols, heraldry, and pageantry of courtly life, and it was the means of inducting noble youths into the complicated relationships and obligations of the age of feudalism.

Since the Middle Ages was a highly religious period in its formal and outward manifestations, strong connections existed between the knightly and religious ideals. The squire was inducted into the knighthood in a way that resembled the entry of a novice into a religious order. Knighthood was a sacred brotherhood, and entry into the brotherhood meant induction through solemn rites of initiation. In many ways the monastic and knightly ideals were intertwined. Monastic elements were found in the great knightly orders, such as the Knights Templar, Knights of Saint John, and the Teutonic Knights. The knight's business was war, but he was also to personify the Christian values of mercy, honor, and protection of the weak. Although often overromanticized, the medieval knight was an unusual combination of a fighting and a religious man.

Stages of Chivalric Education

From the age of seven or eight until fourteen or fifteen, the young boy served at the court of his father's lord. This service related to the system of feudal dues and obligations, and it demonstrated the vassal's trust in his lord. Here the boy learned how to practice the manners and gestures of court life, to be a gentleman, and to sing and play a musical instrument. He might even learn to read and write in the vernacular language.

From fourteen or fifteen until twenty-one, the youth-in-training was a squire, serving as an attendant for the lord of the castle or for one of the knights of the court. During these years, he learned the professional skills of knighthood, such as hunting, warfare, and the care of armor, arms, and horses. The cultural aspects of knightly education might consist of singing, reciting, composing verses, dancing, and storytelling. He studied the chivalric symbols, coats of arms, and heraldry and practiced the exaggerated politeness, minute regulation of social amenities, and strict formalism associated with chivalric etiquette.

At twenty-one the squire became a candidate for knighthood into which he was inducted by his overlord and church officials. Dubbed a knight, the young man dedicated himself to serving his lords, both temporal and spiritual. After the ceremony of knighthood, he officially entered into the life and obligations of his station. He then received some land as a means of subsistence and began to fulfill his obligations as a vassal.

Revival of City Life and Guild Education

Between the fourth and tenth centuries, primitive agrarianism, which sustained manorialism and feudalism, dominated Western European economic life. City life had markedly declined as the old Roman cities deteriorated and the population shifted to self-sufficient manors protected by feudal lords. Moreover, city life is always sustained by agricultural surpluses, and when agricultural production was allocated to support the self-sufficient manor, this surplus was lacking. By the late tenth century, however, the feudal system was sufficiently stable to produce adequate agricultural surpluses. Because not as many people were needed for agricultural production, some were free to specialize in the skills, crafts, and occupations that characterized town life. The eleventh-century crusades also stimulated mobility and produced a more cosmopolitan pattern of life. The revival of city life signified a departure from the manorial-feudal system. Serfs were freed, and feudal lords became landlords of rent-paying tenants. The growth of the city also brought about a major social transformation as a European middle class began to exert a marked influence on the political, social, and economic life.

With the revival of town life came the merchant and craft guilds. The merchant guilds, which bore a superficial resemblance to modern corporations, were formed as traders banded together for mutual protection as they traveled from city to city. They selected leaders, devised trade regulations, and formed common funds. The ideal of the merchant guild was a stable price under stable market conditions. Most importantly, the guilds were able to win monopolies and trade concessions from feudal lords.

City life revived such specialized occupations as bakers, shoemakers, glassmakers, and silversmiths. These craftsmen united in craft guilds, which gained production monopolies and controlled the admission of new members. The guilds regulated working conditions and the number of working hours and set quality standards and wages and prices.

Although the vocational education of the craftsmen was not conducted in formal schools, it was based on systematized and well-defined procedures. There were three essential stages to guild education: apprentice, journeyman, and master craftsman.

The period of apprenticeship could vary from three to ten years, depending upon the complexity of the vocational skills that were needed for admission into the craft. As an apprentice, a boy was assigned to a master craftsman by means of a written contract, which established a set of reciprocal relationships between apprentice and master. The master was obligated to teach the apprentice the skills of his trade, to look after his morals and religion, and to provide food, lodging, and a small stipend. In many of the craft guilds, the master was also required to provide instruction in reading and writing. In return for his training and education, the apprentice was obliged to work diligently, keep the craft secrets, and be obedient to the master. Occasionally, the guilds established formal schools to educate apprentices in reading and writing.

After proving himself sufficiently adept in the trade, the apprentice moved to the higher rank of journeyman, which permitted him to travel about working as a day laborer. He might work with a number of master craftsmen in order to profit from their experience and expertise in the particular craft. When the journeyman had attained the necessary skills, he was admitted to the guild as a full-fledged member. As a master craftsman, he could establish his own shop, hire journeymen, take on apprentices, and serve as an instructor in the guild.

Conclusion

The medieval period in Western history was a long thousand-year expanse of time that extended from the collapse of the Roman Empire to the early attempts at modernization in the Renaissance. It was a time of Western history when men, educated as well as ignorant, were guided by a theocentric world view. The basic educational institutions were conducted under the protective auspices of the Roman Church. Chantry, parish, monastic, and cathedral schools were sustained by religious people and communities. Learning itself became identified with the canonical and the clerical modes of life. Even the more secular guild and chivalric forms of education were affected by the pervading religious orientation of the Middle Ages.

This chapter has discussed the basic characteristics of medieval life and education. The elementary forms of medieval education were examined. Attention was given to the monastic school as representative of early medieval education. Chapter 6 will direct itself to an examination of medieval higher education and to the scholastic method that was used in the universities.

Suggested Readings

Artz, Frederick B. *The Mind of the Middle Ages*. New York: Knopf, 1953.

Broudy, Harry S., and John R. Palmer. *Exemplars of Teaching Method*. Chicago: Rand McNally, 1965.

Daniel-Rops, H. *Cathedral and Crusade—Studies of the Medieval Church*. New York: Dutton, 1957.

————. *The Church in the Dark Ages*. London: J. M. Dent, 1959.

Drane, Augusta T. *Christian Schools and Scholars*. London: Burns and Oates, 1881.

Duckett, Eleanor S. *Anglo-Saxon Saints and Scholars*. New York: Macmillan, 1948.

Easton, Stewart C. *The Era of Charlemagne*. Princeton, N.J.: Van Nostrand, 1961.

Ellspermann, Gerald L. *The Attitude of the Early Christian Latin Writers Toward Pagan Literature and Learning*. Washington, D.C.: Catholic University of America, 1949.

Gaskoin, C. J. *Alcuin, His Life and His Work*. New York: Russell and Russell, 1966.

Godfrey, John. *The Church in Anglo-Saxon England*. Cambridge, England: Cambridge University Press, 1962.

Graves, Frank Pierrepont. *A History of Education During the Middle Ages.* New York: Macmillan, 1919.

Haskins, Charles H. *The Renaissance of the Twelfth Century.* Cambridge, Mass.: Harvard University Press, 1927.

————. *Studies in Medieval Culture.* London: Oxford University Press, 1929.

Hatch, Edwin. *The Influence of Greek Ideas on Christianity.* New York: Harper, 1957.

Hill, Odell T. *English Monasticism: Its Rise and Influence.* London: Jackson, Walford, and Hodders, 1867.

Huizinga, J. *The Waning of the Middle Ages.* Garden City, N.Y.: Doubleday, 1954.

Jaeger, Werner W. *Early Christianity and Greek Paideia.* Cambridge, Mass.: Harvard University Press, 1961.

Kane, William T., S.J. *History of Education.* Chicago: Loyola University Press, 1954.

Knowles, D. D. *The Monastic Order in England.* Cambridge, England: Cambridge University Press, 1950.

————. *Saints and Scholars.* Cambridge, England: Cambridge University Press, 1962.

McCormick, Patrick J., and Francis P. Cassidy. *History of Education.* Washington, D.C.: Catholic Education Press, 1953.

Painter, Sidney. *French Chivalry.* Baltimore: Johns Hopkins University Press, 1940.

————. *Mediaeval Society.* Ithaca, N.Y.: Cornell University Press, 1951.

Pirenne, Henri. *Economic and Social History of Medieval Europe.* New York: Harcourt, Brace, 1937.

Smith, Lucy M. *Cluny in the Eleventh and Twelfth Centuries.* London: Philip Allan, 1930.

Southern, Richard W. *The Making of the Middle Ages.* New Haven, Conn.: Yale University Press, 1953.

Stephenson, Carl. *Medieval Feudalism.* Ithaca, N.Y.: Cornell University Press, 1964.

Thompson, Alexander H. *Bede: His Life, Times, and Writings.* New York: Russell and Russell, 1966.

The Venerable Bede's Ecclesiastical History of England. J. A. Giles (ed.). London: George Bell and Sons, 1894.

West, A. F. *Alcuin and the Rise of the Christian Schools.* New York: Scribner, 1892.

Winston, Richard. *Charlemagne from the Hammer to the Cross.* New York: Random House, 1960.

CHAPTER 6

Scholasticism and the Medieval University

Medieval higher education can be viewed from the perspectives of the university, which was the major institution of liberal and professional studies, and scholasticism, which was the dominant intellectual and educational methodology. Scholastic scholars and teachers occupied the faculty ranks of the major European universities of Salerno, Bologna, Paris, Oxford, and Cambridge. This chapter will examine the origins, development, and significance of the medieval university and will analyze scholasticism as an educational methodology.

Origins of the Medieval University

The medieval university represented the institutionalization of the complex forces that characterized the revival of learning in the twelfth and thirteenth centuries. The eminent scholar Hastings Rashdall described the universities of the Middle Ages as reflections of medieval intellectual views:

> A complete history of the Universities of the Middle Ages would be in fact a history of medieval thought—of the fortunes, during four centuries, of literary culture, of the whole of the Scholastic Philosophy and Scholastic Theology, of the revived study of the Civil Law, of the formation and development of the Canon Law of the faint, murky, cloud-wrapped dawn of modern Mathematics, modern Science, and modern Medicine.[1]

The eleventh-century intellectual renaissance that was initiated in Cluny and other monastic schools spread to cathedral schools as city life revived. In most instances, universities evolved from the expanding studia generalia, or liberal arts curricula, of the cathedral schools. By

[1] Hastings Rashdall, *The Universities of Europe in the Middle Ages*, Vol. I (London: Oxford University Press, 1895), p. 5.

the twelfth century, enrollment at certain cathedral schools had grown so large that the existing patterns of organization were inadequate to accommodate the large numbers of students. For their own protection students and masters organized associations, or *universitas*, that emulated the patterns of the craft guilds and obtained the recognition of secular and religious authorities. The famous medieval universities that originated in the twelfth century grew out of these associations.

Such related factors as the crusades, the revival of commerce, and Western contacts with Arabic scholarship stimulated higher education in the twelfth century and contributed directly to the rise of the university. Between 1100 and 1200, an influx of new ideas came from the Moorish scholars of Spain. The crusades had weakened the feudal provincialism of the early Middle Ages as the crusaders came into contact with new places, peoples, and ideas. The Arab world, in particular, had served as a repository for many of the classical Greek writings that had become obscure or were believed lost. This broadened intellectual experience, which was concurrent with the decline of feudalism and the reinvigoration of the city, contributed to the revival of learning in the twelfth and thirteenth centuries.

The Moorish kingdoms of the Iberian peninsula were an initial point of contact between the European medieval and the Arabic worlds. The erudition of the Arab scholars of medicine and mathematics especially impressed the western European. Through the Arab scholars, the works of Aristotle, Euclid, Ptolemy, and the Greek physicians Galen and Hippocrates found their way into medieval scholarship. The entry of the complete works of Aristotle into western Europe, by way of the Arabic commentaries of Averroës (c. 1126–1198), was of particular significance for the development of scholastic philosophy and education. This flood of newly discovered knowledge burst the bounds of the extant monastic and cathedral schools and eventuated in the growth of the universities.

The crusades not only introduced Arabic learning into western Europe but also revived commercial and city life. The economic revival of the twelfth and thirteenth centuries produced a burgher, or middle, class that possessed the finances needed to make professional studies both possible and profitable. As commerce revived, travel facilities improved and engendered a cosmopolitan spirit that contributed to a scholarly interchange transcending the boundaries of the feudal enclave.

The stimulus of Arabic learning and commercial revival must be viewed in the context of scholastic theology and philosophy, upon which was based the educated medieval Christian's theocentric world view. The ecclesiastical preeminence of the Roman Catholic Church allowed it to dominate the other institutions of western Europe. Mendicant religious orders, such as the Dominicans, whose origins coincided with the European commercial revival, produced a large body of able scholars. Certain of these academics, such as Abelard, Duns Scotus, and Thomas Aquinas, were so acclaimed that thousands of students came to hear them lecture. The attraction that these famous scholars had for the mobile student population also contributed to the rise of the universities. Theological interpretation and investigation were major interests of the medieval scholastics, especially at the University of Paris, where Thomas Aquinas and other scholars sought to reconcile rediscovered Greek rationalism with the revealed scriptural and doctrinal sources of the Christian faith.

An examination of the origins of the medieval university reveals certain general trends:

1. Many of the universities evolved from and frequently absorbed the studia generalia of the older cathedral schools.
2. The general stimulus emanating from the revival of learning contributed to the support and growth of the universities.
3. The introduction of new learning and the rediscovery of classical Greek rationalism created problems of synthesis for the scholastics who tried to reconcile these new intellectual sources with the corpus of Christian doctrine.
4. Revived commercial and city life produced a mobile and cosmopolitan body of scholars and students who populated the universities.
5. The faculties and students of the universities followed the examples of the existing guilds and assumed the powers of self-government, establishing internal structures and enacting internal regulations.
6. The medieval universities established specialized schools for one one or more of the major professional studies of law, medicine, and theology.

Salerno

One of the oldest of the medieval universities was at Salerno, an urban center located close to inland trade routes in southern Italy, a region where the Greco-Roman cultural tradition had survived barbarian invasion. Acknowledging the overlordship of the Byzantine emperor, Salerno was a protected city that attracted numerous visitors because of the alleged healing benefits of the region's mineral springs. A number of physicians settled in the vicinity which was noted as a medical center.

The University of Salerno had its origins in the study of surviving ancient Greek medical works. It functioned as a medical school in the tenth and eleventh centuries and was not chartered as a university until 1231, when Frederick II of Sicily granted the institution a monopoly for medical training.

Sicily had had long contact with Arabic and Greek culture, and Salerno attracted scholars from the various parts of Europe who sought to study Arabic and Greek medicine. The scholar Constantinus Africanus translated a large number of Arabic medical works into Latin, including the treatises of Hippocrates and Galen, which the Arabs had earlier translated from the original Greek. The Persian physician Avicenna's *Book of Healing* and *Medical Encyclopedia* were also translated into Latin. These Latin translations of Arabic works were especially significant because they introduced the superior Arab medical scholarship to the West. Anatomical demonstrations were given in the university classes, and animals were dissected. As medical instruction became more sophisticated, the earlier lists of recipes and cures were replaced by more elaborate commentaries on classical and Arabic medical works.

Bologna

With the exception of the famous medical university of Salerno, the medieval universities originated in the twelfth century or thereafter. Although they shared some common features, a major difference existed between those that followed the Parisian, or northern, pattern of organization and those that followed the Bolognese, or southern, pattern. While the faculty ruled Paris, the students dominated Bologna.

The University of Bologna, which received a formal charter from the Emperor Frederick Barbarossa in 1158, grew out of the excellent schools that were already located in the vicinity. An episcopal school provided liberal studies, a municipal school gave instruction in Roman civil law, and a monastic school stressed canon law. As an important city for the revived study of law, Bologna attracted students both from Italy and from across the Alps. Although the Italian and non-Italian students had organized separate student guilds, they united to coerce the Bolognese townsmen and the university faculty into granting a number of major concessions that gave the students control of the university. They gained the power to elect the university rector, to engage the faculty, and to conduct the academic and business affairs of the university. The student election of the rector was a key factor in controlling the university since he held civil and criminal jurisdiction over both students and professors.

Since the medieval university was a corporation, or guild, of masters and students, it did not depend on extensive physical facilities as does its modern counterpart. The location of the medieval university was determined by the presence of scholars. A university was a source of income and prestige to the city in which it was located. The scholars could deprive a city of income by merely moving in a body to another city. Whenever they sought to win concessions from the townspeople, the scholars threatened to leave the city and to settle elsewhere. At Bologna, as in Paris, the students successfully used the threat of migration to force the town merchants to reduce the charges for books, lodging, food, and other necessities.

As a result of their successful demonstration of student power, the student associations of Bologna gained financial and administrative control of their university. By collecting fees, paying salaries, and issuing academic regulations, they won major concessions from the faculty, who depended on tuition fees for their livelihood. Assuming that competent teachers should also be popular ones, the students fined unpopular masters who attracted less than five students to their lectures. Moreover, they issued academic regulations that required every lecture to last for a specified time; lecturers were expected to read the complete text of a manuscript and not skip any of the pages. They controlled the movement of teachers by requiring masters to secure permission of the rector if they wished to leave the university.

The University of Bologna became a recognized center for specialization in both civil and canon law. Irnerius (c. 1050–c. 1130), one of the founders of the university and a noted expert on Roman civil law, systematically codified and classified Justinian's *Corpus juris civilis*. He also wrote an elaborate set of interlinear glosses that contained explanatory and interpretive notes on the code. Irnerius' scholarship separated Roman law from rhetoric and established it as a distinct subject of professional study.

The revival of interest in Roman civil law, stimulated by Irnerius, also quickened an interest in canon law. By the twelfth century, the medieval Western church contained an elaborate administrative apparatus, which required direction by skilled lawyers who were knowledgeable in canonical law. Gratian (1080–1150), a monk from San Felice, settled at the University of Bologna, where he wrote his *Decretum*, a work that codified a body of often contradictory laws and became the definitive text for the study of canon law.

Paris

Evolving from the cathedral school of Notre Dame, the University of Paris was the model for the scholar-dominated northern European university in which the faculty exercised the controlling power in the corporation. Such scholars as Roscelin, William of Champeaux, and Abelard attracted large numbers of students to their lectures at the cathedral school of Notre Dame. By the end of the twelfth century, master's associations had organized to seek independence from cathedral authorities and to gain greater academic self-government. In 1200, the French monarch Philip Augustus granted a royal charter to the university that created a privileged position for the university community by exempting faculty and students from the jurisdiction of lay courts. This special treatment was advantageous to the scholars since secular, or lay, courts were inefficient and severe in comparison to the more lenient and sympathetic university clerical court. In 1231, Pope Gregory IX approved university statutes and granted the papal privilege *Parens scientiarum,* which gave the university chancellor the power to confer degrees. In giving the university power over its own affairs, the pope recognized the right of the faculty to make constitutions and ordinances regulating lectures, disputations, and academic dress. Papal interest in the University of Paris gave evidence that the pope regarded the theology faculty as a body of expert consultants on doctrinal matters.

The faculty of arts, the largest and most influential association of masters at Paris, elected the rector, who eventually emerged as the most important university official. The deans of the law, medical, and theology faculties acknowledged the rector's authority as the chief financial agent and spokesman for the university. He had the responsibility of presiding over university meetings when all the faculties were represented. As the chief negotiator at the papal court, the rector exercised an extremely significant function as the popes' interest in higher education led them to grant charters and other guarantees of protection to the universities.

A reading knowledge of Latin was the only academic requirement needed for admission into the arts course, the basic course of study. As the prerequisite for advanced professional studies in theology, law, and medicine, the arts included grammar, philosophy, logic, rhetoric, metaphysics, and mathematics. The time devoted to studying the arts varied from four to seven years. According to the scholastic conception of education, learning was arranged in a pyramid, or hierarchy, of studies. Beginning with the liberal arts at the base of the pyramid, the student progressed upward through philosophy and finally reached theology, the queen of medieval studies, located at the summit. Theology served to integrate the various bodies of knowledge into a pattern that conformed to the medieval theocentric conception of reality.

As an educational method, scholasticism was highly verbal and intellectualistic and relied on lecture and disputation. Using Aristotelian logic as a framework for intellectual inquiry, the scholastic lecturer began with a carefully worded question, reviewed the authorities, and proposed a correct answer to the question posed initially; he then refuted objections that were mustered against his conclusion. The chief instructional method was the lecture, consisting of a reading and explanation of the text under consideration together with its glosses. Since students copied the lecture, the professor had to read the passage repeatedly and slowly enough for them to copy it. In fact, regulations prohibited a professor from lecturing too rapidly. At the end of a course, the student's notes would comprise a complete copy of the text, with the lecturer's explanations. For the scholastic educators, authoritative sources were revealed and rational truth. Ignoring scientific and empirical modes of inquiry, they and their students investigated controversies within a framework bounded by Christian Scripture and Aristotelian logic.

The curriculum of the medieval university was directed primarily toward transmitting and diffusing extant knowledge rather than to adding new information or stimulating new interpretations.[2] It was designed to prepare qualified teachers and professionals who had earned their degrees by mastering the necessary subjects. Reflecting its origins in the studium generale, the core of the arts curriculum was the seven liberal studies, which were regarded as the foundation of higher learning. The appearance of Aristotle's works by way of Latin translations of Arabic manuscripts and some direct translations from the Greek had an impact on the arts curriculum. By 1200, Aristotle's logical, scientific, and metaphysical works were generally available in Latin translations for study by medieval schoolmen. The Aristotelian resurgence made the syllogism the authoritative method of reasoning and made Aristotle's logic the focus of study. In addition to translations, such commentaries on Aristotle as Porphyry's *Isagogue*, Boethius' *Categories*, and Themistius' *Posterior Analytics* were studied.

As logic became preeminent in the medieval arts curriculum, the emphasis in rhetoric gradually changed from that of eloquence in speaking to the art of composition, or *ars dictaminis*. As the medieval civil and ecclesiastical governments grew into more complex bureaucracies, trained secretaries were needed in the various church and state offices. Among the major rhetorical texts used to train them were Alberich's *Rationes dictandi* and John Garland's *Parisiana poetria*.

In the study of grammar, the older textbooks of Donatus and Priscian remained in use but were supplemented by such newer treatises as the *Doctrinale* of Alexander of Villedieu and the *Graecismus* of Eberhard of Bethune. Euclid was the standard text in geometry, and Ptolemy was studied in astronomy. In theology, the principal works read were the Holy Scriptures, Gratian's *Decretum*, Peter Lombard's *Book of Sentences*, and Thomas Aquinas' *Summa theologica*. Justinian's *Corpus juris civilis* was used for civil law. Medieval medical students read the Greek writers Hippocrates and Galen.

A student who had studied the arts for six years and had passed all the requirements was awarded the degree of master of arts, which was

[2] For a thorough treatment of the medieval university curriculum, see Gordon Leff, *Paris and Oxford Universities in the Thirteenth and Fourteenth Centuries* (New York: Wiley, 1968), pp. 116–183.

also the *licentia docendi,* the license to teach, and the earliest of the earned academic degrees. In time, the bachelor's degree became a stage toward the master of arts degree. Often recipients of the master's degree taught in the arts college while meeting the requirements for advanced degrees, such as doctor of laws, doctor of medicine, or doctor of sacred theology. At first the distinctions between the titles "doctor," "professor," and "master" were unclear, and all three of them meant that the individual was competent to teach a particular subject. The usual designation for a professor in a medieval university was simply *magister,* or master.

Originally, the students at the University of Paris were organized into four nations according to their birthplace: French; Norman; Picard, comprised of residents of the Low Countries; and English, comprised of residents of England, Germany, and northern Europe. Although the nations persisted as a means of organization, they grew cosmopolitan and accepted students of various nationalities as members.

In Paris, as well as in other medieval universities, there was hostility between the academic community and the townspeople. The students believed that the town merchants charged unjust rates for lodging, food, and supplies; the townspeople regarded the students as a riotous and unruly group. The ill-defined student body attracted many non-scholars who, spending their time in idleness, merely wanted to have a good time and enjoy the privileges accorded to the university community. Despite the rivalry between town and gown, the Parisians took pride in their university. The threat of the scholars and students to withdraw from the city (*cessatio*) and to locate elsewhere was always used as a lever to control local opinion. Merchants feared the economic consequences of a disruption of classes or migration of students to another area. Although the academics of Paris as well as of other universities were often resented by townspeople, the universities continued to enjoy special privileges and to develop as a semiautonomous state within a state, or city within a city.

Student Life

The early medieval universities had no distinct central organization but were a loose association of masters, skilled and licensed teachers, and students. Just as the artisan and craft guilds trained craftsmen, the university corporation prepared students to be scholars and teachers by educating them in the content and method of the scholarly disciplines. Thus, the medieval university's arts faculty provided a liberal education for the students, and the professional schools prepared doctors of law, medicine, and theology.

Students were free to live as best as they could according to their wits, funds, and style. Although wealthy students might live in their own houses with servants and a hired tutor, most students formed associations and rented houses as collective residences. A master, chosen by the students, might be invited to live in the house as its head resident. Gradually, these collective student housing units developed into colleges, which, in time, became directly identified with the studies pursued by the students who lived in them.

As the scholars were free to travel from place to place and from country to country, the medieval university was distinguished by its cosmopolitanism. The use of Latin as the universal language of learning transcended vernacular barriers, and higher learning transcended national and regional boundaries. The medieval scholar spoke a universal language, lived in a universal world, and believed in a universal faith.

Although Paris and Bologna were two of the major medieval universities, others were established throughout Europe between the twelfth and fifteenth centuries. In Italy, the University of Padua was founded by masters from Bologna; Emperor Frederick II created the University of Naples. In France, the universities of Montpellier, Orleans, and Toulouse came into existence. In the twelfth century, a group of masters migrated from Paris to England, where they founded Oxford University. In the thirteenth century, a migration of scholars from Oxford resulted in the establishment of Cambridge University. Scotland had St. Andrews and Aberdeen as universities. The Spanish University of Salamanca was founded in 1220. By the fourteenth century, universities were functioning in Erfurt, Heidelberg, Cologne, Prague, and Vienna.

The Legacy of the Medieval University

The medieval university evolved from a voluntary association of masters and students. Control came to rest either with the students, as at Bologna, or with the masters, as in Paris. Regarding them as important organs of learned opinion, both the church and the state recognized the university corporations and sanctioned them by granting charters and privileges. Disputes between civil and ecclesiastical powers were often referred to the learned doctors of the university for arbitration.

Academic freedom was circumscribed by certain theological limitations. In the medieval theocentric world, theology was regarded as the highest study to which man could aspire and the faculty of theology as superior to all others in the university. The church was regarded as the sole repository of revealed truth. Medieval man conceived truth to be that which had been revealed by the authority of the sacred Scriptures. Faith prescribed the sciences, fixed their boundaries, and determined the conditions of inquiry. Yet within the established framework of medieval Christianity, there was freedom to teach and to learn. Outside of it, there was heresy.

Although scholastic teachers recognized the primacy of medieval Christian theology, this did not mean that a monolithic theological dictatorship ruled the medieval university. Theology, itself, was a discipline that embraced contending viewpoints. The interpretations of various theological schools and the rivalry of the teaching orders neutralized any tendencies to absolute thought control. Much of the scholastic method centered on the disputation, where both sides of controversial issues were presented, argued, and considered. Indeed, the great controversies between the nominalists and the realists indicated the depth of disagreement among the scholastics.

The medieval university made a number of significant contributions to later educational development:

1. Modern universities bear a strong resemblance to the medieval university in organizational structure, customs, and degrees.
2. The privileges granted to medieval scholars contributed to a respect and reverence for learning.
3. The cosmopolitanism associated with higher education contributed to internationalize learning.
4. Professional studies were rendered more sophisticated and specialized by the separate faculty arrangements characteristic of the medieval university.
5. The university was a civilizing force.

Scholasticism

By the eleventh century, theologians had begun to concern themselves with serious study of philosophical problems relating to Christian theology. Their researches led to the development of scholasticism as a formal methodology of inquiry, scholarship, and teaching among the medieval educators. Although the scholastics accepted the general theology associated with Western Christianity, they differed on metaphysical, epistemological, and ethical issues as is evidenced by the academic feuding of nominalists and realists on the problem of universals. Although delicate issues were raised as to the primacy of faith or reason as a methodological authority, the scholastics generally regarded both as complementary sources of truth. In faith, the scholastic accepted the Scriptures as God's revealed Word. He also trusted that his intellect would function rationally and logically. He believed that his mind, reasoning deductively and syllogistically from a priori first principles, was a surer guide to God's universal truth than direct sense experience of the external world.

The issue of nominalism versus realism, centering on the relationship between words and the reality to which they referred, caused major controversy among the medieval scholastics. Such proponents of scholastic realism as Saint Anselm, Saint Bernard of Clairvaux, and William of Champeaux followed the tradition of Platonic idealism, which had been introduced into Christian theology by Saint Augustine. The realists, asserting that universal ideas, or forms, exist independently and prior to individual objects, posited reality in a world of unchanging essences or forms. God, the most universal and abstract Being, is the Source of all reality. Universal concepts of goodness, justice, truth, and beauty derive from the ultimate reality and give form to individual acts of goodness and justice and particular examples of truth and beauty. The realists viewed society organically, as a collective unit in which individuals, like the separate cells of an organism, are participating parts. Realist epistemology was based primarily on the recognition of the universal, or general, idea. Individual members of a species are knowable in that they partake of the general nature of the universal.

Roscellinus of Compiègne was a spokesman for nominalism. Suggesting an empirical outlook, Roscellinus asserted that reality is posited in individual objects. Upon observation, certain objects are found to exhibit similar characteristics. Universals are merely the names used to describe classes of objects that share the same characteristics.

When carried to extremes both realism and nominalism posed dangers for medieval Christian theology. At its logical extremity, extreme nominalism tended to the position that nothing existed that could not be apprehended through sense experience. Although the realist position was more compatible with the doctrines of the medieval Church, it, too, posed problems. When pushed to its logical extreme, realism could involve a total rejection of the material world. A major task of the scholastic theologians and philosophers was to reconcile the realist and nominalist positions.

Peter Abelard

Peter Abelard (1079–1142), a prominent philosopher and a professor of the University of Paris, was a precursor of the sophisticated scholasticism that reached its apex in the *Summa theologica* of Thomas Aquinas. Abelard attempted to reconcile the two major issues facing the medieval schoolmen: nominalism versus realism; faith versus reason. As a synthesis of the nominalist-realist controversy, Abelard offered "conceptualism," which held that universals had existed in the mind of God before being given form in particular objects. Universal qualities are exhibited by those classes of objects that share them; through sensation, the learner is able to recognize those discernible qualities that adhere in classes of objects.

Abelard was struck by the contradictions on doctrinal matters that were found in the writings of the early church fathers. In his famous work *Sic et non* (*Yes and No*), he presented 158 points of dogma and arrayed the contradictory authorities on such questions as: Should human faith be based upon reason? Is God all-powerful? Has God free will? Do we sometimes sin unwillingly? Is it worse to sin openly than secretly?

Abelard did not intend to discredit the early church fathers as authorities, but he believed that reason could support faith, and logic could explain the apparent discrepancies. In telling his students that respect for authority should not impede their efforts to seek truth, Abelard said that the questions raised by seemingly contradictory statements should lead to zealous inquiry into truth. Although the writings of the church fathers were to be examined critically and were to serve as an excellent intellectual exercise in debating questions of language and presentation, Abelard did not question the scriptural authority of revelation.

ABELARD'S SCHOLASTIC METHODOLOGY

In *Sic et non*, Abelard structured the scholastic methodology, which consisted of a number of well-defined procedures:

1. He arranged the conflicting authorities into affirmative and negative columns.
2. Once the point at issue had been stated and the incompatible dicta were marshaled, he explored the context of the citation, including its historical setting. In doing so, he investigated the facts that had led to the issuance of the statement and inquired into the circumstances that had led to the statement.
3. He examined the text for corruptions, distortions, and errors that may have been made by copyists. Textual criticism was concerned with etymology, morphology, examination of grammatical forms, and other elements of linguistic science.
4. Once the citation was clearly established, then he was ready to make a judgment as to its real meaning as distinguished from incidental meanings. In establishing the real meaning, Abelard made sure that there was no recorded retraction of the statement.

If incompatibilities remained after this highly intellectual and laborious work had been completed, the scholar was led to either of two conclusions:

1. The incomplete statement was a mystery that should be believed on faith.
2. The incomplete statements were only in apparent contradiction and were both partially correct. Therefore, a synthesis was needed to incorporate both into a higher and more inclusive truth.[3]

In *Sic et non*, Abelard developed a structured set of teaching and learning materials that contributed to the formalizing of the scholastic educational method. He was a model teacher whose fame rested on a number of related factors:

1. His dynamic personality vitalized his lectures.
2. He was a well-prepared teacher who had carefully organized his lectures.
3. His subject matter dealt with current theological issues that were relevant to his students.

Thomas Aquinas

Scholastic philosophy and education reached its high point in the writings of Saint Thomas Aquinas (c. 1225–1274).[4] Born into an Italian noble family, Aquinas was enrolled at the age of five in the Benedictine Abbey of Monte Cassino, where he received his basic education. Between the ages of fourteen and eighteen, he took the arts course of the University of Naples, where he encountered Aristotelian philosophy through his Dominican teachers. Despite the strong objections of his parents, Aquinas entered the Dominican order, studied at the Monastery of the Holy Cross at Cologne from 1246 to 1252, and was ordained as a priest. In 1252, he went to the University of Paris, western Europe's major theological center, where he taught and engaged in further study, which led to the master's degree in theology. In 1256, he qualified for the licentiate, or certificate that qualified him as professor of theology. From 1269 until 1272, he taught and wrote his most famous work, the *Summa theologica*.

Although he was a theologian who philosophized, Aquinas clearly distinguished between theological inquiry derived from faith and philosophical inquiry derived from human experience. He used both modes of inquiry as he pursued basic questions dealing with the Christian conception of God, the universe, the nature of man, and the relationship between God and man. As a philosopher-theologian, Aquinas was

[3] Harry S. Broudy and John R. Palmer, *Exemplars of Teaching Method* (Chicago: Rand McNally, 1965), pp. 62–63.
[4] For a concise but excellent treatment, see John W. Donohue, S.J., *St. Thomas Aquinas and Education* (New York: Random House, 1968).

acquainted with the corpus of Christian Scripture and doctrine and Aristotelian philosophy. He spent his life seeking to integrate Christian faith and Aristotelian philosophy into a coherent world view, and it was this pursuit that resulted in the writing of the *Summa theologica*.

THEISTIC REALISM

Aquinas developed a scholastic philosophy that can be classified as a form of theistic realism. Drawing from Christian and Aristotelian sources, theistic realism asserted that

1. Reality is both spiritual and material.
2. God is both ultimate Being and a personal and caring Creator.
3. Man, a rational being, can achieve knowledge of reality.
4. Man is endowed with a free will, which he exercises by making choices.
5. Objective truth and value exist as the surest guide to human conduct.

THOMISTIC VIEW OF MAN

Aquinas held man to be a creature composed of a physical body and a spiritual soul who lives on earth for a time but is destined to experience the vision of God in eternity. Following Aristotle, he asserted that man's defining power is his rationality. Although instinctive and behavioral like other animals, man is distinguished by his intellectual, or rational, powers. Following an essentially Aristotelian epistemology, Aquinas asserted that man's knowledge of the world begins with sense experience. Endowed with abstractive, rational powers, man conceptualizes his experience and can weigh alternatives and choose between them in the exercise of his free will. As a self-conscious being, man can transcend the limitations of matter and fact and arrive at universal knowledge. Following Christian doctrine, Aquinas asserted that man possesses a spiritual soul, the principle of his self-awareness and freedom, which is immaterial and deathless. After the demise of the body, his soul is destined for the Beatific Vision of God.

THOMISTIC EDUCATIONAL IMPLICATIONS

Aquinas' conception of the educator drew from the Dominican synthesis that blended faith and learning. By serving his fellowmen, the teacher is called to the love of God. As both a contemplative scholar and an active participant in the learning process, the teacher should master his discipline by quietly pursuing its basic sources and acquiring an expertise in using the methods of inquiry relevant to these sources. When he actively engages in teaching, the teacher should direct his energies to organizing and transmitting the materials of the discipline to the student. Thus, for a scholastic such as Aquinas, there was no contradiction between research and teaching. The good teacher teaches a subject matter that he has carefully researched. Both active teaching and quiet scholarship blend in this scholastic method.

Aquinas distinguished carefully between *educatio,* informal education, and *disciplina,* formal schooling. Educatio involved all the means or agencies that contributed to bring a person to virtue or excellence. Disciplina was the learning that resulted from the formal instruction of teachers and schools. In recognizing the distinctions between informal and formal education, Aquinas determined that schooling should center on "scientia," or bodies of knowledge, based on demonstrated subject matters. Scholastic instruction began with first premises or principles and involved the demonstration of conclusions, through example and analogy, which were deductively derived from these principles.

Scholastic teachers used syllogistic reasoning from evident "first principles" and accumulated an ordered body of demonstrated knowledge. The teacher's task was to aid the students in recognizing basic principles and in developing their implications. Thomistic teaching was an exercise in language in that the instructional act involved the selecting of language that functioned effectively to communicate the teacher's thought to the students. Aquinas also asserted the curricular primacy of the liberal arts and sciences. Logic, mathematics, natural philosophy, moral philosophy, metaphysics, and theology formed the organized subject matters to be pursued as the higher studies.

Conclusion

The medieval university was a community of scholars that represented the institutionalization of the theological, philosophical, and intellectual currents of the late Middle Ages. Although there were variations in the organizational patterns of such universities as Bologna, Salerno, Paris, and Oxford, the two dominant patterns were either the student-dominated southern model or the faculty-dominated northern model. The curriculum of medieval higher education consisted of the core liberal arts and sciences, which were foundational to the professional studies of theology, law, and medicine. The mode of inquiry was scholasticism, which sought to integrate both faith and reason.

In the declining years of the medieval period, scholastic education began to show the signs of an excessive formalism. Trivialities replaced the crucial theological questions that had been faced earlier by

Abelard and Aquinas. It was this decline of scholasticism that contributed to the rise of a new intellectual force in the West—classical humanism. As the medieval period gradually faded into the rebirth of humanism, Western education entered the Renaissance, often called the beginning of modern thought.

Suggested Readings

Conway, Pierre H. *Principles of Education: A Thomistic Approach*. Washington: Thomist Press, 1960.

Daly, Lowrie J. *The Medieval University*. New York: Sheed and Ward, 1961.

Donohue, John W. *St. Thomas Aquinas and Education*. New York: Random House, 1968.

Haskins, Charles H. *The Rise of Universities*. New York: Cornell University Press, 1957.

Kibre, Pearl. *The Nations in the Mediaeval Universities*. Cambridge, Mass.: Mediaeval Academy of America, 1948.

Knowles, David. *The Evolution of Medieval Thought*. New York: Knopf, 1962.

Laurie, S. S. *Rise and Early Constitutions of Universities*. New York: D. Appleton, 1891.

Lawson, John. *Mediaeval Education*. London: Routledge and Kegan Paul, 1968.

Leff, Gordon. *Paris and Oxford Universities in the Thirteenth and Fourteenth Centuries: An Institutional and Intellectual History*. New York: Wiley, 1968.

McKeon, Richard. *Selections from Medieval Philosophers*. New York: Scribner, 1930.

Paetow, L. J. *The Arts Course at Medieval Universities*. Urbana: University of Illinois Press, 1910.

Rait, Robert S. *Life in the Mediaeval University*. Cambridge, England: Cambridge University Press, 1931.

Rashdall, Hastings. *The Universities of Europe in the Middle Ages*. London: Oxford University Press, 1936.

Schachner, Nathan. *The Medieval Universities*. London: George Allen and Unwin, 1938.

Thompson, J. W. *The Medieval Library*. Chicago: University of Chicago Press, 1939.

Thorndike, Lynn. *University Records and Life in the Middle Ages*. New York: Columbia University Press, 1944.

Vinogradoff, Paul. *Roman Law in Medieval Europe*. New York: Barnes and Noble, 1968.

Wieruszowski, Helene. *The Medieval University*. Princeton, N.J.: Van Nostrand, 1966.

CHAPTER 7

The Renaissance and Humanist Education

Historians have termed the humanist revival of interest in the Greek and Roman classics as the Renaissance. As a historical movement, the Renaissance began at the end of the fourteenth century, reached a high point in the fifteenth century, and carried over into the sixteenth-century Reformation. Like all historical movements, the Renaissance was complex and does not fit simple definitions. It did not begin abruptly but drew upon medieval antecedents that had emphasized classical learning. Although some interpreters have designated the Renaissance a rebirth of classical learning, this period was more accurately a shift in perspective as interest revived in the humanistic and secular implications of the Greek and Latin classics rather than in their providential and religious aspects. Although the medieval schoolmen had used classical authorities, especially Aristotle, as a basis for scholastic philosophy, the Renaissance humanist turned to the rhetorical works of Cicero and Quintilian.

The shift in perspective from a providential to a humanistic world view can be illustrated by contrasting the outlooks of the medieval and the Renaissance man. The medieval man had a providential conception of history that directed his life and aspirations toward God. He regarded all creation as being controlled by the Divine Force, which was beyond human interference. Based upon this spiritual orientation, the medieval authorities were the sacred Scripture, divine revelation, and faith. In the framework of medieval scholasticism, all aspects of life were theocentrically related to God or to the church. Although the medieval scholastic might have studied many of the same scriptural and classical sources as did the Renaissance humanist, his interpretation emphasized God's direct intervention in the lives of men.

Although great similarities still existed between the medieval and Renaissance man, the latter's view of history was more humanistic in that it centered on the temporal world rather than the world after death. Like the scholastic, the humanist regarded Latin as the language of scholarship, culture, and education. While concerned with religious themes, he was involved with secular issues and problems. Since the Renaissance embraced both theocentric and humanistic elements, the classical humanist exhibited many symptoms of a dualistic personality. While religious, he was also materialistic. He read the Greco-Roman classical literature and construed it to be intrinsically valuable for its content.

The tension between the providential and humanistic world views was clearly evident in the literary contributions of the major literary figures of the Renaissance. Dante (1265–1321) was a transitional figure between the Middle Ages and the Renaissance. His *Divine Comedy* made use of classical figures such as the Roman poet Vergil, but the emphasis was on Christian concern for salvation. In the late Renaissance, Erasmus (c. 1466–1536) wrote of the dignity of human nature in the light of Christian values.

Currents of the Renaissance: An Overview

The Renaissance is probably best described as a transitional period between the medieval and the modern. Like the medieval scholastic, the Renaissance humanist found his authorities in the past, ignored science, and stressed the editing of classical manuscripts. Despite the scholarly emphasis on classical antiquity, the Renaissance also exhibited sharp political, economic, and religious crosscurrents, some of which were still quite medieval and others of which held portents of modernity.

In western Europe, especially in England, France, and Spain, medieval feudalism was declining before the forces of resurgent political centralization found in the emergent modern nation-state and the strong national monarchy.

The revival of commerce and city life in the late Middle Ages had seriously weakened the decentralized, agrarian manorial-feudal system. By the time of the Renaissance, the process of political consolidation was well advanced in England, Spain, and France. In the German states and principalities of the Holy Roman Empire, local lords and princes retained control. In Italy, the various city-states, the papal states, and the Kingdom of the Two Sicilies were rigidly decentralized, each seeking through a combined use of diplomacy and mercenary soldiers to maintain the balance of power principle.

The growth of national states, each with its ruling house, was of educational significance in that such centralized political authorities require efficient bureaucracies to administer justice, collect taxes, and enforce national policies. In the late medieval and early Renaissance periods a whole complex of civil servants was introduced to enable the national monarch to interfere with and gain control of local and private political and economic transactions. These bureaucracies required educated civil servants. The rise of the nation-state was a sign of the weakening of the medieval synthesis with its priority on service to the church. The clerical scholastic was yielding to the emergent model of the humanistically educated courtier whose loyalties were to king rather than church.

The commercial revival, an aftermath of the crusades, and the consolidation of political power into national states contributed to an age of exploration. As a result, Europeans began to colonize the non-Western world, a colonization that was to continue until the end of the nineteenth century. Although the explorers had various religious, economic, and political motivations, the end result was the diffusion of Western ideas and culture. Prior to the fall of Constantinople to the Turks in 1453, the major trade centers had been the northern German cities of the Hanseatic League and the Italian city-states. When the Turks blocked much of the commerce with the Orient, the commercial center shifted to the Atlantic coastal regions, especially to Spain and Portugal.

The explorations of the fifteenth and sixteenth centuries were facilitated by the use of improved maritime technology, such as the compass and sextant. The economic ambitions of the rising commercial class and the political aspirations of national states coincided to stimulate investment in exploration.

Portuguese explorers such as Prince Henry the Navigator (1394–1460) desired to convert the Indian and Asiatic populations to Christianity and to promote Portuguese power and influence. The Portuguese explorers, who established what was primarily a trading rather than a colonial empire, did little to alter the basic fabric of native life. Portuguese trading colonies were founded at Goa in India, Macao in China, and in Brazil. The Spanish explorations in the Western Hemisphere did effect greater alterations in the cultures of their subject peoples. Cortes' conquest of the Aztecs in Mexico and Pizarro's conquest of the Peruvian Incas permanently imposed the Spanish language, culture, and religion. The Spanish crown maintained a centralized administrative authority to exploit natural and mineral resources of the colony on the behalf of the mother country.

Although the educational effects of exploration and colonization will be treated in greater detail later in this book, certain evident implications might now be considered. The contact between the western European and the American, Asian, and African was a transcultural encounter. Although the European received a non-Western education from the peoples whom he encountered, he also transferred the European language and culture to the conquered people. Religious missionaries and other educators came to convert subject peoples to both Christian and Western ways.

The revitalization of city life inaugurated near the end of the Middle Ages continued unabated into the Renaissance. City dwellers engaged in commerce formed a new class, the middle-class bourgeoisie. It was this class that was most effective in destroying the medieval synthesis. The commercial class was characterized by its upward mobility, whereas the medieval socioeconomic conceptions had excluded social mobility. Coming to possess financial power, the commercial class often allied with the national monarchs to weaken the rule of the feudal lords. The rise of the European middle class had great importance for educational development. It also demanded the literacy, arithmetic, bookkeeping, and commercial skills necessary to sustain commercial and business enterprises. The scholastic educational patterns and content that had been inherited from the medieval period were inadequate to satisfy the needs of this class. The bourgeoisie actively promoted the extension and contributed to the availability of formal education.

Decline of the Roman Catholic Church

The Renaissance ushered in a period of decline for the Roman Catholic Church. The supremacy that it had enjoyed during the Middle Ages was weakened by the Renaissance shift to a more humanistic and secular orientation. The rise of national states, strong dynastic monarchies, and commercial interests all tended to weaken the synthesis that the church had used to order medieval life and society. The popes were often involved in clashes with national monarchs over political power. In 1309, the weakened papacy was transferred to Avignon, where it remained until 1377 as a virtual prisoner of the French king.

Perspectives Within Renaissance Humanism

While the broad currents of the Renaissance might be considered as one movement, differences existed between the southern, or Italian, Renaissance and the northern, or Germanic, Renaissance. The Italian Renaissance was more secular and worldly than religious. The commercial revival and trade monopolies of some of the Italian city-states had produced a financial surplus, which was used to support art, literature, and architecture. The Italian humanists regarded themselves as an aristocratic literary elite whose task was to act as the "custodians of knowledge." They believed that their scholarship could be appreciated only by an initiated elite group. The Italian movement was not a great transforming or reforming social force, and the masses of population were largely untouched by the humanism of the Italian classical scholars.

With Francesco Petrarch (1304–1374) and Giovanni Boccaccio (1313–1375), the classical humanist movement of the Italian Renaissance was born. The classical humanists liberated individuality from the constraints of monasticism, feudalism, and scholasticism. Rejecting Aristotelian scholasticism, they turned to Cicero and Quintilian and to the secular dimension of experience. Humanist scholars and educators claimed that the development and perfection of human nature were best portrayed in the Latin and Greek classical literatures. Standards of literary excellence and appreciation were found in the ancient masterpieces.

Local rulers in the Italian city-states took advantage of the growing disenchantment with papal rule by increasing their political and economic authority. They soon entered into the field of education and claimed the right to control it. While the church was interested in training scholars and clergy for ecclesiastic service, the petty rulers of the Italian states and principalities established court schools to prepare courtiers for state service. As the court schools increased in number, the demand for humanist teachers made education a profitable career. Wealth flowing into the prosperous cities supported humanist education. Teaching, especially when done by classical humanists, grew in public esteem.

The classical humanist scholars of northern Europe, especially those of the Low Countries and Germany, directed their attention to criticizing scriptural and theological writings, many of which had been distorted by medieval copyists. The northern Renaissance continued to emphasize religious concerns but in a more individualistic and subjective manner than the medieval scholastics. They combined a reverence for classical antiquity with an evangelic Christianity that contributed to the Protestant Reformation.

Humanist Educators of the Renaissance

The history of Renaissance education is primarily that of individual humanist educators who developed distinctive pedagogical strategies designed to produce the well-rounded, liberally educated gentleman. These educators generally believed that classical Greek and Latin literatures, by furnishing the basic elements of a liberal education, could produce this cultured gentleman. The style of writing of the classical authors, especially Cicero, would produce, it was believed, an elegance of style and expression.

Vittorino da Feltre

One of the major educators of the southern Renaissance was the famous Italian humanist Vittorino da Feltre (1378–1446). Born in Feltre as Vittorino da Ramboldini, he was educated in the cathedral school, where he exhibited a decided propensity for books and learning. He was popular with his peers and often joined in mock war games, but only when he could be the leader. As a young man, he attended the university in Padua, where he studied Latin grammar and literature with Ravenna, a protégé of Petrarch. He attended the lectures of Vergerio, author of *De ingenuis moribus*, which was a major humanist work. While at the university, Vittorino also studied dialectic and philosophy. In order to supplement the stipend given to him by his father, he tutored a number of students. After earning his *laurea*, or doctorate of arts, in 1411, he decided to remain in Padua to teach and to attend lectures. He studied mathematics under Pelacani and became proficient in the subject.

Vittorino developed a lasting friendship with Gasparino Barzizza, who was a professor of Latin letters at Padua. Barzizza, recognized as one of Italy's most prominent Latinists, had prepared an edition of Cicero's *De oratore*. Vittorino also spent some time studying with Guarino, who had learned Greek from the great scholar Chrysolorus.

In 1422, when he was gaining recognition as the "most capable teacher of the New Learning in Italy,"[1] Vittorino established a school in Venice. The school was well-attended by the sons of wealthy men who were eager to expose their children to his teaching. Because of his fame, the duke of Mantua, Gianfrancesco Gonzaga, sought to attract Vittorino to his court school. In 1423, Vittorino accepted Gonzaga's invitation and took up residence in Mantua. Here Vittorino established his "house of joy" in facilities provided by the duke. The spacious school contained broad corridors and well-lighted and lofty rooms and was surrounded by broad meadows, walks, and trees. The river Mincio flowed nearby. The meadows and the river were used for recreational purposes and student outings. Vittorino believed that learning proceeded more efficiently in pleasant surroundings and sought to create and maintain a physically attractive school.

Although Vittorino's "house of joy" was a court school that was intended primarily for the education of young aristocrats, a few places were reserved for the talented poor, who were fed, clothed, and educated with funds paid from Vittorino's own stipend and from the charity of the duke. Emphasizing the selective function of the school, Vittorino carefully screened the applicants to determine whether a

[1] William Woodward, *Vittorino da Feltre and Other Humanist Educators* (Cambridge, England: Cambridge University Press, 1921), p. 22.

child would be admitted. He preferred to admit younger children since they were unspoiled by a previous miseducation.

Vittorino's philosophy of education included elements of classical and Christian humanism. He saw no contradiction between the study of the ancient classics and Christianity. Like other Renaissance educators, he accepted the ideas of Cicero and Quintilian and believed that an educated man should be able to speak knowledgeably on a broad range of subjects. He also emphasized the moral nature of education by stressing the values of Christianity and humanism. He drew heavily on the classics, from which he extracted examples of noble lives to be used as moral exemplars by his students.

The core of Vittorino's curriculum was a thorough training in classical literature, along with such subjects drawn from classical and patristic sources as mathematics, natural sciences, ethics, history, and geography. The rationale for the curriculum came from such sources as Plutarch's *De liberis educandis*, Quintilian's *Institutio oratoria*, and Vergerio's *De ingenuis moribus*. All discourse in the school, including everyday conversation, was in Latin or Greek. The use of the vernacular was forbidden.

Children of four or five learned to read by means of letter games devised by Vittorino. By the age of ten, the students were memorizing and reciting classical literature. By fourteen they were reading and reciting from the orations of Cicero and Demosthenes, the books of Livy, Sallust, Caesar, and Plutarch, and the poems of Vergil and Homer. Grammar and composition were taught in both Latin and Greek. Vittorino regarded the study of Greek to be of great importance. Like his humanist colleagues, he wanted his students to return to the original sources, which were largely Greek.

Vittorino permitted his students to write original compositions only after they had thoroughly developed the theme that they wished to exposit. Students were expected to develop their arguments, determine the form of the composition, and use copious evidence drawn from their reading of the classical literatures. Vittorino then carefully corrected the compositions.

Vittorino has earned a place in the history of education because of his pedagogical innovations. He emphasized physical fitness and dexterity in the belief that the truly educated man possesses both an excellent mind and body. Regular periods were reserved for gymnastics and physical exercises. Physical education and games were regarded as recreational and as a respite from the rigors of academic learning. Vittorino himself often participated in the students' games. In fact, believing that there should be a close relationship between teacher and learner, he joined them in hiking and mountain climbing, ate at their table, and was available for counsel and guidance.

Vittorino followed Quintilian's recommendations that students be motivated by appeals to interest and pride rather than by coercive corporal punishment. In some ways, he anticipated the methods of the later Jesuits by cultivating a friendly rivalry among his students. As a teacher, he encouraged and praised his students and demonstrated a sincere interest and concern for them. Although the learning atmosphere in Vittorino's "house of joy" was permissive for the time, it was not lax. He demanded quality work; poorly prepared lessons were repeated.

Since Vittorino's school was intended to prepare future statesmen, scholars, administrators, and ecclesiastics, he encouraged student self-government. A form of student council was devised in which the students were divided into the political factions that had characterized Roman political life. Self-government was encouraged as both a means of character education and a method of institutional governance.

Following Quintilian's admonitions, Vittorino's methodology emphasized the recognition of individual differences among the students. A child was not to be forced into a line of rigidly prescribed study but was to be encouraged to develop according to his capacity and interests. As soon as he noticed a particular interest in a student, Vittorino adjusted the method of his teaching. The school at Mantua became a model for other humanist educators who sought to emulate the success of Vittorino.

Da Feltre conceived of the educated man as a humanist gentleman of good physical health and bearing, accomplished in social graces, capable of aesthetic expression, and, above all, possessing liberal ideas and outlook. To prepare such a well-rounded and versatile person, he turned to the classical heritage of Greece and Rome, which he believed to be the gateway of ideas. His pedagogical insights came primarily from the Roman rhetoricians Cicero and Quintilian.

Da Feltre strongly advocated the liberal arts, which formed the basis of his educational system. Like most humanists, he looked upon certain aspects of medieval scholasticism with suspicion, rejecting the scholastic emphasis on logic. He wanted to educate Christian gentlemen but believed that morality should be derived from classical literature rather than from specific catechetical instructions.

Vittorino da Feltre was both a representative of the Italian Renaissance and a precursor of modern education. In his humanism and his concern for the classics, he represented Italian classical humanist education. His court school at Mantua exhibited several characteristics of Italian education during the Renaissance: it was aristocratic in nature; it was designed to prepare courtiers who would be useful to their prince; and the curriculum was based upon the classics, especially Italian rhetorical sources. In wanting his school to be a pleasant place and in providing for recreation, games, and athletic events, he foreshadowed a more enlightened conception of educational theory and practice than was generally present during his lifetime. Da Feltre's attempts to liberalize schooling have made him a significant figure in educational history.

Erasmus

Erasmus (c. 1466–1536) represents a Renaissance ideal, Christian humanism. He was born in Rotterdam in the Netherlands and educated in the elementary schools of the evangelical and pietistical Brethren of the Common Life. After entering religious life in 1492, he studied scholasticism at the University of Paris and traveled extensively throughout Europe. He was a scholar, classicist, critic, and author. As a religious scholar, he edited the Testaments and the writings of the church fathers; as a classical humanist, he devised a methodology for teaching Latin, which he explained in the *Adagia* and *Colloquies;* as a social and educational critic, he wrote *The Praise of Folly;* as a Christian humanist, he wrote *The Education of a Christian Prince*. If there was a universal man, it was Erasmus of Rotterdam.[2]

Major tendencies of the Renaissance are revealed in both the person and the writings of Erasmus. Like many northern humanists, he was interested in social criticism and reformation. Like classicists everywhere, he was vitally concerned with the study of Greek and Latin. Erasmus' most revealing characteristic was his cosmopolitanism. European in outlook, he feared that the emergent contentions of religious sectarianism and nationalism would destroy the community and cosmopolitanism that characterized European intellectual life. Although critical of abuses and corruption within the Roman Catholic Church, he remained devoted to the notion of a universal institution. To appreciate Erasmus' contribution to Western education, he can be examined as: first, a critic who revealed the weaknesses of his time; second, a teacher who emphasized the humanistic content of the classics; third, a social reformer who advocated a Christian and cosmopolitan humanism.

In *The Praise of Folly*, Erasmus criticized the grammarians who devoted their lives to searching for obscure facts and trivialities. As scholars often do, they permitted minute specialization to obscure the realities of life. He criticized philosophers for weaving speculative webs of dialectical arguments that had no real impact nor made any

---

[2] For an analysis of the educational theory of Erasmus, see Frank E. Schacht, "The Classical Humanist: Erasmus," in Paul Nash, Andreas M. Kazamias, and Henry J. Perkinson (eds.), *The Educated Man: Studies in the History of Educational Thought* (New York: Wiley, 1965), pp. 141–162. Also see William Harrison Woodward, *Desiderius Erasmus Concerning the Aim and Method of Education* (New York: Bureau of Publications, Teachers College, Columbia University, 1964).

humane contribution. The theologians, he found, were concerned with corollaries, propositions, conclusions, and definitions rather than with the basic question of man's relationship to God and to the cosmos. Erasmus' critique was directed against both the scholastic philosophers and theologians and the classicist grammarians who, while claiming to seek truth, actually were idling with insignificant trivialities.

Although he did not develop a systematic educational theory, Erasmus recognized the importance of early childhood and advised that children be "brought up gently in virtue and learning." The educational processes were to be begun as early as possible by both fathers and mothers, who were to take their duties seriously. The gentle humanist Erasmus suggested that children receive gentle instruction in good manners and be read fables and poems having a desirable formative effect.

As a humanist educator, Erasmus focused his attention on language. Since they contained all the knowledge needed by man, he said that Latin and Greek were the most important subjects and should not be allowed to be devitalized by pedantic grammarians. Erasmus opposed those classicists who, in slavish devotion, followed Cicero's style so narrowly that they failed to develop their own style of writing. The good teacher of languages should be well read and have a rich background in materials that supplement the basic texts. He should have a knowledge of literature and of etymology and should be acquainted with the subject matter of such fields of knowledge as archeology, astronomy, history, and Scripture, which relate to and complement the study of the classical languages.

In language study itself, Erasmus indicated that it was much more important to understand the content than to master style and grammar. Conversation in the language made learning it more attractive, as did games, plays, and contests. Erasmus suggested a well-defined methodology for teaching the content of classical literatures: (1) presentation of the author's biography; (2) examination of the type of work under consideration; (3) discussion of the basic plot; (4) analysis of the author's style; (5) consideration of the moral applications of the work; and (6) explanation of the broader philosophical themes.

Erasmus' cosmopolitan humanism is most evident in his work *The Education of a Christian Prince*. Although he recognized that the prince exercised power, he urged that such power be used for wise and peaceful rule rather than exploitation of the prince's subjects. The prince should be educated in the "arts of peace" and should strive to find the means of avoiding war. Erasmus' admonitions on the education of the Christian prince can be contrasted to the writings of his contemporary, Machiavelli (1469–1527), who emphasized power politics and the theory that the end justifies the means. While Erasmus urged the Christian prince to employ the "peaceful arts," Machiavelli considered the ruler's task to be that of gaining and maintaining power.

Erasmus advised the prince to be aware of the geography, history, institutions, customs, laws, and traditions of his own kingdom. This knowledge would help him to love his people and to be loved by them. The prince should not attempt to buy the affection of his people since such popularity is not genuine and is temporary. Rather, he should love his people so that they might genuinely love him. As a person, the prince should be worthy of love and respect and should select his counselors from among the most worthy men of the realm. Violence, insult, and greed are ignoble in any man, but especially so in the Christian prince, who should win affection by clemency, affability, fairness, courtesy, and kindliness and maintain his authority by wisdom, integrity, and self-restraint. Erasmus' model of the Christian prince contained a great deal that was reminiscent of the chivalric knight of the medieval era.

Machiavelli, in contrast, believed that the people were to be manipulated rather than loved, for the always fickle populace would follow the highest bidder. The prince should be exclusively occupied with planning for war, although if he could win his demands through diplomatic machinations, this pursuit would be less costly. However, there should be no hesitancy about resorting to war when necessary. The skillful prince should use both diplomacy and force, making and breaking treaties whenever such action suited his ends. While Erasmus urged the prince to cultivate the love of his subjects, Machiavelli cautioned that it was safer for princes to be feared than loved. Erasmus admonished the prince to be fair and affable, but Machiavelli indicated that from time to time the prince would have to use punishment as an example to curb potential opposition. If the prince were too lenient, he would invite only rebellion and disorder.

Like most of those men who believe that man is capable of improving his condition through nonviolent and enlightened means, Erasmus turned to education. The Christian prince was advised that the main hope of the civil state was in educating its youth. If youth were educated by gentle instructors in the teachings of Christ and in good literature, the state would benefit. People would of their own free will follow the course of right action, and the need for many laws and punishments would decrease. Thus, Erasmus believed that it was possible to improve and enlighten both individuals and governments through educational means.

As indicated, Machiavelli found the chief princely occupation to be war or preparation for war. Erasmus, in contrast, found war to be a peril that endangered all mankind. From war came more wars; local war would escalate into widespread conflict; minimal confrontations would become increasingly more violent and bloody. In the education of the prince, care should be taken that he be aware of the serious consequences that warfare brought not only to himself but to his people. If war should be necessary, the prince should put away his personal feelings, rationally estimate the consequences, and be cautious with the lives of others. In any event, Erasmus found it to be the height of folly that Christians should be fighting Christians since the founder of their religion had opposed the very idea of war. He advocated an international Christianity when he said that, instead of blessing armies on their way to battle, bishops and priests should dissuade the parties from conflict. Christian teachers should uproot the ideas of discord and prejudice from the common people. Unfortunately, nationality hated nationality, race hated race, and district hated district. Erasmus asserted that "stupid names" did more to divide mankind than the name of Christ did to unite them.

In addition to being a distinguished classical humanist, Erasmus clearly advocated cosmopolitan education. He believed that education could do much to promote understanding, tolerance, and gentleness between peoples. He argued that men were primarily brothers who shared the earth as a common home. He did not reject the notion of harmonious synthesis of all men under the Fatherhood of God as did some of the humanists. His cosmopolitanism ran counter to the doctrinal clash that would come between Protestant and Catholic with the Reformation and to the nationalism that would lead to a long and continuing series of wars between rival nations.

The differences presented by the humanism of Erasmus and Machiavelli clearly indicate a problem that has faced education since the days of the Renaissance. In the post-Renaissance Reformation era, the goal of education became training for citizenship, which often meant nationalism and even chauvinism. Frequently it meant training for war. As education has become controlled by national governments and designed to serve national interests, it has lost the cosmopolitanism that Erasmus advocated. Some educators would assert that the reality of modern life is that of the national state and would condemn Erasmus as a utopian visionary.

Although the dominant feature of modern education has been service to the nation, there has been a long tradition of educators who have continued to assert that we live in one world and that man's basic interests are derived from his sharing in a common humanity that transcends national boundaries. Contemporary forms of the basic cosmopolitan humanism suggested by Erasmus are the various arguments made for world law, international organization, and intercultural and international education.

Michel de Montaigne

Michel de Montaigne (1533–1592), a French humanist, intellectual, and social critic, criticized both the older scholastic and the formalized classical humanist kinds of education. Montaigne received an excessively formal classical education, studied law, served as mayor of Bordeaux, and then retired to the leisure of his estate. He wrote a large number of essays, the first of which appeared in 1580. Several of them, such as "On Pedantry," "On the Education of Children," and "On the Affection of Fathers for Their Children," directly relate to education.

Although a humanist, Montaigne was very critical of the degeneration of classical humanism into sheer pedantry, idle verbalism, and formalism. Like most educational movements, classical humanism had originated as an exciting, vital, and inspired approach to learning. Over time, however, the original stimulus had been undermined by pedestrian teachers, and the movement deteriorated as it retained the form but lost the spirit of its original impetus. Recognizing the debilitating effects of the formalized version of classical humanism, Montaigne accused the pedantic humanists of stuffing the memories of their students with dull facts while ignoring the meaning of the classics. He felt that they had become overly concerned with educating mere pedantic scholars rather than well-rounded, cultured gentlemen.

Montaigne, who was concerned with the education of children of the aristocracy, believed that proper education should begin with study under a carefully chosen tutor. Provision should be made for moral and physical training, social experience, travel, and philosophical and historical study. Although Latin would remain the language of the educated man, the gentleman should also be conversant in the modern vernaculars. Montaigne's own essays were written in French rather than Latin.

Since the aristocratic child was destined to be a member of the ruling class, he should be prepared to act like a ruler from the time of birth onward. He should know etiquette, courtly manners, proper behavior, music, and dancing. These should be cultivated while the child was still young and flexible enough to learn them easily. Although skeptical about certain aspects of the supernatural such as miracles and demons, Montaigne did not entirely neglect religious formation. For him, religion was an emotional rather than intellectual matter.

Montaigne's social or realistic humanism was directed away from the exclusively scholarly interpretation of Latin classical literature. Although not neglecting these classics, he wanted them studied for their meaning rather than their literary style. Like many humanists, he wanted to educate an intellectual elite rather than the masses of the population.

English Humanists: Vives, Ascham, Milton

Although there were a number of humanist educators in England who contributed to the classical revival of the Renaissance, the development of humanist educational patterns there can best be seen by examining the work of Juan Luis Vives (1492–1540) and Roger Ascham (1515–1568). The cosmopolitan nature of Renaissance classical humanism is exhibited by Vives' own education. He was born in Spain, studied at the University of Paris, was a professor at Louvain and then at Oxford, and served as adviser of Catherine of Aragon, the first wife of King Henry VIII. Unlike many of his contemporaries, Vives advocated the education of women. In *De institutione feminae Christianae,* which he dedicated to Catherine, he stated that the educated noblewoman should be high-principled, moral, an intelligent mistress of her own household, and a cultured and intellectual companion for her husband.

Vives had studied the works of Erasmus and reflected many of his ideas. Like the Dutch humanist, he opposed both scholasticism's slavish devotion to Aristotle's logic and classical humanism's enthronement of Ciceronian style. In many ways, Vives anticipated the sense of realism that developed in the eighteenth century. His general theme held that knowledge was valuable when it was useful. He proposed that apprenticeship schools be established so that the poor might be prepared for useful trades.

Roger Ascham was a tutor of Elizabeth I, a classical scholar at Cambridge, and a Latin secretary to both Queen Mary and Queen Elizabeth. He was primarily concerned with language instruction, and his book *The Scholemaster* is a treatise on the methodology of teaching Latin to young aristocrats. Like many humanists, Ascham was a devotee of Ciceronian Latin. He developed the method of the double translation in which the students would learn to imitate Cicero by studying those Roman authors whom Cicero had himself imitated. The student would translate from Latin into English and then from English into Latin with emphasis being directed to the exact reproduction of the literature being translated.

In addition to teaching Latin, Ascham made several contributions to the development of educational methodology. First of all, he said, the tutor must be a good man who is worthy of imitation by his students. This moral influence should be complemented further by studying the Bible and ancient literatures.

Although he believed that learning should be interesting, Ascham indicated that it involved hard work and diligence. In fact, he preferred the "hard wit," the student who persisted and whose learning might be slow but steady and certain. The diligent student was preferred to the "quick wit," who, although imaginative and ready to respond, often lacked the needed virtues of discipline and persistence.

In addition to Vives and Ascham, mention should be made of Sir Thomas Elyot and John Collette, who also contributed to English humanistic education. Elyot promoted Greek literature in England by his translations of the works of Plutarch and Isocrates into the vernacular. In his *The Boke Named the Governour*, he set down the curriculum that should be used to educate the English gentleman, statesman, and royal official. To be broadly educated, he should know Latin, Greek, rhetoric, logic, geometry, astronomy, music, history, geography, drawing, sculpture, and physical education.

John Collette, who established the famous humanist St. Paul's Churchyard School, was influenced by both the Italian and the northern Renaissance. He believed that classical literature was desirable in improving the general intellectual climate but that morality should be cultivated by exposure to religious truths and doctrine rather than by isolating moral exemplars from classical study.

Conclusion

While the educational history of the Renaissance is largely dominated by the individual classical humanist, certain general patterns and trends that arose during the period affected the subsequent course of Western educational development. Although the church still maintained formal control over educational institutions, secular and political authorities were making inroads into the area. During the Renaissance the church's monopoly over parish, monastic, and cathedral schools was broken as princes, nobles, town governments, and private teachers established their own schools. In Italy, the towns continued the practice of endowing schools, as they had done in the Middle Ages. In Germany, town officials and church officials contended for control of the schools. Numerous court schools, like that of da Feltre at Mantua, made their appearance as noblemen rejected scholasticism in favor of classical humanism. Some of the humanist educators established their own schools and made a living from tuition fees and payments. In terms of educational control, the Renaissance marked the decline of the church's monopoly, but a number of alternative patterns coexisted, and no clear-cut pattern of control emerged.

Within the various patterns of Renaissance education could be seen the origins of the European dual-track system of schools. Classical education, with its emphasis on Latin, was preferred by the upper classes, which consisted of the nobility and the bureaucracy that served the king. The various classical secondary schools maintained by the humanist educators served their pedagogical needs. The rising commercial class—the town burghers and merchants—were more interested in using their own language than studying classical Greek and Latin. They therefore preferred vernacular elementary schools that would provide their sons with the rudiments of reading, writing, arithmetic, and bookkeeping. It was upon this framework of a dual system of educational institutions that western European education would develop.

Although the demands of the bourgeoisie for vernacular schools were heard, the dominant pattern of Renaissance education was classical humanist. Despite their differences in style and method, the humanist educators, with their concern for language, especially classical Latin, believed that, to be educated, one had to master language and literature. Scientific and practical studies were virtually ignored. These verbal, literary, and classical predilections of the humanist educators still have an impact on formal schooling, especially in the secondary school. Until the last two decades of the nineteenth century, Latin remained a mark of the educated man. Proficiency in Latin was an entrance requirement for college and university admission throughout western Europe and the United States. Although Latin has lost its dominance, the verbal and literary emphasis that originated in the Renaissance still dominates secondary education, where learning is construed as the mastery of bodies of literature, textbooks, and language. The various "reform movements" of Rousseau in the eighteenth century, Pestalozzi in the nineteenth century, and Dewey in the twentieth century were directed against forms of education that were exclusively verbal and ignored direct experience, activities, and science. Despite the various educational reforms, the emphasis on grammar and rhetoric still prevails. Contemporary humanists continue to assert that the literary inheritance of the Western world constitutes the most efficient, accomplished, and significant means of cultivating man's rationality.

Suggested Readings

Adams, Robert P. *The Better Part of Valor: More, Erasmus, Colet, and Vives, on Humanism, War, and Peace, 1496–1535.* Seattle: University of Washington Press, 1962.

Allen, P. S. *The Age of Erasmus.* London: Oxford University Press, 1914.

Burckhardt, J. *The Civilization of the Renaissance in Italy.* S. G. C. Middlemore (tr.). London: George G. Hurrop, 1929.

Hay, Denys. *The Italian Renaissance in its Historical Background.* Cambridge, England: Cambridge University Press, 1966.

Hyma, Albert. *The Youth of Erasmus.* Ann Arbor: University of Michigan Press, 1930.

Laurie, S. S. *Studies in the History of Educational Opinion from the Renaissance.* New York: Humanities Press, 1968.

Lehmberg, S. E. *Sir Thomas Elyot, Tudor Humanist.* Austin: University of Texas Press, 1960.

Phillips, M. M. *Erasmus and the Northern Renaissance.* London: Hodder and Stoughton, 1949.

Ryan, Lawrence V. *Roger Ascham.* Stanford: Stanford University Press, 1963.

Schevill, Ferdinand. *The First Century of Italian Humanism.* New York: Russell and Russell, 1967.

Symonds, John A. *Renaissance in Italy: The Revival of Learning.* New York: Scribner, 1907; Magnolia, Mass.: Smith, Peter, n.d.

Watson, Foster. *Vives and the Renaissance Education of Women.* London: Longmans, Green, 1912.

————. *Vives on Education.* New York: Putnam, 1913.

Woodward, William H. *Vittorino da Feltre and Other Humanist Educators.* New York: Teachers College Press, Columbia University, 1963. (First published in 1897.)

————. *Desiderius Erasmus Concerning the Aim and Method of Education.* New York: Bureau of Publications, Teachers College, Columbia University, 1964.

————. *Studies in Education During the Age of the Renaissance, 1400–1600.* New York: Teachers College Press, Columbia University, 1967. (First published in 1906.)

CHAPTER 8

Religious Reformation and Education

The sixteenth-century Protestant Reformation and Roman Catholic Counter Reformation were closely related to the northern Renaissance emphasis on scriptural criticism and personal and social regeneration. Although humanism itself entailed no overt break with Catholicism, the humanist demand for freedom of scholarship contributed to the initial phase of the Reformation. In their antiquarian researches, the classicists had discovered certain textual corruptions in some of the documents of the church. For example, Valla had discovered the "Donation of Constantine," which had granted land to the pope, to be a forgery. Many of the northern humanists, in urging a refocusing of attention on early Christian sources, on the study of the life of Christ, and on the primitive holiness of the early church, anticipated the evangelicalism of certain of the Protestant reformers. Humanists such as Erasmus had criticized Roman Catholicism's formalism, traditionalism, authoritarianism, and scholasticism but, like the earlier Cluniac Benedictines and the Franciscans, urged that internal reformation proceed within the context of a universal Christian synthesis.

Other northern humanists, such as John Calvin and Martin Luther, inaugurated their pleas for reformation within the Catholic framework by protesting against certain corrupt practices. Within a short time, however, the initial controversies centering on practices developed into serious and major doctrinal differences.

Much of the post-Reformation history of Western culture and education is an account of the antagonistic Christian denominations' uncompromising and bitter struggle. Histories of the sixteenth and seventeenth centuries detail various religious wars; in the course of these conflicts, dynastic and national ambitions were intermixed with religious antagonism. Nevertheless, religious intolerance contributed to the interminable hatred, which often led to genocide against many of the smaller dissenting Christian sects. Religious antagonism was a major cause of the struggle of the German Lutheran princes against the Catholic Hapsburg Emperor Charles V from 1546 until 1555, of the French religious civil war from 1562 to 1598, and of the major Thirty Years' War from 1618 to 1648. These violent confrontations resulted in extensive property destruction and loss of life. The German states and principalities in particular were devastated by the various contending armies of Germans, Danes, Swedes, and French.

In 1555, the Peace of Augsburg established the principle that the ruler of an area was to establish his religion as the creed of the inhabitants. The Peace of Westphalia in 1648 reconfirmed this principle and allowed dissenters to migrate. As a result of these settlements and the residue of hatred left by religious war and persecution, continental western Europe was divided into three major contending creeds: Lutheran, Calvinist, and Roman Catholic. As doctrinal differences hardened into acrimonious recrimination, there was virtually no communication between these major religious groups.

The Protestant Reformation profoundly affected Western educational institutions, which had already been influenced by Renaissance humanism. The various denominations developed their own theologies of education, established their own schools, and sought to commit the young members of the church to "defend the faith" against rival creeds. The general Protestant emphasis on individual biblical reading and interpretation fostered a demand for universal literacy.

Although the obvious impact of the Reformation was religious, certain major secular tendencies that had originated in the late medieval and Renaissance periods exerted a powerful effect on Western European life. The political movement to centralized nation-states under the leadership of national monarchs continued. The medieval synthesis proclaiming one church and one people crumbled as national differences and vernacular languages overshadowed the claims of universal authority. For example, the French, recognizing their unique cultural heritage, identified with their nation and their king. Sixteenth-century Spain was one of the strongest national states. The Spanish king, an absolute sovereign who was proclaimed as a "Catholic majesty," was closely identified with the Roman Catholic Church, which he often dominated in his own country.

The French kings asserted their own authority and extended French territory by engaging in a series of wars against England, Spain, Germany, and the Italian states. The English king, although limited by Parliament, consolidated national and royal authority. Henry VIII, seizing monastic lands, disestablished Roman Catholicism and established the Church of England, of which he was titular head.

In the Low Countries, the German states, and the Italian principalities, nationalist sentiment encountered opposition. Dutch nationalism, confronting Spanish imperialism, eventually triumphed in achieving an independent Netherlands. In resisting the Spanish Hapsburgs, the

Dutch asserted their own Calvinist convictions and special commercial interests. In the various German states, the nationalist party, led by Lutheran princes, confronted the Catholic Hapsburg emperor, who preferred a number of weak and disunited German states. The Italian peninsula remained divided into papal states, city-states, and principalities which engaged in Machiavellian intrigues against each other. Surfacing in the Reformation, nationalism exerted a strong and continuing influence on Western history and education. With it came the growing use of vernacular languages, the creation of vernacular literatures, and a sense of national pride, particularities, and values. Nationalism promoted national educational systems that stressed vernacular languages and national loyalties. The nation-state's control was extended over schools, educational aims, organizations, and curricula.

The disintegration of the medieval synthesis and the rise of national states were concurrent with the commercial revolution. Revitalized in the late medieval period, cities became centers of Renaissance humanism and culture. With commercial expansion, significant economic changes occurred in Europe. As money became a more important source of wealth than land, merchants, bankers, and other tradesmen replaced the feudal nobility as the holders of real power. In the early stages of the commercial revival, merchants and kings allied against feudal lords. Since the merchant needed a system of internal security to protect his economic investments, it was in his self-interest that the national state be strong enough to regulate, protect, and promote commerce by erecting tariffs, providing subsidies, and encouraging trade. It was most important that the king be sufficiently strong to check the feudal aristocrats who interfered with commerce by erecting such barriers to internal trade as local dues, excises, taxes, and tributes. This mutual alliance between businessmen and monarch produced mercantilism, an initial stage of modern capitalism. National states acquired and maintained colonies as sources of raw materials and precious metals. The merchants were protected from domestic robber barons and foreign rivals. With the financial support of the middle classes, the kings consolidated their nations and waged foreign wars. Although king and bourgeoisie cooperated initially, the alliance was uneasy. By the later eighteenth century, the bourgeoisie often gained the upper hand in the alliance and, at times, dominated it.

The commercial revolution significantly affected Western educational history. The new commercial class was clearly distinct from the rural aristocracy and peasantry. After it had gained economic power, the new class sought political power commensurate with its economic position. In education, the middle class desired more useful subject matters and often established its own schools through voluntary action and donations. Whenever possible, this class also encouraged the creation of state and municipal educational systems.

These complex economic, political, and social forces as well as religious motivations contributed to the sixteenth-century Reformation and the seventeenth-century dynastic and religious wars. By examining the life and work of Martin Luther (1483–1546), the major innovator of the Reformation, the principal trends of the period can be isolated and analyzed.

Martin Luther: The Personality of a Reformer

On October 31, 1517, Martin Luther (1483–1546) nailed his famous "Ninety-five Theses" to the door of the court church at Wittenberg in the German state of Saxony. Although the medieval synthesis had already shown serious weaknesses, his action signaled the onset of the Protestant Reformation. Luther, an Augustinian monk and scriptural professor at the University of Wittenberg, did not intend to found a reformed Christian church when he publicized his objections to certain corrupt practices in Catholicism. Like many of his fellow northern humanists, including Erasmus, Luther was following the tradition of internal and communal reformation used earlier by the medieval Cluniac Benedictines and the Franciscans. Although the sale of indulgences had precipitated Luther's action, his protest soon reached matters of basic Christian doctrine.

Luther was one of those great historic personages who affect both ideas and institutions. His personality revealed traits that reflected both humanism and medievalism. Like other humanists, Luther had carefully studied the biblical and doctrinal sources of Christianity. He knew that accidental textual corruptions and even some outright forgeries had occurred in the Middle Ages. He believed it possible and desirable for the church to reform itself and thereby aid men to achieve salvation. In many other respects, Luther's outlook was more medieval than humanistic. Feeling alienated from God, he had great fears and anxieties regarding his own personal salvation. His life as an Augustinian monk and priest did little to ease his depression and foreboding.

In Chapter 7, Erasmian Christian humanism was contrasted to Machiavellian realpolitik. Since Erasmus and Luther were contemporaneous and in the tradition of northern humanism, a comparison of the two provides insights into Luther's attitudes. As biblical scholars, both Erasmus and Luther wanted to revive Europe's Christian consciousness by disseminating the sacred Scriptures in their pure form. Both believed that the church had grown too legalistic and needed humanization, and both disagreed with the pope. Luther came to assert that the popes had imperiled the salvation of souls; Erasmus felt that those associated with the papal office had impeded freedom of inquiry.

Although both Luther and Erasmus had these things in common, their personalities were in sharp contrast. While Erasmus was a cosmopolitan social and literary critic, Luther became an uncompromising religious reformer who uttered the famous words:

> . . . my conscience is captive to the Word of God. I cannot and I will not recant anything, for to go against conscience is neither right nor safe.[1]

As a man of action, Luther felt compelled to act when he believed he was right. Erasmus, an intellectual, could examine all sides of an issue but not press for a decision. Desiring to bring Christianity within the range of all men, Erasmus hoped that Christian humanism would check the rising forces of nationalism that were beginning to appear in Europe. The threat of division and war, implicit in both the Reformation and nationalism, frightened Erasmus, who envisioned a universal synthesis that would transcend the regional and institutional particularities that divided men. Luther, in contrast, believed that a man should act on his beliefs and should not compromise, or temporize, them. As both a religious reformer and a German nationalist, Luther was intolerant of Rome's interference in German affairs.

Although they were contemporaries, Erasmus reflected the values of the Renaissance, and Luther those of the Protestant Reformation. A particular attitude toward education can be extrapolated from the life of each man. When it centers upon crucial value issues, teaching involves both commitment and objectivity. Like intellectuals in any period, Erasmus was objective and could dissect arguments, clearly define issues, and caustically criticize inconsistencies in his opponent's views. In preferring these intellectual stratagems and exercises, he opposed those who interfered with the objectivity needed for scholarship. He did not become committed to any particular reform programs to the degree that objectivity was lost. Erasmus' basic commitments were to the rather lofty and abstract values of objectivity, cosmopolitanism, tolerance, and scholarship, which are very difficult to concretize or particularize into programmatic reforms. As an educational theorist, therefore, he might be criticized for being uncommitted, for lacking specific programs of social and personal reform, and for being a compromiser. On the other hand, he might be praised for maintaining scholarship, detachment, and tolerance in an age that considered neutrality and tolerance vices rather than virtues.

Luther, although similarly interested in the scholarly examination of scriptural sources, was not satisfied merely to comment and criti-

[1] Roland H. Bainton, *Here I Stand: A Life of Martin Luther* (New York: New American Library, 1961), p. 141.

cize. His investigations led to conclusions, and upon reaching a decision, Luther translated theory into action. He was not content merely to serve as an intellectual and social critic but became an activist. Once the educator leaves the realm of detached and objective scholarship, he formulates a set of goals that must be implemented by concrete actions. Those who believe themselves to be absolutely correct will not and indeed cannot compromise.

As already indicated, Luther's original protest was against the sale of indulgences. In Roman Catholic practice, an indulgence remitted the temporal, usually purgatorial, punishment of the sinner, whose eternal punishment and guilt had been pardoned by reception of the sacrament of penance. In 1515, the Dominican monk Tetzel had been commissioned to sell indulgences by Albert of Brandenburg, archbishop of Mainz. The funds from this sale were to be donated to the archbishop and to Pope Leo X, who was engaged in building St. Peter's. Luther objected to the indulgence thesis on the ground that each man had to work out his own salvation in fear and trembling. He further questioned the power of the pope to remit punishment due for sin. Through the various debates on the issue, Luther was pressed to defend his position. When debating with the theologian Johann Eck, he questioned the divine institution of the papacy. Despite various pressures placed upon him by church and imperial authorities, Luther remained steadfast and was excommunicated in 1521. Protected by powerful German princes, such as Frederick the Wise, elector of Brandenburg, Luther escaped the fate that had befallen Wycliffe and Huss.

Luther's Theology

Luther became a popular hero in northern Germany for his resistance to papal authority, construed as Italian interference by German nationalists. While in hiding, he developed the theology that served as the doctrinal framework of what was to be the Lutheran Church. Although this book is primarily concerned with educational developments, it is not easy to disentangle the theological from the educational aspects of the Reformation. Luther's religious teachings framed what might be considered a "theology of education."

The concept of "justification by faith" was basic to Luther's theology. Having often experienced feelings of alienation from God, he had been disturbed by his doubts that sins could ever be really forgiven. His scriptural study led him to Christ's words, "My God, My God, why hast Thou forsaken Me?" Luther believed that Christ had so identified with man that He too had experienced the feeling of profound alienation from God. Christ redeemed and won salvation for mankind. Luther believed that what God had worked in Christ, He also worked in man through faith. A gift from God, faith could not be achieved by man through good works or sacraments. Man's willing acceptance of the gift of faith brought salvation.

Luther's insistence on "justification by faith" led him to affirm the corollary of the priesthood of all true believers. Since each man by either believing or disbelieving either accepted or rejected the gift of faith, a special priesthood was unnecessary to forgive or to retain sins. Luther's views contradicted the Catholic insistence that man was saved by both faith and good works and that the priest alone had the God-given powers to secure remission of sins for the laity.

It might be recalled that the medieval church was a hierarchical institution in which authority flowed downward from the pope, to the bishops, to the priests, to the laity. In rejecting this hierarchical flow of authority Luther centered authority in each individual. His emphasis on the priesthood of all believers and on the individual as a free agent meant that each man should read and study the Bible. Luther translated the Bible into German so that each man could read it. The Lutheran reformation gave strong impetus to the movement for universal literacy and education.

Luther's Socioeconomic Views

Although an uncompromising religious reformer, Luther was a socioeconomic and political conservative who believed that both the church and the state were necessary institutions. Although coercive, the state was necessarily so since society would never be completely Christian. Luther relied on the protection of the German nationalist princes and the government officials. When the peasants revolted, he opposed their rebellion and supported the aristocrats who crushed it.

Luther placed a special emphasis on the various vocations by which man earned his livelihood and maintained the economic order, and he recognized the importance of vocational education. He recognized three major vocations: religious, political, and economic, or domestic. Each of these had its own dignity, required training, and functioned in a particular way.

Lutheran Educational Theory and Practice

Although more of a religious reformer than an educational theorist, Luther recognized that reformed education was a necessary ally of a reformed church. Education needed to be conceived of very broadly and informally. The church, the state, and the family were to be enlisted as agents of reformation. Although he recognized the role of formal schools, Luther did not believe that education should be reserved solely to them. In the total process of enculturation, the family environment was a crucial force in forming the dispositions that were conducive to both Christian life and education. In 1530, Luther's sermon "On the Duty of Sending Children to School" urged parents to cultivate literacy and religion in their children and to be aware of their role in forming the children's character. In each family, there should be prayer, Bible-reading, the study of catechism, and, above all, vocational instruction. Earnest tradesmen, craftsmen, officials, and farmers in diligently pursuing their vocations would contribute to a stable, efficient, and Christian community. Once children had been nurtured in the right values and were predisposed to Christian duties, then they would be ready for the more formal program of the schools.

In preparing his educational reforms, Luther was aided by Philipp Melanchthon, an able humanist scholar. Both men rejected the virtual monopoly that the medieval church had enjoyed over the schools and the licensing of teachers, and they looked to the state to exercise these functions. In his "Letter to the Mayors and Aldermen of All Cities of Germany on Behalf of Christian Schools," Luther stressed the spiritual, material, and political benefits that derived from formal education. Schools were necessary for defending the faith, interpreting Scriptures, preparing ministers of the church, and cultivating a literate people. Educated citizens would recognize state authority, and trained craftsmen would contribute to the economic well-being of the society.

The School Code of Württemberg, which Melanchthon drafted in 1559, clearly expressed certain of the Lutheran educational views. According to his Code, vernacular schools were to be established in every village to teach religion, reading, writing, arithmetic, and music; the gymnasium, a classical secondary school, was to provide preparation for higher studies; state officials were to supervise the schools.

Both Luther and Melanchthon distrusted scholastic secondary and higher education. They believed that scholasticism, too closely identified with Roman Catholicism, had come to emphasize Aristotle over the Scriptures. Although Luther strongly advocated the establishment of elementary vernacular schools to cultivate basic literacy and religion, he believed that the Latin and Greek curriculum of the classical humanist schools was necessary to educate the religious and political leadership elite. The German classical secondary school, the gymnasium, followed the educational patterns of Renaissance humanism and added the dimension of a reformed Lutheran theology.

Philipp Melanchthon

Philipp Melanchthon (1497–1560), Luther's trusted aide in educational matters, was born in the German Palatinate.[2] After having been educated by a private tutor in Latin, he attended a Latin school in

2 For a biography of Melanchthon, see Wilhelm D. Maurer, *Melanchthon: Humanist and Reformer* (Karlsruhe: Hans Thoma Verlag, 1960).

Pforzheim, one of the finest preparatory schools of that time. In 1509, he entered the University of Heidelberg, a center of the German Renaissance, where he received his bachelor's degree in 1511; he earned his master's degree from the University of Tübingen at age seventeen. As a lecturer at Tübingen, he taught Cicero, Livy, and Demosthenes and continued his own education by studying the works of Vergil, Homer, Terence, and Hesiod in addition to mathematics, astronomy, and physics. In 1518, he accepted a position as professor of Greek at the University of Wittenberg. It was at Wittenberg that Melanchthon met and was influenced by Martin Luther. Adding theology to his humanistic interests, he earned a second bachelor's degree in 1519 in theology.

Melanchthon accepted Luther's religious reforms and was instrumental in transforming Wittenberg into a Protestant university. With Johann Sturm (1507–1589) and Johann Bugenhagen (1485–1558), he worked to systematize Luther's educational ideas. Melanchthon's *Discourse on Reforming the Studies of Youth* in 1518 reiterated the humanist principles of the Renaissance and argued for an enrichment of the curriculum. As an inspector of Lutheran schools, Melanchthon argued for improved quality, especially in the area of Latin instruction. He wrote the *Visitation Papers,* which were used as the basis for the various school plans adopted in the German states that followed the Lutheran creed. As Luther's educational adviser, Melanchthon prepared school plans for the cities of Eisleben, Nuremberg, Harzberg, Cologne, and Wittenberg and for the states of Saxony, Mecklenburg, and the Palatinate.

By the mid-sixteenth century, Lutheranism had become the state church in many of the states of northern Germany and in the Scandinavian kingdoms of Norway, Sweden, and Denmark. In these areas, education developed according to the ideas expressed by Luther and his associates. A dual system of elementary vernacular schools and secondary classical humanist schools and colleges was organized under the supervision of state officials.

Calvinism

In the French-speaking Swiss city of Geneva, an exiled French lawyer, John Calvin (1509–1564), led the forces of religious reformation. Calvin's *Institutes of the Christian Religion* (1536) broke completely with the Roman Catholic hierarchical and sacramental system. For Calvin, God, an Absolute Sovereign, is so powerful and transcendental that He cannot be sacramentally approached. Rejecting a hierarchical conception of authority, Calvin believed that authority derives from a common commitment to promote righteous living. Reformed and emancipated people will follow their religious leaders and willingly accept the discipline of an enlightened conscience. Calvin attempted to solve the problem of free will and the existence of evil by emphasizing reciprocal doctrines of divine election and predestination. Before creation, God chose some men for eternal salvation without regard for their merits in life; others were left to eternal damnation as just punishment for sins. Man possesses no real freedom until he consciously recognizes God's all-powerful will.

According to Calvin, man is innately corrupt because of Adam's fall from grace. By his very depraved nature, he is motivated by evil desires and a perverse will. God has given certain "elected" men the interior strength to overcome their evil inclination. The elect testify to God's mercy and glorify Him. Other men are doomed to perdition as a just punishment for their own perversity and iniquity.

Rather than bringing a sense of complacent moral self-assurance to the Calvinist, the doctrines of predestination and divine election brought a disciplined and puritanical rigor to Calvinists born of a desire to prove their election. The efficiency, diligence, and industry characteristic of Calvinism were also the virtues that contributed to the prosperity of the middle-class burghers, tradesmen, bankers, and merchants of Switzerland, England, Scotland, and the Netherlands. Calvinism was also the religion of the Puritan colonists in the Massachusetts Bay Colony in North America. The Puritan ethic with its doctrine of stewardship justified and sanctified the existence of the middle-class guardians of wealth who had been denied a place in the synthesis of medieval society.

In rejecting the medieval Catholic hierarchical, traditional, and sacramental authorities, Calvin asserted that the Bible was a self-sufficient authority in and of itself. The Old and New Testaments had revealed all that had to be and could be known about God and man's place in creation. Although Calvin emphasized scriptural reading, man also had to experience internal conversion. Through the internal testimony of the Holy Spirit, God aided the elect in achieving the conversion.

According to Calvin, the church was the foundation of true religion. Declaring His will in the Scriptures, God had ordained the establishment of the church as a visible and organized society to demonstrate the principles of the true and reformed religion to the world. The church, composed of the elect of God, was a company of Christians and was coterminous with cities and nations. It had a definite but independent relationship to civil authorities. The church expected, required, and demanded a rigorous public discipline of all its members. While temporal rulers were not to interfere with the church's moral discipline and teaching authority, governors, magistrates, and other officials had the duty of enforcing the moral discipline required of residents of the city of God, even if it required legal penalties. In

Calvin's Geneva, Presbyterian Edinburgh, and Puritan Boston, all men were to honor God according to true doctrine even if they had to be compelled to do so.

Educational Implications of Calvinism

Calvinism contributed to a particular way of life and a value system that had direct educational implications. Stripped of pageantry and emotionalism, Calvinist liturgy consisted primarily of scriptural reading, preaching of the sermon, singing of psalms, and recitation of congregational prayers. As members of a highly scriptural church, Calvinists were expected to read their Bibles. Calvin's highly intellectual theology required that the ministers of the church be literate and knowledgeable about doctrine. Calvinism also required a literate and educated laity. Since laymen were empowered as trustees of their churches, they were responsible for the collective conscience of their congregations.

For the businessmen of the Netherlands, Switzerland, England, Scotland, and North America, education was necessary for commercial activities. For the middle classes, the most willing adherents to Calvinism, education contributed to profit-making.[3] According to the notion of "stewardship," earning a profit, living an earnest life, and paying attention to business were outward signs of election. Thus theology and economics mutually supported Calvinist educational theory and practice.

According to Calvin's doctrine of human depravity, no human being was free of the inheritance of Adam's sin; all men and their offspring were victims of the legacy bestowed by their first parents. Conceived in sin and born in corruption, children were especially prone to sin and were idle, noisy, and willful. Formal schooling was conceived of as a means of disciplining the child and curbing his inclinations to evil. Calvinist educators rejected play as idleness and justified corporal punishment. Through hard discipline and the application of effort, the child could be brought into conformity and take his place among the citizens of the holy city.

The puritanical conception of innate human depravity associated with Calvinism differed from the Catholic view, which held man to be spiritually deprived. In Catholic theology the reception of the sacraments, especially baptism, penance, and the Holy Eucharist, helped man to overcome his inherited spiritual deficiency. In the Catholic tradition, formal schooling was not to be easy. Here, too, the child

---

[3] The classic study on the relationship of religion and economic development is R. H. Tawney, *Religion and the Rise of Capitalism* (New York: Harcourt, Brace, 1926). Reprinted by New American Library in 1947.

needed discipline, the routine of an orderly environment, and the presence of an authoritative teacher. Thomas Aquinas and other scholastics believed that external discipline was necessary until the child had acquired the habits of self-discipline. Without a firm teacher, he was likely to be willful and disorderly. Once discipline was internalized, then intellect would govern the will.

In the eighteenth century, Jean Jacques Rousseau challenged Calvin, a fellow Genevan, on the matter of human depravity. In *Emile*, Rousseau asserted that children, like all men, were naturally good. Rousseau had an impact on Johann Heinrich Pestalozzi, a nineteenth-century Swiss educator who sought to replace fear with love as a motivation to learning. The later twentieth-century progressive educators were also inspired to oppose coercive and authoritarian educational modes with pedagogical doctrines of permissiveness.

Calvinist Schools

The Calvinists, like the Lutherans, favored the dual-track system of schools. The common people attended vernacular schools whose curriculum consisted of the catechism, psalms, religious materials, reading, writing, arithmetic, and history. Classical Latin grammar schools were maintained for upper-class children who were going on to higher studies. These classical secondary schools sought to prepare future ministers, lawyers, and leaders for higher education by emphasizing Latin, Greek, and Hebrew.

In the Massachusetts Bay Colony of North America, English Puritans established a biblical commonwealth according to the religious, social, economic, and political design prescribed by John Calvin. Objecting to the retention of certain popish practices by the Church of England, these Puritans had dissented from the Anglican religious settlement. Coming to North America in 1620, they established congregations in towns—areas of land ranging from twenty to forty square miles—and enacted ordinances to create a Calvinist social order. Although only recent arrivals in the North American wilderness, Puritan legislators in the Massachusetts General Court enacted laws to promote learning, such as that of 1642 which required the trustees of every town to oversee the "calling and employment of children." Town officials were to make certain that children could read and understand the commonwealth's religion and the laws. In 1647, Massachusetts Bay enacted the "Old Deluder Satan Act," which was premised on the belief that ignorant illiterates were more prone to fall victim to evil than literate citizens. This act specified that Massachusetts towns of more than fifty families were to provide elementary education. Towns of one hundred families or more were to maintain Latin grammar masters to educate boys for college. Fearing to "leave an illiterate ministry to the churches," the Puritans established Harvard College in 1636.

The Anglican Reformation

The religious reformation in England was related to the personal life of Henry VIII (1491–1547), to English nationalism, and to discontent with the Roman Church. Henry desired to have his marriage to Catherine of Aragon pronounced void since no male heir had been born to the Tudor dynasty, which had only recently occupied the English throne. Henry first tried to have his marriage annulled through church channels, but the pope refused to grant the annulment. After obtaining an annulment from his own appointee, Archbishop Cranmer of Canterbury, Henry married Anne Boleyn. The pope responded by excommunicating Henry and declaring Cranmer's annulment invalid. Henry then secured the Act of Supremacy of 1534, which made him the head of the church in England. Although these events in Henry's private life precipitated the English Reformation, more was involved than the king's personal life. A considerable body of Englishmen, especially the prosperous and growing middle class, favored the breach with Rome. Antipapal and anti-Roman sentiment had long been a feature of English nationalism. English humanists were aware of events on the Continent. For example, William Tyndale, who had studied with Luther, had published an English translation of the New Testament in 1526. Henry confiscated monastic lands and distributed them to the nobility and country gentry and further consolidated loyalty to the Tudor dynasty. Here again, economic and political overtones entered into religious reformation.

Although he had abolished monasticism and replaced the pope as head of the Church of England, Henry did not intend to "protestant-ize" the English church but hoped to retain Catholic doctrine and ritual. His compromise satisfied neither Catholics such as Thomas More nor the growing number of militant Protestants. Henry used force against Catholic opposition and parliamentary tactics against those who demanded that the English church follow continental Protestant doctrines and practices. In 1539, Parliament passed the Statute of Six Articles, which reaffirmed the doctrines of transubstantiation, priestly celibacy, and confession. Despite this act, the English church moved steadily toward Protestantism.

Although Henry's heir, Edward VI, leaned in the direction of Protestantism, and his daughter Mary tried to restore Roman Catholicism, Elizabeth I took the middle course between Protestantism and Roman Catholicism and made Anglicanism the official religion. In 1563, Parliament enacted the Thirty-nine Articles as the statement of Anglican belief. These articles rejected the Catholic Latin liturgy, clerical celibacy, and papal allegiance as well as the continental Lutheran and Calvinist doctrines of justification by faith and the priesthood of all believers. The Church of England, or Anglican Church, retaining a sacramental system, used the hierarchical principle in church governance; it became closely tied to the English monarch, who was its head, and to the English establishment.

Educational Implications of Anglicanism

The immediate educational effects of the Anglican Reformation were not as direct as in the case of the Lutherans and the Calvinists. This was probably because those who were attracted to Anglicanism were upper-class aristocrats, gentry, country squires, and small farmers. These landed aristocrats, who found themselves well served by the existing institutions, generally neglected the education of tenant farmers. The urban middle classes preferred to organize dissenting congregations. The Anglicans adopted a laissez-faire educational policy. Upper-class English children attended the various humanist schools and received a classical education which prepared them to enter Oxford or Cambridge, the major universities. The Anglicans conducted parish schools in much the same way as the Catholic church had done. The preferred schools were the famous "public" schools of Winchester, Eton, Harrow, Westminster, Rugby, and St. Paul's.

The establishment of Anglicanism as the official religion did affect academic freedom. The Act of Supremacy of 1562 required all teachers to take an oath of loyalty to the crown and accept the Thirty-nine Articles of the Anglican faith. The Act of Uniformity required all teachers to support the established church. Despite this legislation, the Anglican Church did not exercise the determined control of education found in Calvinist countries.

Catholic Counter Reformation

It should be remembered that certain of the Protestant reformers, notably Luther, had commenced their pleas for reformation within the Catholic framework. Many advocates of internal reformation, such as Erasmus, remained within the Catholic Church. The Catholic Church responded to Protestantism by hardening the lines of hierarchical and doctrinal authority. The Council of Trent, called in 1545 by Pope Paul III (1534–1549), sought to reform religious practices and to combat Protestant inroads. The council ruled out doctrinal compromise with Protestants on the major theological issues. It reaffirmed the role of a specialized priesthood as against the Lutheran concept of a "priesthood of all believers." The council also reaffirmed the seven sacraments and the importance of both faith and good works, and it emphasized both the Scriptures and the church as theological authorities. After holding the line on doctrine, the council addressed itself to religious practices. It insisted on a strict observance of clerical vows, forbade the sale of church offices, and called for the establishment of seminaries to improve priestly education.

To promote discipline among the laity, the council imposed censorship by issuing an Index of forbidden books. The Index came to include the writings of those considered to be heretical, Protestant, and anticlerical.

As a result of internal weakness and external pressures from the dynamic Protestant reformers, the Catholic church initially took a defensive posture. Ruling out doctrinal compromises with the Protestant denominations, it sought to revitalize its resources and to combat what it regarded as the disintegration of religious authority. While the Council of Trent preserved basic doctrines, Catholics tried to regain the offensive by internal reformation and a militant response to Protestantism. Seizing upon education as a potent weapon, Ignatius Loyola, a former soldier who had been converted to an intensely spiritual life, organized the Society of Jesus, or Jesuits, in 1540.[4]

Ignatius Loyola and Jesuit Education

Ignatius Loyola (1491–1556) studied the classics, philosophy, and theology at the University of Paris, where he encountered the Latin classics—Cicero, Livy, Caesar, Vergil, Horace, and Terence—and the *Summa theologica* of Aquinas. His own schooling affected the educational theory that he devised for members of his own order. Regarding Latin as essential for the education of both the priest and the Christian gentleman, Loyola made it a basic component of the curriculum.

In the *Constitutions of the Society* (1541), Loyola set forth the fundamental principles that were to govern the order. The plan of studies outlined in the *Constitutions* was more fully developed in the *Ratio studiorum* (1599). The administration of the Society of Jesus was organized along military lines into provinces, each presided over by a provincial, who was responsible to the general, who in turn was accountable only to the pope.

[4] Among the many books detailing the life of Ignatius Loyola, John W. Donohue's *Jesuit Education* (New York: Fordham University Press, 1963) is recommended for its treatment of the educational principles of the Society of Jesus.

In framing the core of Jesuit education, Loyola adapted elements from both medieval scholasticism and classical humanism to provide both religious and secular education. Jesuit schools were to educate prospective members of the Society of Jesus and other Catholic gentlemen. Concerned with the education of the elite, they devoted little attention to the education of the masses.

The Jesuit Curriculum

As a student at the University of Paris, Loyola had been heavily influenced by the Dominican exposition of Thomistic philosophy and theology. In the *Constitutions,* he prescribed that Jesuit theology classes give lectures on Thomas Aquinas and that metaphysics follow basic Aristotelian outlines. Latin was regarded as a practical necessity because the cultivated gentleman of the sixteenth century was expected to be fluent in that language. Latin was needed not only for the pursuit of higher studies but also for any career in the church, the state, letters, or commerce. Like most humanists, Loyola emphasized the study and imitation of Cicero and Quintilian so that the student might develop eloquence. As one knowledgeable about Quintilian, Loyola stressed that Jesuit educators should recognize and provide for individual differences in their students. Age, education, capacity, character, physical condition, needs, vocational goals, and interests were to be carefully weighed and considered.

The *Ratio studiorum,* first published in 1599 and revised periodically, was an outline of the basic Jesuit curriculum. There were to be three basic faculties: (1) humane letters, consisting of language and literature with emphasis on Latin and Greek classics, some vernacular studies, and work in grammar, poetry, rhetoric, and history; (2) the arts or natural sciences, consisting of logic, physics, metaphysics, and mathematics; (3) theology, the most important components being scholastic and positive theology, and biblical studies. This curriculum plan, which was designed to provide a general and systematic education, preceded specialization. The student began his work by mastering linguistic tools and studying the classics, liberal arts, and finally theology, which dealt with man's relationship to God.

The Jesuit Method

Since the Society of Jesus was primarily an organization of priest-teachers, candidates for the order received an extensive preparation in educational methodology. Prospective teachers were to be prepared by experienced teachers and given practice in methods of teaching reading and writing and of correcting and managing a class. If teachers were deficient methodologically, then the students would suffer.

Classes taught by the Jesuits were divided into small groups in which rivals competed against each other. The entire method rested on the premise that it was better to concentrate thoroughly on a small amount of material rather than to deal superficially with masses of subject matter. Jesuit teachers tried to disassociate punishment from the learning task. Although they were to take a personal interest in the academic progress of their students, there was to be no favoritism. The teacher was to be equally concerned with both rich and poor.

Among the specific and distinctive methods that became associated with Jesuit education were the *Praelectio, Repetitio, Exercitatio, Concertatio,* and *Argumentum scribendi.* The *Praelectio,* prelection, was an introductory explanation of the precepts and content of the assignment. If the assignment was the study of a particular selection from classical literature, the teacher would provide a preliminary interpretation of the significance, rules, and style exemplified in the selection. This was to provide the student with a means of analysis and to clear up any difficulties that might block his study of the assignment.

The *Repetitio,* or repetition, involved a constant and consistent review of subject matter in order to impress it permanently in the student's memory. Each day the previous day's work was reviewed, and on Saturday the work in all subjects studied during the previous week was reviewed. Similarly, at the onset of each school year, the studies of the previous year were summarized and reviewed. The repetition was another indication of the stress that the educators of the period placed upon memorization.

The *Exercitatio* was a written exercise done by the pupil in the classroom under the supervision of the teacher. It was designed to apply grammatical and rhetorical principles to the student's own expression. The *Concertatio,* an oral and public examination, often took the form of class competitions intended to spur a desire to excel in scholastic achievement. The *Argumentum scribendi,* the dictation of a theme to students, who were to develop and elaborate on it, was designed to test the student's ability to imitate the major classical authors who had been studied as models.

The Catholic Gentleman

The ideally educated man that Loyola conceived as the product of his educational method was one who used education to strengthen religious belief and commitment. Jesuit teachers sought to prepare students who could infuse society with the doctrines of a reformed Catholicism and combat the inroads of the Protestant reformers. Although Loyola was well aware of the actuality of social change, Jesuit education emphasized the transmission of bodies of inherited theological, philosophical, classical, and literary knowledge. Loyola's plan of education and his priest-educators followed a pattern of strict military obedience and discipline. Geared to the education of the ruling classes, Jesuit priest-teachers often found themselves close to persons of power and were frequently accused of being more concerned with the manipulation of political power than with religious activities. Often distrusted, they were suppressed by Protestant and often by Catholic rulers.

Comenius: Protestant, Pietist, Realist

In the seventeenth century, European religious lines had been drawn and formally fixed by the Peace of Westphalia (1648). Roman Catholicism remained established in Spain, Portugal, France, the Italian states, the Hapsburg empire, and southern Germany; Lutheranism was established in much of northern and eastern Germany and in Norway, Sweden, and Denmark; Anglicanism was the established church in England; Calvinism drew large followings in the major urban areas of Europe, such as the cities of Switzerland, the Netherlands, and Scotland. It was not easy to draw a religious map of Europe in which particular regions were allotted to particular churches. There were many small sects and denominations that were loosely referred to as Anabaptists or Pietists. Many of these groups established communities and lived as they thought the earlier Christians had lived, in shared brotherhood, work, and prayer. The great diversity of theological interpretation that existed among these various Protestant Pietists makes it extremely difficult to examine each of their particular theologies. Such groups as the Baptists, Quakers, Hutterites, Mennonites, and Amish were among those who dissented from the various religious establishments.

Among these small sects of dissenting Protestants were the Moravian Brethren, a reformed evangelical sect descended from the followers of the earlier pre-Reformation reformer, John Huss, who was burnt at the stake for heresy in 1415. The Brethren were constantly persecuted but managed to survive in the Bohemian and Moravian hill country. This small sect is singled out because of the significant educational contributions made by one of its bishops, John Amos Komensky (1592–1670), better known by the Latin version of his name, Comenius.[5]

Comenius was born in Nivnitz, Moravia, which is in present-day

[5] Good interpretative essays on Comenius' educational theories are: Harry S. Broudy and John R. Palmer, "Teaching According to Nature: Comenius," in *Exemplars of Teaching Method* (Chicago: Rand McNally, 1965), pp. 93–103; Jerome K. Clauser, "The Pansophist: Comenius," in Paul Nash, Andreas M. Kazamias, and Henry J. Perkinson (eds.), *The Educated Man: Studies in the History of Educational Thought* (New York: Wiley, 1965), pp. 165–188.

Czechoslovakia. His family were members of the Moravian Brethren. At the village school, which was maintained by the Brethren, he learned reading, writing, hymn singing, catechism, and arithmetic. At age sixteen, he attended the Latin preparatory school at Přerov. He later went on to the University of Heidelberg, where he was attracted to the study of educational methodology. Comenius returned to his native Moravia and directed the Latin school at Přerov, where he had been a student. In 1616, he was ordained as a minister in the Brethren and was assigned to Fulnick as pastor and inspector of the local school.

In 1618, the outbreak of the Thirty Years' War resulted in the persecution of the Brethren by the invading Hapsburg armies. The Brethren were dispersed, and Comenius was forced into exile. He settled first in Poland as director of the gymnasium at Lissa in 1628; he became rector in 1636. He later migrated to the Netherlands, where he devoted himself to writing and to the care of the Brethren who were now scattered as exiles throughout Europe.

The brutal realities of religious persecution, personal tragedy, and the exile and dispersion of his flock profoundly affected Comenius' educational philosophy. As Erasmus had feared, the possibilities for developing a cosmopolitan Christian humanism had been destroyed by the antagonism of warring religious denominations and rival national dynasties. The dream of a synthesis of Western culture had been wrecked by religious wars and persecutions. Comenius, who has been described as a belated humanist, kept the idea of Western peace and unity alive in his philosophy of pansophism. He believed it possible to acquire universal knowledge. If this knowledge were diffused among all men, they could be educated to live the good life, and world peace would be secured. Through knowledge, men would come to know God, the source of all truth. They would come to realize their common human nature as sons of a universal Father.

In his own day, Comenius was an internationally known teacher and educational reformer. He was a man of broad knowledge interested in many fields of study, ranging from theology to science and psychology. As an exile, he traveled extensively. He composed religious music and wrote some of the major classics in the history of Western educational theory. His educational philosophy was an interesting blend; some of his theories were based on the humanism of the Renaissance, and others anticipated the "sense realism" of the eighteenth-century Enlightenment. As a bishop of the Brethren, his religious convictions also marked him clearly among the genre of religious reformers.

As a humanist educator, Comenius was concerned with making language instruction, especially in Latin, both interesting and efficient.

He believed that language was a necessary foundation for approaching the universal knowledge required for pansophism. In the *Janua linguarum reserata* (the *Gate of Tongues Unlocked*), Comenius departed from traditional language teaching by approaching the study of Latin through the use of the vernacular. His grammar began with short and simple sentences and gradually progressed toward more complex and involved ones. He later prepared a dramatized form of the *Janua* in the *Schola ludus* and a pictorial form in the *Orbis sensualium pictus*, which consisted of a series of engravings that designated objects by both their Latin and vernacular names. Although the emphasis in these works was still on the learning of language, Comenius employed a form of sense realism. The picture of the object in the *Orbis pictus* was intended to combine language learning with a sense perception. Comenius' use of sensation anticipated the nineteenth-century pedagogy of Pestalozzi, who based his educational methodology on concrete objects and direct sensory experience.

Reflecting pansophism, Comenius' *Great Didactic,* first written in Czech in 1628 and then translated into Latin, sought to develop an efficient method of instruction that would make learning joyful and progressive and bring light, order, and peace to the Christian community. Reflecting his evangelical theology, Comenius used the figure of Christ as the desired educational exemplar. The true Christian should be formed on the model of Christ and intellectually enlightened through universal knowledge. Schools should strive to be Christian schools. No matter how pernicious the effects of sin on mankind, Comenius relied on God's grace and on efficient educational methods to restore each man's personal harmony and contribute to the genuine integration of a Christian social order. Since Christ had recognized the dignity of all persons, education should be available to all men and women, regardless of socioeconomic distinctions. The purpose of education should be to prepare man for the future on earth and for eternal life. A pansophic education should cultivate the three qualities of wisdom, virtue, and piety: As a rational being, man requires knowledge of all that the world contains; the virtuous man's behavior is to be guided according to knowledge and prudence; the pious man refers all things to God, the universal Father and Source of all truth and being. Modeled on Christ, the ideally educated man is liberal in intellect, prudent in action, and pious in spirit.

Although committed to Scripture as the source of all authority, Comenius anticipated the naturalism of Rousseau and Pestalozzi. Like Pestalozzi, he believed that nature is orderly and gradual in its basic operations and that it reveals certain stages of growth that can be used as the basis for organizing an educational method. Educators should follow these natural guidelines and recognize that children have stages of readiness for specific learnings. Instruction should therefore be organized carefully into easily assimilated steps so that the student's progress might be efficient, pleasant, and steady.

To accommodate these different stages of development, Comenius believed that instruction should be generally divided into four periods, each of which should be six years in length: during infancy, informal education directed largely by the mother; the vernacular school; the Latin preparatory school; and the university.

Comenius rejected notions of child depravity and the discipline of corporal punishment. Rather than resorting to blows, punishment, coercion, and threats, teachers should make learning attractive and interesting. They should be pleasant and gentle rather than tyrannical. His views on enlightened discipline and interest as a form of motivation were similar to those expressed earlier by Erasmus and later by Rousseau and Pestalozzi.

As an educator, many of Comenius' views ran counter to the general intolerance that characterized the Reformation and Counter Reformation. Although his pansophism was mystical and visionary, he believed that knowledge could be used to reconstruct society along the lines of an evangelical, tolerant, and open Christianity. Comenius' contribution was to emphasize sensation as the basis of learning and to develop learning strategies that recognized, albeit in a rudimentary way, the general patterns of human development.

Conclusion

The Protestant Reformation and Catholic Counter Reformation had serious consequences for Western educational development. Since most of the Protestant reformers emphasized that every man should read the Bible in his own language, there was a corresponding stress on creating wider educational opportunities and universal literacy. Although universal literacy had religious implications, it also responded to the needs of the rising commercial classes.

Educational opportunities were extended through universal education, but the two-track system of formal schools, inherited from the Renaissance humanists, was crystallized. While both the lower and the upper classes were to be educated, they were to receive different kinds of education. A vernacular, basic elementary education was suited for the lower classes so that they might read, write, and know their particular religious creeds. The upper classes, destined to rule, were to receive a classical humanist secondary education designed to prepare them for higher education, the professions, and positions of authority in the church and the state.

The Protestant Reformation ended the monopoly of the Roman

Catholic Church over formal educational institutions. In Lutheran areas, the church had become closely allied with the state. Civil officials gradually assumed the function of supervising schools and licensing teachers. In Calvinist areas, where the state often functioned as an arm of the church, civil magistrates inspected schools. Generally, the trend was to recognize and legitimize the states' role in education. Combined church and state interest led to the establishment of educational standards, some limited taxation and allocation of financial resources, and the licensing of teachers. Doctrinal conformity was often the major requirement for a teaching license.

The Reformation and Counter Reformation revitalized the religious component in formal education, which had been weakened by the secular interests of some of the Renaissance humanists. The revitalization of religious concern was socially divisive as contending sects quarreled with one another. These religious contentions produced a "defense of the faith" mentality designed to fix the religious commitments of the young so that they might be steadfast in their faith and ready to combat deviations from their particular creedal conception of religious orthodoxy.

Suggested Readings

Bainton, Roland H. *Here I Stand: A Life of Martin Luther*. New York: New American Library, 1961.

Clauser, Jerome K. "The Pansophist: Comenius," in Paul Nash, Andreas M. Kazamias, and Henry J. Perkinson (eds.), *The Educated Man: Studies in the History of Educational Thought*. New York: Wiley, 1965, pp. 165–188.

Donnelly, Francis P., S.J. *Principles of Jesuit Education in Practice*. New York: P. J. Kenedy and Sons, 1934.

Donohue, John W., S.J. *Jesuit Education*. New York: Fordham University Press, 1963.

Eller, Ernest M. *The School of Infancy*. Chapel Hill: University of North Carolina Press, 1956.

Farrell, Allan P., S.J. *The Jesuit Code of Liberal Education*. Milwaukee, Wis.: Bruce Publishing Co., 1938.

Fitzpatrick, Edward A. *Saint Ignatius and the Ratio Studiorum*. New York: McGraw-Hill, 1933.

Fleming, Sandford. *Children and Puritanism: The Place of Children in the Life and Thought of the New England Churches, 1602–1847*. New Haven, Conn.: Yale University Press, 1933.

Ganss, George E., S.J. *Saint Ignatius' Idea of a Jesuit University*. Milwaukee, Wis.: Marquette University Press, 1954.

Jelinek, Vladimir. *The Analytical Didactic of Comenius*. Chicago: University of Chicago Press, 1953.

Keatinge, M. W. *The Great Didactic of John Amos Comenius*. London: Adam and Charles Black, 1907.

Maurer, Wilhelm D. *Melanchthon: Humanist and Reformer*. Karlsruhe, Germany: Hans Thoma Verlag, 1960.

McGucken, William S., S.J. *The Jesuits and Education*. New York: Bruce Publishing Co., 1932.

McNeil, John T. *The History and Character of Calvinism*. New York: Oxford University Press, 1954.

Monroe, Will S. *Comenius and the Beginnings of Educational Reform*. New York: Scribner, 1912.

Odlozilik, Otakar. *Jan Amos Komensky*. Chicago: Czechoslovak National Council of America, 1942.

The Orbis Pictus of John Amos Comenius. Syracuse, N.Y.: C. W. Bardeen, 1887; Detroit: Singing Tree Press, n.d.

Sadler, John E. *J.A. Comenius and the Concept of Universal Education*. New York: Barnes and Noble, 1966.

Spinka, Mathew. *John Amos Comenius, That Incomparable Moravian*. Chicago: University of Chicago Press, 1943.

Woody, Thomas. *Fuerstenschulen in Germany after the Reformation*. Menasha, Wis.: George Banta Publishers, 1920.

CHAPTER 9

The Enlightenment and Education

The Enlightenment has often been referred to as the "Age of Reason," a time when man could exert his intelligence to reconstruct the social order according to scientific principles.[1] Ushering in an optimism that colored Western thought until World War I, Enlightenment rationalism had a profound impact on education. This impact can best be appreciated by analyzing the intellectual currents of the Enlightenment, particularly the ideas of "reason," "natural law," and "progress."

Reason

The intellectuals, or philosophes, of the Enlightenment believed that human reason could cure mankind of its social, political, and economic ills and lead to a time of perpetual peace, utopian government, and perfect society. Through reason, man would discover the natural laws governing human existence and with this knowledge be able to guarantee the progress of the human race. The age of the devotees of reason coincided with the emergence of the Newtonian world view. In the *Mathematical Principles of Natural Philosophy*, Isaac Newton (1642–1727) had postulated a natural law theory based on the law of gravitation. The universe was described as an orderly system of atoms moving in absolute time and space. Newton conceived of the universe as a great machine that functioned according to its own intrinsic laws and design. He believed it possible for man to employ the scientific method to discover these natural laws that kept the world in order and motion. Once discovered, these laws could be expressed in mathematical formulas and made intelligible to all men. Newtonian science postulated: (1) a mechanistic universe that functioned ac-

---

[1] Carl L. Becker, *The Heavenly City of the Eighteenth-Century Philosophers* (New Haven, Conn.: Yale University Press, 1932), pp. 1–31.

cording to universal laws, and (2) the possibility of discovering these laws and translating them into mathematical terms.

Although Newton, like Darwin later, was a natural scientist, some philosophes attempted to apply the basic Newtonian premises to human society. For example, Condorcet held that the laws of nature were applicable to man's intellectual and moral faculties. The crucial educational task was to adjust man to natural law. Because of superstition and obsolete economic, social, political, and educational institutions, man's adjustment had been thwarted. As they conceived it, the philosophes' task was to:

1. Expose obsolete institutions to rigorous criticism
2. Destroy those institutions that impeded the progressive adjustment of man to the natural order
3. Construct a new set of institutions in conformity to natural law
4. Reeducate man so that he could exercise his natural goodness and live in perfect harmony with the emergent natural institutions.

The program of the philosophes held both revolutionary and educational possibilities. For example, through revolutions, such as the American and the French, obsolete political institutions could be destroyed. Through natural education, man could be restored to his original goodness and be given the stimulus and preparation to live scientifically, rationally, and progressively. Underlying the program of the philosophes was a basic faith in man's rationality. This optimistic view of human nature came to the surface in the educational ideas of the eighteenth-century theorist Rousseau, the nineteenth-century reformers Pestalozzi, Owen, and Mann, and the twentieth-century progressives Dewey and Kilpatrick.

Progress

The Enlightenment philosophes rejected both the Calvinist view that man was innately depraved and the Catholic view that he was spiritually deprived. Instead, they emphasized man's natural goodness. Evil was not a product of man's nature but was an effect produced by an unnatural, artificial, and irrational society. If man's reason were liberated by natural education, then he could follow his inherent benevolent inclinations, perfect the good life, and construct fair and just institutions. In such a natural order the course of mankind would be progressive, that is, the future would be better than the past. Men were no longer to look backward to ancient classical utopias but were to look ahead to an earthly paradise, a modern utopia where poverty, superstition, hunger, persecution, and war would be forever abolished.

The Enlightenment conception of progress gave a new dimension to education that had significant methodological and sociological implications. If men were innately good, then the hope of the future was the unspoiled child, an uncorrupted and natural being whose interests, needs, and inclinations were the proper beginnings of instruction. Formalized schooling with its emphasis on the written word and discipline based on corporal punishment was seen as inherited pedantic residue that needed to be removed. Rousseau, Pestalozzi, and other reformers stressed the goodness of the child, the importance of his needs, and the liberation of his energies as the basis for a sound natural method of education. In addition to exalting child nature, the educators influenced by the notion of progress conceived of education as an instrument for social amelioration and reform. A number of American theorists, such as Jefferson, Rush, and Webster, argued for a republican system of instruction. The Swiss Pestalozzi saw natural instruction as a means of uplifting the poor. The Englishman Robert Owen wanted to use education to build a new society based on human equality.

Deism

As indicated, the views of the Enlightenment placed great faith in man's reason and benevolence. This faith was a humanistic one and was expressed in the religion known as deism. The philosophes centered much of their criticism on the established churches, which they considered institutionalized impediments to progress. They tended to reject the Judeo-Christian concept of God as a personal Creator who intervened in the lives of men. For them, creation had been the work of an impersonal First Cause, or a Prime Mover, which had created a mechanistic universe operating according to built-in laws. Man was endowed with a reasoning mind in order to work out his own destiny. For the deist philosophe, institutionalized religious orthodoxies were illiberal. As part of their program of social reform, the deists were in the forefront of movements to disestablish state churches and to separate the church and the state.

Laissez-Faire Economics

François Quesnay (1694–1774), who believed that natural laws governed economic affairs as well as natural science, formulated the classic economic doctrine of laissez faire. In advocating a free-market economy, Quesnay was repudiating mercantilism, an economic policy associated with absolutist monarchies that called for government regulation of commerce. Quesnay and his followers, called "physiocrats," attacked mercantilism as an obsolete economic theory that had exaggerated the importance of specie and minimized the significance of natural wealth.

Quesnay emphasized that land and agricultural production formed the basis of natural wealth. The physiocratic stress on agriculture was compatible with Rousseau's ideas of the natural man. Pestalozzi's first school at Neuhof sought to combine farming and handicraft production into a practical system of natural education. William Maclure, an American theorist, attempted to establish agricultural schools in the nineteenth century in both Europe and the United States. Physiocratic economic theory had an influence on educational theorists who sought to formulate an alternative pattern of education to the humanist schools' emphasis on the Latin and Greek classics.

Laissez-faire economic theory found its best-known proponent in Adam Smith (1723–1790). Smith's *Inquiry into the Nature and Causes of the Wealth of Nations* (1776) was a classic statement of liberal economic principles. Like Quesnay, Smith rejected the short-sighted mercantilist view that equated wealth and specie. He attributed national wealth to the efficient production of commodities stimulated by the competition of the open market. Government encouraged national prosperity when it refrained from interfering in economic affairs. Smith reduced the power of the state to that of a passive policeman and exalted individual initiative, economic freedom, and free trade as natural laws.

The economic theories of Quesnay and Smith advocating free trade, economic individualism, an open market, and limited government held great appeal for the rising middle classes. In some ways, the American and French revolutions were middle-class movements in which the men of "new wealth" challenged the entrenched older aristocracy of land and blood. When the English government sought to impose a mercantilist economic policy on its North American colonies, merchants raised the cry of "no taxation without representation."

Political Liberalism

The contract theory of government was closely allied to the Enlightenment concepts of natural law, progress, and economic individualism. In the second of his *Two Treatises on Government* (1690), John Locke (1632–1704) had penned a theoretical justification for England's "Glorious Revolution" of 1688. Locke's argument was based on an assertion of the natural rights of man. In the state of nature, he said, man had lived without organized society, government, or legislation. Each man possessed natural and intrinsic rights of life, liberty, and property. Men had organized society to protect these natural rights against hostile threats. Government arose from the consent of the governed and was intended to secure man's natural rights. Governors continued to rule only by maintaining the social contract that protected the natural rights of each individual member of society. When any government violated the natural contract, then the members of the body politic had the right to revolt, to overturn the government, and to establish a new one in its place.

Locke's contract concept was a significant justification against the "divine right of kings" theory of absolute monarchy. Even kings were subject to the social contract. When the North American colonists revolted against English rule, Thomas Jefferson borrowed heavily from Lockean theory. In the Declaration of Independence, Jefferson accused King George III of violating the social contract and of depriving his North American subjects of their natural and inalienable rights of "life, liberty, and the pursuit of hapiness."

Jefferson realized that the contract theory of government had profound educational implications. Republican political institutions required an educated citizenry who were capable of self-government.[2] Not only were these enlightened citizens to participate in the electoral processes, but they were also to assume the political powers given them by their peers. According to the contract theory, government originated with the consent of the governed. For Jefferson, republican government would ensure progress only if conducted by enlightened and rational men. With the acceptance of the contract theory of government, formal educational institutions assumed much of the responsibility for educating an enlightened citizenry in the arts of self-government.

While Locke and Jefferson presented the case for political liberalism to their English-speaking countrymen, Jean Jacques Rousseau (1712–1778) put forth a continental version of Enlightenment political theory in *On the Origin of the Inequality of Mankind* (1775) and in *The Social Contract* (1762). Rousseau ascribed social inequalities to artificial distinctions based on wealth, property, and prestige. In the state of nature, man had been a "noble savage" uncorrupted by social artificialities. With the acquisition of personal property, men instituted government to protect their possessions. Property had produced inequalities among men, and government had made these inequalities legal. In *The Social Contract*, Rousseau asserted that society was formed by the association of men who agreed to be ruled by the "General Will." Al-

[2] For two very readable accounts of Jefferson's philosophical and educational ideas, see Robert D. Heslep, *Thomas Jefferson and Education* (New York: Random House, 1969); and Gordon C. Lee, *Crusade Against Ignorance: Thomas Jefferson on Education* (New York: Bureau of Publications, Teachers College, Columbia University, 1961).

though each individual's particular will might disagree with it, the individual was obliged to obey the General Will. The formulating of the General Will was the community's task, and it could not be delegated to an institution such as a parliament. Rousseau's concept of the General Will was ill-defined, vague, and romantic. It might be interpreted as community consensus, but it could also mean the collective power of the totalitarian state. While Locke and Jefferson regarded the social contract to be based on an association of individuals, Rousseau's General Will took on mystical overtones that made it more powerful and inclusive than a mutual association of individual men.

Rousseau's Natural Education

The Enlightenment's stress on naturalism was expressed by Rousseau and his pedagogical disciple, Johann Heinrich Pestalozzi (1746–1827). Rousseau, born in Geneva, was left motherless as an infant and then abandoned by his father at the age of ten. He studied for various careers but achieved fame as a social critic and philosopher. He was associated with the French philosophes Voltaire, Diderot, Helvetius, and Condorcet. As an educational theorist, Rousseau is best known for his educational novel *Emile* (1762), which recounts the story of the education of a boy from infancy to manhood.[3] The novel was a reaction against highly verbal and literary education that ignored the interests and inclinations of the learner. He claimed that such excessively verbal education resulted from a civilization that ignored the natural dimensions of life and emphasized artificial social conventions. Civilization had corrupted the natural goodness of man by imprisoning him within artificial institutions, one of which was the school.

Rousseau believed that man was naturally good but had been corrupted by society. In his novel, Rousseau had Emile develop naturally, apart from the social corruption. By following his own inclinations, the boy's natural goodness was cultivated and developed. Such a natural education, Rousseau believed, would help equip the child to withstand the temptations of an evil and corruptive society. Rousseau gave Emile "natural freedom" within a prepared environment. His tutor resembled the modern progressive teacher who, although never dominating, re-

[3] An excellent analysis of Rousseau's social, political, and educational theories can be found in Stanley E. Ballinger, "The Natural Man: Rousseau," in Paul Nash, Andreas M. Kazamias, and Henry J. Perkinson (eds.), *The Educated Man: Studies in the History of Educational Thought* (New York: Wiley, 1965), pp. 224–246. Also see William Boyd, *The Emile of Jean Jacques Rousseau* (New York: Teachers College Press, Columbia University, 1962), and *The Minor Educational Writings of Jean Jacques Rousseau* (New York: Bureau of Publications, Teachers College, Columbia University, 1962).

tains control over the learning environment. Of all the lessons that Emile needed to learn, the most important was that actions had consequences and that the doer is responsible for the consequences of the deed.

Like the earlier Comenius, Rousseau recognized, albeit in a rudimentary way, the existence of stages of human development, at each stage of which, a person exhibited certain characteristics. Each stage required a special kind of activity designed to stimulate and further development. In *Emile*, Rousseau demarcated five stages of growth: infancy, childhood, boyhood, adolescence, and youth.

Rousseau termed the first five years of life as infancy, during which the human was helpless. It was most important that the infant be allowed freedom of movement so that he could exercise his body and encounter objects. A simple diet was recommended for the development of a healthy body. Rousseau cautioned that parents should neither spoil nor coerce the infant.

From five until twelve, Emile was stronger and capable of doing more things for himself. His genuinely personal life was now beginning as he became conscious of happiness and unhappiness. Concerned with his own happiness, the child's egotism was natural to his stage of development. During this period, the child was curious and learned a great deal about the world through his senses. Rousseau referred to the eyes and ears, the hands and feet, as the first teachers. He warned that the substitution of books for the products of sensation did not teach the child to reason. Bookishness taught children uncritical acceptance of the thoughts of others.

During boyhood, ages twelve to fifteen, Emile's strength increased so rapidly that it exceeded his needs. The natural environment provided scientific and geographical lessons. The first book, *Robinson Crusoe*, was introduced, as the story of a man living within an isolated natural environment. The boy was also to learn some manual skill so that he could effect a proper combination of mental and physical labor.

During adolescence, ages fifteen to eighteen, the adolescent experienced an awareness of sex. The tutor was to supply special guidance by answering the questions that were put to him. The tutor's replies to Emile's queries were to be direct and sincere, with no mysteriousness or coarseness. As an adolescent, Emile was also becoming socially conscious of other people and was now to learn about human psychology, social forces, and civil society. In his travels, he encountered poor people; his encounter with poverty aroused a natural pity that stimulated a natural morality. To develop his aesthetic sensibilities, Emile visited museums and the theater, learned languages, and read books. During the period from eighteen to twenty, he met his future wife, the reasonable, simple, and pleasant Sophy. Before marriage, Emile traveled to learn foreign languages, laws, and customs.

Rousseau's novel *Emile* had a significant effect on Western educational thought. It stimulated Pestalozzi to expand, interpret, and implement Rousseau's educational ideas. Although he eventually was forced to conclude that Rousseau was impractical in some instances, Pestalozzi's stress on sensation and on liberating the child resulted from the contact with Rousseau's naturalism. Rousseau himself was a blend of the rationalist and the romantic. Although he was inconsistent as a social and educational philosopher, his ideas were congenial to the rationalist stress on the discovery and social implementation of natural laws. Simultaneously, Rousseau was a forerunner in nineteenth-century romanticism, which was more concerned with expression of "feelings" than with the rational pursuit of natural laws. Morevoer, it is no exaggeration to state that Rousseau had an impact on some of the twentieth-century progressive educators who asserted that education should be based on the interests and inclinations of the child.

The popularity of Rousseau's educational doctrines produced a sharp reaction from those who opposed educational naturalism. Such a critic was William McGucken, who wrote:

> In the 1890's, that decade so feverish in educational activity in the United States, the first attempt to apply some of the principles of *Emile* on a large scale was made. The years that followed have seen the almost complete adoption of Rousseau's philosophy of education in this country. The cult of sentimentalism and utilitarianism in American education is due in large part to Rousseau's *Emile*, that incredibly unreal book, the product of an unreal age, which has become the Koran of the American school with its cry of "back to nature."[4]

Although this chapter is concerned with the Enlightenment, some mention should be made of the resurgence of Rousseauist romanticism in certain recent developments in twentieth-century education. Rather than being concerned with the structures of knowledge and modes of inquiry in academic disciplines, the resurgent romanticism gives priority to emotions and feelings. What is sometimes suggested is the liberation of feelings in an emotional apprehension of truth. The current Rousseauist renaissance is also impatient with the structures of formal learning that were erected in the course of the late nineteenth and the twentieth centuries. As Rousseau attacked verbalism, the new Rousseauists attack the emphasis on science and the quantification of human experience. These current educational movements suggest that Rousseau's educational theory is still a rich source of investigation for students of intellectual and educational history.

[4] William J. McGucken, S.J., *The Catholic Way in Education* (Chicago: Loyola University Press, 1962), p. 6.

Sense Realism

The new world view that Newton introduced into Western thought construed the universe as a vast mechanism functioning according to its own intrinsic laws. When the eighteenth-century philosophe spoke of nature, he most likely meant this all-pervasive, harmoniously functioning world machine. Through carefully constructed scientific experimentation and the accurate compilation of data, man could discern the universal patterns of natural operations and discover natural laws. While the greatest advances were being made in the physical sciences, the philosophes believed that if science was applied to human institutions, society could be reconstructed in conformity with natural law.

Unfortunately, the dominant social institutions of the day were not in accord with natural law. Obsolete concepts of the divine right of kings impeded the formation of republican governments based on the social contract. Mercantilism blocked the free flow of commerce and violated the natural law of supply and demand. According to the philosophes, artificial and archaic educational patterns based on scholasticism, dogmatism, and verbalism impeded the movement to a natural system of education. The residues of the old unnatural, unscientific, and unenlightened eras of the past thwarted human progress.

Most of the eighteenth-century rationalists rejected the idea that man was naturally depraved, a sinful, wounded, willful creature. To cooperate with his original state of benevolence, man's innate goodness had to be developed by a system of natural education that would liberate his intelligence and bring about a moral regeneration.

These views of the Enlightenment were an outgrowth of the eighteenth century's emphasis on science, nature, and reason. If man observed carefully and scientifically, he could extract the laws of nature and establish new governments and social institutions in conformity with natural law. Although much eighteenth-century theorizing rested on crucial a priori assumptions that asserted the existence of natural law and the inherent rights of man, the philosophes of the Enlightenment also relied on empirical methods as a source of knowledge. In the *Essay Concerning Human Understanding* (1690), John Locke asserted an empiricism that profoundly affected educational theory and method. Locke attacked the Platonic conception of the mind as a locus of innate ideas and repudiated the doctrine of reminiscence, which held that the knowing process consisted in recalling these innate ideas by bringing them to consciousness. The mind, Locke asserted, is a tabula rasa, a blank slate, upon which is imprinted the materials of experience that come to it through the senses. Stressing an empiricist epistemology, Locke asserted that knowledge derives from sensory perceptions of objects. Man constructs his knowledge through combinations of simple ideas derived from sensation.

In France, Etienne Bonnot de Condillac (1715–1780), who was simultaneously priest and materialist, adopted Locke's empiricism, denied the presence of innate ideas in the mind, and asserted that sensation is the source of human knowledge. In developing a sensationalist psychology of learning, which anticipated modern behaviorism, Condillac defined sensation as communication between the sensory organs and the brain. In asserting that Condillac exerted a greater influence on European naturalism than is commonly supposed, Isaiah Berlin said:

> Condillac undertakes to reconstruct every human experience—the most complex and sophisticated thoughts or "movements of the soul," the most elaborate play of the imagination, the most subtle scientific speculation—out of "simple" ideas, that is, sensations classifiable as being given to one or the other of our normal senses, each of which can, as it were, be pin-pointed and assigned to its rightful place in the stream of sensations.[5]

Although Condillac might be classified variously as an empiricist, a sensationalist, or a sense realist, the latter designation is most appropriate. He accepted the existence of a natural and objective reality that exhibits patterns or regularities—or natural laws—that man can discover by carefully conducted observation. As stated by Condillac, "this design belongs to nature alone; nature began it without our participation in the design."[6] For Condillac, mind is a feeling, or sensing, substance that is comparable to the eye. Since the sight of the mind is like that of the body, Condillac held that the efficient functioning of both depends upon exercise:

> Indeed, an exercised mind discerns in a subject on which it meditates, a multitude of relations which are not generally perceived; just as the exercised eyes of a great painter, in a moment discovers in a landscape a multitude of things which we see with him, but of which, however, the peculiarities escape our notice.[7]

Although man's sensory organs passively receive data from physical objects, this passive sensation is inadequate to form accurate concepts. Condillac expressed a belief in the existence of a methodology of proper sensation. When sensations are acquired in an orderly manner by the process of analysis, the ideas that result are likewise orderly. However,

[5] Isaiah Berlin, *The Age of Enlightenment: The Eighteenth Century Philosophers* (Boston: Houghton Mifflin, 1956), pp. 266–268.
[6] Etienne Bonnot de Condillac, *Logic of Condillac, Translated by Joseph Neef, as an Illustration of the Plan of Education Established at His School Near Philadelphia* (Philadelphia: Printed for the Author, 1809), pp. 26–27.
[7] *Ibid.*, p. 15.

if the sensations are acquired at random, then the resulting ideas will be disordered, inaccurate, and chaotic.

Condillac's treatment of proper sensation embodies five phases: (1) man observes principal objects; (2) he notes the relationships among them; (3) he observes the intervals that exist between these objects; (4) he observes the secondary objects that occupy the intervals between the principal ones; (5) he compares all of these. After the objects have been recognized as particular and discrete and after their form and situation have been observed and compared, then a collective and simultaneous concept is formed.

Condillac defined sensation as a way of analyzing an object by first mentally decomposing and then recomposing it. Analysis involves the successive observation of the qualities of an object in order to present them to the mind in the simultaneous order in which they exist in the object. His conception of analysis was similar to Pestalozzi's reductionism, which held that proper sensation requires that an object be reduced to its simplest elements or components. According to Condillac and the sense realists, natural education begins with the learner's direct sensory experience of objects found in the immediate environment. These objects are minutely studied in order to isolate their basic or essential qualities.

Condillac distrusted generalized, abstract, and holistic conceptions of knowledge. Such generalizations, increasingly removed from direct sense experience, become clouded by error-producing abstractions. All instruction should begin with immediate sense impressions and avoid the premature introduction of abstract and verbalized definitions. Only after acquiring graduated and analytical series of sense impressions should the learner be encouraged to form general classifications or definitions.

Theorists such as Locke and Condillac moved epistemological research in the decided direction of empiricism. Their emphasis on sensation as the basis of knowledge undermined the school's exclusive concentration on verbalism and bookishness. It was in this spirit of sense impressionism that Pestalozzi was later to devise an educational method that emphasized the child's immediate environment and the objects within it as the source of learning. The sense realism of the eighteenth-century philosophes and their nineteenth-century disciples had a decided effect on the development of educational methodology.

Conclusion

Although Rousseau's *Emile* had expressed a desire for a reformed and liberated education, eighteenth- and early nineteenth-century schooling ignored intellectual and social change. The ideas of Locke,

Condillac, Diderot, and others had stimulated European intellectual history, but the conventional schools resisted the enticements of the Enlightenment in favor of classical humanism, which, although vital in the Renaissance, had grown pedantic and stale. Although enlightened educators might urge pedagogical reform, schoolmasters still practiced a rigid discipline and conceived of education as the recitation of memorized responses.

The elementary, or vernacular, schools remained primarily reading schools that stressed basic literacy, writing, singing, and arithmetic in addition to the preachment of religious doctrine and dogma. The various conflicting denominations had not forgotten, nor forgiven, the contentiousness of the Reformation and the ensuing decades of religious warfare. Children were admonished to defend their particular faiths by memorizing catechisms, psalters, primers, and creeds. Schoolmasters were employed on the basis of their adherence to doctrinal conformity and their skill in maintaining order and discipline. Often heavy-handed, authoritarian, and incompetent bigots were preferred over the educated man for teaching positions.

The various secondary schools—the German gymnasium, the French lycée, and the English grammar school—were somewhat more responsive to the currents of the Enlightenment than were the elementary schools. In Germany, August Hermann Francke enriched the gymnasium's curriculum by adding scientific and naturalistic studies. Although the English grammar school generally remained tied to classical Latin and Greek and theology, certain dissenting academies taught English and the natural sciences in addition to the classical languages. Despite these efforts, secondary education was still dominated by a pedagogical devotion to Latin and Greek as the necessary marks of an educated man. In higher education, professional preparation in theology, law, and medicine was the dominant concern of the Catholic scholastic, the Protestant classical humanist, and even the Enlightenment scholar, who was struggling for recognition in the university. Although the discussions of the Enlightenment period induced an intellectual ferment, schools were not necessarily the most exciting places in the eighteenth century.

Formal education often exhibits a resistance to change. The conventional educators of the eighteenth century regarded themselves as conservators of knowledge. Schooled in the methods of classical humanism, they practiced the educational arts as they had learned them from their masters. Formal educational institutions were often controlled by religious denominations, and the energies of teachers were spent in instructing the young in the creedal and ritualistic components of the various denominations. The impact of denominationalism thus blunted the cutting edges of Enlightenment science.

Formal education usually has lagged behind social and intellectual developments. The curriculum is often the repository of materials that were developed in the past. After a time, however, the school, too, responds to socioeconomic and political changes. Thus, the impact of the Enlightenment was felt in formal educational institutions in the nineteenth century. It was the early nineteenth-century educator Johann Heinrich Pestalozzi who put Rousseau's romantic educational theory into a pedagogical form. Pestalozzi's educational contribution will be treated extensively in Chapter 12.

More than in the realm of formal education, the real impact of the Enlightenment came in politics. The ideas of the philosophes found a ready hearing among the gentlemen of the generation that produced the American and French revolutions.

Suggested Readings

Ballinger, Stanley E. "The Natural Man: Rousseau," in Paul Nash, Andreas M. Kazamias, and Henry J. Perkinson (eds.), *The Educated Man: Studies in the History of Educational Thought*. New York: Wiley, 1965, pp. 225–246.

Becker, Carl L. *The Heavenly City of the Eighteenth-Century Philosophers*. New Haven, Conn.: Yale University Press, 1932.

Berlin, Isaiah. *The Age of Enlightenment: The Eighteenth Century Philosophers*. Boston: Houghton Mifflin, 1956.

Bury, J. B. *The Idea of Progress*. New York: Dover Pub., 1932.

Cassirer, Ernst. *The Philosophy of the Enlightenment*. Fritz Koellin and J. F. Pettigrove (trs.). Princeton: Princeton University Press, 1961.

Condillac, Etienne Bonnot de. *Logic of Condillac, Translated by Joseph Neef, as an Illustration of the Plan of Education Established at His School Near Philadelphia*. Philadelphia: Printed for the Author, 1809.

Cranston, Maurice. *John Locke: A Biography*. New York: Macmillan, 1957.

Green, R. G. *Jean Jacques Rousseau: A Critical Study of His Life and Writings*. Cambridge, Mass.: Harvard University Press, 1956.

Hazard, Paul. *European Thought in the Eighteenth Century*. New Haven, Conn.: Yale University Press, 1954.

Hendel, Charles W. *Jean Jacques Rousseau: Moralist*. London: Oxford University Press, 1934.

Heslep, Robert D. *Thomas Jefferson and Education*. New York: Random House, 1969.

Hudson, William H. *Rousseau and Naturalism in Life and Thought*. Edinburgh: T. T. Clark, 1903.

Jefferson, Thomas. *Crusade Against Ignorance: Thomas Jefferson on Education*. Gordon C. Lee (ed.). New York: Bureau of Publications, Teachers College, Columbia University, 1961.

Jeffreys, M. V. C. *John Locke: Prophet of Common Sense*. London: Methuen, 1967.

Locke, John. *An Essay Concerning Human Understanding*. Raymond Wilburn (ed.). New York: Dutton, 1947.

McGucken, William J., S.J. *The Catholic Way in Education*. Chicago: Loyola University Press, 1962.

Rousseau, Jean Jacques. *The Emile of Jean Jacques Rousseau: Selections*. William Boyd (ed.). New York: Teachers College Press, Columbia University, 1962.

————. *The Minor Writings of Jean Jacques Rousseau*. William Boyd (ed.). New York: Bureau of Publications, Teachers College, Columbia University, 1962.

Yolton, John. *John Locke and the Way of Ideas*. Oxford, England: Clarendon Press, 1956.

CHAPTER 10

Republicanism, Revolution, and Education

The intellectual ferment unleashed by the Enlightenment philosophes was not merely theoretical but had implications for politics, government, society, and education. Basic to the thought of the philosophes was the idea that social, political, and educational institutions should be reformed and brought into conformity with natural law. Adam Smith's economic liberalism and François Quesnay's physiocratic doctrines attacked economic mercantilism and strongly recommended the adoption of free trade, an open market, and laissez-faire economics. The French Encyclopedists Diderot, Voltaire, and others had subjected the established church and aristocracy to the lash of ridicule and criticism. The contract theories of both Locke and Rousseau contained the incipient revolutionary germs of republicanism. Rousseau had suggested the possibility of creating a new educational methodology based on naturalistic principles in *Emile*. The ferment of the Age of Reason brought the established church, state, and school under critical examination and attack. In the English colonies of North America and in France, an unyielding political establishment was unwilling to temper absolutism. The result was revolution, the overthrow of the establishment, and the institution of republican government. This chapter will examine the educational consequences of revolutionary republicanism.

Education in the United States

When the American Revolution abruptly ended British rule in the thirteen rebellious colonies, the task of the revolutionary leaders was to forge a national consensus. The republican experiment involved the establishment of a new government based on the Lockean social contract and the inauguration of a system of checks and balances that distributed power among the executive, legislative, and judicial branches. Although early republican education exhibited the residues of the earlier colonial denominational and Latin grammar schools, American intellectuals sought to devise an educational system that would serve the cause of nation-building by inducting young republicans into a new political and social experience. Old loyalties had to be transformed into new values and commitments based on the republican concepts of self-government.

Under the Articles of Confederation, Congress faced the problem of administering the western lands of the Northwest Territory. The first national educational legislation was included in the Northwest Ordinance of 1785, which required that the Northwest Territory be surveyed and divided into townships of six square miles each. Each township was to be further divided into thirty-six sections, the sixteenth section of which was reserved for education.

The United States Constitution, ratified in 1789, contained no specific reference to education. Thus, education was reserved to the individual states under the "reserved powers" clause of the Tenth Amendment. The persistent tradition of local control and the fear of centralized political power contributed to a decentralized school system in the United States. Educational support and control became a state rather than a national function. This was in contrast to the centralization that was characteristic of education in most continental European nations.

Early American Educational Theories

Although the establishment of a republican government was the paramount issue, American theorists recognized the relationship between the republic and the school. The educational proposals of such men as Benjamin Rush, Robert Coram, and Samuel Smith raised questions about the type of education that would be appropriate to the politics and society of the new republic.[1] Rush urged that a uniquely American type of education be designed to reinforce patriotism and nationalism. In equating republicanism with scientific thought and method, Rush believed that enlightened education should create an attitude that would be progressive, forward-looking, and flexible.

Robert Coram related education to society and economics. He believed that educational equality and social, political, and economic equality were closely related. Coram's recommendation for a uniform

[1] For an analysis of the various educational plans of the republican period, especially those submitted to the American Philosophical Society, see Allen O. Hansen, *Liberalism and American Education in the Eighteenth Century* (New York: Macmillan, 1926). The several essays of Benjamin Rush, Robert Coram, and Samuel Smith are available in Frederick Rudolph's *Essays on Education in the Early Republic* (Cambridge, Mass.: Harvard University Press, 1965).

educational system went unheeded, however. Samuel Smith saw education as a social and political instrument that would make the American republic into a democratic model for the world. The educational plans of Rush, Coram, and Smith shared common themes of (1) using education as an instrument of nation-building, and (2) developing a scientific attitude designed to promote progress. These educational plans were also revealing examples of the transference of Enlightenment ideology to North America. The denominational religious motives that had characterized colonial American education, especially in New England, were completely lacking. For these republican theorists, education was to serve political purposes. The work of Rush, Coram, and Smith pointed to the coming secularization of American education.

The notion of progress, identified with the application of science to society, was also clearly present in the work of the republican social and educational theorists. If Americans were to include science in the curriculum and apply scientific principles to their political and social life, then progress would definitely ensue. The work of the republican theorists also cast aside the Puritan conception of human depravity. An optimism was voiced that the future would be better than the past.

During the early republican period, it grew increasingly evident that the educational residues of the colonial period were unsuited to the forging of national loyalties. Republican government required a different mode of education. The educational ideas of the distinguished American leaders Benjamin Franklin and Thomas Jefferson merit an examination for their insights into the republican attitudes to society and education.

Benjamin Franklin

Benjamin Franklin (1706–1790) was a vocal representative of the rising American middle class. Born into a large family of modest means, Franklin had only a limited formal education, consisting of one year spent at the Boston Grammar School and some writing and arithmetic lessons given by private teachers. After he was apprenticed to a printer, Franklin continued his education on his own by acquainting himself with the English classics and contemporary literature. He moved to Philadelphia, where he became a leading citizen and inaugurated numerous scientific and educational organizations and projects, such as the library subscription society and the Junto, a debating society. It was Franklin who proposed the founding of the American Philosophical Society. His *Poor Richard's Almanack* reached the homes of many Americans. Poor Richard's proverbs and admonitions were readily accepted by the American middle classes since they recommended the utilitarian values of diligence, thrift, and hard work, which had already been part of the liberal ethic. Although Franklin was certainly not a religious man in the orthodox sense, Poor Richard's values were still an expression of a secularized Puritanism.

Franklin's achievements were many. He proposed a plan for colonial unity in the Albany Plan of Union in 1754. From 1753 to 1774, he was the colonial postmaster general. An early advocate of American independence, he served as the Continental Congress' delegate to France from 1776 to 1777, where he was received as an American philosophe and enjoyed great popularity. He was a skilled diplomat who early advocated a foreign policy based on American vital interests. Franklin was instrumental in gaining an alliance with France that was a crucial determinant in the success of the American Revolution. His last major political service came as Pennsylvania's delegate to the Constitutional Convention in 1787. In many ways, Franklin's life was a personal success story that helped to create the popular American myth of the self-educated and self-made man who achieves a realistic education based on his own experiences with life and work. He distrusted classical schooling as too ornamental and as a useless waste of time. His distrust of exclusively intellectual conceptions of education moved him to propose plans for an English grammar school in Philadelphia. His proposal reflects the middle classes' demands for vernacular and utilitarian schooling as opposed to classical humanist studies.

FRANKLIN'S EDUCATIONAL PROPOSALS

In 1749, Franklin authored "Proposals Relating to the Education of Youth in Pennsylvania," which recommended the establishment of an English grammar school.[2] Rather than focusing exclusively on the classical languages as had the old Latin grammar school, Franklin's proposed school would offer a practical curriculum that would include a variety of subjects. English grammar, classics, composition, rhetoric, and declamation were to be the dominant language studies. The emphasis was on English, the vernacular of commerce and common discourse, rather than on Latin. In addition to English, students could elect a second language based on their vocational destination. Ministers might choose to study Latin and Greek; doctors, Latin, Greek, and French; merchants, French, German, and Spanish. Franklin's proposed curriculum included such utilitarian pursuits as carpentry, shipbuilding, engraving, printing, painting, cabinet-making, carving, and gardening. Mathematics was to be taught in a practical manner that would be useful for the keeping of accounts. As an ethical study, history was to provide students with moral lessons.

When Franklin's school was established, however, it was located in

2 See Benjamin Franklin, *Proposals Relating to the Education of Youth in Pensilvania* (Philadelphia, 1749), in Leonard W. Labaree and Whitfield J. Bell, Jr. (eds.), *The Papers of Benjamin Franklin* (New Haven, Conn.: Yale University Press, 1961), III, 395–421.

the same building as the Latin school. The English program was placed under the direction of the Latin master, who headed the school, and it never really developed into a viable form of secondary education. Franklin's proposal for an English grammar school is significant because it was prophetic of the academy that evolved as the dominant secondary school in the United States in the nineteenth century. The American academies offered a curriculum that included various subject matters, ranging from the classics to English and from the fine arts to the practical crafts.

Thomas Jefferson

Unlike Franklin, the self-made man, Thomas Jefferson (1743–1826), the scion of a prosperous plantation family of Albemarle County, Virginia, enjoyed the formal educational opportunities of the colonial American elite. He attended the local English vernacular school and the Latin grammar school and completed his formal education at William and Mary College. As a leading statesman of the revolutionary and early republican eras, Jefferson was a member of the Virginia legislature, a delegate to the Continental Congress, governor of Virginia, minister to France, secretary of state, vice president, and finally president of the United States. His political views, which were derived from an essentially Lockean perspective, were expressed in the Declaration of Independence's assertion that man is endowed with inalienable rights to "life, liberty, and pursuit of happiness." Jefferson was truly an American philosophe, and his interests extended to politics, society, religion, education, architecture, science, and literature. He was elected to the American Academy of Arts and Sciences and was president of the American Philosophical Society. He asserted that his epitaph should bear witness to only three of his accomplishments—writing the Declaration of Independence and the Virginia Bill of Rights and founding the University of Virginia.

JEFFERSON'S EDUCATIONAL PROPOSALS

Although he was concerned with educational affairs throughout his public career and private life, Jefferson's "Bill for the More General Diffusion of Knowledge," introduced in the Virginia legislature in 1779, clearly indicated his philosophy of education.[3] Implicit in this proposal were the following assumptions: (1) republican government requires an educated and literate citizenry; (2) education should fulfill a civic or political function rather than a religious one; (3) the state properly

[3] Thomas Jefferson, "A Bill for the More General Diffusion of Knowledge," in Julian P. Boyd (ed.), *The Papers of Thomas Jefferson* (Princeton, N.J.: Princeton University Press, 1950), II, 526–533.

has an educational responsibility; and (4) a democratic society should provide educational opportunities for both the common man and the gifted leader.

According to Jefferson's plan, the counties of Virginia were to be subdivided into wards, each with an elementary school to provide instruction in reading, writing, arithmetic, and history. All white children were to attend the ward school for three years as beneficiaries of publicly funded elementary education. After three years, their parents could continue to enroll their children in the school if they wished to assume tuition payments.

Jefferson also proposed the establishment of twenty grammar, or secondary, schools in Virginia. The district supervisor was to select the most able student in each elementary school who could not afford to pay tuition. These scholarship students were to continue their education for three additional years, studying Latin, Greek, English, geography, and higher mathematics. The most able of the scholarship students, chosen annually, were to receive additional education. Upon completing their secondary education, half of the scholarship students were to assume positions as teachers in the elementary schools; the remaining ten students were to go on to higher education at William and Mary College.

Although not enacted into legislation, Jefferson's proposal is an interesting historical document that provides insights into early republican educational thought. When compared with his Federalist political opponents, Jefferson appears to be an advocate of frontier agrarian egalitarianism. His educational proposal in the "Bill for the More General Diffusion of Knowledge" shows that he regarded education to have two roles in a republican society: (1) to provide a common core of knowledge to the mass of population, and (2) to identify talented persons and prepare them to assume positions of leadership. Jefferson's bill was in many ways a simplified version of the scheme of education that Plato advanced in *The Republic*. Jefferson assumed that the masses of population, the voters, would recognize and accept the "aristocracy of intellect" that would be identified and brought forth as leaders of the republican society.

Republican Education in the United States

The proposals of Franklin, Jefferson, and the other theorists of the early republican era were attempts to establish agencies to educate men capable of performing the functions necessary for republican government. Although many of the proposals were vague and ill-defined, they gave evidence that political change affects education. They also indicated a shift in emphasis from religious sectarianism to the social and political functions of education. The theoretical formulations of Franklin, Rush, Jefferson, Smith, and Coram were indicators of a republican sense of values. Although these proposals were not enacted directly into legislation, they laid the groundwork for the development of American educational theory. While they contained elements that were distinctly American, they were also part of the total intellectual developments that were surging through the European Enlightenment. The frontier-born distrust of powerful central government contributed to the notion that education should be a function of the local community and not of the federal government. As mentioned earlier, Franklin's proposals anticipated the emergence of the multifaceted nineteenth-century academy. Jefferson's "Bill for the More General Diffusion of Knowledge" revealed the continuing tension that American education experienced as it sought to educate both the intellectually gifted as well as the ordinary citizen.

The republican educational theories also gave clear evidence of the coming dethronement of religious education and values from the curriculum. Although denominational forces were to control formal education in the United States throughout much of the nineteenth century, the republican theorists clearly stated what would become the secularized education of the twentieth century. Rather than serving the purposes of denominational religion, Jefferson and others saw education as a civic, political, and social instrument deliberately designed to advance republican knowledge, skills, and values.

The American Revolution was an inspiration to those Frenchmen who sought to replace Bourbon autocracy with enlightened government. Indeed, such Frenchmen as the Marquis de Lafayette, who had fought in Washington's army, joined in the struggle to give political expression to the Enlightenment's ideas on French soil.

The French Revolution

Although the philosophes had cautiously criticized Bourbon absolutism in France, it was an acute financial crisis that precipitated the Revolution of 1789. The slow-witted King Louis XVI (1774–1792) was unequal to problems posed by a bankrupt treasury and a disintegrating royal government, and the severity of the crisis forced him to call the Estates General into session. The proportions and influence of the three sectors of the population that made up the Estates General serve to indicate the social structure of prerevolutionary France. The first estate, the clergy, which consisted of less than 1 percent of the population, occupied a position of conspicuous importance in France. The French church was a wealthy landowner and the recipient of the tithe. The clergy itself was divided into the higher ecclesiastics—archbishops, bishops, and superiors of religious orders—and the parish priests. Although the Catholic hierarchy generally allied itself with Bourbon absolutism, the parish priests were often sympathetic to the aspirations of the lower classes. The French peasants were usually faithful Catholics, but the bourgeois generally accepted the antireligious views of the philosophes. The working classes were often openly anticlerical and hostile to the church.

In matters of civil authority and education, the influence of the French Roman Catholic Church was extensive. The church kept all public registers, recording all the baptisms, marriages, and deaths in the kingdom; public welfare and charity were under church jurisdiction. Education was almost exclusively conducted in the church-controlled parish schools and the church-oriented universities.

The second estate, the nobility, was less than 2 percent of the population. Holding about 25 percent of the land, enjoying a virtual exemption from taxation, and monopolizing positions of authority, the nobility was decidedly unpopular.

The vast majority of Frenchmen—in excess of 95 percent—fell within the third estate. The small landholding peasants felt the economic pinch caused by land shortage, obsolete agricultural methods, and overpopulation. Although generally ignorant of the reform program of the Enlightenment philosophes, the peasantry was hungry for more land. The leaders of the middle class, who were becoming increasingly aware of their own growing economic importance, were beginning to demand social, political, and educational rights. It was this class—the merchants, lawyers, bankers, storekeepers, doctors, and other professional men—that took the lead in advancing the initial momentum of the revolutionary forces.

When the Estates General met on May 5, 1789, the third estate refused to meet separately to cast the one vote allotted to it and demanded instead that voting be by head rather than estate. By the end of July 1789, three events made it clear that a revolution was under way: (1) the third estate had proclaimed itself the National Assembly; (2) the Bastille had been stormed on July 14, 1789, and a communal government established in Paris; and (3) violent antiaristocratic outbreaks began to occur throughout France. During the period from 1789 to 1791, the National Assembly enacted legislation that destroyed the residues of French feudalism and serfdom, reorganized France into a centralized system of eighty-three departments—which replaced the old provinces as administrative units—enacted more uniform taxes, and reduced the clergy to civil servants. Accused of duplicity and counterrevolutionary activities, Louis XVI was charged with treason and sent to the guillotine on January 21, 1793. France had made a rapid transition from absolute monarchy to republic.

Although the various legislative actions cannot be detailed here, the "Declaration of the Rights of Man and of the Citizen" of August 27, 1789, gives evidence of the essentially liberal spirit of the initial stages of the Revolution. A brief examination of some of the articles of the declaration show it to have been heavily influenced by Enlightenment theories. According to the declaration: (1) men are born free and equal; (2) any political association should preserve man's natural rights of liberty, property, security, and resistance to oppression; (3) sovereignty lies within the nation; (4) man has the liberty to do anything that does not injure others; (5) law expresses the general will; and (6) because the free communication of ideas and opinions is a precious human right, every citizen has the right to speak, write, and print.

Education and the French Republic

From 1789 to 1793, the deputies in the French National Assembly attempted to centralize law and education.[4] An attempt was made to draft a complete civil code. Although it was not promulgated, it served as a basis for the codification of the civil laws that occurred under Napoleon. In 1793, the National Convention, which had been elected in 1792 and acted as the chief legislative body, introduced the compulsory use of the metric system to standardize weights and measures.

The Convention also nationalized the French language so that local dialects and such non-French languages as Italian, German, and Spanish would be eliminated. The Convention assigned instructors of French to the necessary regions to teach French and to expound the Declaration of the Rights of Man to children. The use of education to stimulate national uniformity, loyalty, and patriotism marked a major attempt to apply the doctrine of nationalism to education. Since the citizen was born to live for the republic, the state would indoctrinate him to love and defend his nation. Public games and festivals were organized to generate the sentiments of liberty, equality, and fraternity.

The promulgation of the civil constitution of the clergy and the dissolution of the Catholic teaching orders by the revolutionary French government produced educational dislocations. In many rural areas where Catholic and monarchist sentiment was strong, private and religious schools attracted more support than the national schools that

---

[4] For a history of education during the French Revolution, see H. C. Barnard, *Education and the French Revolution* (Cambridge, England: Cambridge University Press, 1969).

the various revolutionary regimes sought to establish. During the Constituent Assembly, Talleyrand prepared a comprehensive educational plan, and the principle of free elementary education was included in the Constitution of 1791.

Charles Maurice Talleyrand-Perigord (1754–1838), a former bishop who was politically discrete enough to make the various ideological shifts that enabled him to exercise influence in the Revolution, in Napoleon's government, and then in the Bourbon restoration, presented a report on public instruction to the Constituent Assembly in 1791. Talleyrand argued that the old clerical-dominated education was irrelevant to the needs of revolutionary France. Although the republic should be responsive to the expression of the general will, it was necessary that republican education be instituted so that the populace could speak with reason. General education should be made available to citizens without discrimination by age or sex. A three-stage system of schools was recommended: (1) primary schools to provide a general education for all; (2) secondary schools to provide the specialized education that would move men in the direction of particular vocations; and (3) institutions of higher learning, to be located in each department of the republic, for advanced and professional education.[5] Although the Assembly adjourned before taking action on Talleyrand's report, it recommended the report to its successor, the Legislative Assembly.

On April 20, 1792, Condorcet, the leading member of the committee of public instruction of the Legislative Assembly, presented his plan for educational reform, the "Report on Public Instruction." Marie Jean Antoine Nicolas Caritat, Marquis de Condorcet (1743–1794), was a noble by birth and educated at the Jesuit College de Navarre. An able mathematician and scientist, he was elected secretary of the *Académie des Sciences* in 1781. Condorcet had associated with the philosophes in the prerevolutionary period and then supported the Revolution. Because of his moderate views, he was imprisoned by the Jacobins during the Reign of Terror and died, apparently a suicide.

A brief examination of Condorcet's philosophy of education reveals him to be a clear advocate of the Enlightenment's concepts of science and progress. Essentially he believed that man's knowledge was a product of sense experience; he trusted that the course of human history would be the record of man's continuing and unlimited progress and ultimate perfectability; he believed that science was the instrument for securing the progressive development of mankind. According to Condorcet, science and education were intimately related:

> The progress of the sciences ensures the progress of the art of education which in turn advances that of the sciences. This reciprocal

[5] *Ibid.*, pp. 68–79.

influence, whose activity is ceaselessly renewed, deserves to be seen as one of the most powerful and active causes working for the perfection of mankind.[6]

According to Condorcet's proposed plan of education, the state would provide universal education and maintain equality of educational opportunity. He proposed four grades of schools: (1) primary schools to provide basic instruction in reading, writing, measurement, morality, agriculture, and industry; (2) secondary schools—at least one for every town of 4,000 inhabitants—to teach the sciences; (3) institutes—at least one in every department—to teach the applied sciences of agriculture and mechanics; and (4) higher education at the university level to be offered by nine lycées.

According to Condorcet's plan, primary and secondary education was to be free to the student. The emphasis throughout the plan was on scientific and social studies. Like most advocates of the sensationalists' epistemology, Condorcet de-emphasized language study. A system of scholarships would be created to give the poorer classes access to education. Finally, to protect the educational system against political interference, Condorcet proposed a self-perpetuating controlling board, the National Society of Sciences and Arts, which would supervise instruction and disseminate knowledge. Although Condorcet's proposal was tabled, his report was a landmark in educational history and served to inspire other French educational reformers.

The Convention's definitive decree on school organization was passed on October 25, 1795. It provided for the establishment of a limited number of primary schools and also recognized the legitimacy of home and private instruction. One secondary, or central, school was to be established in each department. Five were to be established in Paris. The secondary school curriculum was to consist of languages, drawing, natural history, sciences, literature, grammar, history, and law. After initial difficulties, the secondary schools proved to be prosperous institutions until they were suppressed by Napoleon in 1802.

The Convention was successful in its organization of higher education. The School of Public Works, later the Polytechnic School, was established in 1794 to educate civil and military engineers. In 1793, the Museum of Natural History was subsidized to carry on research and to enlarge its collections. On October 25, 1795, the Convention created the National Institute, with more than one hundred resident scholars, divided into three major divisions: physical and mathematical sciences; moral and political sciences; literature and fine arts.

Although there was evidence of irresponsible and destructive pillag-

[6] Antoine Nicolas de Condorcet, *Sketch for a Historical Picture of the Progress of the Human Mind,* June Barraclough (tr.) (London: Weidenfeld and Nicolson, 1955), pp. 201–202.

ing of churches, monasteries, and private galleries and archives, the Constituent Assembly and Convention sought to safeguard the national artistic and cultural heritage. The Royal Library was reorganized and expanded as the National Library. The National Archives were established to preserve books, manuscripts, and other documents. The Louvre Museum was founded to house the royal collections of paintings and other art works.

Napoleon and the First Empire

After the Reign of Terror of Robespierre, the course of the French Revolution took a more conservative bent as the leaders of the Thermidorean reaction disbanded the remnants of the Revolutionary Tribunal. The Thermidorians, seizing power in July 1794, the month of Thermidor according to the revolutionary calendar, sought to retain the republic and give political power to the upper middle class. From 1795 until 1799, executive power was in the hands of the five members of the Directory. Political and financial instability plagued the Directory and paved the way for the appearance of a strong man, Napoleon Bonaparte (1769–1821), the hero of the Italian campaign of 1796–1797. In November 1799, Napoleon seized power in a coup d'état. In 1802, he was made first consul for life and given the power to designate his successor and amend the constitution at his own discretion. In 1804, Napoleon crowned himself the hereditary emperor of the French. Thus, the Revolution had run its course and culminated in a police state that was more efficient and more highly organized than Bourbon absolutism had ever been.

A charismatic leader, Napoleon was able to win the support of the majority of Frenchmen. He made decisions quickly, was a strong leader, and exuded a personal magnetism that won devoted obedience from his followers. Napoleon's use of coordinated artillery fire and mobile infantry and cavalry revolutionized military tactics. He was an efficient tyrant who skillfully practiced Machiavellian duplicity and eventually brought about his own downfall by overextending his empire. Under his rule, from 1799 until 1815, the French people sacrificed political liberty and initiative for efficient and vigorous, albeit tyrannical, government.

Although personally indifferent to religion, Napoleon believed that Frenchmen were fundamentally Roman Catholic. Moreover, he believed that a reconciliation with the Catholic Church would be advantageous for his own policy and remove the blemish of Jacobinism from his regime. Therefore, on July 16, 1801, Napoleon negotiated a concordat with Pope Pius VII that recognized the Catholic religion as the "religion of the great majority of French citizens" but not the state religion. The Napoleonic government agreed to permit the exercise of Catholic worship.

In 1804, French law was centralized under the Civil Code, often called the *Code Napoléon,* which declared all men equal without regard to rank or wealth. Each man was free to choose his own occupation and religion. The Civil Code maintained the revolutionary separation of civil law from ecclesiastical interference and guaranteed civil equality before the law. It also gave evidence of Napoleonic authoritarianism in that the authority of the father in the home was reasserted and the status of women repressed. Generally, the Civil Code produced a single coherent system of law, but a highly centralized one.

Napoleonic Education

The Napoleonic era was characterized by intellectual repression. Napoleon rejected the liberalism of the philosophes, whom he considered to be intellectual agitators. His regime was a forerunner of the modern totalitarian state with its system of police spying and political arrest. Napoleon also anticipated twentieth-century fascist paternalism. To keep the press muzzled, the number of printers in Paris was limited to sixty, each of whom was required to swear obedience to the government. The number of newspapers declined from seventy in 1800 to four government propaganda organs in 1810. Napoleonic intellectual repression was also extended to the theater and to literature, both of which were severely censored.

Napoleon's thought control was rigorously extended to education. Like the modern dictators, he wanted to make the schools an arm of the state that would indoctrinate men to accept his government's views on all questions. He conceived the school's function to be strictly political:

> The system that we propose is not only moral; it is also a political system. Its purpose is to rally behind the government both the new and the old generation, the old through their children, and the children through their parents, to establish a sort of public fatherhood.[7]

Napoleon's reorganization of the educational system took effect in May 1802. Elementary education was assigned to the voluntary action of the communes. The primary schools established by the revolutionary government were very weak and remained so. He abolished the prospering *écoles centrales*—secondary schools—which were developing into intellectual centers, adequately equipped and competently

[7] Leo Gershoy, *The French Revolution and Napoleon* (New York: Appleton-Century-Crofts, 1933), p. 464.

staffed. Secondary education was given over to a number of local and private schools and to the lycées under direct government control and supervision.

The government-controlled lycées were schools for patriotic indoctrination and were carefully regulated. The national government determined the curriculum, appointed the faculty, provided salaries, prescribed rules of conduct, and inspected the schools. The conduct of the government lycées was highly militaristic. Students wore uniforms, marched to classes, and received military training from army officers.

In 1808, the Imperial University, a teaching corporation encompassing all educational levels, was established as a state monopoly over public instruction throughout France. The entire school system was centralized under the Grand Master, the administrative head of the university, who presided over thirty-four regional subdivisions, or academies. Administrative and teaching members of the university promised complete obedience to the Grand Master as a condition of their appointment and tenure.

The Imperial University was a unified educational system of primary, secondary, and higher schools rather than a single institution of higher learning in the sense of either the medieval or modern university. The Napoleonic government was least concerned with primary schools which were generally entrusted to various Roman Catholic religious teaching orders such as the Brothers of the Christian Schools. In its educational planning, the *Conseil de l'Université*, the central administrative agency of the Imperial University, gave priority to the various secondary schools. Foremost among the secondary schools were the thirty lycées, or state boarding schools, which offered a six-year course that emphasized classics and mathematics. Less prestigious than the lycées, the *collèges* were municipal secondary schools that offered courses in French, Latin, history, geography, and mathematics. There were also some independent secondary schools, or *instituts*, that were on the same academic level as the collèges.

Under the direction of the Imperial University, higher education was entrusted to university faculties of theology, law, medicine, science, and arts which were located in various French cities. The most prestigious institutions of higher education were the *Ecole Militaire* for military officers, the *Ecole Normale Supérieure* for professors of higher education, and the *Ecole Polytechnique* for engineers. Napoleon planned to draw his ruling elite from the graduates of these special professional schools.[8]

Instruction in all schools was intended to train citizens who would

[8] Barnard, *op. cit.*, pp. 217–221.

be devoted to "their religion, to their prince, to their fatherland, and to their family."[9] The curriculum, the method of instruction, and the school milieu were closely regulated in order to produce trained military and administrative personnel who would perform their duties with a sense of patriotic zeal and loyalty to the emperor. In an imperial catechism, the political indoctrination used by Napoleon is clearly evident:

> QUESTION. What are the duties of Christians towards those who govern them, and what in particular are our duties towards Napoleon I, our emperor?
>
> ANSWER. Christians owe to the princes who govern them, and we in particular owe to Napoleon I, our emperor, love, respect, obedience, fidelity, military service, and the taxes levied for the preservation and defense of the empire and of his throne. We also owe him fervent prayers for his safety and for the spiritual and temporal prosperity of the state.[10]

Although Napoleon's empire ended with his defeat at Waterloo in 1815, he established the basic pattern of centralization that has characterized French education. His armies had not only carried revolutionary doctrines but also infected the invaded peoples with nationalism as a counterforce to the French nationalism. As the spirit of nationalism emerged, the schools would forever be in danger of being subverted to the exclusive service of the national state.

Conclusion

This chapter on the revolutionary consequences of the Enlightenment concentrated on the American and French revolutions, which sought to give concrete political expression to the ideas of the philosophes and bore a direct relationship to educational change. As a result of the American and French revolutions, education was tied to the cultivation of nationalism among the young, who were destined to be citizens of national states.

Chapter 11 deals with the social, political, and educational movements of the nineteenth century. In some ways, the nineteenth century was a time when certain of the Enlightenment ideas, such as the concept of "progress" and "science," were emphasized. However, the nineteenth century also gave evidences of a reaction against the Age of Reason when it ushered in a romanticist renaissance.

---

[9] Gershoy, op. cit., p. 465.
[10] "Napoleonic Catechism," in Raymond P. Stearns (ed.), Pageant of Europe (New York: Harcourt, Brace, and World, 1961), p. 424.

Suggested Readings

Arrowood, Charles F. *Thomas Jefferson and Education in a Republic*. New York: McGraw-Hill, 1930.

Barnard, H. C. *Education and the French Revolution*. Cambridge, Mass.: Cambridge University Press, 1969.

Best, John Hardin. *Benjamin Franklin on Education*. New York: Bureau of Publications, Teachers College, Columbia University, 1962.

Condorcet, Antoine Nicolas. *Sketch for a Historical Picture of the Progress of the Human Mind*. June Barraclough (tr.). London: Weidenfeld and Nicolson, 1955.

Curti, Merle. *The Social Ideas of American Educators*. Totowa, N.J. Littlefield, Adams, 1959.

Fisher, Herbert A. *Napoleon*. New York: Oxford University Press, 1945.

Franklin, Benjamin. *The Papers of Benjamin Franklin*. Leonard W. Labaree and Whitfield J. Bell, Jr. (eds.). New Haven, Conn.: Yale University Press, 1961.

Gershoy, Leo. *The French Revolution and Napoleon*. New York: Appleton-Century-Crofts, 1933.

Greene, Evarts B. *Revolutionary Generation, 1763–90*. New York: Macmillan, 1943.

Hansen, Allen O. *Liberalism and American Education in the Eighteenth Century*. New York: Octagon, 1965.

Heslep, Robert D. *Thomas Jefferson and Education*. New York: Random House, 1969.

Honeywell, Roy J. *The Educational Work of Thomas Jefferson*. Cambridge, Mass.: Harvard University Press, 1931.

Jefferson, Thomas. *The Papers of Thomas Jefferson*. Julian P. Boyd (ed.). Princeton, N.J.: Princeton University Press, 1950.

Lee, Gordon C. *Crusade Against Ignorance: Thomas Jefferson on Education*. New York: Bureau of Publications, Teachers College, Columbia University, 1961.

Lefebvre, Georges. *Coming of the French Revolution*. R. R. Palmer (tr.). Princeton, N.J.: Princeton University Press, 1948.

Morgan, Edmund. *Birth of the Republic, 1763–89*. Chicago: University of Chicago Press, 1956.

Reisner, E. H. *Nationalism and Education Since 1789*. New York: Macmillan, 1922.

Rudolph, Frederick. *Essays on Education in the Early Republic*. Cambridge, Mass.: Harvard University Press, 1965.

Woody, Thomas. *Educational Views of Benjamin Franklin*. New York: McGraw-Hill, 1931.

CHAPTER 11

The Nineteenth Century: An Age of Ideology

The nineteenth century was an age of conflicting ideologies that competed for the loyalties of Western man. Sometimes these ideologies were spun from the speculations of social philosophers; at other times they were merely theoretical posturings that disguised special and vested class interests. Given such names as liberalism, conservatism, and socialism, the various sociopolitical dogmas of the nineteenth century replaced the much-eroded inherited commitments to established religions and dynastic monarchies. The ideological clashes of the nineteenth century did not always result from a rational choosing between alternative shades of liberalism, conservatism, or socialism but often were motivated by an emotional fervor that reached the heights of a moral crusade. In terms of their educational consequences, the nineteenth-century ideologies had a twofold effect: (1) they were often used as the rationale for educational philosophies; and (2) the various political parties that were associated with particular ideologies either advanced or retarded the cause of popular education.

In describing the nineteenth century as the first great age of ideology, the historian H. Stuart Hughes has remarked that an ideology lies somewhere between "abstract political and social philosophy and the practical activities of parties and pressure groups." Hughes provides a useful definition in describing an ideology as the

general concept of the actual or ideal nature of society that gives meaning and direction to the lives of large groups of people. In one aspect, it is a theory of history, charting the "inevitable" course of human affairs and assuring its adherents that the future lies with them. It is no accident that it was the historically minded nineteenth century that first began to think in this fashion. From another standpoint, ideology is linked to class, rationalizing and endorsing the aspirations of one social class and attacking those of its enemies. Finally, it may be viewed as a secular cult with its own saints and martyrs, its own creed, and its own system of missionary work, propaganda, and indoctrination.[1]

Extrapolating from Hughes' definition of ideology, it can be seen that ideologies have significant importance for the construction of educational aims. As a theoretical view of the ideal nature of society, ideology acts as a determinant of the kinds of values that are to be cultivated by the school. While a liberal might stress individual competition, a socialist would emphasize cooperative activities and relationships in the school. In a broader sense, the societal concepts that are enmeshed in ideology also serve to establish the definition and function of the school as a social agency. Whereas conservatives see the school as an agency of cultural transmission and preservation, a liberal might envision it as an instrument of change. Ideologies tend, as Hughes says, to chart the "inevitable" course of history, at least for their adherents, who believe that their ideology completely conforms to universal natural laws. The classical liberal's law of supply and demand and the Marxist socialist's dialectical materialism are examples of this sense of historical inevitability. The supposed or alleged detection of inevitable laws of social change profoundly affects the construction of educational aims. While the classical liberal and social Darwinist reject using educational agencies as instruments of deliberate social change, the utopian socialist believes that educational means can bring about a new society. Ideology was often centered on the aspirations of a particular socioeconomic class, and the formal school was also conceived of in terms of these class interests. Since ideologists were creedal and evangelical, they sought to include the study of their heroes and beliefs in the school's curriculum. The propaganda of the ideologists was a form of informal education as the press was used as an instrument to influence public opinion and to win political power.

Industrialism

The nineteenth-century social and political ideologies were not disemboweled thought systems but were developed within the context established by the continuing Industrial Revolution. The process of industrialization, which had begun in the eighteenth century, was an ongoing phenomenon that had a profound impact on nineteenth-century Europe and North America. In the twentieth century, industrialization, under the guise of modernization, has affected almost every nation on earth. The industrial factory system, resulting from the har-

[1] H. Stuart Hughes, *Contemporary Europe: A History* (Englewood Cliffs, N.J.: Prentice-Hall, 1961), p. 11.

nessing of power, the introduction of machinery, and the use of inter-changeable parts, made mass production efficient and profitable. Industrialization not only modernized Western society but also brought into existence a capitalistic middle class of businessmen, entrepre-neurs, and managers that came to exert a profound power on social, economic, and political life. The rise of the middle class to power had educational consequences in that it developed its own class definition of a "good education" and sought to make schools responsive to its needs. Since the middle class was the mobile class, it sought to use education to advance its own upward mobility. Since it was a monied class, it tended to measure educational results in monetary terms. As a practical, entrepreneurial class, it desired utilitarian and scientific education.

In the early stages of industrialization, there was little or no gov-ernment interference with business. Early industrial capitalism's ex-pansion rested on the exercise of the profit motive, free competition in an open market, and private ownership of property. Advocates of free trade, many of whom supported liberal ideology, talked about a natural law of supply and demand in which money and price auto-matically reached their natural levels.

The industrialization of the Western world significantly reordered the socioeconomic class structure. The older aristocracy of birth and breeding was severely shaken by the rise of the *nouveau riche* capital-ists and their professional, technological, and managerial allies. As a power group, the older landed aristocracy was attached to agricultural interests and to conservative ideology. Although their position had been jeopardized by the eighteenth-century French and American rev-olutions, the landed aristocracy and gentry persisted as a potent po-litical force in the less industrialized central and eastern European nations. Generally, the landed aristocrats supported, and in turn were supported by, established churches, hereditary monarchs, and the peasantry. Resistant and fearful of the modernizing tendencies ush-ered in by industrialization, they usually supported political reaction or conservatism. For the landed aristocracy, education followed the doctrine of "appropriateness," which held that there was a predeter-mined and appropriate kind of education for each social class. As they saw it, the function of education was to maintain the political and social status quo by transmitting the cultural heritage.

In contrast to the conservatism of the agricultural aristocracy and gentry, the new claimants for political and social power, the middle class, were attracted to liberalism. Much nineteenth-century history records the power struggles between the old aristocracy and the mid-dle class. As the rising class, the middle class challenged the political status quo, which denied them the power commensurate to their eco-nomic position. When it encountered the obstacles of entrenched custom, tradition, and established religion, the middle class took a revolutionary stance designed to further the course of social change. Although they occasionally resorted to violent revolution as in the American and French revolutions and had participated in some of the revolutionary activities of 1848, the middle class usually avoided violent confrontations that jeopardized their property holdings. They came to prefer either the workings of what they regarded as natural laws of supply and demand or gradualistic attempts to effect change by parliamentary and evolutionary means.

Since the middle class opposed the restraints of the status quo, they also opposed traditional aristocratic education. They were usually dissenters from established churches and opposed the close alliance between school and church. Although often members of nonconformist churches, they actively sought to disengage education from religious domination. Since they preferred evolutionary and peaceful parliamentary processes of political change, they believed that a literate and educated citizenry was necessary for the proper functioning of representative political institutions. Naively, like Horace Mann, they believed that schooling would improve each individual to the point that the whole society would be reformed. A minority of middle-class liberals carried the concept of laissez faire into educational arrangements. This minority asserted that as a private matter educational arrangements were best conducted on a "cash and carry" basis. The majority of the members of the middle class, however, sought to advance programs of popular education but were opposed to the traditional educational modes, which emphasized either religious indoctrination or the exclusive study of classical languages.

The third major class on the nineteenth-century political, social, and economic scene was the industrial working class, which Marx called the proletariat. These were workers who had migrated to the cities, where factory work was available, and formed an industrialized, mass urban population. Urbanization was a significant result of industrialization. For example, the English city of Manchester had a population of 40,000 people in 1774. By 1831, its population had increased more than six times, to 271,000. The concentration of population in large cities was one of the major characteristics of the nineteenth century.

The life of the workers who manned the mills, mines, and factories was the social consequence of industrialization. Uprooted from their rural environment, the working classes soon lost touch with the values and traditions of their former village heritage. Often victimized by the economic and social policies of their employers, the industrial working class became the dispossessed of the early nineteenth century. Yet this discontented class served as the lever that effected dramatic social changes at the end of the nineteenth century and in the twentieth century.

Although the older conservative aristocracy and the newer middle-class liberals halfheartedly competed for their support, the socialist ideology had the greatest appeal to the working class. At first, enlightened utopian socialists like Robert Owen sought to ameliorate the workingman's depressed condition through educational reforms and the creation of model factory communities. When the utopian socialists had little impact in effecting major reforms, the urban factory workers turned to the various "scientific" socialists.

This chapter will examine the various ideologies of liberalism, conservatism, and socialism in terms of their social, political, economic, and educational consequences. These more clearly defined political ideologies must be interpreted against the background of the social conditions already alluded to and must also be considered in the light of romanticism and nationalism, which, although more emotional than rational, had a profound effect on the development of Western culture and education in the nineteenth century.

Liberalism

Liberalism was one of the strong ideological crosscurrents felt throughout the Western world. Of the various nineteenth-century ideologies, it was most closely related to the Enlightenment's ideals of intellectual, religious, and economic freedom. Reflecting the middle-class ethic, liberals stressed individualism in the belief that each man should be allowed to reach that stature and attainment that his abilities allowed. Intellectually, they argued for freedom of thought; economically, they opted for free trade and freedom of contract; politically, they saw the state as a "passive policeman" whose functions were to maintain order, enforce contracts, and preserve property.

One major achievement of nineteenth-century liberalism was that it tended to democratize political life by gradually extending suffrage. For example, the English Reform Bills of 1832 and 1867 both extended suffrage; property qualifications for suffrage were removed in many of the states during the American Jacksonian period. Liberalism placed authority in constitutional forms of parliamentary government and in elected representative assemblies. As a political, economic, and social philosophy, liberalism was supported by middle-class business and professional groups. During the first half of the nineteenth century, liberal forces promoted "negative" legislation that restricted government powers. As advocates of individualism, liberal parties enacted legislation that protected freedom of speech, press, assembly, and religion. Although they disagreed as to the degree and scope to which formal schooling should be made available, liberals generally contributed to the extension of popular education.

By the middle of the nineteenth century, liberalism revealed an inner tension that produced a split in its ranks between those who adhered to the strict interpretation of laissez-faire principles and those who recommended "positive" social legislation to provide welfare benefits for the greatest number of people. The liberal proponents of classical laissez-faire economic and social theories were inspired by Adam Smith's *Inquiry into the Nature and Causes of the Wealth of Nations* (1776), Thomas Malthus' *Essay on the Principle of Population,* and David Ricardo's works on wages and prices. Of the three writers, Smith was most influential in providing the theoretical justification used by nineteenth-century business interests in support of their economic policies of rugged competition. Smith's theories were based on the fundamental thesis that economic institutions originated naturally and are subject to natural economic laws that function progressively when not interfered with by human legislation. Any restriction of the free flow of commerce is mischievously detrimental to the smooth and automatic functioning of these natural economic laws. According to Smith's followers, government's proper functions are restricted to the preservation of life and property. Government should conform to natural conditions rather than try to regulate the economy through legislation. These disciples of unregulated individualism believed that the state's functions should be restricted to those that are absolutely necessary. Rather than being a "positive" institution, government should be restricted to ensuring that free trade and private competition flourish. The liberal proponents of individual initiative believed that genuine progress resulted only from competition and individual effort. In the 1870s, 1880s, and 1890s, the advocates of laissez-faire individualism received support from the works of Herbert Spencer and William Graham Sumner, who were then highly regarded as social scientists. Relying heavily on Darwin's biological theories and transferring them to society, the social Darwinists reasserted Smith's thesis that progress results from individual effort and from competition.

In contrast, those liberals who took a reformed position saw the state in an ameliorative relationship to the individual. Unlike the classical liberals of the Manchester school, they believed that the state, as the largest and most effective of human institutions, had to be relied upon to introduce certain needed benefits to the majority of the population. This group had been influenced by Jeremy Bentham's "philosophical radicalism," which asserted that the goal of society is to promote the "greatest happiness of the greatest number." Bentham said that if each person were free to seek his own happiness with as little restraint as possible, then the end result would ensure the greatest general happiness. In an industrial society, it is necessary, however, to enact some minimum of legislation to raise the general level of life so that this "greatest happiness" might be secured. Those liberals who allocated some minimal powers to the state for the enactment of social legislation began to look upon programs of popular education as a means of ensuring that each man would be sufficiently enlightened to recognize and to pursue his genuine interests.

John Stuart Mill (1806–1873) was an articulate advocate of the doctrines of the new, or "reformed," liberalism. His writings *The Principles of Political Economy* (1848), *On Liberty* (1859), and *Autobiography* (1873) represented a humanitarian modification of the classical liberalism expressed by Malthus, Smith, and Ricardo. Mill's liberalism modified strict laissez-faire economic theory and recognized that social reform was needed. Although the "modern Liberals" believed that most reformation was carried on more efficiently by private rather than public agencies, they came to believe that certain general programs of reform, such as popular education, needed governmental encouragement.

Mill's primary concern was that individual liberty be preserved in the context of an organized society. His problem was to provide a reconciliation of individual and private happiness with that of the general welfare. He recognized that the task of maintaining individual liberties in a mass society is a difficult one. Individual liberty demands, Mill said, freedom of conscience, thought, feeling, taste, and pursuit. It requires the freedom to form opinion by pursuing speculative, scientific, moral, theological, and practical inquiries so that man can weigh alternatives rationally and make the choices that genuinely secure his liberty.

As a true liberal, Mill resisted those conceptions of the organic society that saw the social order as a great vast mechanism in which men are functioning parts. For Mill, society rests upon its individaul members. When men join together in society, their mutual association does not take precedence over their individual rights and freedoms. Rather the liberty of each individual is extended to encompass the whole of the society. Mill, did not however, recommend social anarchy; he believed that each individual's liberty is legitimately limited in that he is not to infringe on the legitimate spheres of action of other individuals. He recognized the dangers posed by the coming of a mass industrialized society, and he opposed the conformity of each individual to the mass. Such conformity would be pernicious to individual liberty and would stifle the development of individual personality. Although the majority has a legitimate right to express itself in opinion and in legislation, the minority also has the right to dissent from the majority view.

It can be seen that clearly defined philosophies of education can be extrapolated from the contrasting doctrines of the two schools of liberalism, classical and modern. Both schools would agree on the primacy of the individual and would insist on his freedom to inquire and to learn. Like the freedoms of speech, press, and assembly, educational freedom would be interpreted as a freedom that is the individual right of each man. Classical liberals resisted state-supported educational systems, fearing that the intrusion of government into education would jeopardize educational freedom, whereas modern liberals accepted an educational role for government and believed that a mass social system requires a large-scale system of popular education. In terms of a social ethic, classical liberals asserted that genuine human progress results from competition. Modern liberals, in contrast, opted for cooperative action in matters that have widespread social consequences.

Liberalism and Popular Education

Although some liberals like Herbert Spencer opposed it, liberals generally supported and sought to advance programs of popular education under state auspices. Liberals had mixed motives for supporting such programs. Some believed that popular education would advance enlightenment and secure human progress by widely diffusing scientific and practical knowledge. Business interests, which usually supported liberal parties and policies, hoped to indoctrinate the working masses in what they regarded as sound economic principles and thus make them resistant to anarchist and socialist propaganda. Generally, liberal political parties regarded popular education under state auspices as a functional instrument for propagating civic, economic, social, and moral responsibility.

Before the 1860s, the vast majority of Europeans were still illiterate. Only Prussia, some of the other northern German states, and the Scandinavian kingdoms boasted widespread literacy. Beginning with the 1860s, the movement to mass systems of popular education was stimulated by several tendencies:

1. Industrialization had provided the necessary surplus funds to establish and maintain large-scale national systems of elementary schools.
2. Urbanization, with its concentration of population masses in cities, facilitated popular education by making it possible to conduct schools more efficiently than had been possible in sparsely populated rural villages.
3. Traditional values and family structures had been weakened by industrialization and urbanization.

The business classes who had reaped the profits of industrialization gradually came to support popular educational systems as a means of maintaining social stability and increasing economic productivity. They came to believe that popular education would counteract the increase of crime and vice that accompanied the migration of peasants to the city and ward off Marxist, socialist, and anarchist enticements that might mislead an ignorant working class.

Under liberal auspices—or at least with liberal support—systems of state-supported and state-directed elementary schools were established throughout most of Europe in the late 1860s, 1870s, and 1880s. Such school systems were inaugurated in Hungary in 1868; Austria, 1869; England, 1870; Switzerland, 1874; the Netherlands, 1876; Italy, 1877; Belgium, 1879; and France, 1881. By the time of the Civil War, the common school movement in the United States had accomplished its aim of achieving popular systems of elementary schools in most of the states. After 1865, common schools were established in the southern states. As various new states entered the Union, they, too, established common elementary school systems.

When state-supported and controlled elementary school systems were established, they generally reflected the liberal antagonism to clerical control of education. Existing religious schools were often stripped of their privileged position, reduced to private status, and deprived of state subsidization. The establishment of state schools was usually followed by the enactment of laws requiring compulsory attendance by every child. The degree to which these laws were enforced varied according to the priority given to education by the various national governments. Nevertheless, the establishment of state systems of education and the enactment of compulsory school attendance laws increased the rate of literacy among the populations of the nations of western Europe and North America.

Conservatism

Conservatism was a reaction against eighteenth-century rationalism—the social philosophy of the French Revolution—and nineteenth-century liberalism. Although he lived in the eighteenth century, Edmund Burke (1729–1797) was a cogent spokesman for the conservative ideology. Burke's *Reflections on the Revolution in France* (1790) attacked the concept of radical, or revolutionary, social reconstruction. Like most conservatives, he believed that genuine change resulted only from gradual historical processes. Burke believed that the "supposed reforms" of the French Revolution had only served to increase the tempo of violence. If unchecked, the disequilibrium that resulted from the premature forcing of social change would destroy society and induce a new age of barbarism. In denying that social institutions could or should be radically transformed, Burke stressed the principle of historical continuity, which was sacred to conservatives. He believed that civilization is a continuum that unites the dead, the living, and posterity. Each generation of man, past, present, and future, is a link in the chain of humanity that transcends the ages. Inherited language, traditions, religion, and rituals meaningfully identify contemporary man with his past and serve to prepare a place for posterity in the social and cultural order. Social class distinctions give each individual a clearly assigned place in the functioning of an organic society.

The conservatives found much of their support among the landed aristocracy, the rural gentry, and the tradition-bound peasantry. They found an important ally in established state churches. They also identified with legitimate dynastic monarchies that provided strong focal points for national loyalty.

Unlike their liberal opponents who emphasized change, conservatives stressed the necessity for social stability. Conservatives like the Austrian diplomat Metternich believed that change, at best, should be reduced to a minimum. When absolutely necessary, social change should be accepted only grudgingly. Moreover, it should be carefully conditioned by the past and occur within the contours of tradition and religion.

Advocates of conservatism held that the proper role of education is to preserve language and tradition by transmitting the cultural heritage to the young so that they can assume their predetermined roles. Education, both formal and informal, should provide class skills and values to the immature so that they can fit into the social order of the state. In short, the basic objective of education should be to preserve the status quo and maintain cultural continuity.

As mentioned above, conservatives were usually allied with established religious orthodoxies. In England, they supported the Anglican Church; in France, Italy, and Spain, the Roman Catholic Church; and in Russia, the Orthodox Church. They believed that the value component in education was best conveyed through the medium of religious education, supported and reinforced by a stable family life. When they favored state systems of education, they did so out of a sense of paternalism and preferred that religious authorities exercise a dominant role. Since they wished to preserve the cultural heritage, they advocated a curriculum that idealized the past and emphasized literature, through which the young would learn traditions, values, and rituals that would unite them with the past in an unending flow of cultural continuity. The literary education conservatives favored often leaned heavily on the Greek and Latin classics.

Socialism

Among the urban working classes, the various types of socialism met with a friendly response. Such utopian socialists as Saint-Simon, Fourier, and Owen hoped to regenerate society by means of voluntary cooperative communities. So-called "scientific socialists" followed Karl Marx, who in the *Communist Manifesto* and *Das Kapital* urged proletarian revolution, or class warfare, in order to seize the means of production. During the course of the nineteenth century, the scientific socialists split into two broad groups: democratic socialists, who believed that society could be socialized through parliamentary means; and Marxist communists, who believed that socialism could come only through revolution.

The French utopian socialist Claude Henri de Rouvroy, comte de Saint-Simon (1760–1825), was an economic determinist, that is, he believed that economic forces determined the course of history. Saint-Simon wrote that the historical process was a record of continuous conflict between hostile economic classes. As a consequence of industrialization, the old military and religious elite was unable to adapt to social change and attempted to obstruct progress. In place of these obsolete ruling classes, Saint-Simon argued that a managerial elite of experts, chosen for technological competencies, should be entrusted with the task of forming a rational government. Although a predecessor of other utopian socialists, Saint-Simon did not underestimate the incentives that property provides in stimulating productive labor.

Unlike Saint-Simon, Charles Fourier (1772–1837) did not trust a government of managerial experts. He felt that mankind everywhere should be organized into small cooperative, self-governing communities, called phalansteries. Machinery, land, buildings, equipment, and natural resources were to be commonly owned by the members of the phalanstery, and profits were to be divided among them. Fourier regarded education as a natural ally. Like most utopian socialists, he believed that his ideas could be diffused by educational means. Education, rather than revolution, was to be the instrument for persuading men to accept the ideals of a cooperative society. The phalanstery itself also held educational implications. As model communities, phalansteries were to be so successful that men would seek to live under such beneficent conditions and would construct their own communities. Eventually, the earth would be governed by federations of phalansteries, peacefully coexisting with one another.

Robert Owen's Communitarian Socialism

Among the utopian socialists, Robert Owen (1771–1858) stands out as an individual who most enthusiastically attempted to forge an ideological and working alliance between communitarian socialism and education. Owen, a rather eccentric philanthropist, has been credited with being a pioneer of factory legislation in Great Britain, the first proponent of the infant school, and an early advocate of popular education. He was a humane capitalist who believed that employers had a moral responsibility to improve the living conditions of their workmen. Believing that man was a product of his environment, he set out to reform and reconstruct that environment. When he took possession of the mills at New Lanark, Scotland, Owen was appalled at the living and working conditions that he found there and quickly set about cleaning streets and dwellings, abolished the sale of liquor, and generally improved hygienic standards in the village of two thousand inhabitants.

As a utopian socialist, Owen relied on the processes of peaceful change to secure social reform. He turned to education, which he believed was one of the most potent instruments that man possessed to shape his environment and ultimately himself. Owen's conception of education was broad enough to encompass both formal schooling and the environment. He recognized that informal educational agencies, such as the family and the community, had a strong formative effect on children. Unlike Pestalozzi who emphasized the loving family as a necessary ingredient in successful education, Owen felt that the family could be an obstacle to the improvement of individual and social character. He preferred, instead, that the entire model community act as a kind of extended family. Among the educational principles that governed Owen's school at New Lanark were the following:

1. Man's character is formed by his environment.
2. Education is a major force in the formation of individual and social character.
3. Education should foster an ethical system based upon the premise of community welfare.
4. Learning should relate to action rather than words and should emphasize the necessary consequences that result from action.
5. Children should be treated with kindness rather than severity.
6. All artificial rewards and punishments should be removed from the school.

Owen's concept of the infant school derived from his belief that children should enter school as early as possible in order to escape being habituated in the accumulated wrong habits and superstitions that parents impose on their children. Like Rousseau and Pestalozzi, he opposed the excessive verbalism that characterized traditional schooling. In Owen's schools, children were not to be annoyed by the premature introduction of books, which he believed hindered genuine character formation. Following a method that bore some resemblance to Pestalozzianism, Owen's students studied natural objects.

Spurred on by his success with early childhood education, Owen was encouraged to establish the Institute for the Formation of Character, which included advanced schools, meeting halls, and community rooms as well as an infant, or nursery, school. Owen's model community and educational institute at New Lanark were so successful that they attracted a steady stream of visitors. Over a ten-year period, twenty thousand visitors inscribed their names in the institute's "Visitor's Book." Like most of the utopian socialists and humanitarian reformers of the nineteenth century, Owen had an unbounded faith that education was the key to human progress:

> . . . I know that society may be formed so as to exist without crime, without poverty, with health greatly improved, with little, if any, misery, and with intelligence and happiness increased a hundredfold; and no obstacle whatsoever intervenes at this moment, except ignorance, to prevent such a state of society from becoming universal.[2]

Owen's eldest son, Robert Dale Owen, wrote a short account of his father's educational and social experiment at New Lanark that clearly revealed the utopian's firm belief that the proper kind of communitarian education would alleviate social ills and reduce socioeconomic class antagonism. Robert Dale Owen's belief that education could unify the interests of all social classes sharply contrasted with Marx's call for class warfare. According to Robert Dale Owen:

> . . . the lower classes cannot receive such an education, and yet remain in their present ignorant and degraded state. We admit, that it will make them intelligent and excellent characters.— That when they are placed in a situation which is really improper, it will necessarily make them desirous of changing and improving it. We admit, that the real distance between the lowest and the highest ranks will be decreased. That the ultimate result will be such an improvement of habits, dispositions, and general character in those in subordinate situations, as will induce us to regard them in the light of assistants rather than of dependents. We admit, that its general introduction will gradually render all ranks much more liberal, better informed, more accomplished, and more virtuous than the inhabitants of Great Britain are at this moment. And that, in short, its direct tendency will be to enlighten the

2 Frank Podmore, *Robert Owen* (New York: D. Appleton, 1924), I, 130.

world, to raise all classes without lowering any one, and to reform mankind from the least event to the greatest.[3]

Robert Owen became increasingly convinced that nonsectarian communitarianism was the only means that could check the social disintegration caused by the excesses of the Industrial Revolution. In 1824, he felt that the time had arrived to extend his social and educational experiment beyond England to North America. He purchased the Indiana town of New Harmony from the Rappite religious community and hoped to establish a "new moral world" on the American frontier. In this community on the banks of the Wabash, private property was to be abolished, and enlightened men were to work to create the cooperative commonwealth. Owen anticipated that New Harmony would be so successful that other communities would be established in emulation. The community was to be equalitarian in all matters:

> All members of the community shall be considered as one family, and no one shall be held in higher or lower estimation on account of occupation. There shall be similar food, clothing, and education, as near as can be furnished, for all according to their ages; and, as soon as practicable, all shall live in similar houses, and in all respects be accommodated alike. Every member shall render his or her best services for the good of the whole, according to the rules and regulations that may be hereafter adopted by the community. It shall always remain a primary object of the community to give the best physical, moral, and intellectual education to all its members.[4]

As a utopian communitarian socialist, Owen wanted to effect social reconstruction through peaceful rather than violent means and turned to education as the instrument to accomplish the desired goals. He was joined in his experiment by a dedicated band of Pestalozzian educators, notably William Maclure, Joseph Neef, and Marie Duclos Fretageot, who were charged with establishing the New Harmony school system. Pestalozzian educational theory was compatible with Owenism since it rested on the premise that social and personal regeneration could be accomplished through education. The Owenites and Pestalozzians who gathered at New Harmony conceived of their communitarian experiment as a lever that could exert upon society the force needed to bring about social reconstruction.

Arthur Bestor, a distinguished commentator on communitarianism, has remarked:

[3] Robert Dale Owen, *An Outline of the System of Education at New Lanark* (Cincinnati: Deming and Wood Printers, 1825), p. 27.
[4] George B. Lockwood, *The New Harmony Movement* (New York: D. Appleton, 1905), pp. 105–108.

More remarkable even than the communitarian's interest in education was the complementary tendency of educational reformers to think in communitarian terms. To begin with, schoolmen of the early nineteenth century were giving increased attention to the social context of education. So long as this wider outlook inspired no more than an adjustment of the curriculum to changes in society, it had few implications for the reform movement generally. But there were educationists to whom the relationship between school and society appeared a reciprocal one. The school should respond to social change, they held, but it should also be an instrument for effecting desirable alterations in society. In their hands educational reform became a branch of social reform.[5]

Owen's "New Moral World" at New Harmony lasted for less than two years before it disintegrated. Its fate was one that befell most communitarian enterprises organized on a nonreligious basis. There was a lack of practical administrative planning. Disagreements between the major principals, Owen and Maclure, weakened the community. The ill-sorted group of intellectual visionaries did more debating than community-building. Nevertheless, Owen's experiment at New Harmony is a valuable episode for study by educational historians since it represented the transfer of European social and educational theories to North America. It also clearly revealed the weaknesses that occurred when utopian socialists sought to translate their theories into actuality.

The scientific socialism of Karl Marx, which had a major impact on Western social and political philosophy, will be treated in detail in Chapter 15. Many of Marx's ideas were derived from concepts enunciated by the utopian socialists. His theory of class warfare was a reaction to the utopians' belief that social reform could be secured peacefully and through education.

Humanitarianism

Although large numbers of the agricultural and industrial poor were victims of an exploitative capitalism during the nineteenth century, this period also revealed a decided inclination toward humanitarianism, which first took the form of private reforming efforts by benevolent individuals such as Pestalozzi and Owen. In the later nineteenth century, humanitarian efforts were increasingly institutionalized into larger corporate agencies. By the beginning of the twentieth century, humanitarianism had reached the point of becoming a governmental activity. Many of the social activities of the

[5] Arthur E. Bestor, Jr. *Backwoods Utopias: The Sectarian and Owenite Phases of Communitarian Socialism in America, 1663–1829* (Philadelphia: University of Pennsylvania Press, 1950), pp. 134–135.

twentieth century "welfare state" regimes in England and the Scandinavian countries grew out of these humanitarian impulses.

Among the various humanitarian crusades that flourished during the nineteenth century were some that had a definite educational impact. The need for humanitarian reform was stimulated by and was symptomatic of the influx of population to the cities. In its raw years, urbanization unleashed a host of social ills that continue to haunt Western man even in the scientific and technological age of the twentieth century.

The transformation that occurred as Western man changed from an agricultural to an industrial mode of life had profound social and psychic consequences as well as economic and political ones. In an obvious physical sense, the haphazard growth of cities ignored human sensitivities. The city dweller was often a former peasant who had been uprooted from his pastoral environment, with its long-established mores, folkways, and traditions. The dehumanizing work routines of mass production destroyed the sense of craftmanship associated with handicraft production. Working conditions under early capitalism were geared to realizing the greatest profit for the manufacturer. Crowded into urban slums, the workers were too often ready to channel their discontent and malaise into socially destructive and personally disintegrative behavior. With long hours being spent in factories, family stability was shaken as entire families worked until exhausted in poorly lighted, unventilated, and unsafe factories, mills, and mines.

As a response to the changing conditions of economic and social life, humanitarian reformers proposed a variety of panaceas to soothe man's ills. In the belief that the consumption of alcoholic drink was the cause of human debilitation, some reformers founded temperance societies to abolish the consumption of alcohol and thus eliminate the social ills by alcoholism. Others turned their attention to penal reform. Prisons, they believed, should be used for rehabilitation rather than punishment. Still others joined movements to bring about a reformed utopian society where poverty, crime, and vice would be forever banished. Other individuals and groups sought to remove the blight of war from mankind by organizing peace movements. In the United States, the humanitarian impulse took the form of the northern abolitionist movement that sought to eradicate Negro slavery.

All the reforming humanitarian movements had educational consequences. Individuals and groups wanted to find a place for their particular social conceptions in formal education. Press and podium were used to propagandize for various social panaceas. In addition, mass education itself was often regarded as a means of alleviating social problems, conflicts, and tensions. Some of the programs for mass education were naively conceived and were reduced to simplis-

tic formulas for achieving basic literacy. The Sunday School movement, originating in England, was designed to impart religious values
and reading, writing, and arithmetic to working-class children who
were released from their toil on the Lord's day. Robert Owen, the
English humanitarian and utopian, proposed a program of infant
schools designed to provide a wholesome environment for the young
children of factory operatives. Johann Heinrich Pestalozzi, the Swiss
educational reformer, devised a system on natural education that attempted to create a wholesome and loving environment in which
children could learn basic skills and habits. Andrew Bell, an Anglican
minister, and Joseph Lancaster, a Quaker teacher, simultaneously
proposed monitorial schools in which large numbers of children could
be made literate at low financial expenditure. The rival systems of
monitorial education were based on the idea that master teachers
could instruct older students, who might then serve as teachers for
younger children. Generally, these various humanitarian reformers
made only a slight impact on the total educational structure since
their proposals and plans were inadequate to cope with the problems
created by the concentration of mass populations in urban areas.

Although in many respects the initial impetus for popular education was a simplistic yearning for a panacea for personal and social
ills, the movement also reflected social class aspirations and status-
seeking. As indicated, popular education was also related to the
various programs of political parties that represented class interests.
Conservative aristocrats saw mass education as a means of fixing
loyalties to national traditions. The liberal middle class saw it as a
way of bringing about universal literacy, which would make workmen more efficient and less prone to radicalism and socialism. The
working classes saw popular education as a means of upward social
mobility, if not for them, then for their children.

Romanticism and Nationalism

The nineteenth century must also be explained in terms of the
forces of romanticism and nationalism, which rampantly cut across
the line of ideological demarcation, as well as by the more clearly
defined socioeconomic and political dogmas of liberalism, conservatism, and socialism. Nationalism in particular profoundly affected
educational development. It was during the nineteenth century that
the national educational systems were either created or extended.
These educational systems invariably stressed the value of loyalty to
the national state.

As an intellectual and aesthetic current of the early nineteenth
century, romanticism was a reaction against the classicism and ra-

tionalism of the Enlightenment. Although both rationalists and romantics emphasized nature as a crucial theme, the rationalist philosophe saw nature as a universal mechanism that operated according to an intrinsic set of natural laws. These discoverable natural laws were believed to contain the means by which man could control his own destiny. In contrast, the romantic saw nature as a mysterious, brooding, and beautiful life force that man could not really analyze but only love with the fullness of his emotions. The nineteenth-century romanticists therefore did not attempt to analyze nature but sought rather to interpret her moods so that man could attain a greater empathy with the universe. While the rationalist believed that man's reason would enable him to control his destiny and reconstruct his society, the romantic protested against an oversimplification of man and society. Insisting on the intricacy and complexity of human nature, the romantic emphasized man as an emotional and volitional being who was directed more by his feelings than by his intellect. While the rationalist view of history held that man through the use of his reason was moving ever onward to a better life, the romantic believed that human destiny was linked to the past in an unbroken flow of experience.

Whereas such eighteenth-century rationalists as Diderot, Condillac, and Condorcet had conceived of nature as an orderly, precise, and logical mechanism, Coleridge, Wordsworth, and other romantics found inspiration in a conception of nature that was vague, misty, and marvelous. Romantic artists favored such themes as the mysteries of the night, the majesty of nature, and the stress of the approaching storm.

The reaction against rationalism was not evident in literature, where the romantic temperament revealed itself by projecting human emotions into natural forces. Sir Walter Scott (1771–1832), the leading prose writer among the British romanticists and one of the creators of the historical novel, expressing a melancholy yearning for the Gothic style of the age of chivalry, portrayed heroic persons and events of that era. England produced a galaxy of romantic poets, such as Byron, Shelley, Keats, and Coleridge. One of the greatest of them, William Wordsworth (1770–1850), conceived of nature as a vitalizing and energetic life force that expressed itself in a myriad number of situations. It was the task of the poet, he believed, to raise these commonplace situations to a higher level of human experience by emphasizing and glorifying them.

In Germany more than in England, romanticism was a reaction against French rationalism. Young German intellectuals, who experienced feelings of uprootedness, uncertainty, and frustration as a result of the humiliation and defeat of Prussia by Napoleon, infused romanticism with the spirit of Germanic cultural nationalism. They turned to poetry and philosophy to create a *Weltanschauung*, a total world and life view, that distinguished German romanticism from the purely literary and aesthetic movement that generally characterized romanticism elsewhere in Europe. German intellectuals like Fichte, Herder, and Jahn united nationalism and romanticism by their patriotic appeals for German unity.

In their request to discover and reassert common Germanic origins, the German romantics turned to the past—to history and to tradition. The idealist philosopher Johann Gottfried von Herder (1744–1803) examined Germanic folklore and believed that he detected therein the presence of a *Volksgeist*, or spirit at work among the German people. Herder sought to purify German literature to free it from what he regarded to be the artificial and devitalizing influences of French style. His primary objective was to install in Germans a sense of identity and pride in their origins. Herder's cultural nationalism, tinged by influences of romaticism and idealism, contributed to the concept of the folk nation. For Herder, each nation was an organic personality distinguished by a unique national heredity, language, traditions, and spirit. In contrast to the Enlightenment doctrines with their emphasis on individual rights, romantic cultural nationalism postulated a community in which men shared an organic association of spiritual and cultural values. In such an organic community, each man could realize himself as an individual only by accepting and identifying with the folk spirit of the national community.

Johann Gottlieb Fichte (1762–1814), a German philosopher who combined aspects of Platonic idealism and Rousseauist naturalism, was familiar with the educational theory of Pestalozzi and incorporated it in his *Addresses to the German People* (1808), which were written to stimulate Germanic regeneration. Fichte believed that a reinvigorated system of education could do much to promote the German national identity and thereby achieve German unification. Herder and Fichte urged the formation of a working alliance between the state and the educator in order to strengthen the Germanic culture and way of life.

Cultural nationalism in Germany, as well as in other nations of the West, was extending from literary and artistic works to political, economic, and social life. Like romanticism, nationalism was an irrational and mystical force that reconciled and unified discordant elements. The French revolutionary and Napoleonic armies, inspired by slogans of "liberty, equality, and fraternity," carried with them the spirit of French nationalism. In response, the Germans, Spaniards, and Russians asserted their own national consciousness. The force of nationalism found entry into both liberal and conservative political camps. Even the socialists, who talked of a working-class unity that transcended national boundaries, were not immune to the nationalistic impulse. As the old attachments to the local community, to the dynasty, or to the church were eroded by the processes of industrialization, the nation became a new unifying and integrating force. A consciousness based on common descent, language, religion, tradition, history, and economic interests cut across class and political lines to achieve a sense of national identity.

The blurred edges of nationalism cut across the neat distinctions of political ideologists and affected all areas of life, including education. The nation-state system was the basis of world-wide political organization. Although individuals might communicate and cooperate across the impediments raised by national boundaries, the national state was the unit upon which political authority rested. According to the concept of national sovereignty, each nation had the right to set its own boundaries, establish its own government forms, and make its own internal domestic arrangements. Closely tied to political sovereignty was the conception of cultural nationality. Each nation claimed a common historical experience, language, religion, and tradition and came to assert a particular style of institutional and aesthetic life.

Since the late eighteenth century, nationalism has been a major force in education. National systems of education were organized not only to bring about popular literacy but also to generate commitment and loyalty to the aims of the nation-state. A major emphasis in the national systems of education was placed on the study of the national language, history, and literature. Good citizenship was construed as the manifestation of obedience and duty to the nation. Although the nationalistic impulse in education fixed loyalties and provided for a core of integration that went beyond socioeconomic class lines, it often had the negative effect of producing a chauvinistic attitude toward other peoples and countries. Nationalism drew support not only from the peoples of the major Western nations but also from the submerged nationalities of Central and Eastern Europe. Although the causes of World War I were many, the precipitating event was the assassination of Archduke Francis Ferdinand, heir to the Hapsburg throne, in the streets of the Sarajevo on June 28, 1914, which resulted from a conspiracy by a group of Serbian patriots who believed that Bosnia should be united to Slavic Serbia rather than be ruled by the Teutonic Hapsburg. It was this initial clash between the rival forces of Slavic and Germanic nationalism that brought about the war that dramatically changed the old order of life.

Nationalism was also a motivating factor in the imperialist quest of the Western European powers for colonies in Africa and Asia. Each nation tried to secure its "place in the sun" by conquering and exploiting the subject colonial peoples. England, France, Germany, Belgium, and Italy sought to establish empires. When the Western powers established their empires, they also exported their educational systems to the conquered lands.

Conclusion

The nineteenth century was an age in which certain of the social, political, economic, and educational ideas of the Enlightenment were cast into the form of particular ideologies and programs, such as liberalism, conservatism, and socialism. It was also a time of reaction to eighteenth-century rationalism. Romanticism, in particular, was such a reaction against the primacy of reason. Even romanticism, however, had origins in Rousseau's social philosophy. The current of nationalism, coming out of the American and French revolutions and the Napoleonic wars, was a strong force throughout the nineteenth and into the twentieth centuries.

A number of the remaining chapters of this book will deal with themes that were born in the nineteenth century. For example, the educational work of Pestalozzi, Froebel, and Montessori were part of the nineteenth-century milieu. Karl Marx's communism and Herbert Spencer's social Darwinism were social, political, and economic philosophies that had strong educational implications.

Suggested Readings

Artz, Frederick. *Reaction and Revolution, 1814–1832.* New York: Harper and Brothers, 1934.

Ashton, Thomas S. *The Industrial Revolution, 1760–1830.* New York: Oxford University Press, 1954.

Bestor, Arthur E., Jr. *Backwoods Utopias: The Sectarian and Owenite Phases of Communitarian Socialism in America, 1663–1829.* Philadelphia: University of Pennsylvania Press, 1950.

Binkley, R. C. *Realism and Nationalism, 1852–1871.* New York: Harper and Brothers, 1935.

Bowden, Witt. *Industrial Society Towards the End of the Eighteenth Century.* New York: Barnes and Noble, 1965.

Brinton, Crane. *English Political Thought in the 19th Century.* Cambridge, Mass.: Harvard University Press, 1949.

Cole, G. D. H. *A History of Socialist Thought.* New York: St. Martin's Press, 1954.

————. *Life of Robert Owen.* New York: Macmillan, 1930.

Dietz, F. C. *The Industrial Revolution.* New York: Henry Holt, 1927.

Dobb, Maurice. *Studies in the Development of Capitalism.* New York: International Publishers, 1947.

Ergang, R. R. *Herder and the Foundations of German Nationalism.* New York: Columbia University Press, 1931.

Harrison, John F. *Quest for the New Moral World: Robert Owen and the Owenites in Britain and America*. New York: Scribner, 1969.

Harvey, Rowland Hill. *Robert Owen, Social Idealist*. Berkeley: University of California Press, 1949.

Hayes, C. J. H. *The Historical Evolution of Modern Nationalism*. New York: Richard R. Smith, 1931.

Hughes, H. Stuart. *Contemporary Europe: A History*. Englewood Cliffs, N.J.: Prentice-Hall, 1961.

Kohn, Hans. *The Idea of Nationalism: A Study in Its Origins and Backgrounds*. New York: Macmillan, 1944.

Laidler, H. W. *A History of Socialist Thought*. New York: Crowell, 1933.

Laski, Harold. *The Rise of Liberalism: The Philosophy of a Business Civilization*. New York: Harper and Brothers, 1936.

Leopold, Richard W. *Robert Dale Owen*. Cambridge, Mass.: Harvard University Press, 1940.

Lockwood, George B. *The New Harmony Movement*. New York: Augustus M. Kelley, Pub., 1969.

Manuel, F. E. *The New World of Henri Saint-Simon*. Cambridge, Mass.: Harvard University Press, 1956.

Mill, John Stuart. *Selected Writings*, Bernard Wishy (ed.). Boston: Beacon Press, 1959.

Owen, Robert. *The Life of Robert Owen, by Himself*. New York: Augustus M. Kelley, Pub., 1967.

Owen, Robert Dale. *An Outline of the System of Education at New Lanark*. Cincinnati: Deming and Wood Printers, 1825.

Podmore, Frank. *Robert Owen*. New York: Augustus M. Kelley, Pub., 1968.

Ruggiero, Guido de. *The History of European Liberalism*. Boston: Beacon Press, 1959.

Silver, Harold. *Robert Owen on Education*. Cambridge, England: Cambridge University Press, 1969.

Smith, Adam. *An Inquiry Into the Wealth of Nations*. New York: Barnes and Noble, 1950.

CHAPTER 12

Pestalozzi and Natural Education

The famous Swiss educator Johann Heinrich Pestalozzi (1746–
1827) was among those who sought to establish an educational philosophy based on a return to nature. The naturalism of the Enlightenment
had both a romantic and a scientific impact on Pestalozzi. An avid
reader of Rousseau's *Emile,* he succumbed to the romantic appeal of
the "natural man" who was unspoiled by social corruption. Like Rousseau, he attacked the excessive verbalism of traditional schooling and
advocated a pedagogical reformation based on the child's interests
and needs.

Pestalozzi was also influenced by Enlightenment rationalism. He believed, as did the eighteenth-century philosophes, that nature exhibits
patterns of regularity, or natural laws, that are relevant to human society and institutions. He hoped to discover the universal natural laws
that govern learning and erect a "natural society" on the foundations of
such laws. Embracing Rousseau's romantic idealization of child nature, Pestalozzi accepted Enlightenment science as an instrument that
would render the misty world of primeval nature into clear ideas. His
theory of natural education thus blended romanticism and rationalism.

Pestalozzi's Life

Pestalozzi was born in Zurich of a middle-class, Protestant family of
Italian origin. The death of his father, Johann Baptiste, in 1751 left the
family of three children in an impoverished financial condition, and
Pestalozzi's mother came to rely on a servant, Barbara Schmid, or
Babeli, to manage the household. Babeli, a strong-willed woman,
effected stringent economies and dominated the Pestalozzi household.
She prevented the children from developing outside friendships, and
Johann Heinrich grew up as a highly introspective and socially isolated
child. In reminiscing about his childhood, Pestalozzi complained of his

shyness and social incompetence with children of his own age: "I knew none of their games, their exercises, their secrets; naturally, I was awkward in their midst and the object of their ridicule."[1]

Pestalozzi received a conventional education in the Zurich elementary vernacular schools and classical Latin secondary schools. He took his higher education in the Collegium Humanitatis, where he studied Latin, Greek, Hebrew, rhetoric, logic, and catechetics, and in the Collegium Carolinum, where he studied philology and philosophy. For the first time in his life, the highly introspective youth overcame his social isolation and joined a group of professors, intellectuals, and students in the Helvetic Society, a movement dedicated to reforming Swiss life and society. One of the founders of the Helvetic movement was Jean Jacques Bodmer (1699–1783), a historian, writer, and poet, who insisted that the regeneration of Swiss life could be modeled only on the simplicity and liberty that had characterized the mountaineer spirit. Pestalozzi contributed a number of articles to the Helvetic Society's journal, *The Memorial*, which attacked certain abuses and corruptions of Swiss life.

As a youth, Pestalozzi was unable to decide upon a profession. For a time, he thought of becoming a minister. Then he decided to become a lawyer, but his association with the Helvetic Society, which had been suppressed as a radical group, blocked a legal career. Finally, inspired by Rousseau's glorification of nature and by the Helvetic Society's romanticizing of rural virtues, Pestalozzi decided to become a farmer. He purchased a farm near the village of Birr in the canton of Berne. In 1769, he and his bride, Anna Schulthess, established their home on the farm, which they called Neuhof. The following year, the couple's only child was born; Pestalozzi named him Jean Jacques after his hero, Rousseau.

Neuhof

In 1774, Pestalozzi added a spinning mill to his farm at Neuhof and established a school for poor children, which was to combine working and learning. He gathered from the vicinity fifty pauper boys and girls, ranging in age from six to eighteen, and fed and clothed them. Pestalozzi's experiment at Neuhof was based on the belief that the child is naturally active. He believed that the educator should capitalize on the child's need for activity by providing exercises that stimulated vocational, moral, and intellectual development. He also believed that the learning of vocational skills would contribute to the child's self-respect and economic independence. Pestalozzi's educational practices at Neuhof also emphasized home education. He wanted his institution

[1] Mary Romana Walch, *Pestalozzi and the Pestalozzian Theory of Education: A Critical Study* (Washington: Catholic University Press, 1952), pp. 3–4.

to resemble a family that worked and learned together. A gentle man by nature, Pestalozzi wanted to preside over his educational family as a father figure rather than as a pedantic taskmaster.

During the summer, the children learned agricultural skills by doing gardening and field work. In winter, they engaged in spinning and handicraft production. As they worked, Pestalozzi attempted to teach reading, writing, arithmetic, and religion by means of group recitations which the children repeated as they worked in the fields or at the spinning wheel. The girls also learned cooking and sewing.

Pestalozzi's experiment at Neuhof failed financially, and the school closed in 1779, having enjoyed only five years of existence. Pestalozzi attributed this failure to his own administrative ineptness rather than to unsound pedagogy. Neuhof gave Pestalozzi his first real experience with the poor, whom he wanted to save from economic and cultural deprivation. Often, however, the very people he tried to help were suspicious of the eccentric reformer and accused him of trying to exploit them for his own profit.

Pestalozzi's Writings

Financially destitute because of his losses at Neuhof, Pestalozzi tried to support his family by writing. From 1780 to 1798, he wrote and articulated his philosophy of natural education. He had already written a short work, *How Father Pestalozzi Instructed His Three and a Half Year Old Son*, in 1774, and *Essays on the Education of the Children of the Poor* and the *Evening Hours of a Hermit* from 1775 to 1778. His successful novel, *Leonard and Gertrude*, appeared in 1781, and its reprinting in 1783, 1785, and 1787 brought fame to its author. In emulation of Rousseau's *Emile*, *Leonard and Gertrude* was intended to publicize Pestalozzi's conviction that natural education could bring about individual and social regeneration. Although widely read as a romantic folk novel, the book's educational message was neglected.

The locale of *Leonard and Gertrude* was the fictional village of Bonnal, where simple but honest villagers were exploited by the corrupt bailiff who also owned the village tavern. Although the introduction of cotton spinning had increased their income, the villagers were victimized by their own ignorance as workers and consumers as well as by the bailiff's machinations. The novel's beneficent forces were the local nobleman, who personified paternalistic government, the pastor, who represented religion, and the teacher, who practiced natural education. These good men rallied around the heroine, Gertrude, the perfect working-class wife and mother, whose home was a true reflection of Pestalozzi's educational philosophy. She gave her children lessons in sensory education and guided their observations of nature. She also trained them in the work that supported the family.

Pestalozzi's plot in *Leonard and Gertrude* was intended to demonstrate his basic educational thesis. Gertrude, the loving mother, was a model that could be emulated by parents and teachers who sought to educate children according to natural principles. Living in an emotionally secure home, Gertrude's children had been able to develop their innate goodness and were capable of resisting the evils that flourished in a corrupt society. If enough individuals were educated according to Gertrude's methods, there was a strong possibility that social reform would occur as these naturally educated men and women took their places in society. The novel demonstrated Pestalozzi's contention that a regenerated society depended on the presence of naturally educated individuals.

Leonard and Gertrude also revealed Pestalozzi's strategy for using both the home and the school as agencies of natural education. Because they were emotionally secure individuals, the members of Gertrude's household were ready to master the skills and knowledge that would contribute to their personal, social, and economic welfare. Pestalozzi felt that natural education would be ineffective in traditional schools, where children were often coerced by incompetent teachers. In contrast, the village school of Bonnal was to be like a loving household. Pestalozzi hoped to see the time when home and school would cooperate as complementary agencies in advancing the child's natural education.

In sum, *Leonard and Gertrude* contained the basic doctrines of Pestalozzian natural education:

1. Evil originates in a distorted social environment rather than in human nature.
2. Education is the surest means of securing both personal growth and social reform.
3. Genuine education should develop man's natural moral, intellectual, and physical powers.
4. Moral development begins in the home as the child responds to the mother's care and kindness.
5. Sensory and vocational education will train economically self-sufficient individuals.

In 1782, Pestalozzi's *Christopher and Elizabeth*, a series of didactic dialogues, appeared but failed to attract significant attention. From 1782 to 1783, he also published his own paper, *Ein Schweizer Blatt*, the *Swiss News*, which carried a number of educational articles. In 1783, his essay *On Legislation and Infanticide* examined the relationships between environment, crime, punishment, education, tradition, and morality. In 1787, Pestalozzi published *Illustrations for my ABC Book*, a series of short illustrated epilogues on morality, society, and education. In 1797, he sought to establish a strong theoretical foundation for his educational system in *Researches into the Course of Nature in the Development of the Human Race*. This work was significant as one of the first attempts to analyze education sociologically by elaborating the thesis that man's discovery of natural developmental patterns would contribute to the formulation of ethical, political, and educational science.

Pestalozzi's *How Gertrude Teaches Her Children* (1801), partly autobiographical and partly pedagogical, was a major articulation of the theme that natural education should harmoniously develop man's moral, physical, and intellectual powers. His essay *Pestalozzi to His Age*, or *Epochs* (1803), reiterated the thesis that man's natural goodness could be restored through education. Pestalozzi's last work, *Swansong* (1826), a defense against his critics, recounted his views on elementary education.

Stans

The last decade of the eighteenth century brought the wars of the French Revolution to Switzerland. The conservative Roman Catholic cantons of Schwyz, Uri, and Unterwalden had refused to give allegiance to the French-supported Helvetian Republic, and a French army detachment was dispatched to compel their submission. Encountering strong opposition, the French soldiers burned the city of Stans, massacred the adult inhabitants, and left a large number of orphans. To care for these children, the Helvetian government established an orphanage and appointed Pestalozzi as director. On January 14, 1799, the first of eighty children were admitted.

Pestalozzi tried to rehabilitate these young victims of war and poverty by creating an environment of love and emotional security. Only when he had restored some degree of security to the children's lives did he begin to employ his natural method of education of "heart, hands, and head." He then began the drawing, writing, reading, and physical education lessons. To build a sense of community, Pestalozzi encouraged the children to cooperate by sharing their work and play.[2]

Believing that all human development results from the proper stimulation of the learner's innate moral, physical, and intellectual powers, Pestalozzi sought to use the child's own spontaneous activities. He refused to permit the highly verbal and literary forms of traditional education to interfere with the paternal relationship between teacher and learner. Unlike his experiment at Neuhof, Pestalozzi no longer tried to use vocational education for immediate profit. He now believed

[2] Johann Heinrich Pestalozzi, *How Gertrude Teaches Her Children* (Syracuse, N.Y.: C. W. Bardeen, 1915), pp. 17–18.

that proper vocational preparation consisted of the gradual exercise of the child's physical abilities.

Unfortunately, Pestalozzi's work at Stans was ended abruptly by the massing of opposing Austrian and French armies in the vicinity. After only five months of existence, the orphanage was commandeered as a military hospital on June 8, 1799. Although the time Pestalozzi spent at Stans was short, his work convinced him of the superiority of sensory and object learning over merely verbal exercises. He was also convinced that simultaneous instruction was more efficient than the individualized recitation.

Burgdorf

In 1801, a group of Pestalozzi's friends raised funds to equip a special school at Burgdorf as a center for educational research, teacher training, and the preparation of instructional materials. With this support and with some assistance from the Helvetian government, Pestalozzi opened an educational institute in the old castle at Burgdorf. His students included some pauper children from the eastern Swiss canton of Appenzell and a number of local children. Pestalozzi was joined by a number of young men, such as Hermann Krusi, Johannes Niederer, Johannes Buss, and Joseph Neef, who served as teaching assistants in order to master the principles of the method of natural education. These educational apprentices became disciples who carried Pestalozzian education throughout the Western world. While at Burgdorf, Pestalozzi developed his famous "ABC of Anschauung" by reducing instruction into its simplest components:

> I sought in all ways to bring the beginnings of spelling and counting to the greatest simplicity and into form. So that the child with the strictest psychological order might pass from the first step gradually to the second; and then without break, upon the foundation of the perfectly understood second step, might go on quickly and safely to the third and fourth.[3]

Pestalozzi tried to perfect a method to make simultaneous group instruction more effective and efficient. He taught spelling by having the children begin with the shortest words and then proceed to longer ones. Movable letters were used to give the first instruction in spelling and reading. In teaching arithmetic, Pestalozzi used concrete objects such as pebbles and beans; to teach fractions, he divided apples and cakes among the children. After becoming completely familiar with arithmetical processes, the children were introduced to the figures that represented the quantities of concrete objects. The initial writing exercises consisted of drawing rising and falling strokes and open and

[3] *Ibid.*, p. 23.

closed curves. These exercises, done on slates, contributed to the children's facility in using their hands for writing. In addition to these more formal exercises, there were frequent occasions for physical exercises, play activities, and nature study excursions.

Pestalozzi enjoyed success in developing his educational method, and the institute flourished for three and a half years. In 1804, however, the canton of Berne repossessed the castle, and the institute was moved from Burgdorf because of a lack of suitable quarters in the area.

Yverdon

After closing his institute at Burgdorf, Pestalozzi moved to Münchenbuchsee, where he briefly cooperated with Philip Emmanuel Fellenberg, who had established an industrial school at Hofwyl. The two educators could not, however, agree on educational aims or methods. On October 18, 1804, Pestalozzi accepted the use of an old castle at Yverdon that was given to him by the municipality. The spacious castle contained large halls, which were converted into assembly rooms, classrooms, and dormitories. Pestalozzi remained at Yverdon for more than twenty years and attained his greatest success there. As he became known in Europe and the United States, Yverdon became an educational mecca for educators who came to observe the natural method of education. Stimulated by Fichte's *Addresses to the German People*, which memorialized the Pestalozzian educational method, the Prussian government dispatched students to study the method so that it might be introduced into the Prussian school system. Such educators as Andrew Bell, developer of the monitorial method, Friedrich Froebel, founder of the kindergarten, Robert Owen, utopian proponent of infant education, William Maclure, an American proponent of industrial schools, and Johann Friedrich Herbart, the educational philosopher, came to Yverdon and were stimulated by their exposure to Pestalozzianism.

Baron Roger de Guimps, who was a student at Yverdon for nine years, left a reminiscence of his school days in his book *Pestalozzi: His Aim and Work*. The basic curriculum, consisting of exercises that Pestalozzi called "elementary education," was designed to exercise the moral, physical, and mental powers of the students. Based on the "ABC of Anschauung," these exercises included the study of form, number, and language. "Elementary education" led to work in geography, natural science, mathematics, drawing, singing, spelling, reading, handicrafts, and gardening. The basic principle that supported all instruction was sensory experience.

De Guimps recounted that the students took part in military drills conducted by Joseph Neef, a teaching assistant who had been a sergeant in Napoleon's army. The pupils formed a small battalion with a flag, drums, and music. There were also regular gymnastic exercises; in winter they skated; in the summer, there were swimming and mountain climbing.[4]

Pestalozzi supervised the entire program of instruction, and the assistant teachers reported to him on the progress of their pupils. The students would also visit with "Papa Pestalozzi," who encouraged them to talk freely about their interests and problems.

Pestalozzi's school at Yverdon attracted a number of teaching assistants who later made an imprint on European and American education. Unfortunately, however, Pestalozzi was an inept administrator, and he was unable to maintain harmony among his staff. Among his methodological principles was his belief that effective education carefully cultivated a "climate of emotional security," but he was unable to maintain the integrity of his institution, and the "homelike" environment was destroyed by family feuds. Because he permitted his assistants a great deal of freedom, some of his educational concepts were diluted or distorted in the process. Although Papa Pestalozzi was a father figure in his educational household, his gentle, but eccentric, personality lacked the necessary firmness to keep order in his institution.

In 1821, a series of charges and countercharges between the municipality of Yverdon and Pestalozzi occurred over the financial support of the institute. After a great deal of controversy, the municipality agreed to pay a small sum to defray Pestalozzi's expenses. However, these quarrels sapped the aging Pestalozzi's energy and detracted his attention from the educational task of the institute. Discouraged, he left Yverdon in 1825 to return to spend his last years at Neuhof, where he had begun his educational career.

Pestalozzi died two years later on February 17, 1827. In 1846, the canton of Argevie erected a monument bearing the epitaph:

Here lies Heinrich Pestalozzi, born in Zurich on the 12th of January, 1746, died at Brugg on 17th February, 1827. Saviour of the poor at Neuhof, Preacher to the people in *Leonard and Gertrude,* Father of the Fatherless in Stans, Founder of the new elementary school at Burgdorf and Münchenbuchsee, educator of humanity in Yverdon. Man, Christian, Citizen. Everything for others, nothing for himself. Blessings be on his name.

Pestalozzi's Philosophy of Education

The concept of nature was crucial to Pestalozzi's educational philosophy. In Pestalozzian terms, nature might be described both as reality and as the totality of the physical environment that appears to

---

[4] Roger de Guimps, *Pestalozzi: His Aim and Work* (Syracuse, N.Y.: C. W. Bardeen, 1889), p. 174.

the senses as a vast array of seemingly discrete and independent objects.[5] As a natural realist, Pestalozzi believed that these objects exist independently of man's knowledge of them and that man can know them through sensation and his subsequent reflective organization of sensory data. Although appearing as a misty sea of multitudinous objects, nature is a highly organized process, governed by its own intrinsic operations, or natural laws, which are uniform, universal, unchanging, and orderly. Although a unity, nature is to be viewed on two levels: (1) as an objective order of reality consisting of myriad objects, each of which is composed of matter organized according to a structure or form; (2) as a set of operations that control and direct development. Pestalozzi wished to perfect man's ability to see nature as both an objective order of reality and an operational mechanism that governs the course of human and natural development.

Pestalozzi accepted a genetic conception of man, and he compared human development to the growth of a tree, the seed of which contains all the innate potentialities of the mature tree. If given a proper environment, the seed will develop into a tree. Like the tree, man also possesses latent germinal powers for moral, intellectual, and physical growth. According to Pestalozzi:

> Man imitates this action of high Nature, who out of the seed of the largest tree first produces a scarcely perceptible shoot, then just as imperceptibly, daily and hourly, by gradual stages, unfolds first the beginnings of the stem, then the bough, then the branch, then the extreme twig on which hangs the perishable leaf. Consider carefully this action of great Nature,—how she tends and perfects every single part as it is formed, and joins on every new part to the permanent growth of the old.[6]

Man, as a participant in the natural process, follows the same laws of growth. He possesses certain germinal powers which, if given proper environment and nourishment, will blossom. Pestalozzi held that

1. Man as a part of nature is subject to its laws.
2. Human nature is distinguished from brute nature by possession of intellectual, moral, and physical powers.
3. The development of these powers should follow the natural laws.
4. A natural education will facilitate the harmonious development of these natural powers.
5. The existence of accidental variations among men does not contradict the essential laws of human development.

[5] For a discussion of Pestalozzi's educational philosophy in the context of its historical setting, see Gerald L. Gutek, *Pestalozzi and Education* (New York: Random House, 1968).
[6] Pestalozzi, *op. cit.*, p. 77.

Pestalozzi defined man as a moral, intellectual, and physical being who, regardless of the contingencies of time, place, and culture, is the possessor of a common human nature. Man's basic nature does not change, although environmental circumstances are alterable. Pestalozzi's concept of the prepared educational environment was based on unchanging laws of human growth.

Art of Instruction

Pestalozzi worked to develop an "art of instruction" to assist man to develop naturally and harmoniously. He believed that such a system of natural instruction is necessary to enable man to apprehend reality clearly. Natural phenomena, manifested in multitudinous objects, appear to man in a confused way, as through a glass darkly. The art of instruction is a method by which man can form clear concepts from this apparent confusion. The development of man's intellectual, moral, and physical powers requires appropriately graduated situations so that growth will be balanced and harmonious rather than one-sided. Education is a means of providing balanced development within a prepared environment. For example, the seed of the plant contains the whole plant. The seed will sprout and the plant will grow, but unless given the proper environmental conditions in terms of moisture, light, and warmth, this growth could be distorted by a tropism. Man can also experience tropism, or a developmental distortion that hinders harmonious development. When formal education overemphasizes intellectual development to the neglect of moral and physical development, the result may be an amoral, physically weak genius. One-sided development is a deviation from the natural man. Since the harmonious development of man's threefold powers is preferred, the accidental occasions for growth in an unstructured learning environment are inadequate.

Pestalozzi believed that the art of instruction is needed for the proper cultivation of man's inherent moral, intellectual, and physical powers. Intelligent control, an efficient method to secure a desired end, implies an art of instruction, which Pestalozzi referred to as the "psychologizing of instruction." Human nature, or the natural man, is also the psychological man. Man's thought processes conform to nature's laws of growth. Pestalozzi's natural education was actually his conception of a psychology of education:

> I now sought for laws to which the development of the human mind must, by its very nature, be subject. I knew they must be the same as those of physical Nature, and trusted to find in them a safe clue to a universal psychological method of instruction.[7]

[7] *Ibid.*, p. 78.

Pestalozzi used the terms "natural education" and "psychology of learning" synonymously. The human mind, like natural phenomena, operates according to the same laws governing physical nature. Psychological principles are derived, theoretically, from the observation of natural phenomena. In actual practice, however, Pestalozzi also carefully observed the children in his schools at Neuhof, Burgdorf, and Yverdon, anticipating the child study movement of the late nineteenth and twentieth centuries.

The primary task in developing an art of instruction, or educational methodology, is to make an accurate identification of man's natural powers, which for Pestalozzi are moral, intellectual, and physical. The second phase requires a strategic organization of exercises, experiences, and materials that can be graded and used to develop these powers. According to Pestalozzi:

> All instruction of man is then only the Art of helping Nature to develop in her own way; and this Art rests essentially on the relation and harmony between the impressions received by the child and the exact degree of his developed powers. It is also necessary, in the impressions that are brought to the child by instruction, that there should be sequence, so that beginning and progress should keep pace with the beginning and progress of the powers to be developed in the child. I soon saw that an inquiry into this sequence throughout the whole range of human knowledge, particularly those fundamental points from which the development of the human mind originates, must be the simple and only way ever to attain and keep satisfactory school and instruction books, of every grade, suitable for our nature and our wants. I saw just as soon, that in making these books, the constituents of instruction must be separated according to the degree of the growing power of the child; and that in all matters of instruction, it is necessary to determine, with the greatest accuracy, which of these constituents is fit for each age of the child, in order, on the one hand, not to hold him back if he is ready, and on the other, not to load him and confuse him with anything for which he is not quite ready.[8]

Anschauung

In his quest to psychologize instruction and develop a natural method of education, Pestalozzi was convinced that a single, unitary operational process is the source of all human cognition. Pestalozzi called this process *Anschauung,* a multifunctional term, usually translated as "intuition," that embraces a host of mental activities. Not merely a mental form or faculty, Anschauung is the functional process of forming concepts, or clear ideas. Although believing his discovery of Anschauung to be his greatest pedagogical contribution, Pestalozzi's confused definition of the term has often confounded his interpreters.

[8] *Ibid.,* p. 26.

He used the term to refer to every mental operation relevant to concept formation, such as sense impression, observation, contemplation, perception, apperception, and intuition.[9] Because of his imprecise usage, Anschauung must be construed to mean man's general cognitive or ideational function. Curtis and Boultwood speak of Anschauung as the fundamental mental processes that embrace all and any of the various stages in conceptualization:

> Sometimes it is the process of reception by the mind of a sense-impression and the resultant production of an idea—an idea of softness, of prickliness, of warmth, of dullness—independent of a knowledge of the appropriate word used to describe it. Sometimes it is the process of idea-formation through a combination of sense-impression and observation—the latter term implying intellectual awareness or attention. Sometimes it is the immediate mental realization of an idea without the intervention of external things. These three versions of Anschauung explain its translation as "sense-impression" or "observation" or "intuition."[10]

Pestalozzi identified five sources of knowledge, all of which depend on sensation:

1. Accidental sense impressions, which, though sources of knowledge, are limited by imprecision
2. Knowledge acquired by instruction, psychologically arranged according to the "art"
3. Knowledge resulting from man's desire to know
4. Knowledge acquired by working
5. Knowledge acquired by the use of analogy, comparisons, and contrasts

Pestalozzi's discovery of Anschauung led him to emphasize sense impression as a necessary process in acquiring knowledge. In seeking to reduce instruction to simple components, or an "ABC of Anschauung," he sought to find those "physicomechanical laws" that enable man's mind to receive sensory data and to abstract the essential qualities of objects through processes of distinguishing, comparing, and classifying. To achieve clearer knowledge of natural phenomena, man must be capable of framing and acting upon valid judgments. While not articulating a neatly structured epistemology, Pestalozzi's views on cognition can be analyzed in terms of the three basic phases of sensation, perception, and cognition. Although passive sensation

[9] Kate Silber, *Pestalozzi: The Man and His Work* (London: Routledge and Kegan Paul, 1960), pp. 138–140.
[10] S. J. Curtis and M. E. A. Boultwood, *A Short History of Educational Ideas* (London: University Tutorial Press, 1953), pp. 340–341.

initiates the thought process, thinking—by way of perception—culminates in the active conceptualization, or framing, of clear ideas.

Pestalozzi distinguished between crude sensation and the art of sense impression. Crude sensation occurs when the qualities of an object impinge upon man's five senses of smell, taste, sight, feeling, and hearing. Sensation is, then, an awareness of the qualities of an object.

Although always chaotic and confused, these sensations are necessary in forming concepts, or clear ideas. Through Anschauung, the mind recognizes the form underlying the diffused sensory data and organizes the sensations into structures. Perception—awareness of the object as a structured whole—is based on the material and formal qualities of the object. Whereas sensation refers to the impinging of the object's material qualities upon man's senses, perception refers to the mind's consciousness of the existence of a form giving structure to these qualities.

The formation of concepts depends upon the validity of the perception, which in turn is based upon the mind's ability to differentiate between the essential qualities of objects as distinct from their accidental qualities. Essential qualities, or necessary conditions, are always present in a particular class of objects; accidental qualities, or contingent conditions, are sometimes present. For example, man as a concept always possesses intellectual, moral, and physical powers. Particular men carry accidental variations of color, size, weight, vocation, or nationality. The validity of a concept rests on the correspondence of the concept with the structure of the object in reality. As Pestalozzi explained it:

> All things which affect my senses, are means of helping me to form correct opinions, only so far as their phenomena present to my senses their immutable, unchangeable, essential nature, as distinguished from their variable appearance or their external qualities. They are, on the other hand, sources of error and deception so far as their phenomena present to my senses their accidental qualities, rather than their essential characteristics.
>
> By putting together objects, whose essential nature is the same, your insight into their inner truth becomes essentially and universally wider, sharper, and surer. The one-sided, biased impressions made by the qualities of individual objects, as opposed to the impression that their nature should make upon you, becomes weakened. Your mind is protected against being swallowed up by the isolated force of single, separate impressions of qualities, and you are saved from the danger of thoughtlessly confusing the external qualities, with the essential nature of things, and from fantastically filling your head with incidental matters to the detriment of clearer insight.[11]

[11] Pestalozzi, *op. cit.*, pp. 80–81.

Art of Sense Impression

For Pestalozzi, sensation is the basis for acquiring knowledge. Instruction for effective sense impression has to be related to natural laws and to Anschauung. Pestalozzi's theory of instruction is geared to deriving clear ideas from chaotic sensations. Conceptualization necessitates the functioning of numerous mental abilities such as memory, imagination, thought, understanding, judgment, and reasoning, all of which are encompassed by Anschauung.

In leading a child to form clear concepts, the teacher must first expose the child to objects possessing the most essential characteristics of the class to which they belong. Such objects are best suited to impressing their essential nature rather than their variable qualities upon the child. The child learns to subordinate the accidental properties of an object to its essential nature. In conceptualization, he recognizes the appearance, form, structure, or outline of the object. He also recognizes the number of objects present, and he names the object by speech. Thus arose the famous Pestalozzian object lesson based upon the teaching of form, number, and language.

Pestalozzi claimed that his fundamental contributions to education were (1) recognizing sense impression as the foundation of knowledge and (2) reducing instruction to three elementary means of form, number, and language. Like his use of Anschauung, Pestalozzi's term "element" is also unclear. Anderson wrote that Pestalozzi believed that individual development parallels race development and that human knowledge develops gradually from the simplest elements.[12] Like race development, individual development is built in a cumulative fashion from the simple to the complex. In ordering instruction, the origins of the fundamental human powers can be used as elements, from which appropriate exercises can be devised to develop these fundamental powers. Anderson concluded that Pestalozzi's natural elements are really a search to identify the logical beginning points of knowledge.

Brubacher claimed that Pestalozzi erroneously confused the logically simple and the psychologically simple. In going from the simple to the complex, the element was arrived at by analyzing a subject. The logically simple, however, might not necessarily be psychologically simple for the child.[13] Broudy and Palmer also referred to Pestalozzi's confused use of "element" and say that, at times, Pestalozzi used the term to refer both to parts of objects and to basic mental acts.[14]

Silber asserted that Pestalozzian "elements" are neither objects nor

---

[12] Lewis F. Anderson, *Pestalozzi* (New York: McGraw-Hill, 1931), pp. 7–8.
[13] John S. Brubacher, *A History of the Problems of Education* (New York: McGraw-Hill, 1966), pp. 210–211.
[14] Harry S. Broudy and John R. Palmer, *Exemplars of Teaching Method* (Chicago: Rand McNally, 1965), pp. 110–111.

qualities of objects but are mental acts by which man constructs an intelligible world. Pestalozzi gave the term "element" a variety of meanings: (1) simple, or uncomplicated; (2) irreducible, or basic, as opposed to complex; (3) early as opposed to advanced; and (4) natural, in contrast to artificial.[15]

Pestalozzi's "elements" of instruction were based upon his equating of the psychological and the natural. He assumed that physical nature follows a set of unalterable laws—one of which is progression from the simple to the complex. Since the human mind is a part of nature, it follows the same laws and moves from the simple to the complex. The elements of instruction are based on a logical order that assumes the existence of: (1) points of origin, (2) developing germinal powers, and (3) cumulative development from the simple to the complex. Pestalozzi attempted to reduce learning to simple acts by analyzing skills and knowledge into parts. He conceived of elements as mental functions, such as numbering, measuring, or speaking, that can be developed by graduated exercises and graded instructional materials. Because of his confusion in the use of the term "element," he prepared instructional activities and materials that were reduced to their smallest part. For example, the smallest part of a word is a letter. Although a letter is logically simpler than a word, the child is more familiar with the word experientially. The logically simple is thus not necessarily the psychologically or experientially simple.

Pestalozzi related conceptualization to: (1) determining the form of objects; (2) determining the number of objects present; and (3) naming the objects. These stages relate to man's powers of calculation, of forming images, and of making sounds. Based upon the threefold powers of form, number, and language, Pestalozzi established that the skills of numbering, measuring, and speaking rather than the traditional literary skills of reading and writing are the proper beginnings of elementary education.

General Method: Emotional Security

Pestalozzi's "General Method" sought to create an emotionally secure educational environment for the child. The success of the method depended on a love relationship between teacher and student. He believed that the impulses of love spring from the child's innermost being. Like a delicate plant, these impulses need warmth, nourishment, protection, and careful attention. Parents, especially the mother, are responsible for cultivating the love impulse. The reciprocal love relationship between the mother and the child is the necessary center of proper emotional development. Pestalozzi's General Method emphasized emotional security as the foundation for all of man's moral, social, religious, and

[15] Silber, *op. cit.*, p. 41.

aesthetic values. Mother love occupies that circle of human environment that is immediate to the infant. In a healthy family, the child receives warmth and affection and reciprocates by giving his parents gratitude and love. Pestalozzi called love that inner sanctity of human nature that contains all that leads to harmonious perfection. It is the "feeling of love" that regulates, directs, stimulates, and restricts man's emotions.

Pestalozzi's General Method was intended to embrace the techniques, experiences, and activities necessary for moral, intellectual, and physical development and to provide the emotional support needed for that development. His attempts to devise a natural method of education were based on the following assumptions:

1. Human nature is unchanging, and the natural method of education is also constant and universally applicable.
2. Every child should develop the moral, intellectual, and physical powers that will define him as a man.
3. Natural education properly provides the sensory experiences that encourage the development of these powers.
4. Because nature develops slowly, gradually, and uniformly, a natural educational method must be based on graduated learning experiences in order to develop all man's powers harmoniously.

The Pestalozzian school was to be specially prepared to provide an environment of love for the child. Continuous with the home and family, it was to extend the range of the familial relationship so that the child could experience a larger number of objects and persons. Pestalozzi saw that the family had been weakened by the ravages of the Napoleonic wars and the changes brought about by industrialism. Where the parents were deficient, the school had to provide love and create a climate of emotional security. Because "Papa Pestalozzi's" greatest desire was to educate and to love neglected orphan children, the various Pestalozzian institutions resembled loving families rather than schools.

Special Method

Pestalozzi's system of natural education consisted of two complementary phases: (1) the General Method of creating an emotionally secure learning environment; and (2) the "Special Method" of instruction in subject matter and skills. Pestalozzi felt that both the General and the Special methods were necessary in successfully implementing his theory of natural education. A school situation that was fearful for children was likely to create emotionally insecure individuals. It was also unlikely that fearful children could effectively study the subjects and skills found in the Special Method. Like the later progressive educators, Pestalozzi wanted to educate the whole child.

Once the climate of love and emotional security had been created, Pestalozzi employed his Special Method, which included instruction in reading, writing, arithmetic, geography, music, and nature studies. He did not teach these subjects according to the traditional practices but rather used his concepts of Anschauung and sense impressionism to reduce instruction to the three basic elements of form, number, and language. Instruction was to begin with the learner's direct experience with concrete objects found in the environment. Pestalozzi's emphasis on sensation and experience led him to assert that all instruction should begin with objects and tasks that were familiar to the child before he proceeded to more abstract kinds of learning.

Instruction in the subjects and skills of the Special Method was a narrower phase of Pestalozzi's General Method. Unfortunately, some Pestalozzian imitators, such as the Mayos of England and Sheldon of the Oswego Normal School, ignored the educational implications of the General Method and stressed only the pedagogical dictums of the Special Method. Their misinterpretation of Pestalozzi's theory of natural education resulted in a very formal kind of object teaching that lacked the General Method's emphasis on the child's affective development.

From the Near to the Far

Educational historians inevitably refer to Pestalozzi's famous dictum that instruction should begin with the "near and move to the far." As with his other concepts of "Anschauung" and "elements," Pestalozzi's admonition held a variety of instructional meanings. Basically, it referred to the literal distance of the perceiver from the object:

> Strengthen and make clear the impressions of important objects by bringing them nearer to you . . . and letting them affect you through different senses. Learn . . . the first law of physical mechanism, which makes the relative power of all influences of physical Nature depend on the physical nearness or distance of the object in contact with the senses. Never forget this physical nearness or distance has an immense effect in determining your positive opinions, conduct, duties, or even virtue.[16]

In a broader context, "from the near to the far" meant that instruction should begin with the learner's immediate environment and the objects that were part of that environmental experience. For example, geography was to begin with the learner's immediate environment before it concerned distant regions. Both Pestalozzi and the American

[16] Pestalozzi, *op. cit.*, p. 17.

educator John Dewey stressed the importance of beginning with the learner's environment and experiences and gradually extending this experience.

Like Rousseau, Pestalozzi distrusted the conventional school's emphasis on books and words. This antiverbalist bias supported Pestalozzi's admonition to begin instruction with the objects found in the immediate environment. Since man comes to know reality through sensation, the nearer he is to the objects the clearer his perception of the objects. When information is introduced verbally and indirectly, the apprehension of reality remains unclear and confused. The experience of others, as found in textbooks, is an indirect experience. Like the twentieth-century progressive educators, Pestalozzi believed such devitalized information tended to be memorized by children who did not really understand it.

"From the near to the far" also applied to vocational education. While believing that all men should be educated generally, Pestalozzi also asserted that there is a particular kind of vocational education appropriate to specific economic groups. The objective conditions of the environment and the objects of experience vary according to the learner's particular economic background and occupation. When instruction begins with the objects found in the environment, the child is more likely to receive the knowledge and skills appropriate to his vocational destination.

The principle of "from the near to the far" also implies a continuity of experience. While the child's immediate environment is the means of developing the lessons in form, number, and language, that immediate environment is a part of a larger one. Ordinarily and naturally, the child moves from his nearest surroundings to those that are successively more remote. In such movement, the progress is gradual, slow, and steady so that a continuity is maintained. Pestalozzi referred to this continuity of experience as the "widening circle of mankind" that leads the child from the home through the socioeconomic environment into the world.

From the Simple to the Complex

Pestalozzi also recommended that instruction move from the "simple to the complex." The Pestalozzian use of "elements" of instruction required a graduated learning continuum in which exercises ranged from the simple to the complex. Hence, the elements of counting, measuring, and speaking are "simple" in the sense of being basic to the more intricate and sophisticated arts of which they are necessary foundations. For example, in Pestalozzi's language lessons, the children went from the simple to the complex by speaking sounds, then words, then phrases, and finally sentences. "Going from the simple to the complex" also meant that the teacher began with a concrete object before developing abstract generalizations. In skill learning, "simple" also meant "easy."

Pestalozzi, a sense realist, believed that natural education should be based on objects that are part of man's environment. Learning was to be a rigorous method of sense experience. The Pestalozzian "art of instruction" was based upon cultivating man's power of Anschauung through the effective use of instructional materials and efforts. Pestalozzi developed a number of insights into learning theory that formed a permanent part of the "progressive" attack upon traditionalism. Among his contributions to educational theory were the emphases on beginning instruction with the learner's experience, on using the educational possibilities existent in the environment, and on maintaining a continuum of experience in instruction.

Conclusion

Pestalozzi's inconsistent and unsystematic theorizing about education was detrimental to the precise application of his method of natural education. His basic concepts of "Anschauung," "element," "psychologizing," and even "natural education" were vague terms to which he gave multifactored definitions. Despite this weakness, Pestalozzi made major contributions by: (1) cultivating a reverence for the nature of the child and (2) introducing the concept that teaching should be related to the child's experiences and environment. His rejection of "child corruption" was based on his view of man as being naturally good. He regarded childhood as a uniquely valuable stage of development. Early childhood education, in particular, was essential in developing proper attitudes and values. Pestalozzi's General Method of education—the creation of a loving environment for the child—anticipated later developments in child psychology. The doctrines of the "child-centered school" and "child permissiveness," which originated at Neuhof, Stans, Burgdorf, and Yverdon, were significant contributions to an enlightened view of child nature.

Pestalozzi's General Method of education was similar to the educational strategies employed by those who work with culturally disadvantaged children, who are often the victims of poverty. Before particular verbal skills are emphasized, the teacher often seeks to instill confidence in the learner so that he can experience a sense of self. Only after a sense of security and personal identity has been cultivated in the learner does the teacher seek to develop the cognitive skills associated with traditional schooling.

The valuable part of the Special Method rested on its relationship to the child's experience. Pestalozzi insisted that the continuity of experience be maintained. As the home circle led to the school, the child's experience was unbroken by the intrusion of verbalized and abstract ethical or literary materials. Such materials were meaningless for children who, if coerced, would memorize rather than understand them. Pestalozzi's stress on maintaining a continuum of experience caused him to examine and to use the learning possibilities that existed in the child's immediate environment. When used in an experiential context that related to environment, Pestalozzi's principles of "from the simple to the complex" and "from the near to the far" were valuable additions to educational practice.

Although Pestalozzi considered that education could advance social reform, such reformation was always regarded as coming from individual efforts. A gradualist, Pestalozzi relied almost exclusively on educational processes to bring about social reform. He was aware that industrialization necessitated a new method of education.

Pestalozzi's model of the educated man was one who harmoniously developed his moral, intellectual, and physical powers. Fearing the harmful effects of industrial specialization, he cultivated the model of the generally educated man. Despite some of the methodological eccentricities that crept into his work, he never lost sight of his vision of the generally educated natural man. Basically, Pestalozzi was a humanitarian, a lover of all mankind. "Love" was the center of his educational theory and practice. "Mother love," "the loving home circle," "love of man and of God," were persistent Pestalozzian themes.

Chapter 13 will deal with Pestalozzi's impact on nineteenth-century education. Although his conception of natural education was frequently distorted by those who claimed to be his disciples, the influence of the Swiss educator's method did much to stimulate educational theory and practice. In part, the popularity of Pestalozzian education contributed to the national system of education that arose in the nineteenth century.

Suggested Readings

Anderson, Lewis F. *Pestalozzi.* New York: McGraw-Hill, 1931.

Barnard, Henry. *Pestalozzi and His Educational System.* Syracuse, N.Y.: C. W. Bardeen, 1906.

Biber, E. Henry. *Pestalozzi and His Plan of Education.* London: J. Souter, 1831.

Broudy, Harry S., and John R. Palmer. *Exemplars of Teaching Method.* Chicago: Rand McNally, 1965.

Brubacher, John S. *A History of the Problems of Education.* New York: McGraw-Hill, 1966.

Curtis, S. J., and M. E. A. Boultwood. *A Short History of Educational Ideas*. London: University Tutorial Press, 1953.

Green, J. A. *The Educational Ideas of Pestalozzi*. New York: Greenwood Press, 1969.

————. *Life and Work of Pestalozzi*. London: University Tutorial Press, 1912.

————. *Pestalozzi's Educational Writings*. London: Longmans, Green, 1912.

Guimps, Roger de. *Pestalozzi: His Aim and Work*. Syracuse: C. W. Bardeen, 1889.

Gutek, Gerald L. *Pestalozzi and Education*. New York: Random House, 1968.

Holman, H. *Pestalozzi: An Account of His Life and Work*. London: Methuen Co., 1908.

Kilpatrick, William H. *Heinrich Pestalozzi: The Education of Man*. New York: Philosophical Library, 1951.

Krusi, Hermann, Jr. *Pestalozzi, His Life, Work, and Influence*. New York: American Book, 1875.

Pestalozzi, Johann Heinrich. *How Gertrude Teaches Her Children*. L. E. Holland and F. C. Turner (trs.). Syracuse, N.Y.: C. W. Bardeen, 1915.

————. *Leonard and Gertrude*. Eva Channing (tr.). Boston: D. C. Heath, 1907.

Pinloche, A. *Pestalozzi and the Foundation of the Modern Elementary School*. New York: Scribner, 1901.

Silber, Kate. *Pestalozzi: The Man and His Work*. London: Routledge and Kegan Paul, 1960.

Walch, Mary Romana. *Pestalozzi and the Pestalozzian Theory of Education: A Critical Study*. Washington: Catholic University Press, 1952.

CHAPTER 13

The Diffusion of Pestalozzianism

After Pestalozzi's death in 1827, his method of natural education was carried throughout Europe and North America by his educational associates at Burgdorf and Yverdon. The European and American visitors to Yverdon also took with them a conception of Pestalozzi's work, which unfortunately was often a pale version of the original. Since Pestalozzi's educational theory was a loosely defined and often unclear pedagogical structure, some of his disciples' work was handicapped by their limited perspectives of the method. Further, the most important phase of the "General Method" was the cultivation of emotional security. It was much easier to diffuse the narrower instructional components of the method rather than a sense of emotional security and commitment.

The gentle Pestalozzi was a father to the children who attended his schools at Neuhof, Stans, Burgdorf, and Yverdon, but not all of his followers were psychologically suited to fulfill that role. Many of the later Pestalozzians failed to understand that the "method" required the full implementation of the "love climate" of emotional security before the Special Method's graduated exercises in teaching skills could be employed. As frequently occurs with educational reformation and innovation, once the dedicated reformer passes from the scene the work is left to more pedantic persons who lack the reforming spirit.

Despite the general weakening of the original impetus of Pestalozzianism, it was a major theory of pedagogical and social reformation. This chapter will consider the implementation of certain aspects of Pestalozzianism in Germany, England, and the United States. A major emphasis in the chapter will be placed on the work of Joseph Neef as a popularizer of Pestalozzianism in the United States.

German Educational Developments

Pestalozzi had been a German-speaking Swiss, and his works were readily available in German language editions. Three major German educational theorists, Johann Gottlieb Fichte (1762–1814), Johann Friedrich Herbart (1776–1841), and Friedrich Froebel (1782–1852) were familiar with Pestalozzian pedagogy and helped to popularize it in the various German states during the nineteenth century. As a result of Fichte's *Addresses to the German People,* delivered during 1807 and 1808, general interest was stimulated in Pestalozzian education. Fichte's *Addresses* were essentially a plea for the regeneration of Germany after the defeat of the German armies at Napoleon's hands in 1806 at the Battle of Jena. Believing that Pestalozzian educational ideas could be used to restore German life by instilling in German youth a sense of cultural identity, order, patriotism, and dedication, Fichte felt that German children should be trained in sense perception, physical education, practical vocational skills, and moral principles.

Herbart, a leading German philosopher and educational theorist, had visited Pestalozzi's schools and written about his educational theory. His writings, especially *Pestalozzi's Idea of an ABC of Observation Scientifically Investigated,* familiarized German educators with the method of natural education. Although Herbart later developed his own educational method, he accepted the Pestalozzian emphasis on sensory perception, vocational education, and civil responsibility.

Like Pestalozzi, Froebel, founder of the kindergarten, was deeply concerned with early childhood education. However, although Froebel generally accepted Pestalozzi's themes of child freedom and emotional security, he was much more prone to symbolic and mystical interpretations of the child's behavior. The Froebelian kindergarten centered around the object lesson, but the Froebelian object lesson was decidedly more symbolic than that of Pestalozzi. Froebel believed that the objects that he had carefully selected had powers of awakening latent ideas in the child's consciousness.

English Pestalozzianism

A number of English visitors had ventured to Yverdon to study Pestalozzi's educational methods. Among them were Maria Edgeworth and John Synge, who wrote short accounts of their early visits with the Swiss educator. Andrew Bell, an Anglican clergyman who popularized monitorialism, visited Yverdon in 1816, but he was very critical of Pestalozzi's method, claiming that his own system of monitorial education was far superior and would in time be more widely accepted than Pestalozzi's method of natural education. Robert Owen, who like Pestalozzi tried to base education on nature, also visited Pestalozzi's school at Yverdon. Although he was impressed by Pestalozzianism, Owen had developed his own system of education, which attracted considerable fame and brought a steady stream of visitors to his school at New Lanark, Scotland.

Pestalozzi himself sought to familiarize English educators with his method by writing a series of letters to James Pierrepoint Greaves (1777–1842), who had been an assistant at Yverdon from 1818 until 1821. These *Letters on Early Education,* published by Greaves in 1827, emphasized the importance of cultivating a strong climate of emotional security in schools and stressed the need for loving mother-child relationships.[1] As secretary of the London Infant School Society, Greaves attempted to popularize Pestalozzianism in England. Of the various English Pestalozzians, Greaves best understood the educational implications of the General Method. Although he actively promoted the cause of natural education throughout his life, Greaves' influence was overshadowed by the educators who emphasized only the Special Method and neglected Pestalozzianism's broader humanism.

Unfortunately, the later English Pestalozzians, influenced by Charles and Elizabeth Mayo, lost sight of the "love environment" of the General Method. Charles Mayo (1792–1846), a clergyman, and his sister Elizabeth (1793–1853) founded a school for upper-class children at Cheam Surrey in 1826. Although the first teachers were Swiss, the school later came to resemble a typical English preparatory school. The Mayos attracted considerable attention and came to be regarded as the most able proponents of Pestalozzianism in the English-speaking world. To popularize their conception of Pestalozzianism, they founded the Home and Colonial School Society in 1836. The society established a model school and a normal school in London, the latter to prepare teachers according to the Mayos' version of Pestalozzianism, which emphasized the object lesson, as is illustrated by the following lesson on glass:

TEACHER: What is this which I hold in my hand?
CHILDREN: A piece of glass.
TEACHER: Can you spell the word glass? (The teacher then writes the word "glass" upon the slate, which is thus presented to the whole class as the subject of the lesson.) You have all examined this glass; what do you observe? What can you say that it is?
CHILDREN: It is bright.
TEACHER: (Teacher having written the word "qualities" writes under it—It is bright.) Take it in your hand and feel it.

[1] Johann Heinrich Pestalozzi, *Letters on Early Education Addressed to J. P. Greaves* (London: Sherwood, Gilbert, and Piper, 1827), pp. 148–149.

CHILDREN: It is cold. (Written on the board under the former quality.)[2]

The preceding object lesson developed by Elizabeth Mayo was one of a series of lesson plans on common objects that was widely imitated in both England and the United States. Pestalozzi did not intend, however, that his principles of natural education and sensory learning should be distorted into a mechanical rote and catechetical method in which students responded to previously set questions. Although the formal object lesson corrupted Pestalozzi's theory, it could be used efficiently by pedestrian practitioners who erroneously called themselves educational reformers and innovators. Thus, the highly verbal and conventional lesson made an inroad into, and subverted, Pestalozzi's liberalized educational practice.

Joseph Neef, an American Pestalozzian

The first major introduction of Pestalozzian education to the United States was conducted under the auspices of the philanthropist William Maclure (1763–1840), who had visited numerous European schools, including Pestalozzi's. Maclure, interested in establishing schools of agriculture and industry, strongly advocated Pestalozzian methodology with its emphasis on sensation and practical skills. He persuaded Joseph Neef (1770–1854) to come to the United States from France to establish Pestalozzian schools.

After his arrival in the United States in 1806, Neef conducted a number of schools in Pennsylvania and Kentucky and was associated with Robert Owen's New Harmony community from 1826 to 1828. Neef published two books that attempted to popularize Pestalozzian education in the United States, *Sketch of a Plan and Method of Education* (1808) and *The Method of Instructing Children Rationally in the Arts of Writing and Reading* (1813). Neef, a convinced Pestalozzian, wrote:

His pupil always sets out from the known and plain, and proceeds with slow speediness to the yet unknown and complicated. He leaves no point behind him without being perfectly master of it. Every point of knowledge which he acquires is but a step to acquire a new one. All his faculties are displayed; but none is overstrained. All his proceedings are subject to the minutest gradation.[3]

[2] Elizabeth Mayo, *Lessons on Objects as Given to Children Between the Ages of Six and Eight in a Pestalozzian School* (London: Seeley and Burnside, 1835), pp. 5–6.
[3] Joseph Neef, *Sketch of a Plan and Method of Education* (Philadelphia: Privately Published, 1808), p. 7.

Since educational historians have long regarded Neef as an American Pestalozzian, an assessment of his educational contribution requires an examination of his particular conception of Pestalozzianism. Throughout his life, Neef tried to be a faithful disciple of Pestalozzi. Like Pestalozzi, he believed that sensation is the source of knowledge and education and opposed the excessive verbalism and authoritarianism found in traditional schools. Yet, like all disciples, he emphasized certain aspects of his master's educational philosophy and method and neglected others.

Neef accepted Pestalozzi's definition of man as a being who possesses moral, intellectual, and physical powers and agreed that natural education should aid nature in developing these three germinal powers. Since these powers do not develop simultaneously or harmoniously, the educator should stimulate their harmonious growth and integration. Neef believed that traditional schooling, by overemphasizing the intellectual, had frequently neglected the threefold development of these powers. Although some educators had erroneously construed the arts and sciences as the end of education, Neef considered them as instruments in bringing man's powers to maturity.

Neef's Adaptation of Pestalozzian Methodology

Neef had worked with Pestalozzi at Burgdorf, where the Swiss educator had developed his educational theory, and was familiar with both the General and Special phases of method. Pestalozzi's emphasis on creating a climate of love and security had been influenced by Rousseau's emotional romanticism; he believed that man's moral power derived from an intrinsic germ of benevolence. Neef however, being more of a rationalist than a romanticist, did not stress Pestalozzi's emphasis on benevolence or love.

Nevertheless, in his *Sketch of a Plan and Method of Education*, Neef made clear that he would be a friend and guide to his students. His schools were generally much more liberal than conventional nineteenth-century American schools. He was a permissive teacher who rejected the use of corporal punishment, ridicule, and fear. Like the twentieth-century progressive educators, he believed that the child could exercise his intelligence more freely in an open environment than in one dominated by fear and authoritarianism. Although he did not romanticize the child, Neef believed that childhood was a crucial period of human development. He thus did not completely lose the spirit of Pestalozzi's General Method as did the English Pestalozzians Charles and Elizabeth Mayo and the American object lesson teachers trained later in the nineteenth century by Edward Sheldon at the Oswego Normal School.

Neef was faithful to the Special Method's object lesson and to the graduated exercises of form, number, and language. He never deviated from the gradualism of Pestalozzian instructional strategy, which cautioned the teacher to proceed slowly and gradually.

Neef's Object Lesson

Neef adapted the Pestalozzian object lesson into an eleven-step set of exercises designed to train students in careful observation, analysis, and reductionism. He indicated that his teaching would always begin with a concrete object and by analysis "descend from decomposition to decomposition till the whole subject is fully exhausted."[4] Neef's object lesson not only followed Pestalozzi's principles but also incorporated ideas derived from Condillac, the French sensationalist philosopher.

In the first step of Neef's object lesson, the teacher presents to the children an object that is to be examined and recognized as a whole. Only after the students have become familiar with the object does the teacher give its name.

Neef's second step was designed to give students experience in determining the relationships between two objects or between a whole object and its parts. To teach relationships—coherence, subordination, connection, and the like—Neef used as examples the subordination of the hand to the body and the leaf to the tree. For example, the leaf is part of the twig, the twig of the branch, the branch of the trunk, the trunk of the tree; the entire tree comprises all of these components. This step is similar to Pestalozzi's method of beginning with an element—the simplest part of an object—and gradually proceeding to a more complex part. It is also related to Condillac's sensationalist epistemology of decomposing or analyzing an object by reducing it into parts.

The third step is an exercise in counting the number of elements or objects involved in the particular lesson. For example, a child may count the number of fingers on his hand. Neef was clearly following the Pestalozzian number exercises by beginning with concrete objects rather than with abstract symbols.

The position, location, and situation of an object are described in the fourth step. Here, Neef drew upon his translation of Condillac's *Logic*, which had discussed the recognition of principal objects, the subordination of secondary objects to principal ones, and the relationships of principal objects to one another and to secondary objects.[5] Neef wanted his students to exercise their skill of observation so that

---

[4] *Ibid.*, p. 8.
[5] *Logic of Condillac, Translated by Joseph Neef, as an Illustration of the Plan of Education Established at His School Near Philadelphia* (Philadelphia: Printed for the Author, 1809), p. 23.

they could recognize both the general setting in which particular objects appeared and the relationships of objects to each other. The recognition of the location, position, and situation of objects was an important part of the method and was frequently used in the field trips and nature excursions led by Neef.

In the fifth step, the teacher asks the children to point out the qualities of the object. Such common objects as snow, water, lead, or wood are used. Neef followed Pestalozzi's theory of conceptualization, which held that objects possess essential, or necessary, qualities, and contingent, or accidental, ones. The purpose of such sensory instruction is to help the children to distinguish and to isolate the necessary qualities upon which clear concepts are formed.

Neef's sixth step helps the learner to recognize the shape, or form, of an object. The children are asked to describe the shape of a table, a finger, or an arm and to identify objects that are spherical, cylindrical, triangular, circular, conic, or prismatic.

The different functions that organic bodies and their parts perform are examined in the seventh step. The functions of the sensory organs —the eyes, ears, and tongue—are given particular attention. The functions performed by plants and their parts are also studied. Neef's emphasis on man's sensory organs was intended to aid students in understanding the relationship of these organs to sensation and conceptualization.

In the object lesson's eighth step, the students examine man's use of various instruments, such as a hammer, pen, knife, plough. What are the uses of iron, steel, coal, wood, and cotton, for example? This step was designed to examine the consequences that certain objects and instruments have when man uses them. Neef shared Pestalozzi's belief that education should be practical and should contribute to vocational efficiency. At Neuhof, Pestalozzi had attempted to combine learning and industry. Maclure, Neef's American patron, advocated an industrial education to advance the production skills of workers and farmers.

Steps nine and ten are designed to make comparisons and contrasts between various objects. In the eleventh step, the students are to arrive at "plain, accurate, exact" definitions of given objects. The definition is expected to be a collective word that amalgamates all that has been observed, examined, investigated, analyzed, and determined in all the preceding steps. These definitions are to be based on sense experience.[6]

Neef's object lesson, a crucial component of his educational method, rejected highly verbalized, bookish instruction. Students were to examine the objects in their immediate environment rather than memorize

[6] Neef, *op. cit.*, pp. 8–11.

abstract definitions that were experientially meaningless. The care that Neef gave to the Special Method revealed that he was more attuned to this aspect of Pestalozzianism rather than to the more emotional aspects of the General Method. Neef affirmed his loyalty to Pestalozzi's instructional strategy when he said:

> "Imitate nature," says the good Pestalozzi, "begin by what is simple, plain, known, by what you find in the child; dwell on each point till the learner is perfectly master of it; and never mix heterogeneous, known, and unknown matters." These precepts are sacred to me, and I shall always endeavor to keep them in mind.[7]

Neef fully accepted Pestalozzi's instructional strategy, which used a series of graduated exercises based on the learner's readiness. He believed that the skillful teacher recognizes the child's readiness for particular instruction and does not retard or prematurely force the child's growth. In his *Sketch*, Neef affirmed that his students would always set out from the "known and plain" and proceed with "slow speediness" to the "unknown and complicated." This affirmation followed Pestalozzi's rule that instruction begin with objects located in the child's own environment. Accurate conceptualization also depends on the literal distance of the perceiver from the object. Pestalozzi had warned:

> Never forget this physical nearness or distance has an immense effect in determining your positive opinions, conduct, duties, or even virtue.[8]

Instruction that moved from the known to the unknown meant that the learner's progression in experience was to be unbroken. In studying geography, for example, the learner began with his immediate home environment before studying more distant regions such as oceans and continents. In his field trips, nature studies, and excursions, Neef led his students from their immediate environment to adjacent but more remote regions. Eventually, the student's experiences would be broadened to include Pestalozzi's "widening circles of mankind," which led from the home, through the socioeconomic environment, to the world.

Neef's instructional method was distinctively Pestalozzian in that it emphasized sensation, rejected verbalism, and used the object lesson and graduated exercises. He attempted to refine Pestalozzi's number, form, and language exercises into a more sophisticated teaching method.

---

[7] *Ibid.*, p. 121.
[8] Johann Heinrich Pestalozzi, *How Gertrude Teaches Her Children* (Syracuse, N. Y.: C. W. Bardeen, 1907), p. 79.

Barnard and Sheldon

Henry Barnard (1811–1900), an educator who was to become the first United States Commissioner of Education, made a contribution to Pestalozzianism by popularizing the theory among American educators. Barnard had become familiar with Pestalozzi's educational work through visits to his schools in Europe. After returning to the United States, he conducted teacher institutes, where he lectured on Pestalozzi's educational theory and practice. Moreover, he wrote an influential volume, *Pestalozzi and Pestalozzianism* (1859), which included sections on Pestalozzi's life and educational philosophy and extracts from his writings.[9]

Barnard was a member of a New England educational circle that included Bronson Alcott, William C. Woodbridge, and William Russell, men who were familiar with Pestalozzianism and tried to incorporate it into their own educational enterprises.[10] The major work of these men consisted of their educational writing and their limited experiments.

The work of Edward A. Sheldon (1823–1897) and his associates at the Oswego Normal School constituted a major phase of the Pestalozzian movement in the United States.[11] Sheldon, superintendent of the school, introduced American teachers to the English conception of the formal object lesson. The basic operating principle at Oswego was that all knowledge derives from sense perception and that all instruction should be based on real objects. Sheldon and his associates, Margaret Jones, formerly a teacher in the Mayos' Home and Colonial School Society, and Herman Krusi, Jr., the son of one of Pestalozzi's teaching assistants, developed an extensive program of teacher preparation based on the object lesson. Like Elizabeth Mayo, Sheldon published books of lesson plans based on sensory examination of a number of common objects. Unfortunately, the "lessons on glass, water, and coal" were very formalized and followed the prestructured, question-and-answer approach developed by the Mayos. The Oswego object teaching method attracted widespread attention among American educators, and in 1865 the National Teachers' Association Committee on Object Teaching reported:

[9] Henry Barnard, *Pestalozzi and Pestalozzianism* (New York: F. C. Brownell, 1862).
[10] Will Seymour Monroe, *History of the Pestalozzian Movement in the United States* (Syracuse: C. W. Bardeen, 1907), pp. 147–155.
[11] For a history of the Oswego phase, see Ned H. Dearborn, *The Oswego Movement in American Education* (New York: Teachers College, Columbia University, 1925).

Whenever this system has been confined to elementary instruction and has been employed by skillful, thorough teachers, in unfolding and disciplining the faculties, in fixing the attention and awakening thought, it has been successful.[12]

Sheldon stated that the object lesson was designed to broaden the child's sphere of observation. Education, he said, consists of leading children to observe the objects that surround them and to describe their observations accurately. In his *Lessons on Objects*, Sheldon told teachers to (1) base instruction on definite objects, (2) call each of the child's senses into action in order to strengthen them through exercise, and (3) link the ideas gained to appropriate words in order that the child might acquire a command of language. The following object lesson, "A Basket, For Its Parts," is an example of Sheldon's method of object teaching:

Require the children to name the object, and to tell its use—as to hold potatoes, peas, bread, tea, sugar, books, work, paper, &c.; and then to point out its parts, as the lid, the handles, the sides, the bottom, the inside, the outside, and the edges; to describe the use of the lid—to cover the things contained in the basket, and to prevent them being seen; and to tell also the use of the sides and of the bottom. What would happen if the basket had no lid? The things it contained would be seen, and the dust would get in. What would happen if it had no handle? . . . Then make the children repeat together the names of the various parts of a basket. "The basket has a lid, a handle," &c.[13]

Sheldon's work at Oswego probably improved and systematized the preparation of common school teachers. Although it was formalized, the Oswego object lesson was an improvement over the memorization of highly verbal materials. The object lesson plan organized instruction to the degree that the teacher could exercise greater planning and control in classroom teaching. The Oswego method was not, however, "natural education" as it had been conceived of by Pestalozzi. It was rather an extension of the formalized English object lesson into American pedagogy.

In *Democracy and Education*, John Dewey's comments on Pestalozzianism provide revealing insights into the strengths and weaknesses of the method of natural education. He felt that Pestalozzi was an intelligent theorist who recognized the shape of things to come. For example, Pestalozzi had realized that the rise of state systems of natural education was necessary to implement his educational theory

12 Monroe, *op. cit.*, pp. 183–184.
13 E. A. Sheldon, *Lessons on Objects, Graduated Series* (New York: Scribner, 1863), p. 25.

successfully. Dewey also believed that Pestalozzi's stress on the child's natural growth was useful in liberating the child from the confinement of authoritarian schools. Dewey's major objections to Pestalozzianism were directed against the routines of the object lesson as practiced by the Mayos and Sheldon. Although the insistence on active use of the senses contributed to pedagogical theory, a major error was made in requiring that the learner know the qualities, or properties, of objects before using them. Dewey opposed the teaching of properties in isolation from the functional uses of objects.[14]

The diffusion of Pestalozzi's philosophy was accomplished by his disciples, who made their own interpretations of natural education as Pestalozzi, himself, had once done with Rousseau's ideas. While Greaves and Neef remained faithful to Pestalozzi's conception of natural education, Mayo and Sheldon emphasized the object lesson, which was the most obvious but not the most important aspect of the method. The major educational contribution of the Pestalozzians was their work in adapting instruction to the nature of the child.

Conclusion

Although only one of many influences on progressivism, Pestalozzi's General Method, based on cultivating an environment of emotional security, greatly resembled the American progressive's permissiveness in regard to the interests and needs of the learner. Unfortunately for both the nineteenth-century Pestalozzi and the twentieth-century progressive, traditional schools resisted change. Rather than bringing about a major educational revolution, the reforming Pestalozzi and the later progressives secured only limited changes, which were incorporated into the fabric of conventional schooling and led to a very gradual transformation of the school rather than to its sweeping reformation.

Chapter 14 will deal with the work of two educators who dedicated themselves to reforming early childhood education. The influence of Pestalozzi was evident in the work of Friedrich Froebel, as was mentioned earlier. Maria Montessori proposed a theory of education that also was designed to liberate the child's energies.

[14] John Dewey, *Democracy and Education* (New York: Macmillan, 1916), pp. 93, 116, 199.

Suggested Readings

Barnard, Henry. *Pestalozzi and Pestalozzianism.* New York: F. C. Brownell, 1862.

Calkins, N. S. *Primary Object Lessons.* New York: Harper, 1872.

Dearborn, Ned Harland. *The Oswego Movement in American Education.* New York: Teachers College, Columbia University, 1925.

Mayo, Elizabeth. *Lessons on Objects as Given to Children Between the Ages of Six and Eight in a Pestalozzian School.* London: Seeley Burnside, 1835.

Monroe, Will S. *History of the Pestalozzian Movement in the United States.* Syracuse: C. W. Bardeen, 1907.

Neef, Joseph. *Sketch of a Plan and Method of Education.* Philadelphia: Printed for the Author, 1809.

Pestalozzi, Johann Heinrich. *Letters on Early Education Addressed to J. P. Greaves.* London: Sherwood, Gilbert, and Piper, 1827.

Sheldon, E. A. *Lessons on Objects, Graduated Series.* New York: Charles Scribner, 1863.

CHAPTER 14

Froebel and Montessori:
Early Childhood Education

Early childhood education has attracted dedicated and sincere people who have sought, like Pestalozzi, to discover the universal laws of child development. Ever since Plato proposed the creation of state nurseries in *The Republic,* educational theorists have been proposing programs for the education of the very young. Educators have sought to cultivate the proper predispositions in the very young. Since early childhood education has attracted such earnest practitioners, it has been a controversial area of pedagogy. Teachers have often found themselves arrayed in opposing ranks as they have adhered to the various philosophies of early childhood education. Among the most interesting have been the kindergartners and the Montessorians. This chapter will examine the contributions of two leading educators, Friedrich Froebel and Maria Montessori. Froebel lived in the first half of the nineteenth century, whereas Montessori's life spanned the end of the nineteenth century and the first half of the twentieth century.

Friedrich Froebel

Friedrich Froebel (1782–1852), like other nineteenth-century German educators, was influenced heavily by philosophical idealism and romanticism. He was the son of a pastor in the Thuringian village of Oberwiessbach in central Germany and grew up in an intensely religious environment. His mother's death when he was a young child left him lonely and neglected. Although he had many interests, his shy, highly introspective, and melancholy temperament made it difficult for him to give sustained concentration to any one of them. As a youth, he was apprenticed to a forester and acquired a thorough knowledge of plant life and a deep appreciation of nature. His scientific interests took him to the University of Jena, where he enrolled as a student for a brief period until he was forced to withdraw because of financial indebtedness. Once again unable to locate himself in a satisfying vocation, he drifted from occupation to occupation, working as a naturalist and then as a chemist before fixing his attention on educational study and practice.

Having decided to become a teacher, Froebel studied for two years with Anton Gruner, a Pestalozzian disciple who headed the Frankfurt am Main model school. Then in 1808 he journeyed to Yverdon with a group of young German teachers who went to apprentice as teaching assistants with the famous Pestalozzi. As a result of his experiences at Yverdon, Froebel became committed to his educational vocation, and accepted certain aspects of Pestalozzi's educational theory. For example, he agreed with Pestalozzi that certain natural laws could be discovered and used as the basis for a natural method of education. Both educators are noted in the history of education for their exaltation of childhood as an intrinsically valuable period of growth that is necessary to man's development. Further, both educators urged that the senses and emotions as well as the intellect be used fully in education. Froebel believed, however, that Pestalozzi's method needed to be refined and systematized. When he elaborated his own educational theory, it was decidedly more mystical and transcendental than Pestalozzi's.

When he returned to Germany, Froebel resumed his formal university education by enrolling in the University of Göttingen, where he studied such natural sciences as physics, chemistry, mineralogy, and natural history and also delved into philosophical and historical treatises. His studies were again interrupted, this time by a call to military service in the campaign of 1813 against Napoleon. Upon release from active military service, Froebel opened a small experimental school at Griesheim in 1816 that emphasized music, play, and self-activity. In 1818, he moved his school to Keilhau, where he inaugurated his method of early childhood education. In 1831, at the invitation of the Swiss government, he agreed to prepare elementary school teachers. He next became director of an orphanage at Burgdorf in Switzerland, an experience that deepened his insights into the patterns of child development. Returning to Germany in 1837, he established his first kindergarten for children between the ages of three and eight in the village of Blankenburg, where he elaborated his theory of kindergarten education and developed games, plays, songs, and occupations designed to stimulate the child's self-activity. Froebel's work *Mother and Play Songs* (1843) was based on materials used at Blankenburg. His kindergarten school attracted a stream of visitors to Blankenburg in much the same way that Pestalozzi's educational experiments had earlier attracted them to Yverdon. Froebel's ideas began to have a respectful audience in Germany and throughout the Western world.

Froebel's Educational Philosophy

In his own education, Froebel had studied the most divergent fields of thought. In *The Education of Man* (1826), he attempted to unite idealism, mysticism, Christianity, romanticism, and natural science into a philosophical synthesis upon which to base his ideas on education. Froebel asserted that all existence originates with, and is united in, God, the divine and universal Presence. All beings comprise an external natural dimension and an internal spiritual dimension and are sustained by the divine energy, or effluence, that is their essence. Since the purpose of existence is to reveal God, it is man's destiny to become conscious of his divine interior essence and to reveal this dynamic inner force through its externalization. It was upon these premises that Froebel asserted that the purpose of education is to lead

> . . . man, as a thinking, intelligent being, growing into self-consciousness, to a pure and unsullied, conscious and free representation of the inner law of Divine Unity, and in teaching him ways and means thereto.[1]

In asserting that the world comes from, but still remains in, God, Froebel meant that natural phenomena represent the concretizing of the ideas that exist in the mind of God. Further, all existence, including human nature, is subject to the universal law of development that manifests divine essence. Froebel believed in a divinely ordained and established universe functioning according to spiritual laws. Development occurs when the divine essence unfolds according to a prescribed and patterned sequence.

Like Pestalozzi and Comenius, Froebel discovered a parallel between nature and man. Since both have a common origin in one divine and eternal Being, the same developmental laws govern both. Basic to these developmental stages is Froebel's doctrine of preformation in which he defined human development as essentially the unfolding of those potentialities that have been preformed in the person. Like the perfect seed, which is in reality the whole plant in miniature with root, stalk, and leaf, all that the child is to become is already present within the embryo and is attainable only through development from within in an outward direction.

Applying the premises of philosophical idealism to educational method, Froebel leaned heavily on the doctrine of interconnectedness, which asserts that all beings are related in an organic unity. Although nature appears to the superficial observer to be a diversity of many separate individuals, these separate individuals form one great spiritu-

[1] Friedrich Froebel, *The Education of Man*, W. N. Hailman (tr.) (New York: Appleton, 1896), p. 1.

ally coherent unity. Froebelian education sought to impress upon the child that he was part of a higher and more complex community of spiritual beings. Although his kindergarten children worked and played with discrete objects, he believed that the objects that they encountered should be interrelated.

In Froebelian methodology, the teacher functions as a cooperative agent who stimulates the process of unfolding the potentialities present in the child's divinely endowed human nature. In order to cooperate with the process of child growth, Froebel urged educators to

1. Study the eternal laws of human development
2. Construct an educational theory that specifies the directions to be followed in cooperating with human development
3. Apply these directions actively to achieve the development of rational beings
4. Direct education to realize a faithful, pure, and holy life that actualizes the divinely implanted potentialities

According to Froebel, education should be passive rather than prescriptive and permit the child to express his inner divine nature through self-activity. In rejecting the notion of child depravity and the need for unduly prescriptive schooling, he asserted that the teacher's major obligation is to provide the space and time that the child needs to develop properly according to the laws that are working within him and to ward off influences that might hinder that development. As a leading proponent of child freedom, Froebel believed that every human being should be respected and accorded the dignity due him as the manifestation of the divine spirit in human form.

Froebel believed that the child's self-activities stimulate him to express his inner impulses in outward action. The manipulation of objects found in the environment stimulates the child's strong interior impulses. Froebel rejected the traditional schoolman's condemnation of play as a form of degenerate idleness that ought to be suppressed. In contrast, he praised children's play and incorporated it as one of the basic kindergarten activities. In fact, his kindergarten was an institution founded on play. Through play, he said, the child exhibits his simple and natural life. In games, he imitates adult activities and practices social and moral values.

The Froebelian Conception of the Child

Froebel, an idealist, believed that the human race could be viewed as one human being. The development of a single human being recapitulates the spiritual and cultural history of the human race by passing through all the preceding phases of human development.

Through this cultural recapitulation, the child unifies his spirit and nature and experiences the spiritual harmony of family life. From family life he is united to the wholeness of the entire human community.

As one who believed in the spiritual relatedness of all existence, Froebel emphasized that a major objective of education should be to develop the child's sense of community. Like Pestalozzi, he believed that the child's sense of communal awareness and identification depends on his discovery that his father, mother, brothers, sisters, and all human beings are united in a universal community through and with God. The feeling of kinship with humanity is the general beginning of the religious spirit that yearns for an unhindered unification with God.

Basing this view on his idealist premises, Froebel asserted that human industries and vocations concretize the thoughts of God. When God created man and the universe, the divine thoughts had been rendered into concrete works, deeds, and products. Made in the image of God, man should also strive to objectify his own thoughts by giving order and form to raw material. Work is a productive and creative activity that gives substance to thought.

Although he was definitely inclined toward greater freedom for the child, Froebel also believed that children need some degree of external guidance within the context of the prepared educational environment. Without some planned and rational guidance by the teacher, children's whims can degenerate into aimless activities. But when properly cultivated, their interests, needs, and play have a significant importance to adult work and society.

Froebel's conception of the school was based on his idea that the inner lives of all beings are interrelated. The major aim of the school should be to give the student insight into the universal unity that permeates all reality so that he can penetrate the external reality of objects and discern a higher order of spirituality. As a person, the teacher should be a model worthy of the child's trust and love.

Basing his views on his observation of nature and the stages of human development, Froebel asserted that the kindergarten curriculum should incorporate the principles of self-development, activity, and socialization. Through such a natural and spiritual curriculum, the school can lead the child to knowledge of (1) himself; (2) human relations; (3) nature and the external world; and (4) God, the Divine Source and Cause of all existence.

Songs, stories, and games were a most important part of Froebel's kindergarten. The songs and stories stimulated the child's imagination and introduced him to his cultural literature. The games gave the child a sense of community and an opportunity to share in cooperative activities that contributed to his socialization and motor competencies.

As the core of the kindergarten curriculum, Froebel devised a series of two types of play materials to stimulate the child's motor expression and skill and develop his symbolic, constructive, and aesthetic powers. He believed that these instructional materials conformed to the laws of human life and development and constituted a medium that the child could manipulate in work and play.

The first of these instructional play materials Froebel classified as "gifts," which were objects given by God to the child to stimulate his development. They were objects whose form was fixed, such as cubes, spheres, and cylinders. These basic kindergarten materials, in his view, have a special power to awaken the child's process of conceptualization and to lead him to recognize ultimate truths. The sphere and the circle, for example, have profound interest for the child. The ball represents the spherical shape of the earth and the concept of unification of all reality in the Absolute. Froebel also believed that children have a compulsion to pursue circular action games. Other symbolic gifts in his kindergarten were cubes, brick-shaped blocks, squares, triangles, straight splints, metal and paper rings, and points represented by stones and seeds.

"Occupations," which were Froebel's second category of instructional materials, referred to activities with certain specified malleable materials. Unlike the gifts, whose form was fixed, these were materials whose form changed with use, such as clay, sand, cardboard, and mud. He felt that these materials involve the child in activity and develop physical and manipulative skills. Through sewing, for example, the child learns to connect points into lines. By weaving, he forms surfaces from lines. In the Froebelian kindergarten, the child was encouraged to use his imagination to practice activities normally associated with adult life. For example, a child making mud pies takes a raw material and, by using his imagination, practices cooking. Such activities enable children to act out their observations of adult life.

Froebel related his conception of occupations to the work that is performed in the child's own family. Since children naturally want to share in family activities, parents should encourage them to do so. Ignoring or rebuffing the child adversely affects his development.

Like Pestalozzi, Montessori, and other childhood educators, Froebel insisted that a definite sequence be employed in using these basic kindergarten materials. The ball, for example, should be the first in the series of gifts introduced to the child. As an undifferentiated unity, it is the symbol from which differentiated entities are derived. In other words, the other gifts—cube, brick, surface, and point—are implicit in the sphere. The child's mind proceeds from an undifferentiated, unconscious unity to one that is differentiated and conscious.

Froebel emphasized activities and games that he believed reflected the cumulative unity associated with genuinely constructive work. He would not permit children to destroy an old form in order to obtain materials to build a new one but insisted, instead, that new forms be made from existing ones. This, he believed, would cultivate a sense of orderliness in the child.

He believed that the introduction of constructive activities in the school provides physical exercise conducive to the child's bodily development and prepares him for his future work. Play, construction, and modeling prepare the child for an industrious, diligent life. By conceiving of God as the eternal Creator who works through eternity to manifest His thoughts into concrete entities, Froebel drew a close relationship between religion and work. Religion without work is idle, while work without religion degrades man. Froebel listed woodcutting, making kitchen utensils, weaving and binding, ruling slates and paper, collecting natural and artistic objects, basket-making, caring for animals, cutting, mounting, weaving, whittling, and a variety of other activities as suitable for the school.

Froebel's Object Lesson

As mentioned earlier, Froebel's educational method was heavily influenced by his predilection for symbolism. Such contemporary commentators on educational theory as Broudy and Palmer, in referring to Froebel's emphasis on symbols, have described Froebelian methodology as "dialectical gardening" employing the "symbolic object lesson."[2] Froebel believed that the child possesses the germ of an idea or concept that he is destined to bring to full consciousness as an adult. This concept is symbolized by some object within the child's range of experience, which he becomes interested in playing with or otherwise using. This activity with the object awakens the concept, which is then developed toward full consciousness.

Froebel's emphasis on symbols often led him to interpret the child's interests and activities in a mystical light. Noticing that children enjoy playing in water, he concluded that the child wants to see his image reflected in water in order to glimpse his soul. Children's occupation with sand and clay reveals a desire to experience the plastic element of life and to shape and master raw materials. Children's desire for membership in the human community is manifest as they join in group occupations. The sense of community identification is strengthened as children work together to complete a common enterprise.

Although modern educators have disregarded much of the symbolic mysticism associated with Froebelian kindergarten practices, the total impact of Froebel's work contributed to the liberalization of, and the

[2] Harry S. Broudy and John R. Palmer, *Exemplars of Teaching Method*, (Chicago: Rand McNally, 1965), pp. 117–129.

legitimizing of the role of play and activities in, early childhood education.[3]

The Kindergarten Movement

Froebel achieved success in his kindergarten school at Blankenburg. By 1850, his methods and ideas had attracted sufficient attention to stimulate the acceptance of the kindergarten. Unfortunately, the reactionary ministry of education of the Prussian government believed that the kindergarten concept was contrary to government policy and banned the institution in 1851. In 1861, however, the prohibition against the kindergarten was lifted, and the popular educational institution reappeared and flourished.

Froebel had trained a number of women in the kindergarten method, and, as disciples, they established kindergartens in their own nations. In England, kindergartens were established by Bertha Ronge, Adele von Portugall, and Eleanore Heerwart. This English movement grew under the aegis of the Froebel Society, which was founded in 1875. In Switzerland, Henriette Breyman worked on behalf of the kindergarten.

Baroness Bertha von Marenholtz Bulow-Wendhausen (1810–1893) had helped to support Froebel's work and became a devoted disciple of the Froebelian method. Lecturing and writing for the Froebelian kindergarten in Germany, England, France, Italy, and the Netherlands, she was a tireless advocate of the kindergarten.

Froebel's ideas, as well as those of Pestalozzi, exerted an influence on the Finnish educator Uno Cygnaeus (1810–1888), who was a major proponent of manual training. Cygnaeus sought to combine the Froebelian concepts of gifts and constructive activities of working with sand, clay, and colors with handicrafts, such as metal work, basket-weaving, and wood-carving. The Finnish government encouraged Cygnaeus' manual training idea by making it compulsory for boys in rural schools and by requiring that male teachers be taught the methods of teaching manual training as a part of their professional preparation.

Sweden also accepted the manual training philosophy, which was introduced into Swedish schools under the name of "sloyd." By 1877, manual training was being offered by Swedish Folk Schools under the encouragement of the government, which believed that it might remedy the depressed condition of Swedish home industries. The Swedish educator Otto Salomon (1849–1907) was impressed by the Finnish system of manual training and introduced many of the methods that Cygnaeus had pioneered.

---

[3] William H. Kilpatrick, *Froebel's Kindergarten Principles: Critically Examined* (New York: Macmillan, 1916), pp. 195–200.

The Growth of the American Kindergarten

The kindergarten concept was originally introduced into the United States by immigrants from Germany. A kindergarten opened by Caroline Frankenberg in 1838 lasted only a brief time, but the refugees from the abortive Revolution of 1848 established a number of German-language kindergartens. Among these immigrants, who came from the most liberal sections of the German population, was Mrs. Carl Schurz, who established a kindergarten in Watertown, Wisconsin, in 1855.

In their European travels, Henry Barnard and other American educators encountered the Froebelian kindergarten and were enthusiastic in their reports. Elizabeth Peabody, one of Froebel's leading disciples in the United States, worked to popularize the kindergarten among English-speaking Americans. When she encountered objections that the kindergarten was better suited to German children than to American, she responded that Froebel had developed a human method of education rather than a national one. In 1860, she established the first English-language kindergarten in Boston, and she was also instrumental in establishing a training school for kindergarten teachers there in 1868. Her book *Lectures in the Training Schools for Kindergartners* (1893) helped to introduce Froebelian educational theory and practice to American teachers. In her enthusiasm for Froebel's educational method, she said:

> It begins to be realized in Europe as well as in America, that Froebel's idea of education, in making character the first thing, and knowledge the hand-maiden of goodness, is the desideratum of the age, and promise of the millennium.[4]

In 1873, the superintendent of schools in St. Louis, Missouri, William Torrey Harris, himself a follower of Hegelian philosophical idealism, established the kindergarten as a part of a public school system. By 1900, the kindergarten was enthusiastically accepted by Americans, who established numerous kindergartens, both private and public.

Maria Montessori

The life of the Italian educator Maria Montessori (1870–1952) spanned parts of both the nineteenth and twentieth centuries. Like her predecessors Pestalozzi and Froebel, she offered new insights into child development and education. Her own training and experience provided an excellent background for the contributions she made to

[4] Elizabeth Peabody, *Lectures in the Training Schools for Kindergartners* (Boston: D. C. Heath, 1893), p. 80.

early childhood education. Montessori was born in Chiaravalle, Italy, on August 31, 1870. Her strong will and independent character were revealed by her departure from the conventional educational norms that applied to girls when she enrolled in a preengineering curriculum in a boys' technical school. She later turned from her interest in engineering to biology and medicine. Despite parental and social opposition, she enrolled in the University of Rome to study medicine and experimental psychology. Completing her studies in 1896, she was the first woman to receive the doctorate in medicine from that university. She remained at the university's psychiatric clinic as an instructor specializing in the education of mentally defective children. In 1899, she became directress of an experimental school, *Scuola Ortofrenica*, which cared for children regarded to be mentally handicapped and uneducable. Under Montessori's direction, these children learned to read and write to the degree that they succeeded in passing the public examinations required of normal children.

Montessori's work with the mentally deficient children stimulated her to investigate child development from biological and psychological perspectives and led to her appointment as lecturer of pedagogical anthropology in 1900. In her research, she encountered the work of Jean Marc Itard (1775–1838) and Edward Sequin (1812–1880), whose investigations into mental retardation were pedagogical as well as medical. Sequin believed that intellectual development could be stimulated through manual work, and he emphasized sensory and motor skills, making use of such concrete materials as pictures, papers, clay, and sand. The research of Itard and Sequin influenced Montessori's own educational theorizing, and she derived many of her pedagogical principles from their pioneer efforts. Her experiences and research confirmed her conviction that earliest childhood education was the most crucial phase of human development.

Montessori's work with mentally deficient children led her to a number of pedagogical insights that she believed were also applicable to normal children:

1. Children are capable of sustained mental concentration when genuinely interested in their work.
2. They love order and especially enjoy the repetition of actions that they have already mastered.
3. They prefer work to play and prefer didactic materials to toys.
4. Rewards and punishments are unnecessary to motivate them.
5. The child has a deep sense of personal dignity that is easily offended.[5]

[5] E. M. Standing, *Maria Montessori: Her Life and Work* (New York: Mentor Omega Books, 1962), pp. 40–43.

When Montessori was asked to organize a school for culturally disadvantaged children in Rome's San Lorenzo district in 1907, she took this opportunity to apply her theory and methods. Her *Casa dei Bambini* ("Children's House") was opened in one room of a tenement house and was furnished with small tables and chairs, proportioned to the size of the students. With the help of two assistants, she undertook the education of sixty undernourished and deprived children from the Roman slums. At the San Lorenzo school, Montessori developed what she called her "observational method" of investigating child growth, which she asserted was based on the idea that children should be permitted to "express themselves freely" by revealing their hidden and often repressed needs and aptitudes[6] and the role of the teacher should be that of a sensitive and scientific observer. In commenting on her work in the *Casa dei Bambini*, Montessori said:

> It was here that there occurred surprising manifestations like the "explosion of spontaneous writing and reading," "spontaneous discipline," "free social life," which have roused the curiosity and admiration of the world.[7]

Gradually, Montessori elaborated an educational theory and method that incorporated her insights into child nature and development. Although she claimed that her theory was scientific rather than romantic and mystical like those of Pestalozzi and Froebel, certain similarities existed between her work and that of these earlier educators. Like Froebel, she believed that the child carries within himself the germinal potentialities that determine his adult development. She also referred to "spontaneous" activities of reading, writing, socialization, and discipline, which were not unlike the Froebelian conception of the unfolding of the child's own latent, preformed potentialities through his own self-activity.

Montessori's method of instruction was to take place in a "prepared environment" in which the child would be guided by trained direction to realize the mental and physical potentialities inherent in his nature. In order to fashion methodological procedures and didactic materials conducive to child growth, she classified two broad sets of functions that must be developed in the child:

1. Those motor functions that secure balance and coordinated movement
2. Those sensory functions that lay the foundations of intelligence by exercising the child's capacity for observation, comparison, and judgment.

[6] Maria Montessori, *The Discovery of the Child* (Adyar, India: Kalakshetra Publications, 1948), p. 75.
[7] *Ibid.*, p. 62.

Like Comenius, Rousseau, Pestalozzi, and Froebel before her, Montessori believed it possible to discern clearly defined stages of human development. She recognized two such stages: the years from birth through age six, during which the child's mind is absorbent and particularly sensitive to learning about the environment; and the years from seven through eighteen, when the child is emerging into adulthood. Although she commented that the stage of emergent adulthood is a time of great physical and mental development, Montessori's greatest concern was with the period of the "absorbent mind," which she subdivided into two chronological developmental periods: one to three years, when the child's mind functions unconsciously; and three to six years, when his mind grows increasingly conscious of its operations. She made it her task to fashion instructional materials and learning experiences that would exercise the child's motor and sensory functions during these periods of greatest sensitivity.

Montessori also referred to "sensitive" times in the child's life when he has a compelling desire to learn such particular skills as language usage, socialization, and mathematical computation. She designed an instructional method and didactic materials to exploit these sensitive periods to their fullest educational advantage in the belief that once the child has lived through a particular sensitive period, he will never again be as adept in mastering the particular skill that is appropriate to that period. The teacher should study the child's activities to detect when he is entering one of these periods of greatest sensitivity and then allow him the greatest possible freedom to develop the appropriate skill. Montessori recommended "auto-education" by which the child selects his own activity and solves his own difficulty. If the child is ready for a task, he can find the proper solution to a problem or difficulty. Only when the child's activities are dangerous to his own person or detrimental to the general good, should he be redirected to another activity. Montessori advised the teacher to exercise caution in interrupting a child's activity since it is easy to wound his dignity and he may be diverted to an activity that he regards as trivial. Montessori's "sensitive" periods were no more than stages of readiness for specific learnings based upon the child's interests, needs, experiences, and maturity. Readiness for learning is a concept that was also shared by Pestalozzi and Froebel.

Although an advocate of child freedom in the sense of emphasizing "sensitivity" or "readiness," Montessori believed in a highly structured, or prepared, environment designed to expedite learning.[8] Although some twentieth-century American progressive educators believe that Montessori's "prepared environment" unduly restricts a child's freedom to experiment, Montessori saw no conflict between a child's

[8] Maria Montessori, *Spontaneous Activity in Education* (New York: Schocken Books, 1917), pp. 67–72.

freedom of activity and a structured learning environment. She believed that the teacher's responsibility is to prepare the environment, direct the activity, and function as the authority but that the actual learning is the responsibility of the child as he persists in, and accomplishes, his task. No human being can be educated by another person; he can learn only through his own efforts.[9]

Montessori's Curriculum

Montessori devised a curriculum that comprised three major kinds of activities and experiences: (1) practical life; (2) sensory training; and (3) formal skills and studies. Upon entering the Montessori school, the child was introduced to such practical activities as setting a table, serving a meal, washing dishes, tying and hooking wearing apparel, and performing the basic social amenities. Sensory and muscular training and coordination also received special attention. Montessori believed that sense education's main objective was to refine perception through repeated exercises. She believed that it was possible to sharpen the capacity for observation, comparison, and judgment through her didactic system.

It was the third area of the Montessori curriculum, the formal skills and studies, that attracted the greatest acclaim. Advocates of the method attested to the great success that had been achieved in teaching reading, writing, and arithmetic to preschool-age children. After they had mastered a series of muscular coordination exercises, children in the Montessori schools were introduced to the alphabet through unmounted, movable sandpaper letters that they used to spell out words. Reading was taught after writing. Colored rods of various sizes were used to teach arithmetic.

Montessori designed various didactic materials that were used to develop the practical, sensory, and formal skills included in the curriculum. Through the regular and graded use of the didactic materials, the children were expected to gain manipulative and judgmental skills that would contribute to their sensory, physical, and intellectual development. Among the didactic materials were such items as lacing and buttoning frames, long and broad stairs, weights, and packets to be identified according to their sound or smell. According to the Montessori method, the materials were to be used in a prescribed manner so that the child would obtain the desired outcome, either skill mastery or intellectual training. It is interesting to note that both Froebel and Montessori were exacting in their specifications of the materials that were to be introduced to the children in their prepared learning en-

---

[9] Dorothy Canfield Fisher, *The Montessori Manual* (Chicago: Robert Bentley, 1913), pp. 18–19.

vironments. Froebel's gifts were intended to be both play and work materials and, as symbols, were to stimulate the recall of latent concepts. Montessori's didactic materials were intended to produce the desired mental effects and skill learning. Disciples of Froebel and those of Montessori have rarely agreed on the nature of the prepared environment and on the use of didactic materials. Froebelians have found the Montessorian prepared environment to be overly structured and rigid. Disciples of Montessori, on the other hand, are likely to believe that the kindergarten is overly sentimentalized and romantic and fails to cultivate the child's possibilities for skill mastery and intellectual achievement.

Montessori also rejected the Froebelian practice of using fairy tales, fables, and fantasy to stimulate the child's imagination. Although she agreed that imagination ought to be stimulated, she believed that science was a more effective vehicle for stimulating the imagination of the modern child. The Froebelian kindergarten teacher was a storyteller, a song leader, and an organizer of group games, plays, and dances. The Montessori directress, in contrast, was a trained observer of children who permitted them to select their own individual activities. Since the child was often involved in individualized activity, the Montessori prepared environment required much more apparatus than did the Froebelian kindergarten.

Both Froebelians and progressive educators have criticized the Montessori method for failing to encourage sufficient socializing. However, although much of the Montessori method is designed to permit the child to develop at his own individual rate, the method does have certain elements of group association and social control. Children are required to conform to standards of cleanliness and behavior that are conducive to group comfort and welfare. They work together in cleaning their classroom and in setting tables for meals. During the 1930s, the Montessori method was suspected by the totalitarian regimes of being contrary to their principles. In 1935, the Nazi regime suppressed the German Montessori Society. In 1936, Mussolini's Fascist government abolished all Montessorian institutions and agencies. During the last two decades of her life, Montessori was in exile from her native Italy. During this period, she encouraged her disciples to implant her educational method throughout the world. As a result, strong groups of Montessorian educators established schools in the United States, India, the Netherlands, and the United Kingdom.

Montessorianism in the United States

Montessorian educational principles made their way to the United States in the early years of the twentieth century. The articles and books of such advocates as Anne E. George, who translated Montessori's *Pedagogia Scientifica,* and Dorothy Canfield Fisher, who published *A Montessori Mother* in 1912 and *The Montessori Manual* in 1913, helped to introduce the method in the United States. Montessori herself visited the United States in 1913 on a lecture tour sponsored by such notables as Thomas Edison, Alexander Graham Bell, and Margaret Wilson, the President's daughter.[10]

Although Montessori attracted a favorable audience in certain quarters of the American public, many professional educators remained unconvinced. At the convention of the National Education Association in 1913, Elizabeth Ross Shaw delivered a number of stinging criticisms. She alleged that Montessori's method was neither new nor scientific. Shaw criticized Montessori's early introduction of writing and reading as being premature and pedagogically unsound. Her most direct attack was on Montessori's sensory exercises, which involved excessive repetition. In attacking the sensory exercises as an archaic form of "intellectual gymnastics," Shaw alleged such concentration

> . . . deliberately tries to make the child an efficient automaton. That is why so many observers of her work have remarked on the striking resemblance between her methods and those of animal trainers.[11]

The Froebelian kindergartners also tended to be suspicious of the Montessori method, which some felt to be an unworthy rival approach to early childhood education. They disapproved strongly of Montessori's rejection of imaginative myths and fables. Some of the Froebelians also felt that Montessori had not given adequate emphasis to play as the child's natural mode of living and learning.

Some progressive educators were also critical of Montessori's emphasis on didactic materials and the principle of auto-education as a lockstep and rigid approach to schooling. Genuine education, they felt, should offer real life situations in which the child can formulate and test his own hypotheses in solving problems. It was also felt that Montessori's emphasis on individualized learning did not offer sufficient opportunities for the child's socializing.

Montessorianism failed to take hold in the United States after its initial introduction. Devoted kindergartners refused to abandon their discipleship to Froebelian pedagogy. Experimentalist progressive educators preferred to look to John Dewey and to William Heard Kilpatrick's project method rather than to Montessori. As of 1934, the

[10] Norak Smaridge, *The Light Within* (New York: Hawthorn Books, 1965), pp. 114–117.

[11] Elizabeth Ross Shaw, "The Effect of the Scientific Spirit in Education Upon the Kindergarten in Relation to the Distinctive Characteristics of the Montessori Method," *Journal of Proceedings and Addresses of the National Education Association of the United States* (1913), pp. 439–445.

respected American educator Ellwood P. Cubberley dismissed Montessorianism as having "its greatest value for subnormal children."[12]

The American Montessori Revival

In the decade of the 1950s, there was a marked revival of interest in the Montessori method in the United States. Progressive education was under attack as "soft pedagogy" by a number of critics. The Soviet Union's space success with the launching of Sputnik in 1957 unleashed a barrage of criticism against the American public school's alleged neglect of basic skills and intellectual subject matter. In 1958, the Whitby School of "pure Montessori" was established in Greenwich, Connecticut, by Nancy McCormick Rambusch. Montessorian literature again became popular as the major works were reprinted.

The revival of Montessorianism brought into being more than two hundred schools, most of them private. These schools appealed primarily to the upper middle class who sought new ways to advance their children's intellectual abilities. In the 1960s, American energies were enlisted in a war on poverty, and some educators began to recommend the method for children who were victims of "cultural disadvantagement."[13]

Conclusion

It can be seen that there were similarities and also differences between the educational theories of Froebel and Montessori. Both educators emphasized the liberation of the child's energies. Both believed that the child possesses innate energies that need to be stimulated by a properly prepared educational environment. Although both theories contain a share of mysticism and idealism, Froebel's kindergarten gifts were more symbolic than Montessori's didactic materials. The kindergarten was probably also more of a socializing agency than was the "prepared environment" of pure Montessorianism. Both methods of early childhood education had an impact that was world-wide.

The nineteenth century was rich in political, social, and educational alternatives as is represented by Froebelianism, Pestalozzianism, and Montessorianism. Chapters 15 and 16, which deal with the educational implications of Marxism and Darwinism, will return to the ideological currents and controversies of the nineteenth century.

[12] Ellwood P. Cubberley, *Public Education in the United States* (Chicago: Houghton Mifflin, 1934), p. 460.
[13] G. L. Stevens, "Implications of Montessori for the War on Poverty," in R. C. Orem (ed.), *Montessori for the Disadvantaged* (New York: Capricorn Books, 1968), pp. 36–37.

Suggested Readings

Baylor, Ruth M. *Elizabeth Palmer Peabody: Kindergarten Pioneer.* Philadelphia: University of Pennsylvania Press, 1965.

Blow, Elizabeth. *Letters to a Mother.* New York: Appleton, 1899.

Elliot, Henrietta R. *Mottoes and Commentaries of Friedrich Froebel.* New York: Appleton, 1895.

Fisher, Dorothy Canfield. *The Montessori Manual.* Chicago: Robert Bentley, 1913. (New edition 1964.)

Froebel, Friedrich. *Education by Development.* New York: Appleton, 1899.

———. *The Education of Man.* W. N. Hailmann (tr.). New York: Appleton, 1887.

Hughes, James L. *Froebel's Education Laws for All Teachers.* New York: Appleton, 1892.

Kilpatrick, William H. *Froebel's Kindergarten Principles: Critically Examined.* New York: Macmillan, 1916.

———. *The Montessori System Examined.* Boston: Houghton Mifflin, 1914.

Lawrence, Evelyn (ed.). *Friedrich Froebel and English Education.* New York: Philosophical Library, 1953.

Lilley, Irene M. (ed.). *Friedrich Froebel: A Selection from His Writings.* Cambridge, England: Cambridge University Press, 1967.

MacVannel, John A. *The Educational Theories of Herbart and Froebel.* New York: Teachers College, Columbia University, 1905.

Montessori, Maria. *Pedagogical Anthropology.* New York: F. A. Stokes, 1913.

———. *Spontaneous Activity in Education.* Cambridge, Mass.: Robert Bentley, Inc., 1964.

———. *The Absorbent Mind.* New York: Holt, Rinehart, and Winston, 1967.

———. *The Child in the Family.* Chicago: Regnery, 1970.

———. *The Discovery of the Child.* Wheaton, Illinois: Theosophical Publishing House, 1966.

———. *The Montessori Method.* Cambridge: Robert Bentley, 1912. (New edition 1965.)

———. *The Secret of Childhood.* Calcutta: Orient Longmans, 1963.

Peabody, Elizabeth P. *Lectures in the Training Schools for Kindergartners.* Boston: D. C. Heath, 1893.

Rambusch, Nancy. *Learning How to Learn: An American Approach to Montessori.* Baltimore: Helicon Press, 1962.

Shaw, Elizabeth Ross. "The Effect of the Scientific Spirit in Education Upon the Kindergarten in Relation to the Distinctive Characteristics of the Montessori Method," *Journal of Proceedings and Addresses of the National Education Association of the United States* (1913), pp. 439–445.

Smaridge, Norak. *The Light Within.* New York: Hawthorn Books, 1965.

Smith, P. Woodham. *Friedrich Froebel and English Education.* New York: Philosophical Library, 1953.

Standing, E. M. *Maria Montessori: Her Life and Work.* New York: Mentor Omega Books, 1962.

———. *The Montessori Method: A Revolution in Education.* Fresno, Cal.: Academy Library Guild, 1962.

Stevens, Ellen Yale. *A Guide to the Montessori Method.* New York: F. A. Stokes, 1913.

————. "The Montessori Movement in America," *McClure's Magazine*, XL (February 1913), 222.

Stevens, G. L. "Implications of Montessori for the War on Poverty," in R. C. Orem (ed.), *Montessori for the Disadvantaged*. New York: Capricorn Books, 1968.

Wakin, Edward. "The Return of Montessori," in Lucille Perryman (ed.), *Montessori in Perspective*. Washington, D.C.: National Association for the Education of Young Children, 1966.

Weber, Evelyn. *The Kindergarten: Its Encounter with Educational Thought in America*. New York: Teachers College Press, 1969.

Wiggin, Kate, and Nora Smith. *The Republic of Childhood*. Boston: Houghton Mifflin, 1898.

CHAPTER 15

Marxism: Educational Implications

Communism, one of the major revolutionary forces of the twentieth century, arose as an ideological, philosophical, and political movement in the nineteenth century. Its originator, Karl Marx, often referred to as the founder of "scientific socialism," drew together the theories of the various socialist ideologies of the nineteenth century into an architectonic system. Marx rejected the peaceful and gradualistic procedures of such utopian socialists as Fourier and Owen and relied instead on the instruments of class warfare and violent revolution to effect social change. Lenin's revolution in Russia in 1917 and Mao Tse-tung's revolution in China in 1949 drew ideological support from Marx's theory.

Born in the city of Trier in the German Rhineland, Karl Marx (1818–1883) was the son of a prosperous middle-class lawyer who was a civil servant in the Prussian government. He received a conventional education in the schools of Trier and went on to higher studies at the universities of Bonn and Berlin. After studying law for a short time, he concentrated on history and philosophy and was awarded a doctorate in 1841. His student years made a profound impact on him and on the ideology that he elaborated in his later years. Like many of his fellow students, Marx was disillusioned by the course of events in Germany. Although Frederick William IV, who had ascended the Prussian throne in 1840, had promised enlightened rule, Prussia was dominated by an unenlightened coalition of bankers, industrialists, and Junker aristocrats. Although foremost among the German states, Prussia had not taken the lead in either liberalizing or uniting the various German principalities and petty kingdoms.

Intellectual Influences on Marx

By briefly examining some of the theoretical influences on Marx's thought, one can discern both the shaping of Marxian scientific socialism, or communism, and the intellectual currents associated with working-class discontent. Marx and his fellow socialists were reacting to the exploitation resulting from industrial capitalism, which they believed dehumanized and victimized industrial factory workers in the urban proletariat. Unlike the utopian socialists, who had relied extensively on education to effect social reform, Marx did not develop a systematic educational theory. Nevertheless, an examination of Marxism and its pedagogical implications can aid the student of educational theory in seeing nineteenth- and twentieth-century social and educational patterns from a perspective that was critical of liberalism.

Among those exerting an intellectual influence on Marx was Moses Hess (1812–1875), a social critic of nineteenth-century industrial capitalism.[1] Hess' critique of capitalism drew heavily on traditional Judaism, humanitarianism, and Hegelian philosophical idealism. From Hess, Marx acquired the belief that private property was the source of all human ills. What came to be Marx's own call for world-wide communism was initially stimulated by Hess' humanitarian plea for an organized international society resting on a rational and collective base. Hess also influenced Marx's notion of economic determinism which Marx developed into a major concept in his own communist ideology. As chief editor of Hess' journal, *Rheinische Zeitung*, Marx attacked the Prussian government, censorship, and the unenlightened ruling classes. In 1843, the Prussian government suppressed the journal.

Like most German university students, Marx had encountered the philosophic idealism of Georg Hegel (1770–1831) and was profoundly influenced by Hegel's conception of history as a dialectical process. According to Hegel's view, history consists of a ceaseless succession of ideological conflicts. Every idea embodies both a partial truth (thesis) and its contradiction (antithesis). From the conflicts of thesis and antithesis emerges a synthesis, a newer and higher idea that, in turn, becomes a thesis generating new conflict. Through these dialectical forms of thesis, antithesis, and synthesis, human history is the unfolding of the Absolute Idea.

Marx rejected the spirituality of Hegelianism. Like the eighteenth-century philosophes, he believed that the "heavenly city" was to be built on this earth and not in a supernatural realm. Although he incorpo-

---

[1] For a very readable discussion of the various influences that affected Marx, see Isaiah Berlin, *Karl Marx: His Life and Environment* (New York: Oxford University Press, 1959).

rated into his own theories the Hegelian view of history as a dialectical process, he transferred this concept to the material realm. Instead of an ideational conflict, he saw the dialectic as a history of the struggle between conflicting economic classes.

In his economic interpretation of history, Marx was influenced by the materialism of Ludwig Feuerbach (1804–1872), author of *Theses on the Hegelian Philosophy*. Feuerbach rejected the Hegelian concept that historical events are determined by the unfolding of a spiritual force, the Absolute Idea. Asserting that the causal force in human history is the totality of material conditions that appear at any given historical period, Feuerbach claimed that society, thought, religion, and politics are products of man's physical environment.

In 1843, Marx and his young wife, the former Jenny von Westphalen, left Germany and went to Paris, where he worked on the German language periodical *Deutsch-Franzosische Jahrbucher*. By this time, he had already accepted the notions of a materialistic universe, dialectical processes of social change, economic determinism, and class struggle, all of which would find expression as elements in his evolving synthesis of scientific socialism. In France, he studied the doctrines of such leading socialist theorists as Saint-Simon, Fourier, Proudhon, and Bakunin.

Claude Henri, Comte de Saint-Simon (1760–1825) believed that the basic changes wrought by industrialization required a restructuring of social institutions. He urged that a new cooperative society governed by scientific and technological experts replace rule by kings and nobles. Saint-Simon's advocacy of government by a technological and managerial elite contributed to Marx's emphasis on the small elite, or the vanguard of the proletariat, that would lead the coming revolution.

Although Marx considered syndicalism a simplistic political alternative, he accepted certain of the ideas expressed in the pamphlet *What Is Property?* by Pierre Joseph Proudhon (1809–1865). Proudhon asserted that unregulated competition would produce aggregates of capital that would magnify the economic disparity existing between classes. He charged that a self-seeking and despotic plutocracy was destined, under the guise of liberalism, to seize and manipulate state power on behalf of its own selfish interests. Instead of competitive capitalism, Proudhon advocated a mutualist cooperative system in which all society would be organized into a single organic whole. Although Marx agreed that competition would concentrate wealth into fewer and fewer hands, he rejected Proudhon's belief that capitalism could be reformed. Instead, he believed that the entire capitalist system had to pass away and yield inevitably to a proletarian classless society.

Marx also came into contact with the Russian anarchist Mikhail Bakunin (1814–1876), who wanted to destroy all social restraints that limited personal freedom. A violent anarchist, Bakunin asserted that destructive violence that seeks to break down and destroy all authority is a positive good. Such violence, he believed, is a fundamental form of creative self-expression. Urging the abolition of all forms of privilege, Bakunin insisted on absolute equality between races, sexes, and nationalities. All human activities should be carried on by free associations forming and dissolving at will. All coercive institutions, especially the church and state, should be destroyed. Although appalled by the wild individualism and anticollectivism of the anarchists, Marx believed that violent methods could be used to advance the revolutionary cause.

Responding to the revolutionary fervor unleashed by the series of revolutions that swept Europe in 1848, Marx and his colleague Friedrich Engels issued *The Manifesto of the Communist Party,* which began with the words, "A spectre is haunting Europe—the spectre of Communism." At the onset of the Revolution of 1848, Marx had returned to his native Germany to organize a communist faction. When the revolution failed, Marx left Germany and took refuge in London, where he spent the rest of his life studying and writing his famous book on economic theory, *Das Kapital.*

The Marxist Synthesis

Although Marx abandoned the spirituality of Hegelianism, he was true enough to his Hegelian origins to define the dynamics of economic and social change as the inevitable products of an unfolding dialectical process whose operations are inherent in the structure of the universe. Human freedom, in the Marxian sense, is reduced to following historical laws that are embodied in the dialectical process. The following examination of Marx's synthesis is designed to illuminate Marx's theory of social change.

Marxian economic determinism rested on the premise that the production and exchange of products form the basis of the social order. As such, these economic factors determine the very origin of social classes, are responsible for class divisions, and produce class conflict. The overall type of economic system in the society—whether it is feudalism or capitalism, for example—depends upon the "means and modes of production," that is, upon the combination of productive forces, such as workers, machines, and raw materials. The control of these productive means is the key to power in Marx's economically determined society. Erected upon the economic foundation of society is an educational, legal, political, and religious superstructure.

In every society, there are always an exploiting class and an exploited one. Because it possesses property, the exploiting class tries to maintain the status quo and prevent change in the existing relations of production. However, the exploiting class faces an internal contradiction: it must maintain the property arrangements that guarantee its power and, at the same time, allow technological innovations designed to increase its wealth. By following this contradictory course of encouraging technological change but discouraging sociopolitical change, the ruling class inevitably affects the means and modes of production and its own base of power. As the technological conditions of production change, the ruling class's accustomed sociopolitical situation also changes. New classes arise that seek to displace the ruling class by taking its power. History, then, becomes a class struggle over the control of the means and modes of production, the very base of all power.

Marx identified four major stages in historical development. The first stage is primitive, communal, nomadic communism. According to the terminology of dialectical materialism, primitive man—the antithesis—was in conflict with nature—the thesis. From this conflict came a new synthesis—the second historical stage, or slave society. The master—the thesis—controlled the means of production through the slave—the antithesis. The third stage was feudalism in which the feudal lord—the thesis—was in conflict with the serf—the antithesis. The fourth historical stage, capitalism, was reached when the industrial factory system made the feudal guild system of craft production obsolete. As the bourgeois merchant class gained economic power, it struggled with and bested the feudal nobility. With industrialization, factory owners came to political power. The system of feudal dues yielded to capitalism's laissez-faire economy. When the means and modes of production associated with medieval feudalism became obsolete, the social and political superstructure was also jeopardized by the processes of industrialization. In the American and French revolutions, the rising bourgeois overthrew the feudal aristocrats. The final stage of class struggle was that of the bourgeois capitalists—the thesis —against the proletariat—the antithesis.

Marx and Engels' *Communist Manifesto* saw wealth in a capitalistic society as an immense accumulation of commodities, or external objects, that satisfy human needs and can be exchanged for other products. Because it satisfies human need, a commodity has a "use value." The degree of that value is determined by the amount of labor needed to produce it. Labor power is also a commodity that the worker exchanges for a wage, which sustains him for further production. Since labor creates more exchange value than it is itself worth, surplus value, a price higher than the costs of production, provides the capitalist with profit.[2]

[2] E. A. Burns, *A Handbook of Marxism* (New York: International Publishers, 1935), p. 549.

Modern society, according to Marx, is therefore arrayed into two great opposing camps: capitalists and proletarians. The capitalists, defined as the owners of the productive resources upon which the proletariat works, live on the receipt of surplus value. Marx conceived of surplus value as a fund, arising out of the exploitation of labor, from which the capitalists receive rent, interest, and profits.

Modern capitalism resulted from a long series of developments in the modes of production and exchange. The capitalists had once been a revolutionary class that had exerted a revolutionary role in destroying feudalism. As the feudal system had engendered the bourgeoisie, capitalism also contained its own antithesis—the proletariat. The exploitative methods of capitalism brought into existence and increased the numbers of exploited, propertyless laborers, who would eventually destroy the system that had brought them into existence:

> In the proportion as the bourgeoisie, i.e., capital, is developed, in the same proportion is the proletariat, the modern working class, developed.[3]

In its early stages of development, the proletariat had allied with the capitalists in the American and French revolutions to destroy the remnants of feudal society. In these struggles, the whole historical movement had concentrated in the capitalist ascendancy.

The proletariat, dependent for its living on the sale of labor power, could live only by resigning all claim to the product of its labor. As factory workers, the proletariat was denied ownership of the means of production. In creating wealth by laboring upon machines and materials that were not its own, the proletariat was actually alienated from, and exploited by, the system of capitalist industrial production.

Marx predicted in *The Manifesto* that the final struggle for control of the means of production would be a class war, or proletarian revolution. In this last struggle between historic classes, the capitalists would be pitted against the proletariat, their economically determined successors. Although it was the unalterable course of history that the proletariat would gain control of the means of production, the capitalists would resist historical inevitability by vainly trying to keep power. As a result of the proletarian revolution, the capitalist system would be violently overthrown.

In the light of Marx's analysis of the revolutionary process, the capitalist and proletariat were the only significant social classes. Other groups that could not be neatly classified within either of the two main conflicting classes were really satellites of these major contenders for power and had no power to create an alternative social pattern. However, a significant role was to be played by a small group of bourgeois

[3] *Ibid.*, p. 30.

ideologists who would detach themselves from their class, join the proletariat, and lead the proletarian revolution. (Among this group could be numbered the authors of *The Communist Manifesto,* Marx and Engels.) Since they were far removed from the actual means and modes of production, these intellectuals were sufficiently detached to escape their class status and comprehend history's inevitable course.

This concept that certain intellectuals were to be trusted by the proletariat and accepted as the leadership elite had tremendous educational consequences for Marxian revolutionary doctrine. Lenin and Trotsky, in Russia, were two such individuals. This elite, or vanguard of the proletariat, had to be properly educated in the laws of dialectical materialism and economic determinism. The proletariat, because it was alienated from the economic processes and indoctrinated by the capitalist-controlled church and school with propaganda that was irrelevant to its real needs, was likely to be ignorant of its revolutionary destiny. The vanguard of the proletariat, the leadership of the Communist party, therefore had to be both educators and agitators. As educators, they had to go among the working class and spread the Marxist message, translating the complicated formulas of dialectical materialism into meaningful language. When Lenin harangued the working classes of Petrograd on the eve of the Bolshevik Revolution, he did not speak about dialectical materialism but used the simple slogan "Land, Bread, and Peace."

As agitators, the Marxist leaders had to be aware of the discontent that could erupt into violence. At times following the anarchist propensity toward violence, the Marxist agitator had to use situations of confrontation between capitalists and workers as incidents that could be enlarged in scope and intensity into the inevitable revolution.

Marx also recognized a subclass of small manufacturers, shopkeepers, artisans, and peasants as another group that could not be identified immediately with the working class. As unregulated competition consolidated wealth into fewer and fewer hands, this group would sink gradually into the proletariat since its own puny capital was insufficient for the scale of production required by modern industry. These lower middle classes would join the proletariat in order to escape extinction at the hands of the industrial capitalists. Marx also identified a group of social dregs from the lowest levels of society. Although this "scum" might be swept by the revolutionary impetus into the proletariat, it was more likely to be among the paid agents of bourgeois reaction, working as secret police, agents, provocateurs, and other petty servants of the capitalist class.

While other subgroups and subclasses might engage in revolutionary activity, only the proletariat was a fully revolutionary class. The inevitable revolution could be made only by the workers, who alone had the strength and will needed to accomplish it. All the other classes would decay and disappear in the face of the inexorable laws of history. Although the communists might form temporary alliances with other classes and parties, any permanent compromise between the proletariat and the other classes was impossible.

Marx's analysis of capitalism also focused attention on the modern national state, which, arising from the economic base into the sociocultural superstructure, was the political institution that served the interests of the dominant economic class, the capitalists. As an arm of capitalism, the nation-state functioned through its subsidiary agencies—the army, the courts, police, and civil service—to repress the exploited proletariat.

Marx believed that the parliamentary structures of government that had evolved in such Western nations as England, France, and the United States could not be used as vehicles of social change. Western parliamentary systems of government were, in his eyes, no better than the more overtly coercive autocratic despotisms such as that of czarist Russia. Although at a higher historical stage, the Western parliamentary governments, creatures of bourgeois liberalism, were merely reflections of capitalism. The schemes of liberal political parties were merely subterfuges designed to delude the working classes. The so-called "democratic socialists" who participated in the parliamentary process were misguided sentimentalists.

The modern industrial nation was fashioned by the processes of the Industrial Revolution. Large urban centers of population were created as workmen came to the cities from rural areas. As old loyalties and values disintegrated, the capitalists used nationalism to divert the proletariat from their real interests. Rather than uniting behind the single cause of proletarian revolution, misguided workmen, by giving their loyalty to the national state, allowed themselves to be divided into Frenchmen, Englishmen, or Germans.

As subsidiary institutions of the national state, the church and the school were also instruments of the dominant capitalist exploiters. With the rise of industrialism, capitalism, and liberalism, large-scale systems of mass education had been erected to indoctrinate the working-class child with a patriotic loyalty to the nation in the hope of blinding him to his real interests. Capitalist schools used curricula designed to instill the child with an exaggerated devotion to national myths, often presented as factual history. He was made literate so that he would be receptive to the capitalist-controlled press, which stimulated patriotism. Although most teachers could be expected to be creatures of the system, a few enlightened individuals could infiltrate the schools and act as agents of the coming proletarian revolution.

For Marx, real social change was determined by transformations in the economic base that supported the sociocultural superstructure. Like history, social change was economically determined. It could not be induced by liberal parliamentarism, social reformism, utopian socialism, or by educational programs. Definite social change would occur only when technological transformations had accumulated to a degree that was sufficient to break the old system and to supersede it by a new productive system that embodied a different set of class aims and ideas. Since any form of political state and any educational system merely reflected the underlying economic base, the capitalist state was a repressive instrument, and capitalist schools were agencies of indoctrination used by the dominant class in enforcing and protecting its special interests. Any policy that attempted to conciliate the class struggle through political or educational means was an illusion since the entrenched exploiting class could be overthrown only by force.[4]

As a productive system, capitalism sows the seeds of its own destruction by spirals of overproduction that lead to the crises, slumps, and social chaos of economic depression. Capitalist productivity would reach a point beyond which it could not be coordinated. Economic crisis would result since the capitalists would be compelled to reinvest capital to effect greater production without being able to guarantee the consumption of the commodities so produced. When home markets were exhausted, capitalist nations would turn to imperialism. In the name of national interest or destiny, capitalists would use the nation as a vehicle of finding new colonial markets to exploit. Wars of imperialism would ensue as the capitalist nations rivaled one another for mastery of markets and sources of materials. Although the working class was likely to be deluded because of the nationalistic indoctrination it had been given in support of imperialist adventurism, its support for imperialism would be but temporary. Foreign markets would be only temporarily supportive of capitalism. Unemployment, once periodic, would become chronic. As the proletariat grew more oppressed and miserable, the conditions would become ripe for revolution.

Inevitably, the proletarian revolution, led by the Communists, would succeed and wrest control of the means and modes of production from the capitalists. A dictatorship of the proletariat would be established to centralize all productive instruments and make the reforms needed to bring about a classless society. Until the time that a classless society was realized, the dictatorship of the proletariat would govern and use the state to destroy the remnants of the old system. When the residues of capitalism had completely disappeared, a classless society would emerge. The state, an instrument of class oppression, would then disappear since it would be unnecessary. Thus, the order of sequential events from the initiation of the revolution to the classless society was to be: (1) proletarian revolution, (2) capture of the state

---

[4] George H. Sabine, *A History of Political Theory* (New York: Henry Holt, 1950), p. 834.

machinery by the working class, (3) establishment of the dictatorship of the proletariat, (4) elimination of opposition and remnants
of capitalism, (5) emergence of the classless society, and (6) withering away of the state. In speaking about the free association of pro-
ducers that was destined to replace the repressive state, Engels wrote:

> At a certain stage of economic development, which was necessarily
> bound up with the cleavage of society into classes, the State became
> a necessity owing to this cleavage. We are now rapidly approaching
> a stage in the development of production at which the existence
> of these classes has not ceased to be a necessity, but it is becoming
> a positive hindrance to production. They will disappear as inevitably
> as they arose at an earlier stage. Along with them the State will in-
> evitably disappear. The society that organizes production anew on
> the basis of a free and equal association of producers will put the
> whole State machine where it will then belong: in the museum of
> antiquities, side by side with the spinning-wheel and the bronze
> axe.[5]

Although neither Marx nor Engels speculated about educational institutions, content, and processes under the dictatorship of the proletariat, some inferences can be made regarding the educational
implications of their theory of social change. First of all, the informal
or milieu education could be expected to change. Since the economic
base of the sociocultural superstructure would be in proletarian control, a proletarian culture could be expected to emerge. The values
associated with private ownership of property, individualistic competition, supernatural religion, and nationalism would probably be replaced by a collectivistic, egalitarian, materialistic, cooperative, and
internationalist set of values. Literature, journalism, and art could
be expected to respond to this new proletarian morality.

As the proletariat captured the machinery of state government, it
could also be expected to capture the machinery of the formal educational structure. Those teachers who retained a loyalty to the old
order would be eliminated and the curriculum purged of its capitalistic, individualistic, and nationalistic biases. Teachers would be re-
cruited for their proletarian dedication and their knowledge of the
processes of dialectical materialism. In a proletarian society, the curriculum could be expected to respond to utilitarian needs. Art forms
and aesthetic education would concretize the aspirations of the proletariat.

There is no reason to believe that Marxian schools under the dictatorship of the proletariat would be centers of continuing revolutionary
thought. With the achievement of the proletarian revolution, schools
would be used to eradicate capitalist sentiments and instill proletarian

[5] Burns, p. 732.

values and knowledge. As such, schools would become agencies of transmission of the proletarian culture.

It is even more difficult to speculate about the conditions of education in the classless society that was to follow the dictatorship of the proletariat. Although the state would wither away, the school system would probably remain. Since Marx and Engels' concept of the "withering away of the state" is patently utopian, it is fair to assume that repressive educational forms would also wither away and be replaced by utopian educational structures and situations.

Conclusion

In Chapter 21, a detailed analysis will be made of education in the Soviet Union. Marx had a profound effect on the course of both Western and global civilization. His ideas inspired Lenin, Trotsky, and the Bolshevik Revolution. They exerted influence on Mao Tze-tung and the Chinese Communists. Marxist ideology was supportive of much of the revolutionary climate of the twentieth century.

Marx also made a contribution to the thinking of the non-Marxist historian, social thinker, and educator. Although he exaggerated economic forces and ignored the impact of ideas, culture, and tradition, he focused attention on economic processes. After Marx, history could no longer be interpreted solely in military or political terms, and culture could not be studied without some attention being paid to economic agencies and productive processes.

Suggested Readings

Berlin, Isaiah. *Karl Marx: His Life and Environment.* New York: Oxford University Press, 1959.

Burns, E. A. *A Handbook of Marxism.* New York: International Publishers, 1935.

Cole, G. D. H. *What Marx Really Meant.* New York: Knopf, 1937.

Hook, Sidney. *Towards the Understanding of Karl Marx.* London: Victor Gallancz, 1933.

Plamenatz, John. *German Marxism and Russian Communism.* London: Longmans, Green, 1954.

Nyberg, Paul. "The Communal Man: Marx," in Paul Nash, Andreas M. Kazamias, and Henry J. Perkinson (eds.), *The Educated Man: Studies in the History of Educational Thought.* New York: Wiley, 1965.

Sabine, George H. *A History of Political Theory.* New York: Henry Holt, 1950.

CHAPTER 16

Evolution, Social Darwinism, and Education

As mentioned in earlier chapters, the nineteenth century was a time when the ideologies of liberalism, conservatism, romanticism, nationalism, socialism, and communism competed for supremacy. Although the spokesmen for these conflicting ideologies argued for either the preservation of the status quo or for radical social change, it was a scientist rather than a politician who profoundly altered Western man's conception of his universe. Charles Darwin proposed an evolutionary theory that profoundly affected Western thought and education. Like Marx's dialectical materialism, the theory of evolution was a synthesis that Darwin developed through observation, experimentation, and insight. Scientists such as Laplace in astronomy, Lamarck in biology, Baer in embryology, Lyell in geology, and Comte in sociology had argued earlier for an evolutionary interpretation of the universe, man, and society.

Evolution

Charles Darwin (1809–1882) devoted his life and scientific energies to expositing and substantiating his thesis that life on this planet had evolved slowly through processes of natural selection. In 1831, he sailed on the *Beagle* and spent five years in the South Atlantic and Pacific collecting, classifying, and studying a wide variety of life forms. Upon returning to his native England, he experimented further in breeding domestic plants and animals. Applying the principle of natural selection to all organic life, ranging from plants, to animals, to man, Darwin concluded that originally simple life forms had grown increasingly differentiated through a long progression of purely natural steps. He published his evolutionary thesis in two works: *The Origin of Species by Means of Natural Selection, or The Preservation of Favored Races in the Struggle for Life* (1859) and *The Descent of Man* (1871). In expounding his thesis, Darwin wrote:

> Let it also be borne in mind how infinitely complex and close fitting are the mutual relations of all organic beings to each other and to their physical conditions of life; and consequently what infinitely varied diversities of structure might be of use to each being under changing conditions of life. Can it then be thought improbable, seeing that variations useful to man have undoubtedly occurred, that other variations useful in some way to each being in the great and complex battle of life, should occur in the course of many successive generations? If such do occur, can we doubt (remembering that many more individuals are born than can possibly survive) that individuals having any advantage, however slight, over others, would have the best chance of surviving and procreating their kind? On the other hand, we may feel sure that any variation in the least degree injurious would be rigidly destroyed. This preservation of favorable individual differences and variations, and the destruction of those which are injurious, I have called Natural Selection, or the Survival of the Fittest.[1]

A brief examination of Darwin's theory of evolution illustrates some of the major concepts that were adopted by various social and educational theorists, such as Herbert Spencer and William Graham Sumner, who applied them to society and education. At first, evolution through natural selection seemed antagonistic to orthodox Christianity's conception of Creation as recorded in the Book of Genesis. Since every organic being is so carefully related to the complex of life conditions, Darwin held it improbable that any being had been "suddenly produced perfect." Within the intimate relationship that exists between the organism and its environment, a struggle for existence occurs as the various species compete for food, water, and other necessities of life. Because of this intense competition, those profitable variations that enhance the survival possibilities of the individual members of a species are transmitted to their offspring. The process of natural selection preserves each useful variation in the species, regardless of how slight. The Darwinian struggle for existence can occur between individuals of the same species or between the organism and the environment. "Struggle for existence" became a key argument of the social Darwinists, for it justified economic and social competition between individuals and condemned any interference with "natural laws" as socially disruptive.

Unlike the eighteenth-century philosophers who saw nature as a perfectly functioning world mechanism governed by intrinsic designs

[1] Charles Darwin, *The Origin of Species by Means of Natural Selection, or The Preservation of Favored Races in the Struggle for Life* (New York: American Publishers Corporation, n.d.), pp. 69–70.

and patterns, Darwin held nature to be a dynamic process. Of greatest importance in this process is natural selection, which Darwin also referred to as "survival of the fittest," by which favorable individual differences are preserved and injurious variations destroyed. Describing existence as a "continually recurring" battle, Darwin defined nature as a dynamic struggle that produces constant but slow changes as victorious individuals survive because of their adaptability to the environment. For him, survival of the fittest was not a pessimistic but rather an optimistic and positive process:

> It may metaphorically be said that natural selection is daily and hourly scrutinizing, throughout the world, the slightest variations; rejecting those that are bad, preserving and adding up all that are good; silently and insensibly working, whenever and wherever opportunity offers, at the improvement of each organic being in relation to its organic and inorganic conditions of life.[2]

Social Darwinism

Darwin's evolutionary thesis pertained to biology. However, it was soon appropriated by social theorists who keenly admired what they believed to be the exactness of the natural sciences. The German biologist Ernst H. Haeckel (1834–1919), a leading Darwinist on the Continent, asserted that natural law made progress necessary, inevitable, and irresistible. Haeckel also claimed that the developing organism was reliving its evolutionary history as it passed through stages that recapitulated those of its ancestors. In England, Thomas H. Huxley (1825–1895), in *Man's Place in Nature*, popularized Darwinism for the general public of the late nineteenth century. The historian James Anthony Froude (1818–1894), who wrote a twelve-volume *History of England*, asserted that superior people had a natural right to govern their inferiors. The Russian writer Nicholas Danilevsky (1822–1885), in *Russia and Europe* (1871), saw human history as a record of particular racial groups, governed by natural laws, passing through different stages of development. Danilevsky made an early application of Darwinism to Pan-Slavic nationalism by asserting that the Slavic peoples were a distinct and superior species. As the largest and leading subspecies among the Slavs, the Russians were obliged to lead all of the Slavic groups. Among those who transferred Darwin's biological theory to social, educational, and political spheres, Herbert Spencer achieved notoriety in both Europe and in the United States. A closer look at his work will elaborate the social Darwinism thesis that was current in the second half of the nineteenth century.

[2] *Ibid.*, p. 73.

Herbert Spencer

Herbert Spencer (1820–1903), a lower-middle-class, nonconformist Englishman, was the most representative and thoroughgoing of the social Darwinists. Although he was educated as a civil engineer, Spencer's predilection for social, economic, and political theorizing led him to attempt to construct an architectonic sociology of knowledge that encompassed evolutionary theory and stressed the concept of survival of the fittest. In seeking to adapt Darwin's biological theory to social science, Spencer incorporated his interpretation of it with a blend of old-fashioned classical liberalism, which comprised free trade, laissez-faire economic theory, antiestablishment nonconformism, and individualism.

Spencer saw the universe as a self-contained system in which indestructible forces of matter and energy exert themselves in constantly changing forms. He built his philosophy on the principle of "persistence of force," which is manifested by matter and motion. According to his theory, the operation of the universe involves a constant redistribution of matter and motion. Evolution—the progressive integration of matter—is accompanied by the dissipation of motion; dissolution —the disorganization of matter—is accompanied by the absorption of motion. Following this universal pattern, the life process is an evolutionary series of stages, developing from simple, incoherent homogeneity to complex, coherent heterogeneity. Spencer believed that these universal principles were applicable to society. In their "natural course," simple, homogeneous societies develop into more complex social systems characterized by an increasing variety of individual roles.

Influenced by Malthus' theory of overpopulation, Spencer asserted that the pressures of subsistence upon population would be beneficial to the progress of the human race. The fittest of each generation survive by their skill, intelligence, diligence, and ability to adapt to change. As a result of the competition for survival, the more intelligent and adaptive individuals will inherit the earth, populating it with equally intelligent and effective offspring.

In the hands of Spencer and his colleagues, social Darwinism became the rationale for those nineteenth-century classical liberals who scrupulously followed Adam Smith's laissez-faire economic doctrines and resisted all attempts at social reform through governmental or educational means. Spencer's Social Statics (1850) gave the economic theories of the Manchester school an apparently "scientific" justification. As a defender of classical liberal economic and social theory, Spencer asserted that every individual has the natural right to do as he pleases if he does not violate the rights of others. True to laissez-faire dicta, the state's only function is to insure the inviolability of the individual's natural freedom. Spencerian social Darwinism was a rationale used by those who opposed the legislative alleviation of poverty and state-supported education, housing, medicine, banking, and postal systems. All forms of governmental control, aid, and regulation were opposed on the grounds that they interfered with natural law, impeded progress, and maintained incompetents whom nature had marked as unfit in the struggle for survival.

In his interpretation of history, Spencer asserted that Western society, in reaching the age of industrial capitalism, was on the threshold of an era that would be most beneficent for mankind. In industrial society, relations are governed by contract rather than by military despotism. The conditions of industrial production provide a greater security for life, liberty, and property. The kind of man who is most likely to survive in an industrial society is independent, thrifty, diligent, kindly, and honest. Successful men, in such an era, are able to adapt to the conditions of life. Evil, resulting from the inability of individuals to adapt to conditions, will eventually disappear as the industrial system expands, and a new civilized, moral state will emerge. While Marx saw capitalism as a predatory stage of history, Spencer saw it as culminating in man's prosperity. Although their ideologies were diametrically opposed, both men believed that social change is produced by inevitable universal patterns over which man has little or no power.

Both Spencer and Marx rejected theology and speculative philosophy as means of explaining the universe and attempted to formulate architectonic "scientific" sociologies of knowledge. Marx's theory of social change was adopted by communists and other "scientific" socialists as a design for revolution. As previously mentioned, Spencer's social Darwinism was adopted by classical liberal ideologists as an apology for unregulated industrial capitalism and a defense against attempts to inaugurate social legislation. In the *Study of Sociology* (1896), Spencer argued for the claims of social science, resting on a body of sociological theory against the older authorities, which were based on theology, speculative philosophy, or strictly literary history. His arguments contributed to the demands for a utilitarian rather than a classical or literary education.

Spencer opposed those who held that social ills are the result of some environmental malfunction. Like the eighteenth-century social philosopher Rousseau, these social reformers asserted that man is good by nature and, if he is corrupted, then the source of corruption is in the environment. In the early nineteenth century, the utopian socialist Robert Owen had proclaimed that man is a product of his environment and that a good environment will produce good men. The nineteenth-century social reformers, such as the welfare-state liberals, the various socialists, and the humanitarians—as well as twentieth-century progressives, social engineers, and planners—generally have sought to regenerate mankind by reordering and repairing the environment. Their basic premise is that human ills are products of the environment rather than man's nature. This view is shared by educators who argue that the key to successful education lies in preparing a learning environment that will permit the release of man's humane tendencies and stimulate their growth. Advocates of deliberate programs of social reform in both the nineteenth and twentieth centuries have relied on legislation and education.

Spencer saw sociology and the allied social sciences as having both a descriptive and a prescriptive function. Descriptively, they recount the normal and natural course of social evolution so that men might be educated to recognize the dynamic natural laws that will eventuate in progress. The prescriptive aspect is designed to discourage those who seek to tamper with the workings of society, the natural laws of supply and demand, individual self-assertion, and competition. In the second half of the nineteenth century, Spencer's social Darwinism provided a theoretical justification for an expansive industrial capitalism.

SPENCERIAN EDUCATION

Spencer's evolutionary sociology and defense of classical economic liberalism influenced his views on education. He was part of a group of nineteenth-century educational reformers who based their educational concepts on a naturalistic ethic. Although he certainly would have disagreed with the social theories of Rousseau, Pestalozzi, and Owen, Spencer's antagonism to classical education as being artificial, dogmatic, and excessively verbal would have been shared by these critics of educational traditionalism. While Owen was a utopian socialist and Spencer a classical liberal, both of these Englishmen advocated the "natural rights" of children against coercive parents and teachers.

Spencer and the other naturalist educators rejected the conventional patterns of nineteenth-century formal education, which they regarded as bookish, authoritarian and still laboring under the impact of an archaic classical humanism. The formally educated man of the time was a master of classical Latin and Greek and was conversant with philosophy, literature, and history. Nineteenth-century formal education, like schools at any age, had failed to incorporate many of the current discoveries, ideas, and modes of inquiry. Spencer felt that conventional schooling was impractical, ornamental, and irrelevant to the needs of an industrial society.

In 1860, Spencer expounded his theory of education in *Education:*

Intellectual, Moral, and Physical,[3] which explored the social and political foundations of education and urged a revision in the curriculum to place more emphasis on science. In answer to his own question in his widely read essay "What Knowledge Is of Most Worth?," Spencer said that the most valuable education provided the learner with a scientific attitude and training in the physical, biological, and social sciences. In this essay, Spencer developed a rationale for curriculum construction based on classifying human activities into a hierarchy according to their priorities for survival. To survive, he said, man must be able to perform a variety of life-sustaining activities efficiently. Therefore, the curriculum should be based on these activities and should place special emphasis on scientific education since it is most relevant to their efficient performance.

Spencer's rationale for curriculum was based on his belief that five major kinds of activities support human life:

1. Activities directly related to self-preservation
2. Activities indirectly related to self-preservation that secure the necessities of life
3. Activities related to the rearing of children
4. Activities related to the maintenance of proper social and political relationships
5. Activities related to leisure time that gratify tastes and feelings

Spencer's rationale for curriculum raised the issue of efficiency: Were the consequences of studying a particular subject matter or skill worth the expenditure of time and energy? He asserted that certain knowledge and skills had a more valuable effect on man's life than others. His functional determination of curriculum clearly departed from the humanistic and classical educational patterns, which were concerned primarily with the learning of languages and literature rather than with human functions. Spencer's five basic human activities were interrelated, and the position of each activity in the hierarchy of priorities was based on its necessity for the succeeding activities. Spencer gave the first priority to activities that contribute to self-preservation since these are basic to all the others. A scientific education should include knowledge of the principles of physiology from which are derived the information and skills needed to preserve the body against disease, for the maintenance of physical health is necessary to the performance of all other activities. Those activities that indirectly support self-preservation, such as earning a livelihood,

[3] Herbert Spencer, *Education: Intellectual, Moral, and Physical* (New York: Appleton, 1881). A recent analysis of Spencer's educational theory is provided in Andreas M. Kazamias, *Herbert Spencer on Education* (New York: Teachers College Press, Columbia University, 1966).

were assigned to the second order of priority. Spencer recognized the immediate utilitarian values of reading, writing, and arithmetic as basic tools. He asserted, however, that modern man living in an industrial society needs more than basic literary skills. He needs an education that contributes to technological, industrial, and scientific efficiency. Such efficiency results when man successfully unites science and industry. Man needs competence in the physical and biological sciences, the applied sciences of engineering, and the social sciences of economics and sociology. While industry depends on technology and science, the schools, Spencer said, neglect these vital subjects and prefer to waste energy, time, and money on dead languages.

Spencer charged that schools had neglected the activities that he assigned as third in priority, those related to rearing of children. He asserted that both men and women should be educated for responsible parenthood. In discussing early childhood education, Spencer echoed the criticisms that such "naturalists" as Rousseau and Pestalozzi had levied against schools for being too formal, abstract, and isolated from meaningful experience. Like Rousseau and Owen, Spencer felt that motivating children by artificial rewards and punishments is harmful to their proper development. The best discipline derives from the pleasures or pains that come as consequences of action. Because it relied so heavily on books and designated experiences, Spencer felt that traditional education had unnatural consequences. He also believed that it had educated improperly because too much of it was book-centered rather than based on experiences. Teachers should motivate children by capitalizing on their natural curiosity rather than by stressing secondhand facts. Like Pestalozzi, Spencer recommended that children study objects and perform activities that are related to their immediate environment.

Spencer's own predilections for a sociology of knowledge were evident. The activities he assigned to the fourth area of the curriculum were related to society and politics. Like many twentieth-century educators, he felt that the conventional study of history concentrating on individual biography or dynastic accounts wastes valuable time. Although the study of biographies of great men and accounts of battles might be diverting and entertaining, such historical materials do not illustrate the principles of right social and political action. Instead of conventional historical accounts, he recommended the study of descriptive and comparative sociology. Educated men living in an industrial era, he felt, need to be aware of the science of society, of the phenomena of social progress, of social and political structures, and of scientific technology. The interpretation of social phenomena requires that educated men possess the competency needed to formulate scientific generalizations from the mass of sociological data. It is of crucial importance that the processes of social change be examined in order to estimate the alterations that occur in institutions and customs.

The activities that relate to leisure time were assigned to the fifth and last major area of the curriculum. Spencer listed such activities as the enjoyment of nature, literature, and fine arts under the general category of aesthetic culture. Only after he has conquered the natural environment and perfected the means of production can man devote more of his time to leisure.

Spencer's relegation of aesthetic and literary education to the area of least importance in the curriculum was a significant departure from conventional educational patterns, which emphasized languages, classics, literature, and the arts as the basis of a well-rounded education. The functional criteria that Spencer used in curriculum construction also signified a rejection of the Aristotelian conception of education, which differentiated it into the liberal arts for free men and technical training for those in servile occupations. Underlying Spencer's rationale for a functional curriculum was a strong belief that scientific knowledge and methods were indispensable for the individual who wished to function efficiently in a technological and industrial era.

SPENCERIAN EDUCATIONAL METHODOLOGY

Spencer's conception of instructional methodology and of teaching and learning embraced the concepts of mental discipline and evolutionary development. In the nineteenth century, most educators subscribed to the view that certain subject matters were valuable in disciplining the mind. These advocates of "faculty psychology" asserted that such subjects as mathematics, Latin, Greek, and logic were potent instruments for exercising and developing certain mental powers, or faculties, such as memory or reasoning. Spencer did not challenge this mental discipline, or faculty psychology, but rather he asserted that scientific study could also produce the desired mental training. Not only did science train the mind as did Latin and Greek, but it was also a functional study that had consequences for life in an industrial society.

To a degree, Spencer believed that man's mental development recapitulates the developmental stages that occurred in the history of the human race. The child's mind, similar to that of primitive man, is unable to deal with abstract and complex relationships. If a teacher wishes to develop the child's mental powers, his method of instruction has to follow evolutionary patterns. Spencer's argument that instruction should follow developmental stages was similar to that enunciated by Comenius in the seventeenth century, Rousseau in the eighteenth century, and Pestalozzi in the early nineteenth century.

Like these educational theorists, who had recognized a pattern in human development that was exhibited by clearly defined stages, Spencer argued that instruction should proceed from the simple to the complex, from the concrete to the abstract, and from the empirical to the rational.

Although Spencer's social theory emphasizing individual competition was often attacked by twentieth-century progressive educators, much of his discussion of educational methodology should have found a sympathetic response with child-centered advocates of the permissive classroom. Spencer asserted that education should encourage the learner's own self-development. When it derives from the learner's interests and needs, learning will be a pleasurable experience.

SPENCER'S VIEWS ON STATE CONTROL OF EDUCATION

During the nineteenth century, the English government had extended suffrage to more individuals as a result of the Reform Bills of 1832 and 1867. By 1884, with the passage of the Third Reform Bill, universal male suffrage had been achieved. Moreover, factory legislation had been enacted during this period to ameliorate the social and economic condition of the masses.

In this context of gradual reformism, demands were made for increased educational opportunities. Liberals were divided, however, on the issue of the state's role in education. This division in liberal ranks reflected a more basic disagreement over the role of government in society. The "welfare-state" liberals believed that government should play a planning and coordinating role in society. They therefore formed organizations to advance the cause of compulsory education under government auspices. The classical liberals like Spencer were opposed to government control of education. They believed that society was composed of a number of discrete individuals—or social atoms—who moved up or down the socioeconomic scale, depending upon their energies, skills, intelligence, and competitive powers. The exercise of government powers would, in their view, restrain this natural process. To give government a role in education, Spencer believed, would imply that the state was an all-powerful source of wisdom. A state educational system would become a corrupt bureaucratic monolith that would be unable to function efficiently. Furthermore, he feared that the Conservative party might cede control of education to the established church. Finally, although he advocated representative government as the most desirable system for an industrial society, he did not believe that conventional elementary education—reading, writing, and arithmetic—would improve the intelligence of the electorate.

Victorian Education

Because of her long reign (1837–1901), Queen Victoria's name has been used to describe the condition of English culture during most of the nineteenth century. The Victorian era saw the queen proclaimed empress of India. Writers such as Macaulay and Kipling convinced most Englishmen that it was their mission to create an empire on which the "sun would never set." Yet although the period was one of surface stability and tranquility, England was making a difficult transition from a rural to an urban society and from an agricultural to an industrial one. Social and political reform bills had ameliorated the lot of the common man, but the rapid growth of large cities brought with it depressing industrial slums.

An age of political ideologies, the Victorian era was characterized by the clashes between liberals and conservatives. It was also an era of intellectual ferment, especially in the realm of religious, ethical, and cultural values. The rise of natural science, particularly influenced by Darwinian evolution, had challenged religious orthodoxy and theology. The assertions of Lyell in *Principles of Geology* that the earth was millions of years old and of Darwin in *Origin of Species* that man had evolved from some form of brute life were regarded as blasphemous by people who were accustomed to think that the world had been created in 4004 B.C.

Like other areas of Victorian culture, education exhibited tensions as science came to challenge both religion and classical literature for educational supremacy. While the natural sciences were challenging and perhaps destroying old values, it was not easy to create meaningful alternatives. The clash between scientific and humanist attitudes in intellectual circles was exemplified by the opposing positions taken by Thomas Huxley (1825–1895) and Matthew Arnold (1822–1888).

Huxley believed that scientific education would produce the knowledge that would be of most worth for men living in a modern era. Although he did not deny the value of a literary education, he believed that an exclusive concentration on literature resulted in a narrowly rather than a liberally educated man. A genuinely scientific education would prepare man to cope with the radical changes in belief and value that the modern age engendered.

Huxley's educational ideal can be described as a scientific humanism that used science to interpret the universe, discover natural processes, and the human condition. Although Huxley recognized the beauty of fine arts, literature, and music, he believed that the growing interdependence of people in a technological world demanded that civic and social responsibilities be subject to scientific scrutiny.

Matthew Arnold looked to the humanism of the Renaissance and a reemphasis on classical thought for the mainsprings of his educational philosophy.[4] Despite scientific and material innovations, man's nature remained the same, and the educational quest was still a search for righteousness and wisdom. Arnold did not, however, see a humanist education confined exclusively to the Greek and Roman classics. The broadly educated man knew not only Pindar, Plato, Vergil, and Shakespeare but also the scientists Copernicus, Galileo, Newton, and Darwin. Although Arnold did not deny the significance of scientific knowledge, he believed that a general education stressing humane letters rather than the natural sciences would be of greatest value for most people.

Social Darwinism in America

In the United States, the industrial, political, and social leadership of the last half of the nineteenth century can aptly be termed the "social-Darwinist generation." In fact, the social and intellectual historian Richard Hofstadter has referred to the United States as the "Darwinian country."[5] Herbert Spencer, who made the most ambitious application of evolutionary theory to society, perhaps enjoyed a greater audience in the United States than he did in his native England.

The years following the Civil War witnessed a tremendous industrial expansion dominated by such men as John D. Rockefeller, J. P. Morgan, and Andrew Carnegie, who have been variously characterized—depending upon the historian's point of view—as "captains of industry" for leading this expansion or "robber barons" for ruthlessly exploiting natural resources and human life. Classical liberal politics and economics had encouraged this growth of industrial capitalism, and social Darwinism provided a timely "scientific" justification for it that could be used to prevent interference by government or by trade unions in what were referred to as "natural laws" of supply and demand and the open market.

In the United States, the social Darwinist jargon of "struggle for existence" and "survival of the fittest" meant that the most effective competitors would survive and win in a competitive situation. Through competition—in economics and in other areas of life—the

---

[4] See Paul Nash, *Culture and the State: Matthew Arnold and Continental Education* (New York: Teachers College Press, Columbia University, 1966), for an introduction to Arnold as a comparative educator, a bibliography, and representative selections.

[5] For an excellent account of the impact of social Darwinism on American life, see Richard Hofstadter, *Social Darwinism in American Thought* (Boston: Beacon Press, 1955).

human race would be gradually improved as the unfit were weeded out. The competitive ethic preached by the social Darwinists was not, of course, new to Americans, for it resembled the old Protestant ethic implanted in the American soil by the Calvinist Puritans. Instead of justifying hard work, discipline, and thrift on theological grounds, the social Darwinist did so on the basis of the "latest scientific theory." The Puritan, the capitalist, and the social Darwinist could thus all subscribe to an ethical code that was suspicious of waste, idleness, and leisure, that held economic activity to be the most effective means of developing solid character, and that saw poverty as a deserved punishment for the shiftless, inefficient, and wasteful.

William Graham Sumner

In the hands of William Graham Sumner (1840–1910), social Darwinism became more than an ideology imported from England or a rationale for capitalism. Sumner, a professor of political and social science at Yale University, was the author of *Folkways* (1906) and the *Science of Society,* published posthumously.[6]

Sumner's works fused together the theoretical underpinnings of American capitalism in a synthesis that embraced classical economic theory and Darwinian natural selection. In *Folkways*, he treated the origin of social systems, values, and change and described social change as a product of slow evolution rather than of deliberately induced planning and execution. His work had a decided impact on American thought.

Sumner accepted the Darwinian assumption that man's evolution occurs in groups and derives from his interaction with the physical conditions of life. Man brings to this interaction sets of biological needs or drives. In association, men meet their needs under the conditions imposed by the physical environment. Over time, certain group responses—ways of doing things common to the group—develop. Gradually, the group evolves folkways, a preferred way of satisfying its needs that is not determined rationally but results from trial-and-error attempts to obtain the basic necessities of life. As certain folkways become identified with the common good, they take on an emotional overtone as values and become identified with the survival of the group. According to Sumner, mores are the instruments by which man elaborates his pattern of social values. Mores define the ethics of the group, and, as social prescriptions, are the basis for morality, philosophy, and law. In such a system, philosophy becomes the means of refining and rationalizing group mores. Law is merely the elaboration of group mores. Laws may be enacted, but

[6] William Graham Sumner, *Folkways* (New York: New American Library, 1960).

they must be based on the accepted mores if they are to be enforced.

In a general and informal sense, mores are educative since they provide the context within which an individual develops his personality and social role. Sumner viewed education as a process of inducting the immature individual—the child—into the knowledge, skills, and values of the group. As he learns the knowledge and skills that have proved successful in satisfying and maintaining group life, the child is conditioned to accept the value systems that rationalize, explain, and protect group behavior and beliefs.

According to Sumner, social change, including educational change, is always a gradual evolutionary process and is caused by a change in the physical environment induced by either natural causes or technological innovation. Sumner discounted revolution as an instrument in producing major social changes. Although mass revolutions may appear to generate major social changes, they merely cause brief periods of violence and chaos, especially when taken up by the lower socioeconomic classes, and, in the long run, are aberrations. After the period of violence, social, economic, and political life revert to their accustomed patterns.

Sumner minimized the role of education in stimulating deliberate social change. Schooling, he said, is a matter of transmitting the approved group norms of behavior to the young through patriotic and religious rituals. For a genuine change to be felt in education, it must first occur at the level of physical life conditions. According to Sumner, educational changes follow the same patterns as other kinds of social change:

1. The raw materials of change originate in the basic conditions of life—that is, in the physical environment—through trial-and-error processes.
2. Significant innovations when repeated often enough become a preferred procedure, or a folkway.
3. Certain significant folkways become mores as they take on emotional overtones.

Clearly, in the Sumnerian sense, education is a matter of transmitting group culture from the mature to the immature. Educators and educational institutions exercise a conservative role by preserving the cultural heritage, for education is a means of preserving the societal status quo, which contains group survival patterns as expressed in the mores and folkways. This is a most important function since survival depends on man's successful adaptation to the environment. If the school were used as an instrument to reconstruct society, then this attempt would fail, as would all efforts at forced or revolutionary change.

Conclusion

Clearly, the work of Charles Darwin in biology and Herbert Spencer and William Graham Sumner in sociology had an impact on Western thought and education. Darwin's work in the natural sciences led to new interpretations in the social sciences. In turn, education reflected the Darwinian impact in both its cognitive and value dimensions. There was an increased emphasis on science both as a component in the curriculum and as a method of inquiry. The natural sciences entered the curriculum, and social Darwinism had an impact on the values or attitudes that schools transmitted. In the United States in particular, individual initiative and competition were emphasized as desirable personal and social values. Darwinian natural science and social Darwinist social science were used as theoretical ammunition in the attack on the inherited patterns of classical and language-centered education.

For educational methodology, Spencer, Sumner, and other social Darwinists supported the concepts that had been developed by such earlier naturalists in education as Comenius, Rousseau, Pestalozzi, and Owen. Spencer's conception of education as a process of unhurried evolutionary development supported the notion that instruction should be graduated and unhurried. In the broader sense of educational aims, the social Darwinist concept of the unhurried development of the learner also meant that the school was to be a conservative social agency whose aims came from, and reflected, natural and societal values. At the same time, the school was to provide a sufficient amount of competitive activities to bring the fittest to the surface.

At the close of the nineteenth century and on into the twentieth, reactions to Darwinism were varied. Some interpretations were supportive of racism, colonialism, and imperialism. Certain progressive social reformers and pragmatic philosophers, such as John Dewey, were stimulated by Darwin. These theorists accepted the Darwinian concept of a changing universe but rejected Spencer's and Sumner's sociological interpretations.

Suggested Readings

Bibby, Cyril. *T. H. Huxley: Scientist, Humanist, and Educator.* New York: Horizon Press, 1960.

Carnegie, Andrew. *The Gospel of Wealth and Other Timely Essays.* Cambridge, Mass: Harvard University Press, 1962.

Daniels, George. *Darwinism Comes to America.* Waltham, Mass.: Blaisdell Publishing Co., 1968.

Dewey, John. *The Influence of Darwin on Philosophy.* New York: Peter Smith, 1951.

Greene, John C. *Darwin and the Modern World View.* Baton Rouge: Louisiana State University Press, 1961.

Hayes, Carlton J. H. *A Generation of Materialism: 1871–1900.* New York: Harper, 1941.

Himmelfarb, Gertrude. *Darwin and the Darwinian Revolution.* Garden City, N. Y.: Doubleday, 1962.

Hofstadter, Richard. *Social Darwinism in American Thought.* Boston: Beacon Press, 1955.

Huxley, Thomas H. *Man's Place in Nature.* Ann Arbor, Mich.: University of Michigan Press, 1959.

Josephson, Matthew. *The Robber Barons.* New York: Harcourt, Brace, 1934.

Kazamias, Andreas M. *Herbert Spencer on Education.* New York: Teachers College Press, Columbia University, 1966.

Loewenberg, B. J. "Darwinism Comes to America, 1859–1900," *Mississippi Valley Historical Review,* XXVIII (1941), 339–368.

Mayer, Frederick. *American Ideas and Education.* Columbus, Ohio: Charles E. Merrill, 1964.

McCloskey, Robert G. *American Conservatism in the Age of Enterprise: A Study of William Graham Sumner, Stephen J. Field, and Andrew Carnegie.* Cambridge, Mass.: Harvard University Press, 1951.

Nash, Paul. *Culture and the State: Matthew Arnold and Continental Education.* New York: Teachers College, Columbia University, 1966.

Rumney, Jay. *Herbert Spencer's Sociology: A Study in the History of Social Theory.* New York: Atherton Press, 1966.

Spencer, Herbert. *An Autobiography.* New York: Appleton, 1904.

————. *Education: Intellectual, Moral, and Physical.* New York: Appleton, 1881.

————. *Essays: Scientific, Political, and Speculative.* 3 vols. New York: Appleton, 1910.

————. *Facts and Comments.* New York: Appleton, 1902.

————. *Social Statics: or The Conditions Essential to Human Happiness Specified and the First of Them Developed.* New York: August M. Kelley Publishers, 1969.

————. *The Man Versus the State.* New York: Appleton, 1885.

————. *The Principles of Sociology.* 3 vols. Hamden, Conn.: Shoe String Press, 1969.

————. *The Study of Sociology.* Ann Arbor, Michigan: University of Michigan Press, 1961.

Sumner, William Graham. *Folkways.* New York: New American Library, 1960.

Thayer, V. T. *Formative Ideas in American Education.* New York: Dodd, Mead, 1965.

Wilson, R. *Darwinism and the American Intellectual: A Book of Readings*. Homewood, Ill.: Dorsey Press, 1967.

Young, G. M. *Victorian England: Portrait of an Age*. New York: Oxford University Press, 1964.

CHAPTER 17

Freud, The Unconscious, and Affective Education

While Charles Darwin's work had revolutionized the natural sciences, the psychological theories of Sigmund Freud altered basic conceptions of human relations. Freud's discovery that the unconscious is a major determinant of personality and behavior transformed the Western world view and conception of human nature. This chapter will deal with Freud's impact upon man's awareness of the nonrational side of his nature and the Freudian contribution to affective education; it will conclude by briefly examining recent developments in the interpersonal aspects of education.

Sigmund Freud

Sigmund Freud (1856–1939), who was a Viennese physician, had been trained in the conventional nineteenth-century rationalist medical tradition. Early in his career, he became intrigued by mental illnesses in which patients exhibited symptoms of organic disturbance without identifiable organic causes. Freud's clinical studies of hysteria and hysterical symptoms led him to develop the system of psychoanalysis, which has profoundly influenced psychology and psychiatry.

Gardner Murphy has distinguished two phases in Freud's work: (1) his investigation of the unconscious from the 1880s until 1913, and (2) his later studies of the integration of the individual within society.[1] Initially, Freud's ideas drew attention in Viennese medical circles and among German-speaking psychologists. The first stage was followed by a period of clarification and dissension among the Freudians, which led to the serious defections of Alfred Adler and

[1] Gardner Murphy, *Historical Introduction to Modern Psychology* (New York: Harcourt, Brace, 1949), p. 321.

Carl Jung. Adler, a Viennese psychologist, had begun to direct psychoanalysis away from its basic emphasis on the individual's unconscious emotions to issues of conscious social participation. Jung, a Swiss psychologist, developed a rather vague psychoanalytical world view. His interest in Oriental religions and philosophies led him to believe that a vast "collective unconscious" existed. Jung stated that the same myth symbols and episodes repeated themselves within human history at various times and places. Unlike Freud, Jung emphasized the therapeutic value of religious belief systems.

Freudian psychoanalytic theory entered English-speaking psychological circles after World War I. By the mid-twentieth century, psychoanalytic theory and its variants were diffused in American medicine.[2] In addition to its significance in psychology, psychiatry, and medicine, Freudianism has had an impact on twentieth-century art, literature, and culture. Freud's stress on early childhood experiences and his emphasis on the unconscious stimulated new approaches to educational theory and practice.

Freud was a prolific author. A brief examination of his major works will give an indication of the way in which his psychoanalytic theory developed. In 1895, Freud and his colleague, Josef Breuer, wrote *Studies on Hysteria,* describing their initial work with analysis. Freud's *The Interpretation of Dreams* (1900) expressed his views on the unconscious and the dominance of the pleasure principle. *Psychopathology of Everyday Life* (1901) made it clear that Freud was enunciating a general psychological theory rather than one confined to pathological mental conditions. His controversial *Three Essays on the Theory of Sexuality* (1905) traced the development of the human sexual instinct from birth to maturity. In 1913, Freud moved from the study of the individual to the study of society. In that year, his *Totem and Taboo* attempted to apply psychoanalysis to anthropology. *On the History of the Psycho-Analytic Movement* (1914) and *Introductory Lectures* (1917) gave general accounts of his views and movement. *Group Psychology* (1921) and *The Ego and the Id* (1923) treated the division of the mind into an id, ego, and superego. Freud's concentration on the historical and cultural implications of psychoanalytic theory was marked in 1927 by the appearance of *The Future of an Illusion,* a critical discussion of religion from the perspective of atheistic humanism. *Civilization and Its Discontents* (1930) presented a Freudian view of history that included an extensive treatment of man's destructive instinct. Freud's last major work, *Moses and Monotheism* (1938), traced the tragic history of the Jewish people to their creation of a monotheistic deity.

[2] *Ibid.,* p. 329.

Freudian Psychoanalysis

After experimenting for a time with hypnotic methods of treating hysteria, Freud developed his psychoanalytic method in which the patient was encouraged to talk about anything that entered his mind. In contrast to hypnosis, psychoanalysis took place while the patient was in a waking state. Through free association, the patient's gradual recollection of repressed emotional episodes led to the source of the conflict that had precipitated the neurosis. The therapeutic aspects of psychoanalysis were intended to help the patient overcome the resistances that resulted from repression and discover the problem that was at the root of his emotional difficulty. A basic premise was that the patient's own self-awareness was an indispensable part of his adjustment. If the neurotic individual understood his behavior and recognized his particular problem, then it was anticipated that he would face his problem and make an adjustment that would enable him to lead a normal life. By releasing pent-up emotion, psychoanalysis would terminate the conflict within the patient's psyche.

Freud's psychoanalytic method was initially a technique for healing mental illnesses by exploring the relationships between the patient's psychic and physical functions. According to Freud, a neurotic is an individual who represses his instinctual drives into his unconscious so that they cannot find suitable outlets. These drives are then expressed through abnormal outlets that manifest themselves in some form of neurosis or phobia. Although maladjusted, the neurotic is nevertheless able to function in society, unlike the completely mentally ill, or psychotic, individual, who fails to recognize reality and lives in an unreal subjective world of his own making. Through psychoanalysis, the neurotic individual searches his childhood memories for concrete details so that the analyst can identify the significant ones that point to the repression contributing to the neurotic behavior. The analysis of dreams plays an important role in psychoanalysis. Freud believed that the unconscious manifests itself while the individual is dreaming. The repressed forces that are kept out of consciousness during waking are expressed in symbolic terms in dreams.[3]

Freud's *Three Essays on the Theory of Sexuality* called attention to the crucial significance of sexuality in the individual's psychological development. In this work, Freud claimed to have discerned evidence of sexuality in infantile behavior. Because of parental and social pressures, he said, children are usually forced to repress their sexuality. Such sexual repression in childhood frequently causes

[3] *Ibid.*, pp. 309–312.

neurosis in the adult because he finds difficulty in achieving normal sexual relationships. If the individual indulges his sexual urges, on the other hand, he will usually experience guilt feelings. Although there had been periods of sexual freedom, Western tradition has, for the most part, emphasized the repression of sexuality, especially in its early manifestation in children. Freud's use of the term "sexual" was a general one that went beyond its conventional meaning, but his emphasis on the sexual instinct provoked both popular and professional controversy. Although disagreeing with each other in other respects, Freud's former disciples Jung and Adler agreed that he had oversimplified and overemphasized the importance of the sexual drive.

The Freudian Psychological System

Freud's system of psychology was based on a set of drives that he claimed are inborn in every person. These instinctual drives arise in the unconscious and are expressions of the "id," which, as the oldest mental agency in the human being, contains everything that is inherited and present at birth. The id expresses the individual's true purpose, which is to satisfy the instinctual needs that are biologically rooted demands upon mental life. As his theory matured, Freud reduced the number of instincts to two basic ones: Eros and the destructive instinct. While Eros (the love instinct) aims to establish ever greater unities and to preserve them by further binding and integration, the destructive (or death) instinct aims to reduce living things to an inorganic state. The interaction of these two basic human instincts that produce all other drives gives rise to the phenomena of life.

It was Freud's emphasis on the unconscious that cast human relationships in a new perspective. In dealing with the unconscious drives, Freud avoided the conventional moralism that had been traditionally applied to human desires. Although the satisfaction of these basic desires would give pleasure to the individual, he learns to repress them because of social pressure. The infant is uninhibited and can satisfy his needs without the restraints of the conscious mind. Soon, however, the pressures of restraint, emanating from parents or guardians, come to play upon the child. As he matures, he becomes aware that some of his desires are objectionable to those on whom he depends. Therefore, he represses certain drives emanating from the id. The unconscious self, or id, contains, then, the instinctual drives, or impulses, repressed from consciousness.

With his growing consciousness of the external objective world, the individual develops another part of his psyche, which acts to censor his drives. This part of the psyche Freud subdivided into the "ego" and the "superego." The ego is a group of tendencies, or a mental agency, that acts as an intermediary between the id and the external world. The ego's task is the self-preservation of the individual. It may control instinctual demands in any one of three ways: (1) by allowing the satisfaction of the instincts, (2) by deferring satisfaction until circumstances are more favorable, or (3) by suppressing the instinctual drives. The ego thus acts as a private censor indicating to the person that certain drives emanating from the id cannot succeed.

In the Freudian system, the "superego" is a special mental agency that is a collection of conscious and unconscious values derived from the culture that restrict the id's instinctual drives and impulses. In the superego, the parental influence is prolonged and extended as it takes on contributions from such parental successors as teachers, admired public figures, and other exemplary persons and from ethical and moral codes. The relationship between the ego and superego originates in the child's experience with his parents' personalities and value systems and is subsequently affected by racial, national, religious, and family traditions as well as the social milieu from which they are derived.

The Freudian psychological system comprises the interactions of the id, ego, and superego. Both the id and the superego represent the individual's personal history. The id is a product of heredity and the superego of social interaction and experience. The ego is influenced by the individual's current experience. An action of the ego is satisfactory when it fulfills the demands of the id and superego and conforms to reality. The mentally healthy individual satisfies enough of the id's desires to feel contented. However, all individuals must repress a great many of the drives emanating from the id. Through the process known as sublimation, the successful individual finds socially approved outlets to express these desires. The psychoneurotic individual, however, cannot satisfactorily express his instinctual desires.

Freud's Social Theory

In contrast to Freud's earlier volumes, which exposited the central concepts and methods of psychoanalysis, his later, more speculative works sought to develop the social and historical implications of his theories. Of these later works, *Civilization and Its Discontents* (1930) is of greatest interest to social, intellectual, and educational historians. Freud saw a parallel between the processes of individual and cultural development. In his view, the sublimation of certain aggressive and sexual instincts in the individual had contributed to intellectual, scientific, aesthetic, and ideological developments and was therefore an important determinant of cultural evolution. In other words, civilization resulted as the gratification of some instincts was channeled along socially approved avenues.[4]

Freud gave a psychoanalytical interpretation to the various stages of cultural development. Human group association arose when primitive man discovered that it was more efficient to improve material life conditions by working with others than against them. Driven by the sexual instinct, primitive man formed families. The power of love caused the male to keep the female near him and caused the female to keep her children near her. Within the context of primitive group association, the members of the human band evolved a set of taboos, or restrictions and sanctions, that they imposed on one another in order to maintain the fragile embryonic society.

Just as he had attached great importance to the sexual instinct in the development of the individual, Freud found it to be a major determinant in cultural evolution. Since man's greatest gratification comes through sexual love, he sought pleasure through sexual relationships. In seeking sexual gratification, man was forced to depend on his chosen lover. This exposed him to the painful sufferings of being rejected or of losing his lover through death or desertion. In the course of time, a small minority of men, by transferring the specific love relationship into a more generalized act of loving, made a far-reaching psychological transformation that profoundly affected cultural development. Such individuals turned away from sexual love and modified the sexual impulse into a more generalized but inhibited aim. As it was slowly encased in religious, philosophical, and ethical systems and codes, this tendency to a generalized love of humanity or nature came to be revered as the highest state of mind that man could possibly achieve.[5]

Abstract and highly generalized philosophical, religious, and ethical expressions of love contributed to form the cultural superego. Derived from the impressions left behind by leading personalities and great men, the superego of any given epoch of civilization originated in the same manner as it did in individuals. The cultural superego elaborated ideals and standards for human behavior. The ethical systems that pertained to interpersonal relationships were especially significant. The cultural superego established high ideals and standards that prescribed human behavior to such a degree that failure to satisfy these moral codes was punished by an anxiety of conscience.

The two basic human instincts of Eros and destructiveness are manifested in a number of ways, the most compelling of which are

---

[4] Sigmund Freud, *Civilization and Its Discontents*, Joan Riviere (tr.) (New York: Doubleday, 1958), pp. 41–53.
[5] *Ibid.*, pp. 56–67.

sexuality and aggressiveness. In Western civilization, the cultural superego traditionally prescribed sexual relationships according to certain standards of monogamy and legitimacy. Western European civilization, in particular, censured any manifestation of sexuality in children in order to cultivate predispositions that curbed their adult expressions of sexual desires. Freud held that men, despite the sanctions of abstract ethical codes, are aggressive creatures who exploit other men. Most men love in a specific context and have difficulty accepting abstract ethical systems that enjoin them to love all men or all creation. This innate tendency to aggression disturbs interpersonal human relationships and makes it necessary for society to enact restrictions on the tendency to aggression through the cultural superego and social sanctions. Because of the primary hostility that men have toward one another, civilized society is perpetually threatened by cultural disintegration manifested by social discontent, violence, strife, and war. For self-preservation, therefore, civilized men construct cultural and social barriers to channel their aggressive instincts.

The meaning of the title *Civilization and Its Discontents* becomes increasingly clear. Civilization is created by the repression of the desire for certain instinctual gratifications. Social relationships are the means of repressing human aggressiveness and antagonism. In every individual, however, are two tendencies: one that seeks happiness through personal gratification and another that seeks greater unity with the rest of humanity through interpersonal association. These two tendencies result in a basic struggle between the individual and society since the processes of individual and cultural development are in perpetual conflict. Thus, Freud's later works attempt to deal with the basic dichotomy in human nature that he believed his psychoanalytical theory had revealed. As an individual, man is a creature of impulse, emotion, and instinct. But as a participant in culture and history, man seeks rationality, self-control, and social order. Although Freud used his psychoanalytic theory to develop a theory of cultural evolution, his conclusions were not unique or even new. The ancient Greek theorists and dramatists had recognized the conflict between the individual and society.

The tone of Freud's later writings revealed pessimism about man's prospects, thereby reflecting the general feeling of anxiety that has characterized Western civilization in the twentieth century, especially in the period between the world wars. This pessimism is in sharp contrast to the confident enthusiasm of the late eighteenth and the nineteenth centuries. Freud asserted that man has made extraordinary advances in the modern era in scientific knowledge and its technical application. While these scientific discoveries and the resulting rise of a technological society have increased man's domination over nature, they have failed to increase human happiness. Along with material progress, Western civilization has also experienced a profound sense of foreboding.

The pervasive anxiety that Freud saw in twentieth-century civilization has been caused in part by the social controls that have increasingly limited the areas of individual action that satisfy instinctual impulses. As civilizing tendencies increase, so does the degree of individual and social discontent. As larger and more complex social aggregates were organized, Freud predicted, the sense of guilt arising from the struggle between the Eros and destructive tendencies would reach such magnitude that individuals would no longer be able to bear it.

Freud raised the specter that certain epochs of human history might be neurotic and that humanity itself might become increasingly neurotic under the pressure of civilizing trends. It was in the area of dealing with such "collective neuroses" that psychoanalytical theory was admittedly inadequate. In the therapy of an individual, the analyst can presume that the environment in which the patient lives is normal. In the case of the neurotic society, however, no such environment exists. Although Freud raised basic questions concerning the pathology of civilized communities, his death in 1939 cut short further research and commentary. Although *Civilization and Its Discontents* was written in 1930, it anticipated the mood of unrest, dejection, and apprehension that resulted in the post-World War II era as man realized that he possessed instruments capable of exterminating the human race.

Freud's Impact

Sigmund Freud parted company with the rationalist tradition that had dominated much of the eighteenth and nineteenth centuries. Whereas the rationalists believed that human behavior is subject to reason's dictates, Freud believed that man's behavior is substantially the product of his unconscious. For Freud, reflective thought is only a fractional part of human behavior. A great part of what appears to be conscious thought is actually rationalization based on the noncognitive, instinctive desires of the id.

The educator who tries to translate Freudianism into pedagogical terms can detect a similarity between Freud and the nineteenth-century Swiss educator Pestalozzi in their emphasis on emotions. Although Freud would have certainly challenged Pestalozzi's naive assumption that man is endowed with an innate propensity to benevolence, he would have agreed with the Swiss educator's contention that the harmonious development of the child's personality depends upon an environment of love and emotional security. Both men would have agreed that healthy emotions are a necessary precondition for man's personal, social, and educational growth. Although Pestalozzi's less sophisticated theory did not identify the unconscious, he emphasized the "will" as the dynamic agency that initiates and, to a large extent, governs behavior. With Freud's discovery of the unconscious, there came a strong impetus for the examination of the irrational aspects of behavior.

Freud's emphasis on the unconscious contrasted with the Western educational tradition that had emphasized the cultivation of reason as defined and elaborated within a variety of social and cultural contexts. The older philosophies of idealism, realism, and Thomism conceived of education as a means of cultivating and exercising reason and intelligence. Philosophers holding such disparate metaphysical views as Plato, Aristotle, and Aquinas agreed that the emotions of a properly functioning human being should be subjected to the dictates of reason. The practical educational consequences of this emphasis on reason called for a restraint of the will or the emotions so that reason could govern behavior. The authority of either the teacher or the group was used as a vehicle to secure the child's conformity to preferred behavioral patterns. Generally, the mainstreams of the Western educational experience have stressed rational development as the preferred aim of education. In the context of schooling, rational behavior has been defined in logical, scientific, or literary terms. The emphasis on rationalism has led to the suppression of the emotional or volitional components of behavior. Although Rousseau and Pestalozzi had called attention to the role of the emotions in the process of natural education, more conventional educators have tended to ignore the irrational side of behavior or to condemn it as a deviation from proper functioning.

The educational crises of the 1960s and 1970s, characterized, in part, by student protests against institutionalized educational patterns, stemmed from the conflict between expressions of rational and nonrational modes of behavior. While more traditional educators have viewed education as a process of acquiring the structures of knowledge and methods of disciplined inquiry, others have become impatient with what has been referred to as the cultivation of rationality. Their impatience has taken the form of vague appeals and often strident demands for the liberation of emotions and for recognition of the importance of "feeling" as well as thinking.

Although Freud's influence on psychology was direct, the Freudian impact on philosophy, art, and education was dispersed but significant. Nevertheless, his work tempered the impact of both eighteenth-century rationalism and nineteenth-century science. The significance of his discovery of the unconscious is just beginning to be felt in formal education. Although Freudian psychoanalysis was only one of several psychological theories that have stimulated interest in the affective dimension of education, it served to focus the educator's attention on the emotional and interpersonal aspects of behavior.

A recent example of interest in the affective aspects of education is provided by the group training movement, which uses social psychology to examine the interpersonal relationships of group behavior. This movement is particularly interesting to educators who feel that interpersonal conflicts, often of an emotional nature, frequently impede group problem-solving efforts. The development of the group training movement illustrates that Freud's interest in man's affective nature is being pursued by contemporary educators.

The Group Training Movement and Affective Education

Although the group training, or laboratory, movement had its origins in Freud's investigation of the subconscious sources of man's behavior, an even greater impact came from the studies in social psychology that were done at the close of the nineteenth century. Gabriel Tarde's *The Laws of Imitation* (1890) and Gustave LeBon's *The Crowd* (1895) investigated pathological suggestibility and paved the way for the study of nonrationalistic group behavior.[6] In *An Introduction to Social Psychology* (1908), William McDougall established the thesis that social life is based on reciprocally related instincts and emotions. Because of these studies, psychologists and social scientists were stimulated to conduct more extensive investigations into social behavior.

During the 1920s, social scientists began to study the functioning of social groups and interaction within the groups. In the 1930s, educators began to be receptive to the idea of applying principles derived from social psychology to education. Some individuals in the socially oriented wing of the progressive education movement began to emphasize the group as a democratic means of problem-solving. The economic depression of the 1930s brought the doctrines of self-assertion and competition into disrepute and engendered an interest in social welfare.

In the late 1930s, the development of social psychology and the investigation of group functioning were stimulated by the work of Kurt Lewin, who conducted a number of investigations in experimental child social psychology. Lewin became interested in research into the means of effecting social change and developing such research into an academic discipline. He and his associates, Ronald Lippitt and Ralph White, formed a group to investigate the psychology of small groups, and, in 1944, Lewin established a Research Center in Group Dynamics at the Massachusetts Institute of Technology to investigate

[6] Murphy, *op. cit.*, pp. 402–403.

social groups and their leadership with a view to reducing tensions stemming from ethnic, religious, and other social cleavages.[7]

The training group, or T-group, was developed in 1946 during a project in which Lewin, Leland Bradford, Ronald Lippitt, and Kenneth Benne were training a group of community leaders to deal with inter-racial problems. They also used this project as an opportunity to study group discussion methods as an educational procedure. As a result of their work, this educational research team became impressed with the possibilities of group self-evaluation as a means of teaching the de-velopment of group processes that could be applied to community problem-solving.[8]

Interest in group problem-solving techniques led to the establish-ment of the National Training Laboratories at Bethel, Maine, where from 1949 to 1955 a number of experiments were conducted to refine and develop group training methods. Two different methods emerged: the T-group, a small group of people from diverse backgrounds who were not given any assignment other than to analyze their immediate interactions; and the A-group, or action group, which was given spe-cific problems to solve. Since 1955, the training laboratory movement has developed in a number of directions. Laboratories—frequently autonomous from the National Training Laboratories—have been es-tablished throughout the United States in such variety that submove-ments have developed with diverse goals and methods.

During the late 1950s and 1960s, there was a continued interest in the use of group training to examine the factors that promote or hinder human relationships. The T-group—or such variants of it as the action group, sensitivity group, encounter group, and personal growth labora-tories—became popular among some industrialists, social scientists, and educators.[9]

The use of the T-group has produced contention between its advo-cates and detractors. Gottschalk and Pattison have listed both the assets and the liabilities of the method. They cite the following advantages:

1. The T-group is a means of teaching interpersonal relations within a functioning group rather than relying on description.
2. It sharpens perceptual skills and teaches individuals to use a number of specific techniques for interpersonal communication.
3. It provides the theory and practice for effective community par-ticipation.

[7] Ibid., pp. 304–305.
[8] Louis A. Gottschalk and E. Mansell Pattison, "Psychiatric Perspectives on T-Groups and the Laboratory Movement: An Overview," American Jour-nal of Psychiatry, 126:6 (December 1969), 824.
[9] Ibid., p. 823.

4. The emphasis on human relations as a means of nurturing growth may be incorporated into the educational structure.

These authors have also listed the limitations of the T-group approach:

1. If the screening of participants is inadequate, some individuals may be involved who cannot tolerate intensive interpersonal group experience.
2. Since few reliable criteria exist for determining the competence of leaders, incompetent or neurotic leaders may use the group for their own aggrandizement or permit destructive group tendencies.
3. Relationships may develop that are inappropriate to the reality of the participants' social and occupational roles.
4. It may emphasize participation or experiencing without appropriate self-analysis or reflection.
5. Groups can be just as tyrannical and destructive as individuals.[10]

When used with appropriate professional safeguards, the T-group method may prove beneficial in such educational situations as the interaction between teaching and learning since it focuses attention on the affective dimension of learning. It can help teachers to identify their own emotional reactions as well as those of others and can focus attention on nonverbal as well as verbal participation.

The training group movement has often drawn criticism from individuals who are identified with academic university departments, well-defined research fields, and the clinical professions. The movement has drawn support from individuals who prefer to use a loosely structured interdisciplinary approach to social problems. These supporters have come from a variety of backgrounds, and because of this diversity, the practices of "trainers" have been extremely varied. In addition, strong similarities exist between the various forms of T-groups and group psychotherapy, and the distinctions between training and therapy have sometimes been dangerously blurred. Since the training group procedure can produce dramatic psychopathological reactions in individuals, the method should be used cautiously and only by carefully prepared group leaders. Gottschalk and Pattison conclude that the T-group method, if used improperly, can have destructive results.[11]

Although it is far too early for the historian to assess the impact of the group training movement upon the affective dimension of education, the interest of educators in seeking to improve interpersonal rela-

[10] *Ibid.*, pp. 833–836.
[11] *Ibid.*, p. 823.

tionships has made this movement a relevant educational concern. The group training movement has sought to extend educational emphasis beyond the cognitive to the emotional dimensions of learning. Although only a few schools of education in the United States have actually established group training laboratories for their students, increased professional attention is being given to the study of training in interpersonal relations in professional education. In the United States, where the movement has enjoyed its greatest popularity, the group training method has attracted both zealous advocates and zealous opponents. A truly objective history of the movement will require both time and the maturing of the movement.

Conclusion

In the twentieth century, man's view of himself was radically reshaped by Sigmund Freud's theory of psychoanalysis, which focused attention on the unconscious. Through Freud's efforts, man began to recognize a side of his nature that had been hidden or ignored. While the comforting rationalism of earlier times may have been eroded, the Freudian contribution to man's self-awareness initiated liberating tendencies. Freud's work had an impact on educational theory in that it called for a rethinking of the conceptions of childhood and behavior. As a result, the twentieth-century educator has grown more concerned with the affective dimension of education and with nonrational as well as rational aspects of learning.

Suggested Readings

Batchelder, R. L., and J. M. Hardy. *Using Sensitivity Training and the Laboratory Method.* New York: Association Press, 1968.

Beckhard, R. *Conferences for Learning, Planning and Action.* Washington, D.C.: National Training Laboratories and National Education Association, 1962.

Bradford, L. P., and Kenneth D. Benne (eds.). *T-Group Theory and Laboratory Method: Innovation in Re-Education.* New York: Wiley, 1964.

Brown, Norman O. *Life Against Death: The Psychoanalytical Meaning of History.* Middletown, Conn.: Wesleyan University Press, 1959.

Crawshaw, Ralph. "How Sensitive is Sensitivity Training?" *American Journal of Psychiatry,* 126:6 (December 1969), 868–873.

Edelson, M. *Ego Psychology, Group Dynamics, and the Therapeutic Community.* New York: Grune and Stratton, 1964.

Freud, Sigmund. *Civilization and Its Discontents.* Joan Riviere (tr.). New York: Doubleday, 1958.

—————. *A General Introduction to Psychoanalysis.* New York: Liveright, 1920.

—————. *An Outline of Psychoanalysis.* James Strachey (tr.). New York: Norton, 1949.

Gottschalk, Louis A., and E. Mansell Pattison. "Psychiatric Perspectives on T-Groups and the Laboratory Movement: An Overview," *American Journal of Psychiatry,* 126:6 (December 1969), 823–839.

Lewin, Kurt. *A Dynamic Theory of Personality.* New York: McGraw-Hill, 1935.

Murphy, Gardner. *Historical Introduction to Modern Psychology.* New York: Harcourt, Brace, 1949.

Schoenwald, R. L. *Freud: The Man and His Mind.* New York: Knopf, 1956.

Weschler, I. R. *Issues in Human Relations Training.* Washington, D.C.: National Training Laboratories and National Education Association, 1962.

CHAPTER 18

English Education

The nineteenth and twentieth centuries witnessed the creation of national education systems in both Europe and America. While the national systems of the countries of the European Continent were usually highly centralized, those of England and the United States were decentralized. This chapter will treat such developments in nineteenth- and twentieth-century English education as (1) the efforts to combat massive illiteracy through programs of voluntary and charity education, (2) the educational consequences of the enactment of reform legislation, (3) the persistence of the laissez-faire tradition, (4) the continuing influence of the public schools, and (5) the gradual emergence of the welfare-state philosophy and its educational implications.

Chapter 11 described the nineteenth century as an age of alternative and often conflicting ideologies. As a reflection of the attitudes, philosophies, and politics of the people of England, English educational policies and programs were often based on the rival ideologies of liberalism and conservatism, which vied for hegemony in the nineteenth century. In the twentieth century, the rise of the British Labour party added a third social and political philosophy to the framing of educational policies. This chapter will examine some of these major developments in modern English education.

Early Efforts to Combat Illiteracy

During the early nineteenth century, the overwhelming majority of the lower socioeconomic classes in England could neither read nor write. Some of the more reactionary of the English aristocrats believed that ignorance was a safeguard against popular discontent and rebellion. They feared that popular education would enable the working classes to read seditious pamphlets and books that might make them insubordinate to their social betters.

Despite the existence of high illiteracy rates, education in early nineteenth-century England exhibited a great deal of variety. There were parish schools, privately endowed chantry schools, dame schools, private venture schools, and an assortment of charity schools maintained by churches or voluntary organizations such as the Society for the Propagation of Christian Knowledge. Private and religious schools were the dominant types of educational institutions during this period. The old public schools, modeled after the classical humanist grammar schools, continued to educate the sons of the wealthy upper and middle classes and to prepare them for entry into the prestige universities of Oxford and Cambridge. The charity schools sought to offer some rudimentary education to the rapidly growing numbers of urban poor children. Robert Raikes was promoting the Sunday school to provide some slight degree of learning for children who were engaged as factory operatives during the week. Infant schools provided a nursery school education to three-, four-, and five-year-old children whose mothers were working. Robert Owen's infant school at New Lanark pioneered in educational reform, permissive practices, and nature studies. In most of these schools, however, teachers were untrained, conditions chaotic, and instruction haphazard.

In the early nineteenth century, monitorialism was proposed as an educational innovation that would revolutionize schools and make learning available to all. Its chief proponents were Joseph Lancaster (1778–1838), a Quaker schoolmaster, and Andrew Bell (1753–1832), an Anglican clergyman who had been a missionary in India. The two educators were bitter rivals who each claimed that the other had usurped his educational idea.

Lancaster hoped to devise an inexpensive and efficient educational method that would make mass schooling possible. In his proposed system, students were to learn the maximum skills in a minimum of time.[1] He started by using the older boys enrolled in his school as monitors; he gave them charge of instructing the younger students in some of the basic skills and routine tasks of school management. Lancaster was successful in publicizing his monitorial method and attracted a number of supporters who contributed to the establishment of a model Lancastrian school.

Andrew Bell had also devised a mutual instruction system similar to Lancaster's method. Bell had published a report, *An Experiment in Education*, in 1797 upon his return from Madras, India, where he had been in charge of an orphanage. After a heated controversy developed between the followers of Bell and Lancaster, two separate societies

[1] For Lancaster's description of his method, see Joseph Lancaster, *Improvements in Education, as it Respects the Industrious Classes of the Community* (London: Darton and Harvey, 1805), and *The British System of Education* (London: Royal Free School Society, 1810).

were established to support the rival monitorial methods: the National Society for the Education of the Poor in the Principles of the Established Church to support Bell and the Royal Lancastrian Society to promote his rival.

Lancaster devised elaborate instructions for organizing and conducting monitorial schools. Careful planning was regarded as necessary for the success of the method. His instructions extended to such matters as the amount of space required for each student, arrangement of desks, construction of school furniture, and the mechanics of keeping school. He recommended that one monitor be appointed to supervise ten students. These monitors were selected from capable students and were assigned to supervise or instruct lower groups. Lancaster believed that children learned most efficiently from one another and tried to incorporate this into his method. The role of the master teacher was really that of organizing his subordinates and supervising instruction. The monitorial schools established by both Bell and Lancaster attempted to teach reading, writing, and simple arithmetic. They attracted widespread attention and were copied in England, on the Continent, and in North and South America. The popularity of monitorialism was quickly spent, however. After enjoying a period of enthusiastic acceptance, the method was generally discarded. While it might prove useful in teaching a few basic skills, it was generally agreed that it could not genuinely educate.

Factory Reform and Education

The various developments of English education were related to the course of industrialism. The factory system, with its system of mass production, had been established in England at the end of the eighteenth century. There was widespread use of child labor as operatives in English factories, mills, and mines. It is obvious that the general use of child labor was antagonistic to the development of large-scale mass systems of education. Correspondingly, the higher the incident of child labor, the greater were the rates of illiteracy.

By the 1830s, certain reform-minded political leaders focused their attention on the plight of the industrial poor. Among the most prominent of these reformers was the Earl of Shaftesbury (1801–1885), who concentrated on working conditions in the factories. An associate of Shaftesbury, Michael Sadler, introduced a bill in Parliament that called for regulation of the working conditions of child laborers in textile mills. This bill was referred to a committee, with Sadler as chairman. The Sadler Committee heard copious testimony regarding the general state of English working conditions. They also found numerous cases of inhumane treatment of child laborers. The following excerpts from the Sadler Report provide a clear indictment of the conditions of child labor in early nineteenth-century England:

> Mr. Matthew Crabtree, called in; and Examined.
> What age are you?—Twenty-two.
> What is your occupation?—A blanket manufacturer.
> Have you ever been employed in a factory?—Yes.
> At what age did you first go to work in one?—Eight.
> How long did you continue in that occupation?—Four years.
> Will you state the hours of labour at the period when you first went to the factory, in ordinary times?—From 6 in the morning to 8 at night.
> Fourteen hours?—Yes.
> With what intervals for refreshment and rest?—An hour at noon. . . .
> State the condition of the children towards the latter part of the day, who have thus to keep up with the machinery?—It is as much as they can do when they are not very much fatigued to keep up with their work, and towards the close of the day, when they come to be more fatigued, they cannot keep up with it very well, and the consequence is that they are beaten to spur them on. . . .
> Do you find that the children and young persons in those mills are moral in other respects, or does their want of education tend to encourage them in a breach of the law?—I believe it does, for there are very few of them that can know anything about it; few of them can either read or write. . . .
> What, in your opinion, would be the effect of limiting the hours of labor upon the happiness, and the health, and the intelligence of the rising generation?—If the hours are shortened, the children, may, perhaps, have a chance of attending some evening-school, and learning to read and write; and those that I know who have been to school and learned to read and write, have much more comfort than those who have not.[2]

The strongest opposition to factory reform legislation often came from the industrial manufacturers, many of whom were prominent members of the Liberal party. John Bright, a leading Liberal, opposed factory legislation as being injurious to the national interest and to personal liberty. A staunch classical liberal of the laissez-faire school, Bright believed that any governmental interference with working conditions violated individual liberty and freedom of contract. Some of the initial impetus for the reform of working conditions came from landed aristocrats, who were prominent in the Conservative party. While some of the Tory Conservatives were genuinely paternalistic, others hoped to embarrass their rivals for political power, the manufacturers. Chapter 16 mentioned how liberals also tended to divide into two opposing groups on the question of social welfare legislation.

[2] *Report From the Committee on the Bill to Regulate the Labour of Children in the Mills and Factories of the United Kingdom* (London: House of Commons, 1832), pp. 94–104.

In 1833, however, through the efforts of Sadler and Shaftesbury, Parliament passed the *Bill to Regulate the Labour of Children in the Mills and Factories of the United Kingdom*. This initial factory legislation sought to ameliorate the harsh conditions of child labor. Children under nine were prohibited from working in the textile mills. Those between the ages of nine and thirteen were restricted to a forty-eight hour workweek; those between thirteen and eighteen to sixty-eight hours per week. The Sadler Report had alerted public attention to the human problems caused by an unregulated industrialism. In the 1840s, a series of royal commissions investigated and reported on the consequences of unregulated capitalism—the deplorable living conditions in factory towns, the lack of adequate housing, water, and sanitary facilities, and the shameful working conditions. These reports engendered reform movements that cut across Liberal and Conservative party lines. Although the strict laissez-faire liberal adherents of the Manchester school's economic doctrines were opposed to them, a number of legislative acts were passed to remedy the working conditions of the poor. Ashley's Act of 1842 prohibited the employment of women and of children under ten years of age in the mines. Graham's Factory Act of 1844 provided for factory inspection to ensure the observance of safety regulations. In 1847, Fielden's Act established a normal working day of ten and a half hours for women and for young people in factories. By implication, the provisions of this act were also extended to adult male operatives. The factory reform legislation was significant in establishing recognition that the government had some degree of regulative responsibility in maintaining the welfare of its citizens.

The passage of child labor legislation had an impact on educational developments in England and other Western nations. When children were freed from labor as factory operatives, they had more time for formal education. As a result, the school increasingly replaced the informal kind of educational arrangements that had once prevailed on the farm, in the mill and factory, and at home. As children between the ages of ten and sixteen were gradually emancipated from factory work, this period of youth, or adolescence, was increasingly used for education beyond the elementary stage. One of the factors of nineteenth- and twentieth-century industrialization has been the recognition that adolescence is a unique and necessary part of human development. In primitive societies that have not felt the impact of industrialization, the socialization of a person often proceeds from childhood directly to adulthood without an intervening period of adolescence. As adolescent education became a possibility for more young people, the conception of secondary education as strictly college preparatory was scrutinized and subjected to criticism.

Laissez-Faire and Educational Reform

Unlike the educational system of the Germans and French, who had centralized educational authority in the national government, English elementary education throughout most of the nineteenth century was a product of the voluntary efforts of private philanthropic and religious organizations. According to both the Anglican tradition and the principles of laissez-faire economic liberalism, education was a private matter, best left to parental discretion. A meager educational charity was provided only in the case of the indigent child. It was this tradition of individual and private initiative that supported the "voluntary" elementary school.

The first significant effort of the government in education came in 1833 when Parliament began to provide limited national grants to schools. It appropriated £20,000 (about $100,000) as an annual grant to be distributed among the various voluntary schools. Although this was a faint move in the direction of popular elementary education, the amount appropriated was pitifully small in terms of the needs of an industrial society. Attempts to establish a national elementary school system were vigorously resisted by an unusual alliance of established churchmen and classical liberals. The orthodox Anglicans feared that a national elementary school system might tend in the direction of disestablishment and secularization. Classical liberals of the Manchester variety were suspicious of any attempts at government intervention in the social sphere.

Although the Parliamentary Act of 1833 had revealed a national interest in elementary education, it was not until the latter half of the nineteenth century that a serious effort was made to inaugurate universal elementary education. During the period from 1850 to 1870, a series of royal commissions were appointed to investigate the universities, public schools, endowed grammar schools, and elementary schools. Frequently, the recommendations of these commissions were implemented through parliamentary legislation. The educational thrust of this period of investigation and recommendation was significant in two respects: (1) Efforts were made in the direction of creating an effective national educational system; (2) attempts were made to build Victorian social mores into the educational system.[3] In 1850, the National Public School Association was organized to work for free and compulsory education supported by government taxation. Despite the efforts of the association, the Newcastle Commission in 1858 advised

[3] Brian Simon, "Classification and Streaming: A Study of Grouping in English Schools, 1860–1960," in Paul Nash (ed.), *History and Education* (New York: Random House, 1970), p. 117.

against establishing a tax-supported educational system. According to this commission, compulsory education would restrict individual rights, and its evil would far outweigh any benefits. Although a national education system did not emerge during the period from 1850 to 1870, the outlines of a tripartite school system were discernible: prestigious "public" schools, actually highly selective private institutions, provided secondary education for the upper class; less selective, privately endowed grammar schools provided secondary education for the middle class; and elementary schools provided primary education for working-class children.

In 1862, the Revised Code of Regulations inaugurated the school grant system, which was popularly referred to as "payments by results." According to the provisions of this Code:

1. Each child was expected to attain a specified level of achievement in the basic subjects of reading, writing, and arithmetic by the end of each year.
2. Each child was to be examined annually to determine his or her competency in the required subjects.
3. The amount of the grant awarded to each school was to be calculated according to the number of children who passed the examination in each of the subjects and by the total number of attendance days recorded per child.

In conjunction with the administration of these large-scale national examinations, officers of the Education Department, known as Her Majesty's Inspectors, carried out regular inspections of elementary schools. The Education Department, established earlier in 1856, gradually shaped the curriculum as the elementary schools came to emphasize success on the examinations as a major educational objective. Classes in the elementary schools were organized on the basis of homogeneous ability groups so that children might be prepared more efficiently for the examinations. Although the "payment by results" system of examinations stimulated the emergence of a national elementary school system, it also contributed to a rigidly defined and narrow curriculum.[4] Religious instruction remained the primary concern of the denomination or private association, called a "voluntary body," maintaining the school; the government's major interest was to improve instruction in the basic elementary subjects. The elementary schools became a separate track with the aim of providing mass literacy rather than attempting to prepare students for entry into secondary schools.

[4] *Ibid.*, pp. 118–119.

Gladstone and Educational Reform

William Ewart Gladstone (1809–1898), leader of the Liberal party throughout most of the nineteenth century, was motivated by a desire to reform English life, society, and politics. Son of a Liverpool merchant, he had attained scholastic success at Oxford and served in a number of cabinet posts, including chancellor of the exchequer, before becoming prime minister. His first term of office, from 1868 to 1874, was characterized by a number of legislative reforms, among them the Forster Act, or Education Act of 1870. This legislation divided the country into local school districts, under the jurisdiction of local, secular school boards, and it authorized taxation to establish and maintain elementary schools. As a result of this legislation, the "board" school, jointly supported by local taxes and national grants, appeared as a rival to the "voluntary" school. In contrast to the board school, the voluntary church schools received national grants but did not receive local tax support. In the case of both voluntary and board schools, the receipt of government grants depended upon the favorabe report of the government inspectors.

According to the Education Act of 1870, denominational religious doctrines were not to be taught in the board schools. In these schools, nondenominational religious instruction took the form of Bible reading and recitation of the Lord's Prayer and the Ten Commandments. In the voluntary schools conducted under church auspices, religious instruction reflected the particular creed of the denomination that established and conducted the school.

Although the Act of 1870 did not establish completely free and compulsory elementary education, it gave a tremendous impetus to the movement for popular education. Since the question of popular elementary education raised a number of religious fears, the Act itself contained a number of compromises designed to quiet the suspicions of churchmen and classical liberals. The division of the country into a number of local school districts with locally elected authorities was designed to dispel the fear of state dictation in educational matters. In districts that already had adequate elementary school facilities, no basic changes were made. The existing school merely had to submit to government inspection and apply for parliamentary aid. Districts without schools could elect local school boards to organize and supervise new schools and to levy local taxes to support them. Districts burdened with exceptional poverty could establish free schools. In general, however, it was expected that parents would pay their children's tuition.

The Education Act of 1870 reflected the major beliefs of the liberals. It still trusted to private enterprise, even in educational matters, by encouraging private educational efforts and requiring individual tuition payments. The Act also revealed a suspicion of established religion that was characteristic of liberal philosophy. Although religious instruction was permitted in both voluntary and board schools, it was to be nondenominational in the latter institutions. Parents could also have their children excused from attendance if they so desired. While the Act of 1870 inaugurated an elementary school system, it also stimulated considerable rivalry between the board and voluntary schools.

Secondary Education

In the nineteenth century, English secondary education generally served the needs of the upper and middle classes who sent their sons to private schools of various types. Unlike the system of articulated elementary and high schools that arose in the United States in the late nineteenth century, there was no comparable educational ladder that linked English primary and secondary schools. The elementary and secondary schools were separate sets of institutions serving different social classes. While the primary schools attempted to provide basic literacy for working-class children, the secondary schools sought to educate upper- and middle-class children and to prepare them for entry into colleges and universities. Secondary education was not completely restricted to these favored classes, however. A few scholarships were available to poor children.

Among the most prestigious of the private schools were the famous "public" schools, which included the nine "great schools" of Charterhouse, Eton, Harrow, Merchant Taylor's, Rugby, St. Paul's, Shrewsbury, Winchester, and Westminster. Winchester, the oldest of them, was founded by William of Wykeham in 1382 to prepare students for entry to Oxford. The public schools provided classical studies, which were necessary for college admission, and prided themselves on developing the characters of their students as "English gentlemen." The nine great public schools served as models for English secondary education; less famous institutions sought to emulate their character, curriculum, and style.

The famous public schools had their origins in the classical humanist grammar schools of the Renaissance, and, proud of their classical traditions, they were resistant to change. When change did occur, it took the form of very slight modifications of the basic institutional structure. Criticism of these institutions in the years between 1828 and 1848 led to moderate reforms. Thomas Arnold, headmaster of Rugby, did make some attempt to modernize and expand the curriculum. Yet although Arnold questioned the educational benefits to be derived from the traditional method of memorizing classical literature, his work was not designed to effect a radical transformation of the English public school.

His son, Matthew Arnold (1828–1888), Inspector of Schools from 1851 to 1882, had a thorough knowledge of educational systems both in England and on the Continent.[5] Arnold's *Reports on Elementary Schools, 1852–1882,* pressed his views on the Education Department and on both teachers and public. His ideas on public school education reflected the dualism that besets the educator who seeks both to modernize and to maintain the traditional. While he revered the public school tradition, Arnold also felt that these institutions needed to change in the light of altered social conditions. Although he advocated a democratic society, he believed that such a society should be led by an enlightened elite.[6] He believed that the public schools performed a national service by educating generations of Engish statesmen but nonetheless felt that they needed some outside policing so that they might be responsive to change. Just as Arnold's educational beliefs represented a tension between tradition and change, his conception of the curriculum reflected both a love of the classics and a recognition of the importance of the natural sciences. For a truly humane education, Arnold believed that the study of classical Greek literature was indispensable. Simultaneously, the genuinely educated man should be conversant with science and more modern studies.

It was the thoughtful questioning of educators like Arnold as well as the political infighting of the Conservatives and Liberals that brought the public schools under scrutiny and into controversy in the 1860s. The historian Edward C. Mack in his authoritative work *The Public Schools and British Opinion* saw the period from 1800 to 1860 as a time of some modification of the public schools. The pace of this change was slow and haphazard. It was a gradual modification of the original structure of the schools rather than a deliberately planned reconstruction.[7]

According to Mack's analysis, public school education reflected the social, political, and economic forces that determined upper-class behavior. Drawing their support from the favored classes, the public schools reinforced the social and political status quo. The values of public school education were classical and traditional and inclined toward religion, patriotism, and manliness. As a result of growing demands for secondary education, the number of public schools had increased by 1860. Although the classics remained the core of the

[5] For a treatment of Arnold's work as a comparative educator, see Paul Nash, *Culture and the State: Matthew Arnold and Continental Education* (New York: Teachers College Press, Columbia University, 1966).
[6] Edward C. Mack, *Public Schools and British Opinion Since 1860* (New York: Columbia University Press, 1941), p. 69.
[7] *Ibid.,* p. x

curriculum, provision was made for other subjects. They were also beginning to concentrate on organized athletics. Mack has characterized the public schools of the 1860s as a

> number of highly individualized institutions which looked for guidance to their own past, taught chiefly the classics, relied for discipline largely on flogging, and, through being miniature worlds, imbued their pupils with self-reliance and group solidarity.[8]

In spite of the changes that had taken place, critics of the public schools felt that they were still too rigidly bound to tradition. After a series of debates, Parliament appointed the Public School Commission (or Clarendon Commission) to investigate endowments, revenues, administration curricula, and instruction. The commission's report in 1864 recommended a number of moderate reforms but reaffirmed the commitment to classical studies. For example, it recommended that eleven of the twenty hours of classroom instruction be devoted to the classics and to religious study. Although the reforms were based largely upon the demands of the upper class for curricular and instructional modifications, the report also reflected middle-class pressures in its recommendation that the curriculum be broadened to include mathematics, foreign languages, music, drawing, history, geography, English, spelling, and natural science. The liberalism of the middle class was also reflected in the recommendations calling for increased academic competition, tightening of standards and requirements, and more thorough examinations. It is interesting to note that the commissioners were generally satisfied with the moral education given by the public schools to their students. By providing the English upper-class adolescent male with a microcosmic world based on the larger society, the public school was adjudged to be admirably successful in cultivating the virtues of self-control, leadership, orderliness, manliness, and strength. Indeed, the commission praised the public schools as being the "chief nurseries of our statesmen."[9]

As a result of the Public School Commission's recommendations, Parliament enacted the Public School Act of 1868, which provided for an executive commission to see that the public schools created a new system of securing governing bodies, which were to enact new statutes to embody and implement the commission's recommendations. These new statutes provided for some degree of government scrutiny over public school endowments. The legislation of 1868 made only a slight impact on the public school's educational program and curriculum.

Despite the reforms of the 1860s, the English public school gener-

[8] *Ibid.*, p. 10.
[9] *Ibid.*, pp. 36–38.

ally remained a bastion of pedagogical traditionalism. The educational milieu was conservative, intellectual, and cultural. Attendance at chapel and religious services was required. The model of an English public school education was the well-rounded gentleman, at home on the playing field as well as in the library. The community life of the public school introduced many upper-class adolescent males to the roles that they were expected to play as adults and as leaders in English politics, business, and letters. Although it has produced many of the leaders in British life, the public school continues to be attacked for its conservatism, elitism, and resistance to change. A major criticism has been that it cultivated, encouraged, and perpetuated class divisions and antagonisms.

Since the Clarendon Commission had examined only upper-class public schools, its report did not answer the critics who wanted reforms in the secondary schools that served the middle class. As in the case of the public schools, the immediate controversy originated in allegations that endowments had been improperly used. This issue, however, was only a symptom of a more general discontent with the condition of secondary education. In 1864, Parliament established the Taunton Commission (or Schools Inquiry Commission) to investigate those endowed schools which had not been examined by the Clarendon Commission. Attesting to the general inadequacy of English secondary education, the commission recommended the creation of a central authority to

1. Study the reorganizing of secondary educational endowments
2. Appoint inspectors of endowed schools
3. Audit the accounts of such schools
4. Divide the nation into administrative areas under authorities entrusted to coordinate secondary schools
5. Create an examining body to examine pupils, certify teachers, and publish annual reports
6. Establish a variety of schools to meet the needs of students from diverse socioeconomic backgrounds

Despite the reports of the Clarendon and Taunton commissions, Parliament failed to take effective action in regard to secondary education. In 1869, the weak Endowed School Act provided only for the appointment of a Board of Endowed School Commissioners, who were to plan a reorganization of endowed schools. In 1874, this vague responsibility was transferred to a body of Charity Commissioners, who exercised the authority until 1900. A significant aspect of the various commission reports was the recognition that secondary education needed to be expanded and conceived of in a variety of ways. In a modern industrial nation, secondary education needed to offer opportunities to youth that included alternatives to the traditional college preparatory curriculum.

Although only slight progress was made in changing the patterns of secondary education during the nineteenth century, some limited responses were made to satisfy the demands for increased secondary educational opportunities. The Technical Instruction Act of 1869 made the county and county borough councils responsible for providing technical training. Some of the local boards of education established higher primary schools for adolescents who desired education beyond the basic elementary level. The Technical Instruction Act of 1889 permitted school boards to establish scholarships for able students to attend "higher" or "technical" schools. Teachers, parents, and school authorities began to press for greater flexibility in classifying elementary pupils so that the more able students would qualify for the scholarship examinations, which were administered between the ages of ten and twelve.

In 1894, a royal commission headed by James Bryce was appointed to consider the establishment of a well-organized secondary education system. In 1895, the Bryce Commission's report offered a plan for a national system of education that included: (1) establishment of a central governmental educational authority, (2) creation of an advisory educational council, and (3) provision of secondary education by local authorities. In 1899, the Board of Education was established as the central educational authority.

The Education Act of 1902 laid the foundation for the establishment of a secondary school system by recommending that the counties and county boroughs provide tax revenues for education. These units of local government were encouraged to promote the general coordination of education and to provide adequate secondary education. The secondary school system that resulted was separate from, and parallel to, the elementary school system. Catering to the middle classes, the secondary schools charged tuition fees. Although there was a limited scholarship program providing for the passage of a few students from elementary to secondary schools, a dual-track system resulted. The elementary and the secondary schools served two different social classes. Despite the legislation of 1902, the development of English secondary education was gradual. The majority of youths terminated their formal schooling by completing elementary education.

The Code of Regulations of 1904 attempted to define the relationships and objectives of the different types of English schools. The elementary school was to provide for the education of the mass of children and was to identify children of exceptional ability so that they might be properly prepared for secondary education. In 1907, the Liberal party, then in power, enacted a provision for a "free place system," which required that secondary schools, aided by government grants, provide 25 percent of classroom seats to pupils from elementary schools. This provision facilitated the entry of a larger number of students from the elementary to the secondary school.

Twentieth-Century Developments

As England entered the twentieth century, the basic educational patterns of its laissez-faire past were still dominant. The momentous events of the twentieth century, World Wars I and II and the depression of the 1930s, demonstrated that Englishmen were loyal to their beliefs in parliamentary government and freedom of expression. The twentieth century did witness, however, a concerted demand for basic socioeconomic changes as the working classes demanded greater economic security and increased social welfare guarantees.

A very evident indication of class consciousness came with the formation of the British Labour party in 1906. Discontented with the piecemeal reforms of the Liberal and Conservative parties, trade union members, intellectuals, and social reformers joined together in a political movement to advance the socialization of English life. In the forefront of the new movement was the Fabian Society, founded by a group of intellectuals in 1883 to promote a socialized democracy. The Fabians dedicated themselves to securing social control over the means of production. They rejected the Marxist thesis that socioeconomic class conflict was inevitable. Also rejecting the use of force, the Fabians believed that socialization would be attained by gradual means within the framework of English legal institutions and processes. Playwright George Bernard Shaw, novelist H. G. Wells, and historians Beatrice and Sidney Webb were among the most prominent, persistent, and persuasive of the Fabian socialists. At first, the Fabians followed the older utopian socialist technique of trying to educate the masses through pamphlets and lectures. When the Labour party was organized, the Fabians joined and actively campaigned for social change through political means.

After World War I, the Labour party displaced the disintegrating Liberal party as one of the two major parties. While the old Conservative party remained a major force, the Liberals lost popular support and became a small faction in the Parliament. In the period between World War I and World War II, the Labour party formed the government on two occasions—in 1924 and from 1929 to 1931—under the leadership of Ramsay MacDonald. The greatest succes of the Labour party came in 1945 when Clement Attlee defeated wartime prime minister, Winston Churchill, a Conservative.

Great Britain emerged victorious but exhausted from World War

II. The English economy had been weakened, half of her foreign investments were depleted, and she was now the world's largest debtor. Although England had heroically defeated Hitler's Nazi onslaught, a drastic restructuring of the English economy and society was necessary. Given a mandate in the election of 1945, the Attlee government introduced the welfare state, based on socialist patterns, to extend economic security to all citizens. In 1946, three major social welfare laws were passed to establish a national minimum of subsistence. The National Insurance Act provided for compulsory insurance of all wage earners; the Industrial Injuries Act improved and extended workmen's compensation for injury and death arising out of employment; the National Health Service Act established a system of socialized medicine. During the period from 1945 to 1950, the Labour party secured the passage of legislation that nationalized the basic industries, including coal, iron, and steel. Even when the Conservative party was returned to power in 1950, it did not challenge the basic social welfare legislation enacted by its political rival. As a result, the United Kingdom has continued to be a thoroughgoing welfare state.

Education in the Twentieth Century

A major piece of educational legislation was enacted in 1918 to reform, coordinate, and reorganize English education. This Act of 1918, which resulted from the efforts of H. A. L. Fisher, the president of the Board of Education, provided for:

1. The establishment of nursery schools for children under five
2. Compulsory school attendance from ages five through fourteen
3. Inspection of private schools
4. Creation of scholarships and financial aid to increase educational opportunities
5. Abolition of child labor up to age twelve
6. Increased medical and physical education facilities

The provision of early childhood education was a major development. Local authorities were permitted to establish day nurseries for infants ranging in age from one month to three years. Nursery schools were to accommodate children from two to five years of age. The Board of Education was to contribute to the financial expenditures needed to maintain these early childhood institutions.

The Act of 1918 asserted that inability to pay tuition fees should not deprive children and young persons of education from which they could profit. However, the number of secondary school pupils increased rapidly after World War I, and the demand for classroom places exceeded the facilities available. In 1919, some 18,000 children who had qualified for admission to secondary school had to be excluded.[10] Because of the press for admission into secondary schools, the Board of Education established a committee to examine the system of scholarships and free places. Although this committee asserted that 75 percent of the nation's children should have some form of secondary education, it also recommended as a realistic immediate goal an increase in the proportion of free places from the 25 percent figure of 1907 to 40 percent. In order to identify the children who were to have secondary education, the committee further recommended that formal examinations be used to determine capacity and promise. To implement this recommendation, the Board of Education began to develop tests to measure the capacity of eleven-year-old children for admission to secondary schools. The result of the Board's efforts was the "eleven-plus examination," comprised of tests in English, arithmetic, and intelligence.

Despite the Act's reforming intent, English secondary education was still inadequate in terms of the educational needs of adolescents living in a modern industrialized society. The Labour party's policy statement of 1922, *Secondary Education for All*, demanded increased educational opportunities for working-class children. In calling for a reconstructed conception of secondary education, the party recommended the creation of a variety of secondary schools in addition to the traditional academic grammar school. In 1926, a committee headed by Sir Henry Hadow was established to study the organization of schools, and curriculum objectives for children who continued their education up to age fifteen. The Hadow Committee was not concerned with academic secondary schools. It recommended that elementary education be divided into two phases: primary and post-primary, with the division coming at age eleven. It also recommended that all senior children in elementary schools be transferred at age eleven to schools or departments that were organized as senior schools.[11] Thus, age eleven became a crucial year in the education of English children.

The English educational historian Brian Simon has carefully traced the history of the concept of "streaming" that has characterized English education since the Hadow Report of 1926. Simon defined streaming as the grouping of children of a given age into parallel classes on the basis of scholastic achievement and intelligence tests. The objective of streaming was to form homogeneous groups of children of the same age, intelligence level, and competence in basic subjects so that instruction could be graduated accord-

[10] Simon, *op. cit.*, pp. 124–125.
[11] *Ibid.*, pp. 132–133.

ing to the capacity of the class. Streaming not only influenced instruction in a particular classroom but also became a major determinant in the structure of English elementary and secondary education. In primary schools, children were divided on the basis of their anticipated academic performance. From age seven onward, they were allocated to particular streams that determined their place within the individual school and within the general school system.[12]

According to the rationale for streaming, intelligence was conceived to be an innate capacity that could not be influenced by teaching or training, emotion or industriousness. With the stress placed on classifying the intelligent child, English education became wedded to traditional academic concepts rather than to more progressive attempts to educate the whole child. Secondary education, in particular, continued to be conceived of as the transmission and mastery of specific academic knowledge and skills. Education became a competitive race in which the intellectually fit mastered academic knowledge and skills at a rapid pace in order to outdistance those who had been labeled as slower and intellectually unfit by the system.

The Butler Act of 1944 introduced major innovations into English education. The National Board of Education was reorganized as the Ministry of Education, headed by a minister of education, who had cabinet rank. For purposes of greater efficiency, the large number of local educational authorities were consolidated. The Act divided education into three major stages: primary, from ages two to eleven; secondary, from twelve through fifteen; and advanced schooling. Primary education was further subdivided into nursery school and kindergarten, until age five; infant school, from five through seven; and junior school, from seven through eleven. The Butler Act also provided for three types of secondary school: grammar school, with a college preparatory curriculum; technical and vocational; and modern, which provided nonpreparatory and nontechnical general education consisting of cultural and work experiences. According to the provisions of the Act of 1944, further education, both part-time and full-time vocational education, was made available by the local education authorities for youth until age eighteen. School was made compulsory until age fifteen, and provision was made for its later extension to sixteen.

It should be pointed out that the Education Act of 1944 continued to emphasize the concept of streaming. Secondary education was provided according to the age and ability of students. It continued to be based on a structure of rigid grade divisions, and the retention of the eleven-plus examination maintained the selective function of the secondary school.

12 *Ibid.*, pp. 115–116.

The Butler Act was noteworthy for its provision on social welfare arrangements. Special schools were established for the physically handicapped. Boarding accommodations were provided for students who lived long distances from schools. The spirit of the social welfare state was also clearly present in provisions for free medical and dental treatment, increased recreational and physical educational facilities, and free milk and a noon meal for all pupils.

The Butler Act also dealt with the controversial issue of religious instruction. All schools were to begin the school day with an act of worship and were to provide regular religious instruction. However, if parents objected to these instructions and exercises, their children would be exempted upon request. In schools supported entirely by public funds, religious instruction was to be nondenominational and based on the agreed syllabus approved by the Ministry of Education.

Simon asserted that after World War II a rigid bipartite school system developed in England. Only 20 percent of the population of secondary school age attended the highly selective grammar schools, the path to the colleges, universities, and professions, whereas the mass of the population attended secondary modern schools. While middle-class children were likely to pass the eleven-plus examination and enter the grammar school, the number of working-class children who did so was quite small. The result of the intensive pressure for entry into the grammar schools led to increased streaming and greater segregation of the school age population. By the 1960s, Simon reported, critics of streaming appeared among English educators and psychologists. The more general economic prosperity, the high rate of employment, and technological changes contributed to demands for a genuinely comprehensive secondary school. Process-oriented education, developed by the followers of Dewey in the United States, also had an impact on English education. More sophisticated sociological examinations of streaming produced evidence that the measurement of intelligence was heavily related to socioeconomic class influences.[13]

Conclusion

At midpoint in the twentieth century, education in England was clearly moving from its nineteenth-century laissez-faire moorings into the twentieth century. With the Butler Act of 1944, education responded to the welfare-state programs of the Labour party. It should be noted, however, that the social benefits of the welfare state were more apparent in the areas of health and housing than in education. In the late 1950s and 1960s, dissatisfaction was being expressed

[13] *Ibid.,* pp. 144–148.

against the existence of social-class bias in education. Criticisms were directed at the procedure of streaming, which resulted in social segregation based on rigid academic grouping of children. English education, like all systems of national education, reflected the political, social, and economic context of which it was a part.

Suggested Readings

Adamson, John W. *English Education, 1789–1902.* New York: Cambridge University Press, 1964.

Armytage, W. H. G. *Four Hundred Years of English Education.* Rev. ed. New York: Cambridge University Press, 1970.

Arnold, Matthew. *Culture and Anarchy.* Edited with an introduction by J. Dover Wilson. Cambridge, England: Cambridge University Press, 1946.

———. *A French Eton.* London: Macmillan, 1864.

———. *Reports on Elementary Schools, 1852–1882.* F. S. Martin (ed.) London: His Majesty's Stationery Office, 1910.

Banks, O. *Parity and Prestige in English Secondary Education.* London: Routledge and Kegan Paul, 1955.

Barnard, H. C. *A Short History of English Education from 1760.* London: University of London Press, 1961.

Baron, George. *Society, Schools and Progress in England.* Oxford, England: Pergamon Press, 1965.

Birchenough, Charles. *History of Elementary Education in England and Wales.* London: University Tutorial Press, 1930.

Burston, W. H. (ed.) *James Mill on Education.* New York: Cambridge University Press, 1969.

Connell, W. F. *The Educational Thought and Influence of Matthew Arnold.* London: Routledge and Kegan Paul, 1950.

Curtis, S. J. *History of Education in Great Britain.* London: University Tutorial Press, 1948.

Dent, H. C. *The Education Act, 1944: Provisions, Possibilities, and Some Problems.* London: University of London Press, 1947.

———. *The Educational System of England and Wales.* London: University of London Press, 1961.

Gribble, James (ed) *Matthew Arnold.* New York: Macmillan, 1967.

Kazamias, Andreas M. *Politics, Society and Secondary Education in England.* Philadelphia: University of Pennsylvania Press, 1966.

Mack, Edward C. *Public Schools and British Opinion, 1780 to 1860.* New York: Columbia University Press, 1939.

———. *Public Schools and British Opinion Since 1860.* New York: Columbia University Press, 1941.

Nash, Paul. *Culture and the State: Matthew Arnold and Continental Education.* New York: Teachers College Press, Columbia University, 1966.

Norwood, Cyril. *The English Tradition of Education.* London: John Murray, 1929.

Sampson, George. *English for the English: A Chapter on National Education.* Cambridge, England: Cambridge University Press, 1970.

Simon, Brian. "Classification and Streaming: A Study of Grouping in English Schools, 1860–1960," in Paul Nash (ed.), *History and Education.* New York: Random House, 1970.

————. *Education and the Labour Movement, 1870–1920.* London: Lawrence and Wishart, 1965.

————. *Studies in the History of Education, 1780–1870.* London: Lawrence and Wishart, 1960.

Wardle, David, *English Popular Education, 1780–1970.* Cambridge, England: Cambridge University Press, 1970.

Weinberg, Ian. *The English Public Schools.* New York: Atherton Press, 1966.

CHAPTER 19

French Education

The antecedents of nineteenth- and twentieth-century education in France were established in the revolutionary and Napoleonic eras. French education also exhibited the divergent tendencies of Rousseau's naturalism and Roman Catholic supernaturalism. Until their expulsion from France in 1762, the Jesuits had been largely in charge of secondary education. The Christian Brothers and other religious teaching orders had been active in elementary education before the Revolution. It should also be recalled that the University of Paris had been a strong theological center in the medieval period. When the French philosophes of the eighteenth century objected to the old order, they also attacked the religious and classical orientation of an educational system dominated by the church.

When the Bourbon regime was overthrown, the revolutionary government sought to destroy this influence of the church on education. The Constitution of 1791 stated the intention of establishing a public system of education, open to all citizens. In 1792, the Committee of Public Instruction abolished all religious corporations, including church-controlled schools, and the state assumed control of all educational institutions. The enthusiasm of the French revolutionary government led to an energetic discussion of proposals for a new system of education. Talleyrand and Condorcet, for example, authored proposals that would have established a national system based on republican educational principles. Although these proposals were not enacted into law, they supplied many of the ideas upon which the later French system was built.

Throughout the nineteenth century, the major trend in French education was the emergence of a highly centralized state educational system. Napoleon I had laid the groundwork for it. The Law of 1802 had provided for nationally controlled secondary schools. In 1806, all French education was brought under the emperor's direct and personal control. The University of France was established as a centralized administrative structure to coordinate and supervise all French education.

As a result of Napoleon's defeat at Waterloo, the victorious allies were able to restore the conservative Bourbon monarchy, which remained in power from 1814 to 1830. The conservatives, showing their usual propensity for forging an alliance with the church, restored the privileges and status of Roman Catholicism. The licensing of private teachers was delegated to bishops rather than secular officials, and priests were often appointed as principals and teachers in public schools. Since the Bourbon restoration was unpopular, the reactionaries could not, however, completely restore the privileges the aristocracy and clergy had under the *ancien régime*. Louis XVIII, attempting to pursue a moderate course, retained the Code Napoléon, the Concordat, and other legislation of the revolutionary and Napoleonic periods. The moderate Louis XVIII was succeeded by Charles X (1824–1830), who tried to restore autocracy by increasing royal prerogatives and shackling the opposition forces.

The July Monarchy

In July 1830, a revolution spearheaded by liberal forces swept the repressive Charles from power and installed his bourgeois cousin Louis Philippe as a constitutional monarch. The so-called July Monarchy, lasting from 1830 to 1848, was really a government controlled by upper-middle-class liberal capitalists who wanted only very gradual and restricted moderate reforms. They were classical liberals who believed that the primary function of government was to maintain public order.

Personifying this right-wing liberalism of Louis Philippe's bourgeois monarchy was François Guizot (1787–1874), a university professor and historian who was its leading statesman. Guizot believed that only the upper middle class had the talent and intelligence to rule.[1] He favored property requirements for suffrage as a means of maintaining upper-middle-class rule. Such requirements, he believed, did not necessarily discriminate against the lower classes since they too could enter the ranks of the middle class if they were sufficiently industrious and diligent.

As a youth, Guizot revealed a scholarly bent and received a broad liberal education. He especially enjoyed the study of languages and

[1] For treatments of Guizot's political and philosophical views, see Elizabeth P. Brush, *Guizot in the Early Years of the Orleanist Monarchy* (Urbana: University of Illinois Studies in the Social Sciences, 1929), and Sister Mary C. O'Connor, *The Historical Thought of François Guizot* (Washington: Catholic University Press, 1955).

mastered German, English, Italian, Latin, and Greek. He also took pleasure in reading German literature and philosophy. Although he studied for the law, he decided to follow a literary and historical career. He wrote a number of articles for the popular Parisian daily *Publiciste,* which dealt with the fine arts, literature, history, and philosophy. In 1812, Guizot began to lecture in history at the Sorbonne, where he proved a popular professor. Entering politics in 1814, he became the rare combination of an active politician and a historian. He joined the *Doctrinaires,* a small liberal faction that opposed both absolutism and popular government. As an advocate of limited representative government based upon upper-middle-class rule, Guizot ardently supported Louis Philippe's government.

Guizot was elected to the Chamber of Deputies in 1830 and served Louis Philippe in such various posts as minister of interior, minister of foreign affairs, and president of the Council of Ministers. He served as minister of public instruction from 1832 to 1836 and was responsible for devising and introducing the Law of 1833, which provided primary education in the communes of France and gave to the state the responsibility for supervising this instruction. When the July Monarchy was overthrown in 1848, Guizot fled to England.

Guizot wrote a number of significant historical works: *General History of Civilization in Europe* (1828), a *History of French Civilization* (1829), a series of works on English history (1850 to 1856), and *Meditations on the Essence of the Christian Religion* (1864). He disliked attempts to write strictly factual or scientific history. Although agreeing that the historian should be meticulous in selecting his data, Guizot believed that historical writing involved the elaboration of broad generalizations that were capable of inspiring men.

Guizot's *General History of Civilization in Europe* revealed his world view. His attitude reflected a moderate conservatism that saw civilization as a cumulative process in which each century was augmented by the culture of preceding ages. However, Guizot was also a liberal who conceived of civilization in progressive and dynamic terms. His conception of civilization revealed his educational philosophy: He believed that both individuals and societies were moving forward progressively and that ameliorative social systems, including education, would liberate individuals and societies.

A cultural nationalist, Guizot believed that European civilization was of the highest order because it had been based upon cultural, political, and social checks and balances. As he explained it:

> European civilization has . . . penetrated into the ways of eternal truth—into the scheme of Providence. In other civilizations in the course of the struggle between the various principles of the social order, the excessive preponderance of control of one of them led to tyranny. However in the European scene these principles strug-

gled for control without any one of them gaining dominance. This has given birth to European liberty.[2]

Guizot distinguished three major stages in the development of European civilization:

1. Various social groups and elements disengage themselves from anarchy and chaos by assuming a definite cultural existence and form.
2. A period of experimentation and social and cultural regrouping occurs in which various social elements enter into a variety of combinations without producing a stable civilization.
3. Society reaches the stage of cultural development exemplified by European civilization in which it moves in an orderly and progressive direction.

As a Frenchman, Guizot also had a marked preference for French civilization:

There is not a single great idea, not a single great principle of civilization, which in order to become universally spread, has not first passed through France. . . . whenever France has set forward in the career of civilization, she has sprung forth with new vigor, and has soon come up with, or passed by, all her rivals.[3]

The Law of 1833

Guizot and the government of Louis Philippe were interested in establishing a national primary school system. Intrigued by Prussian successes with national education, they dispatched Victor Cousin to investigate the Prussian system. In 1831, Cousin's *Report on Public Instruction in Germany* was issued, and it guided French lawmakers in their deliberations concerning a national system of primary education.

It was primarily Guizot's influence that led to the enactment of the Law of 1833, which established the framework for French primary education. Each commune in France was to establish a public primary school, pay teachers, and provide for a school building. Children coming from families with sufficient income were to pay tuition; pauper children were to receive free schooling. The central government was to subsidize communes that were too poor to establish schools. The Law of 1833 also specified that the curriculum of the primary schools should consist of reading, writing, spelling, grammar, composition, and arithmetic.

[2] Francois Guizot, *General History of Civilization in Europe* (New York: Appleton, 1842), pp. 39–40.
[3] *Ibid.*, p. 16.

Although the Law of 1833 made some compromises with the Roman Catholic Church on educational matters, it also revealed the liberals' basic distrust of religious control of schooling. Public and elementary schools were established, but private schools were permitted to function. True to liberal policies, the church's educational prerogatives were circumscribed. All private teachers were to be certified by the mayor of the commune. Church schools were to be visited by state inspectors, and their teachers were to have state certificates.

The liberal interest in utilitarian education was also revealed by the law, which extended opportunities for practical and vocational training. Higher primary schools were to be established in the principal cities of each department of France for the purpose of offering vocational education in commercial, agricultural, and industrial subjects.

The Law of 1833 preserved the dual school system characteristic of European education. Separate school systems were to be maintained for lower and upper socioeconomic classes. The new primary and higher primary schools were established for the common people, while the upper classes continued to receive secondary education in the colleges and lycées.

The upper-middle-class liberal industrialists, financiers, and bankers who formed the governing clique in Louis Philippe's regime favored some degree of popular education but were unwilling to embark on a program of massive educational support. They believed that formal education should be appropriate to the socioeconomic class of the student rather than be equally available to all.

Second French Empire: Louis Napoleon

In 1848, the regime of Louis Philippe was overthrown, and a confused political situation developed as factions of monarchists, Bonapartists, republicans, and socialists competed for power. An insurrection of Parisian workingmen was bloodily crushed in the "June Days" of June 23–26, 1848. In the midst of this political unrest, Prince Louis Napoleon Bonaparte appeared on the scene and was elected president of France by popular vote. After a period of struggle with the monarchist-controlled Legislative Assembly, Louis Napoleon followed his uncle's course. On December 2, 1851, he engineered a coup d'état, dissolved the Assembly, and used the plebiscite to give the appearance of popular approval to his action. In 1852, he was proclaimed Napoleon III, Emperor of the French.

Although the appearances of a constitutional monarchy were maintained, Napoleon III subverted representative institutions. Parliamentary debate was not permitted. Decrees were framed by the Emperor's Council of State and presented for ratification. Coercive licensing practices muzzled the press. Like most autocrats, Napoleon III sought to control education. In the French universities there was substantial opposition to his rule. A number of distinguished academicians such as the philosopher Jules Simon and the historians Michelet and Quinet were dismissed. The teaching of history and philosophy were carefully scrutinized.

In 1850, the Falloux Law was promulgated, which gave the Roman Catholic Church control over French education. Catholic schools were to be given state support. Religious teachers of the recognized religions—Roman Catholic, Protestant, and Jewish—were eligible without examination for appointments in the public schools, although laymen were required to be certified by the state before being appointed to teaching positions. The clergy was given power to supervise instruction in the elementary schools.

The Third Republic

After the French armies experienced a crushing defeat in the Franco-Prussian War of 1870, Napoleon III abdicated and fled to England in disgrace. Although there was considerable political uncertainty, France returned to a genuinely republican government in what was termed the Third Republic. The leading educational direction in the Third Republic came from Jules Ferry (1832–1893), the minister of public instruction, who sought to modernize French education through a series of laws passed in the 1880s, which had the effect of further extending educational opportunities and of reducing religious influences in government schools. In 1881, tuition fees were abolished in the primary schools. In 1882, compulsory attendance was required between the ages of six and thirteen. In 1886, education was further centralized as the minister of public instruction was given detailed control over curriculum, textbooks, teacher certification and appointments, and primary teachers' salaries. This reduced local variations in formal schooling.

In order to eliminate religious influence in public education, the central government no longer permitted members of religious communities to teach in the public schools. Religious instruction in the public schools was also forbidden. Only the public schools were eligible to receive financial support from the state; however, it was left to parents to decide whether their children would attend a public school or a church school. The enactment of the Ferry legislation produced a bitter antirepublican reaction on the part of the supporters of the church. A law enacted in 1904 placed even more

stringent restrictions on private education and provided for the closing of all private schools by 1914. The law was not enforced, however, because of the outbreak of World War I, so French private and
religious schools continued to operate.

Between the Wars

Between World War I and World War II, France was plagued
by internal divisions that historians have labeled the "Three Frances."
The most conservative group was composed of aristocrats, landowners, and conservative Catholics; the middle classes, small landowning peasantry, retailers, businessmen, teachers, and civil servants
formed the second group; and the third group consisted of industrial
workers. This threefold division was also reflected in French politics,
where a host of parties ranging from the extreme right to the Communists on the far left competed against one another. In the period between the wars, France was usually governed by a number of coalition
governments comprising center parties.

The depression made its greatest impact on France after 1934. The
very conception of parliamentary government was attacked by both
the extreme right and the extreme left. A number of fascist organizations sprang up emphasizing French nationalism above everything
else, among them such groups as the *Action Française* and the *Croix
de Feu*, which advocated an authoritarian, anti-Semitic, and corporate state. In opposition to the right-wing threat, a Popular Front was
formed in 1935 consisting of a coalition of Socialists, Radical Socialists (really a center party), and Communists. Securing a majority
in the election of 1936, the Popular Front formed a government
headed by Léon Blum.

Educational enactments that occurred in the period between the
wars tended to consolidate rather than innovate. In 1933, the principle of free tuition was established for both secondary and technical
education. In 1936, schooling was made compulsory through age
fourteen. As in other Western nations during the depression of the
1930s, France had to retrench its educational expenditure.

Vichy France

Since the French Revolution, French public opinion has been
divided on the fundamental principles of government and a desirable
form of social order. Although democratic principles had triumphed
in the Third Republic, a strong preference for authoritarianism
lingered among those who cherished the monarchical tradition and

the Napoleonic legend. When the Third Republic collapsed before the blitzkrieg of the invading German armies in June 1940, this reactionary minority emerged under the leadership of Marshal Henri Pétain, the aged hero of the World War I Battle of Verdun. The demoralized National Assembly conferred authority on Pétain, who promised to safeguard the rights of labor, family, and fatherland. After the French surrender to Germany, Pétain's government, established at Vichy, sought to create a semifascist corporate state in the part of France that was not occupied by German armies. Not all Frenchmen were willing to go along with Pétain's capitulation to Nazism, however. General Charles de Gaulle was recognized as the leader of the Free French forces in exile. There was also considerable underground resistance to both the German occupation and to Pétain's Vichy collaborators.

The Vichy regime of the aging marshal was decidedly reactionary. It tried to turn French interests away from foreign involvement and the German occupation. Pétain and Pierre Laval, his associate in the Vichy regime, had long believed that the French republic, with its proliferation of political parties, was decadent. In the belief that the time was ripe to undo what they regarded as the excesses of liberalism and socialism, Pétain and Laval established an authoritarian regime, modeled on the lines of corporate fascism, that enacted repressive legislation and excluded Freemasons and Jews from legal protection. Pétain's government tried to reestablish the old order and, with it, traditional education along clerical, conservative, and classical lines.

In 1941, Pétain published a pamphlet on national education that condemned the modern forces of liberalism, democracy, and industrialism. Exalting the spirit of paternalism, Pétain asserted that education should be based on respect for authority and firm discipline and called for a reinvigoration of the authority of the family in French life. The Vichy regime also prepared a syllabus on moral instruction for use in the schools that specified the individual's responsibilities to God, state, and family. The paternalistic and authoritarian regime hoped to eradicate permissive, liberal, and individualistic attitudes from the schools and from French society.[4]

Pétain based his educational philosophy on the concept of the corporate state, which was the theoretical foundation of the Spanish and Italian fascist regimes. He felt that industrialism had undermined the sense of French craftsmanship. Therefore, basic elementary education was to emphasize the manual vocations. Further, each profession,

---

[4] For a treatment of comparative education in historical perspective, see Robert Ulich's *The Education of Nations* (Cambridge, Mass.: Harvard University Press, 1967). For Ulich's analysis of French education, see pp. 129–174.

craft, and trade was to have its own elite of artisans as a governing body.

The Vichy regime directed its attention to the preparation, selection, and certification of teachers. Political undesirables, Jews, and Free-masons were barred from teaching positions, and professional teacher organizations were suspended. In 1941, the regime closed the teacher training schools that had hitherto prepared primary school teachers, regarding them as unfit to prepare teachers suited to the new fascist social order. Primary teachers were now required to complete the more classically oriented secondary course, which culminated in the bac-calaureate, and then to enroll in a short training program in pedagogy.

Although the French army was disbanded according to the provisions of the surrender of June 25, 1940, the Vichy government organized a number of young men into a youth movement, the *Chantiers de la Jeunesse*, under the command of General La Porte du Theil, a former scout commissioner. The aim of this youth movement was to expose young men to the physical rigors of outdoor life and give them a basic indoctrination in approved French history and philosophy.

Although Pétain's Vichy regime represented the surfacing of French fascism into a position of power, it was not supported by the majority of Frenchmen, who considered it to be a traitorous government of pro-German collaborationists. After the invasion and liberation of France by the allied English, American, and Free French forces in 1944, the Vichy regime disintegrated. Pétain was tried for treason by the Fourth Republic and imprisoned until his death.

French Education After Liberation

In 1944, an educational commission under the leadership of Paul Langevin, a distinguished humanist, met to consider plans for the postwar reform of French education.[5] After his death, Langevin was succeeded by the psychologist Henri Wallon. Both of these leaders of the reform movement in education were Communists, a fact that stimulated opposition to their recommendations. Among the reforms suggested by the Langevin-Wallon Commission were the following: (1) recognition of individual aptitudes and differences among children; (2) the use of guidance so that every child could receive the education appropriate to his talents; (3) a respect for the dignity of labor. The commission's report was decidedly antibookish and conceived of education in both cultural and vocational terms.[6]

[5] A very readable volume on French education is W. D. Hall's *Society, Schools and Progress in France* (New York: Pergamon Press, 1965).
[6] *Ibid.*, pp. 26–30.

In terms of sequence and structure, the Langevin-Wallon plan proposed that schooling be available for students from ages seven through eighteen. The first phase, from ages seven to eleven, would emphasize the acquisition of basic skills and powers of observation and appreciation. The second phase, from eleven through fifteen, would emphasize guidance so that the student could become aware of and consider the various career and vocational alternatives that were available. This second phase was also to stress the vocational arts, aesthetic appreciation, and academic subject matters. In the third phase, from fifteen through eighteen, the student would determine his dominant interest and pursue it. Those students who were academically inclined would pursue the baccalaureate, which had modern, classical, technical, and artistic options. Those who were not academically oriented were to be provided with vocational and practical training programs.

The Langevin-Wallon proposals were not accepted by the National Assembly. It was alleged that their implementation would be too costly for the available resources, which were limited because of the reconstruction of facilities needed in the aftermath of World War II. The Langevin-Wallon recommendations were significant, however, in that they indicated the direction that French education would take in the postwar world.

During the 1960s, students expressed their discontent with French secondary and higher education. Militant student groups organized strikes, protests, and demonstrations. This was particularly true of university students, who opposed what they regarded to be the obsolescence and formalism of higher education. Student protests were directed not only against the kind of education they were receiving but against the prevailing social order and the Gaullist regime.

The unrest among French students stemmed from both political and educational factors. Some university students actively participated in political movements that sought to radically transform French politics and society. In May 1968, a workers' strike for higher wages incited the more militant students to disrupt the universities and take to the streets in violent demonstrations against the government. Although there was some initial cooperation between students and workers, trade unionists were disinclined to effect a permanent alliance with students. Although some of the political agitation by students was only remotely related to educational reform, it was symptomatic of the more pervasive discontent of the students with the highly centralized and rigorously selective university system.

As is true in most advanced nations, higher education is the means to success and material security in France. While the numbers of French students seeking entry to universities increased in the post-World War II era, the universities did not make adequate preparations to increase enrollments. Students resented the slowness of the Ministry of Education and of university officials in increasing the opportunities for university attendance.

French students also resent the rigorous examinations that lead to the *baccalauréat,* a diploma awarded after the successful completion of seven years of secondary education. The possession of the *baccalauréat* is necessary for university matriculation and for many civil service and business positions. Some student critics regard it as a highly selective device designed to limit the numbers of students admitted to institutions of higher learning and thereby restrict entry to positions of power to a favored minority.

As a response to the unrest of university students, the Gaullist Ministry of Education in 1968 agreed to introduce reforms to permit greater popular participation and to encourage more institutional autonomy in higher education. These reforms have not satisfied critics who have felt them to be piecemeal attempts that fail to deal with the basic issues confronting higher education in France. For example, the critics charge that the Ministry of Education has proposed to decentralize the highly bureaucratic university system but still insists on retaining control of the distribution of funds and of faculty appointments.

Conclusion

French education responded to the political forces operative in France during the nineteenth and twentieth centuries. This was especially true in the area of religious education and religious schools as power shifted back and forth between proclerical and anticlerical forces. The tensions between authoritarianism and democracy also had their effect on French educational legislation. In many ways, French schools have been exceedingly formal and resistant to the forces of modernization. It was this resistance, in part at least, that stimulated the student protests of the late 1960s.

Suggested Readings

Barnard, H. C. *Education and the French Revolution.* Cambridge, England: Cambridge University Press, 1969.

Buisson, F., and F. E. Farringon. *French Educational Ideals.* New York: World Book Co., 1919.

Farrington, F. E. *French Secondary Schools.* London: Longmans, Green, 1910.

———.*The Public Primary School System of France.* New York: Teachers College, Columbia University, 1906.

Fraser, W. R. *Education and Society in Modern France.* London: Routledge and Kegan Paul, 1963.

Hall, W. D. *Society, Schools, and Progress in France.* New York: Pergamon Press, 1965.

Kandel, Isaac. *The Reform of Secondary Education in France.* New York: Teachers College Press, Columbia University, 1924.

Miles, Donald W. *Recent Reforms in French Secondary Education.* New York: Teachers College, Columbia University, 1953.

Talbott, John E. *The Politics of Educational Reform in France, 1918–1940.* Princeton: Princeton University Press, 1969.

Ulich, Robert. *The Education of Nations: A Comparison in Historical Perspective.* Cambridge, Mass.: Harvard University Press, 1967.

U.S. Office of Education. *Education in France.* Washington, D.C.: Government Printing Office, 1963.

German Education

As a result of the Lutheran Reformation of the sixteenth century, a two-track system of education was impressed upon the various German states and principalities. A system of vernacular elementary schools was established to supply education to the masses of the population. Luther and Melanchthon accepted classical humanist education, usually supplied in the gymnasium, as the preferred type of secondary education. The northern German states, in particular, were characterized by widespread literacy.

In the early nineteenth century, Germany was not yet a united country but still a collection of large princely states, such as Prussia and Bavaria and smaller principalities, free cities, and duchies. Since the days of Luther and his princely supporters, the forces of German nationalism had been tending to the surface. German intellectuals and students had been in the forefront of movements designed to unify Germany. German unification was retarded, however, by the rivalries of the various princely rulers and the machinations of the German states' powerful neighbors, France and Austria, who preferred a weak, divided Germany.

Prussia

Prussia became the leader among the various German kingdoms and principalities under the enlightened despotism of Frederick the Great (1740–1786), who organized an efficient administration based on monarchical authority, a strong and highly disciplined army, and an efficient bureaucracy. Frederick perfected the concept of the service state that protected the life and property of its citizens and required efficient state service in return. To secure state benefits, the citizen had special obligations to fulfill for the good of the state.

In the battles of Jena and Auerstädt (October 1806), Napoleon defeated the Prussian armies and further humiliated Prussia by occupying Berlin. Frederick William III (1797–1846), the Prussian king, was treated insolently by Napoleon and at the Treaty of Tilsit (1807) was forced to cede Prussian territory west of the Elbe River to France, to allow the presence of French troops in Prussia, and to limit the size of the Prussian army to a maximum of 42,000 men. Humiliated by their defeats, the Prussians responded to Napoleonic imperialism and French domination with a fierce nationalism. The Prussian government circumvented the restrictions imposed upon the size of its army by introducing universal military conscription and by instituting a system of army reserves. Military recruits were intensively trained and then assigned to reserve units. The process would be repeated as each new class of recruits was called up for military training. Army organization and morale improved greatly. The rise of Prussian nationalism became identified with the army that was later used to effect German unification.

The rise of Prussian nationalism also stimulated a cultural emphasis on Germanic pride. Teachers and writers encouraged German patriotism. Songs, poems, pamphlets, and plays were written that attacked the French and praised the German heroes of the past. Although Frederick William III and his ministers were basically conservative, the Prussian government encouraged this reaction against French domination and allowed such liberals as Stein, Fichte, and Humboldt to express their ideas. Johann Gottlieb Fichte (1762–1814), whose *Addresses to the German People* (1808) called for a rebirth of German idealism and nationalism, urged a reform of German education according to the pedagogy of Pestalozzi.

A brief examination of Fichte's philosophy provides an insight into the spirit of cultural nationalism that characterized Prussian and German education. Fichte's *Addresses* were directed toward regenerating the German people by awakening their sense of national and moral unity. After German armies had been humiliated by the Napoleonic victory at Jena, Fichte hoped to reawaken Germany's slumbering greatness. He believed that an inherent genius and greatness existed among Germans that could be rekindled through a new universal education that would be accessible to all Germans.

Fichte believed that humanity was in a transitional state in the continuing progress of civilization. He envisioned a world that would be progressively better if it were based on a society in which all men knew their proper roles. The key to advancing the course of civilization, Fichte thought, was in the German race, which needed to be united into a single entity. German culture could then be diffused to all nations by the German nation, which would be the great world educator.

Friedrich Jahn (1778–1852) combined romantic cultural nationalism and Prussianism in his work *German Folkdom* (1808). Like

Fichte, Jahn wanted to free Germany from Napoleonic control. He believed that German regeneration could be stimulated by a dedication to the *Volk,* or folk community. To instill an awareness and love for Germanic folkdom, Jahn argued that a new education was needed to reshape the national conscience. The ultimate goal of his educational philosophy was the creation of a genuine national unity centered in the folk state, or *volksstaat.* The universal education of all German children would break down class divisions, which interfered with the nationalization of the masses of people. To inculcate patriotic and nationalistic values, Jahn recommended that the curriculum be restructured to include the study of a patriotic history and literature.

A proponent of physical education, Jahn conceived of education as a total process that included the child's entire physical and cultural environment. He emphasized gymnastics and physical exercises to cultivate team work and good health. In 1811, he established the *Turnerschaft,* a gymnastic society, to inspire national awareness and physical fitness in German youth. Jahn has been accused of being a forerunner of the educational philosophy of National Socialism since he stressed nationalism, physical fitness, and minimized intellectual pursuits.

After Napoleon's defeat and exile to Elbe, the Congress of Vienna sought to reimpose conservative monarchical rule in Europe. The Prussian government increasingly came under the domination of the Austrian diplomat Prince Klemens Metternich (1773–1859), who urged the reassertion of the principles of conservatism and monarchical legitimacy.

In his *Confession of Faith,* Metternich emphasized the conservative view and attacked as evil the views of presumptuous individuals who sought to perfect or reform too many things too quickly. As a defender of paternalistic rule by an aristocratic elite, Metternich asserted that presumption and ambition were middle-class vices that needed to be isolated from the peasant masses. Politically, he believed that the principle of monarchical legitimacy was man's best hope of avoiding political and social ruin. Legitimate monarchs supported by a loving and obedient people would maintain the stability of political and cultural institutions.

German Youth Movement of the Early Nineteenth Century

In the divided states, kingdoms, and principalities of the German Confederation during the early nineteenth century, the focal point of opposition to rule by reactionary princes and to Austrian interference came from youth, especially students. Imbued with a mixture of romanticism, liberalism, and nationalism, German youth wanted to achieve a united Germany governed by liberal principles. Within the universities, student societies known as *Burschenschaften*, or brotherhoods of young men, were organized. The members of these societies pledged themselves to moral and patriotic lives designed to bring about the goal of a united Germany. The *Burschenschaften*, founded as a national movement, adopted a black, red, and gold flag and agitated for a united and free Germany.

On October 18, 1817, the *Burschenschaften* sponsored a national patriotic festival to arouse the German people through patriotic speeches and ceremonies. Large numbers of students and their sympathizers met in Wartburg to demonstrate for a united Germany. In the aftermath of the Wartburg festival, a reactionary journalist, Kotzebue, was assassinated by a student. The Wartburg assassination produced a reaction from the various German princes, who believed that their position was threatened by an incipient student revolution. The various German state authorities denounced the *Burschenschaften* movement and the universities as breeding places of violence and discontent in which the younger generation was being encouraged to resist authority.

Metternich of Austria, the champion of conservatism, called a conference of the German princes at Carlsbad in 1819, which produced a number of decrees designed to curb the youth movement and restore conservative intellectual ideology. The Carlsbad Decrees provided for the appointment of special officials in all the German universities to supervise student and teacher conduct and to report any deviation from conservative principles. Teachers who were considered to be subversive of public order and safety were to be dismissed, the *Burschenschaften* movement was dissolved, and press censorship was established.

Certain individuals who had participated in the liberation movement that stimulated the German reaction against Napoleon were now imprisoned or removed from their positions. For example, Jahn's patriotic gymnastic societies were suppressed and he was jailed. Republication of Fichte's *Addresses to the German People* was also forbidden. Liberal professors were removed from university posts, and intellectual life was constrained for more than a generation.

Revolution of 1848

In 1848, a series of popular uprisings swept across Europe. In France, the bourgeois monarchy of Louis Philippe was overthrown. In Austria, the conservative Metternich was forced to flee. In Prussia, King Frederick William IV (1840–1861) tried to avert a revolution by summoning a United Diet. However, it soon earned his displeasure by rejecting a loan requested by the king and was dismissed. An insurrection broke out in Berlin, and Frederick William hastily agreed to grant a constitution and parliamentary rule.

A self-constituted body of liberals met in Frankfurt to devise means of uniting all Germans and drew up a plan for a national assembly to be elected on the basis of universal male suffrage. The Frankfurt Assembly, composed primarily of intellectuals, lawyers, and professors, quickly bogged down on several key issues. Those who favored a "Greater Germany" that included Austria quarreled with those who wanted Austria excluded. Those who favored a republic argued with those who wanted a constitutional monarchy. By the time the Assembly had finished its deliberations and adopted a constitution, the forces of reaction were again ascendant.

Frederick William had retained the support of the powerful Prussian army and the great numbers of conservative peasants. The rebellion was crushed in Berlin, and the Frankfurt Assembly was dismissed. Some of the most prominent liberal leaders of "1848" fled Germany and emigrated to the United States. Among them was Carl Schurz, who became a prominent Republican politician and United States senator. In Prussia, reaction followed the brief flowering of liberalism, and all popular demonstrations were severely repressed. In 1850, the king promulgated a constitution that provided for a parliament elected by a three-class system of suffrage, heavily weighted to ensure domination of the propertied classes and the Junker aristocracy. The king was given full executive authority and had a veto over all legislation. Not only was autocracy firmly entrenched in Prussia but the failure of 1848 profoundly affected the course of German history. Many Germans, despairing of the possibility of uniting the various German states under liberal direction, increasingly came to rely on unification through authoritarian means.

Prussian Education

Like the Prussian army, Prussian education was efficient, well-organized, and militaristic. During the administration of Baron Karl von Altenstein, Prussian minister of education from 1817 to 1838, education came under rigid bureaucratic control. Altenstein and his supervisor of secondary schools, Johannes Schulze, were fervent disciples of Georg Friedrich Hegel. During their tenure in office, many of Hegel's students obtained teaching positions in the *gymnasien* and universities. In their hands, Hegelian philosophy was rigidly and inflexibly interpreted and regarded as a metaphysical justification for the autocratic exercise of state power. Their version of Hegelianism became a semiofficial state philosophy of education that held that: (1) the individual's life acquired meaning only through complete identification with the state, the temporal manifestation of the Absolute; (2) the state, as the highest form of terrestrial authority, was justified in exercising unrestricted power.

The organizational structure of Prussian schools followed socioeconomic class divisions. Ninety percent of the population received a basic education in *Volksschulen,* elementary vernacular schools that were usually conducted under religious auspices and with state support. The remaining 10 percent of the school-age population, drawn from the favored socioeconomic classes, attended the gymnasium, a college preparatory school with a heavily classical curriculum. School boards in each community represented the various religious denominations, and school inspections were conducted by religious leaders, either priests in the predominately Catholic communities or evangelical ministers in the Protestant ones.

Prussian teacher educational institutions became models for teacher preparation in both France and the United States. Victor Cousin's report on Prussian education had been used by Guizot as a model for the French School Law of 1833; Calvin Stowe's report to the Ohio legislature introduced Prussian conceptions of teacher education to the United States. The annual reports of Horace Mann and Henry Barnard also lauded Prussian teacher education.

Prussia's teacher training institutions and seminaries functioned under government control. Those who were trained in them had the benefits of a broadened curriculum, pedagogical courses, and practice in teaching methods. Seminary preparation was intended not only for teachers destined for primary schools but for secondary teachers as well. The subjects offered were designed to prepare teachers for the rigorous certification examinations that were given in the classics, mathematics, science, history, and geography. In addition to passing these examinations, a year of carefully supervised practice teaching was required of teachers.

Later on, Prussian teacher education directly reflected the two-track system of schools. Prospective elementary school teachers attended the *Volksschulen* and then three-year teacher training schools. Prospective secondary teachers attended the nine-year secondary school, or gymnasium, and then a university, where for four years they studied the specialized subject matters that they would later teach.

Herbartianism

The development of German pedagogical theory owes much to Johann Friedrich Herbart (1776–1841), a philosopher, psychologist, and university professor who was most concerned with developing a systematic method of education.[1] He critically analyzed the learning processes and wrote a number of books, of which *The Science of Education* (1806) and *Outlines of Educational Doctrine* (1835) made a significant impact on both German and Western education.

Herbart, an advocate of a realist philosophy, held that moral development was the ultimate goal of education. His morally educated model, the "cultured man," epitomized five basic virtues of freedom, perfection, good will, righteousness, and ethical responsibility. Essentially, the morally educated man, was a person of many interests who had been provided with the broadest possible cultural experiences.

Basic to Herbart's educational method was the concept of interest, which he described as an internal tendency that facilitates the retention of an idea in consciousness or contributes to bringing it to consciousness. The retentive power of interests are increased by the frequency with which an idea is presented to consciousness and by the association of ideas in what Herbart called an "apperceptive mass." Basing them upon the doctrine of "many-sidedness of interests" and "apperceptive mass," Herbart arrived at two pedagogical laws: frequency and association. When an idea is repeatedly presented to consciousness, the tendency for that idea to lodge in the learner's apperceptive mass is increased. Ideas tend to cluster, and similar ideas lodge among one another in apperceptive masses. The teacher's task, according to Herbart, is to emphasize those ideas that are to dominate the student's life. The teacher should repeat the desired ideas in order to impress them on the mind and indicate the similarities between clusters of related ideas.

Since he considered the ultimate aim of education to be the cultivation of a morally sensitive man, Herbart emphasized the value-rich subjects of history and literature as a cultural core around which the other areas of the curriculum should be correlated. The Herbartian emphasis on literature and history encouraged their entry into the curriculum at a time when secondary education was still dominated by classical Latin and Greek and mathematics.

As a result of his philosophical-psychological inquiries and research, Herbart concluded that since the mind assimilates all ideas in the same manner, it is possible to devise one instructional methodology to teach any subject. Although Herbart's original methodology contained the four steps of clearness, association, system, and method, later Herbartians generally elaborated five clearly defined phases of teaching method:

[1] For the fullest treatments of Herbart and Herbartianism, see Harold B. Dunkel, *Herbart and Education* (New York: Random House, 1969), and his *Herbart and Herbartianism* (Chicago: University of Chicago Press, 1970).

1. Preparation, in which the student's mind is readied to assimilate the new idea. Past ideas, memories, and experiences are recalled and related to the new idea being introduced in the lesson. The apperceptive masses needed to assimilate the idea are stimulated into consciousness. In other words, the initial stage in teaching is really designed to motivate learners by deliberately referring to their past experiences.
2. Presentation, or the actual teaching of the new material, which occurs when the new idea is presented, analyzed, and clarified so that the student fully understands it.
3. Association, during which the new material is contrasted and compared with older ideas. This is designed to facilitate the assimilation of the new idea with the previously acquired clusters of ideas.
4. Generalization, involving the formation of a general idea, or principle, based upon the combination of the new and the old learning.
5. Application, in which the student's grasp of the general principle is tested by appropriate problems and exercises.[2]

The Herbartian method of education was accepted by both German and American educators. Herbart himself had suggested the possibility of devising scientific bases for pedagogy and had furthered the acceptance of education as a subject of university study. In Germany, the popularity of Herbartianism began when Tuiskon Ziller's *The Basis of the Doctrine of Educative Instruction* appeared in 1865. Ziller became the influence behind the Association for the Scientific Study of Education, which attracted Germans as well as others to Herbartianism. Another influential German Herbartian was Karl Stoy, who founded a teacher training school at the University of Jena. A number of American educators had studied in Germany and were familiar with Herbart's educational philosophy and method. Herbartianism became popular with the professors of education who were beginning to occupy chairs of pedagogy in American universities at the turn of the century. Charles and Frank McMurry and Charles de Garmo were especially active in popularizing Herbartian pedagogical ideas in the United States through their writing and lecturing. By 1892, Herbartianism was well on the way to dominating American educational theory and practice. In that year, the National Herbartian Society was formed to serve as a means of communication among those who sought to develop an educational science. Within a decade, however,

[2] A popular American translation of Herbart's ideas was Johann Friedrich Herbart, *Outlines of Educational Doctrine*, Alexis F. Lange (tr.), Charles de Garmo (annotat.) (New York: Macmillan, 1901). De Garmo was an active popularizer of Herbartianism in the United States.

American Herbartianism began to wane, eclipsed by John Dewey's educational philosophy. Its demise was as rapid as its rise.

On the positive side, the achievements of Herbartianism were three-fold: (1) the curriculum was enriched by the inclusion of literature and history as a cultural core; (2) precise lesson planning according to a logical methodology was encouraged; (3) teaching was professionalized as instructional methodology more closely geared to subject matter. Negatively, Herbartianism fastened a rigid, lock-step, and somewhat verbal approach on the teaching-learning process. It overemphasized the teacher as planner, presenter, and director of learning. The student's role was minimized to that of passively receiving information. Although Herbartianism had broadened the scope of the curriculum, it also overemphasized the subject to the neglect of the learner.

Also among the nineteenth-century German educational theorists was Friedrich Froebel. Although a detailed analysis of his educational philosophy has been presented in an earlier chapter, Froebel should also be considered within the context of German education. Although he shared a basic philosophical orientation to idealism, as did Fichte, he differed in that he was more concerned with early childhood education than with the political regeneration of German nationalism. Froebel's major educational contribution was his humanizing influence on childhood and the early years of formal schooling. He stressed the importance of childhood as a formative time in man's life and worked to overcome the residues of the doctrines of child depravity. Froebel, who emphasized play as the highest phase of the child's development, placed a great emphasis on activity and good social relationships. Froebelian educational methodology recognized the child's capacities and respected the child's individuality. Although Froebel was really a nonpolitical person, his kindergarten was banned by the Prussian government for a time.

German Unification

As a result of the French defeat in the Franco-Prussian War of 1870, the various allied German kingdoms and principalities were joined into one empire under the Prussian king, who was proclaimed emperor of Germany. Much of the credit for achieving German unification belonged to Otto von Bismarck (1815–1898), the Iron Chancellor, who was a keen practitioner of Machiavellian realpolitik. Bismarck's masterful diplomacy and the precision-like Prussian army had succeeded in eliminating Austrian and French interference in German affairs. Because of Bismarck's success, William I (1871–1888) became emperor of a united Germany. It was significant that German unification was achieved under the conservative and aristocratic Bismarck, a representative of the Prussian Junker class. Further, it was the military success of the Prussian army that had crushed both the Austrians and the French. In the future, the army, the aristocracy, and the autocratic monarchy were regarded as the forces that had achieved German unity and not the liberals who had been earlier discredited by the abortive revolution of 1848.

Although Germany was finally unified, many Germans believed that other nations had conspired to keep them in the position of a second-rate power. The years between German unification in 1871 and the outbreak of World War I in 1914 saw Germany's attempt to redress what she considered to be centuries of injustice. German unification coincided with the period of large-scale industrialization that was occurring in western Europe and North America. Germany, rapidly emerging as the leading industrial nation in Europe, challenged the United Kingdom's long-established industrial primacy. In attempting to rise to the position of a major world power, Germany's leaders embarked on a program that included: (1) accelerated industrialization; (2) strengthening of the army and navy; (3) establishment of a colonial empire in Africa and Asia; and (4) cultivation of a patriotic and nationalistic esprit de corps among the German people. Education was used as an instrument in achieving this program by inculcating strongly nationalistic and patriotic values. Vocational and adult technical schools became popular institutions for training skilled workers and technicians for Germany's factories.

In the early years of the German Empire, Bismarck sought to consolidate central authority and establish a homogeneous and united modern national state. Although Prussia was the dominant state, the other German kingdoms, Bavaria, Saxony, and Wurttenberg, retained considerable powers in what was a federal system of government. In the Reichstag, the lower house of Germany's Diet, Bismarck cooperated with the National Liberals, the majority party, which supported centralization, laissez-faire economic policies, and secularization. Through this cooperation, he secured legislation that brought about uniform coinage and uniform legal and banking procedures. However, Bismarck's coalition with the National Liberals led him to an ill-fated campaign against the Roman Catholic Church in which he sought to reduce the church's educational powers.

Although the campaign against the influence of the Roman Catholic Church in German life was called the Kulturkampf, or battle for civilization, Bismarck was politically motivated in that he wanted to reduce the political power of the Center, a Catholic party. In 1873, he launched a two-pronged attack on the Catholic Church in both the imperial Reichstag and the Prussian legislature. From 1873 through 1875, Prussia enacted a series of anti-Catholic laws that placed clerical education under state control, made civil marriage mandatory, and dissolved religious orders. In retaliation the papacy severed diplomatic relations with Prussia, and the German bishops declared that Catholics could not obey these laws in good conscience.

Instead of having the political results that he envisioned, Bismarck was dismayed to find that evangelical Protestants came to regard the Kulturkampf as an attack on organized religion. After the Center party's representation grew as a result of the election of 1877, Bismarck, realizing that he had erred politically, ended his anti-Catholic campaign. In 1879, he slowly began the process of revoking the anti-Catholic legislation. Religious orders, with the exception of the Jesuits, were permitted to return to Germany. By 1881, church-state relations had been restored to normal.

In 1888, Emperor William I died, and he was succeeded briefly by his son Frederick III, who reigned for only three months before his death, which brought William II (1888–1918) to the imperial German throne. The young William II was an impetuous ruler who disliked Bismarck's tight reins and reluctance to build an overseas empire. On March 15, 1890, Bismarck was dismissed from the chancellorship. After that time, the Emperor William II exercised an increasingly direct influence on the government. The expansionist policies of the emperor and his ministers contributed to the tinderbox situation in Europe that erupted in World War I.

Education in Imperial Germany

As has been indicated, German unification was achieved under conservative and military auspices. The educational system that served Germany during the imperial period from 1871 to 1918 was also conservative in social values, and it was used to instill nationalistic attitudes.[3] Because unification had been achieved under Prussian leadership, Germany came under the influence of Prussian centralization, efficiency, and bureaucracy. Formal schooling was intended to produce efficient and obedient citizens who would do their duty for the fatherland.

When Germany became a united nation, it was already embarked on a course of vigorous industrialization, and a number of the local communities had established vocational schools. In the late nineteenth century, it was general practice for young workers to attend continuation school on a part-time basis in order to learn or maintain vocational and technical skills. Industrial, technical, and vocational

[3] For a sophisticated analysis of German education, the reader is directed to Robert Ulich, *The Education of Nations* (Cambridge, Mass.: Harvard University Press, 1967), pp. 175–224.

education became widespread and was popularized by the noted German educator Georg Kerschensteiner. German technical education advanced beyond the basic stages and was differentiated into specializations designed to prepare skilled craftsmen, foremen, supervisors, and personnel workers.

When the German empire was established in 1871, the inherited two-track system, which divided the children of the lower and higher classes into separate educational institutions, persisted. Education was compulsory between the ages of six and fourteen. Lower-class children usually attended the folk school, or Volksschule, where the curriculum included instruction in religion, the German language—including literature, reading, writing, composition, and grammar—arithmetic, drawing, history, geography, science, music, and gymnastics for boys and needlework for girls. Regulations promulgated in 1872 were designed to reconcile various religious groups. The government elementary, or folk, schools were designed as either Protestant, Catholic, or Jewish, and religious instruction was given in the particular faith. In communities where all children attended only one school, the ministers of the various denominations provided religious instruction. Although the Volksschule inculcated nationalistic values and perpetuated the status quo, the same charge could also be levied against nineteenth-century French, Russian, English, and American schools. As of 1888, the Volksschule was financed entirely by public funds and was tuition-free.

In 1872, a new institution, the *Mittelschule,* was introduced to occupy an intermediate position between the lower folk elementary schools and the secondary schools. The Mittelschule was usually attended by children of the lower middle classes who were destined to become artisans, shopkeepers, small businessmen, or minor officials. Although the Mittelschule course varied from three to nine years, it generally was six years in length. Children usually transferred to the Mittelschule after doing some preliminary work in the folk school. The curriculum was somewhat more advanced than in the folk school, and foreign languages, such as English, French, and Latin, were offered. Although educational and social mobility was rare, the Mittelschule made it possible for a few students to enter secondary school and possibly the university.

During the imperial period, there were three types of secondary school in Germany: the traditional gymnasium, which had been established in the Renaissance; the *Realgymnasium;* and the *Oberrealschule.* After three years in a public or private preparatory school, or *Vorschule,* the upper-class boy entered one of these institutions at the age of nine to prepare for university entrance. The gymnasium remained the prestige school. Its curriculum was heavily classical, and its graduates were given preference in university admissions. The

Realgymnasium, supposedly a more modern school, continued to offer Latin but dropped Greek as a required subject in the curriculum. The Oberrealschule, the newest of the three secondary schools, emphasized mathematics, science, and modern languages and eliminated both Latin and Greek. The complete course at these three secondary schools lasted nine years, but some schools offered a six-year course. In addition to the emphasis placed on the major subjects cited above, all the schools also required religion, German, history, music, manual work, physical education, and other subjects.

There was some controversy between the classicists and the modernists in secondary education. In 1890, Emperor William II spoke in favor of a more modern curriculum for secondary education that would emphasize German language and culture rather than classical Greek and Latin. The kaiser spoke of the need to prepare youth as soldiers to defend the fatherland and as competent officials ready to administer German affairs. In 1900, all three secondary schools were proclaimed as being equally valuable from the viewpoint of general culture. However, the universities continued to prefer graduates of the gymnasium.

During the imperial years, German higher education was characterized by sound scholarship, scientific research, and vital intellectual activity. The discoveries of German natural scientists were a remarkable page in the history of science. Hermann Ludwig Helmholtz invented the ophthalmoscope, Gustav Kirchhoff invented the spectroscope, Wilhelm Roentgen discovered x-rays, Max Planck formulated the quantum theory, and Einstein conducted his first studies on relativity. In the social sciences, historians Theodor Mommsen and Heinrich von Treitschke, philosopher Wilhelm Dilthey, sociologist Georg Simmel, and Max Weber, who was both a sociologist and an economist, conducted major research and developed theses that had a profound impact on their disciplines.

The University of Berlin, founded in 1810, set the patterns of research, scholarship, and teaching that came to characterize German higher education. At Berlin, each professor was expected to be a specialist in his area of expertise and to carry on specialized research. Through seminars, he and his graduate students investigated limited areas of knowledge. The University of Berlin became a center for specialized research in philology, archeology, anatomy, zoology, chemistry, physics, history, psychology, and other learned disciplines. The German university attracted students from the United States and other nations, who came to study with the famous scholars whose research and writing established standards for scholarship throughout the world. In the United States, for example, returning scholars brought with them the concept of German university life with its stress on graduate studies, research, and specialization.

After World War I: The Weimar Republic

Despite the widespread literacy and prodigious scholarship of Germany, the kaiser's government, like that of most Western nations, found itself trapped by the events, alliances, and diplomatic machinations that culminated in World War I. Although Ludendorff, Hindenburg, and the other German generals almost succeeded in crushing the allied French, British, Italian, and American forces, the tide turned against the Germans. In 1918, the German armies crumbled, the kaiser abdicated, the Hohenzollerns fled Germany, the overseas empire was disassembled, and Germany surrendered. As a result of these events and the Versailles Treaty, the Weimar Republic was established in Germany. Although the Weimar Republic was liberal, democratic, and representative, the future did not augur well for it. In the minds of many Germans, it had been born in defeat and in Versailles' humiliating terms. Ruinous inflation and then the depression of the 1930s played havoc with the German economy and produced massive unemployment.

Despite its tortured short existence, the Weimar government had a very creditable list of educational achievements. Its constitution provided that the schools would work to develop moral education, a sense of civic responsibility, personal and vocational competence, and a spirit of reconciliation with other nations. According to the Weimar Constitution, the central government would seek to develop an integrated public school system in which secondary and higher schools would be extensions of a common school. The School Law of 1920 did not, however, achieve this ladder system of education, but it did establish a four-year public elementary school, or *Grundschule,* a foundational institution. The law also provided that the existing preparatory schools, which had contributed to the differentiation of children at an early age, would be gradually phased out.

The Weimar government continued to permit the existence of private schools if they were approved by the state. Following the deep-rooted ideas about religious education, religious instruction was made part of the curriculum in the public schools. However, the clergy no longer had the right of school inspection.

In secondary education, the previously established gymnasium, Realgymnasium, and Oberrealschule continued to function. A new kind of secondary school, the six-year *Aufbauschule,* was organized to educate academically gifted children from the lower classes in order to enhance their opportunities for entry into the universities.

Although the Weimar government sought to democratize German life, its existence was ended by the rise of Adolph Hitler's National Socialist party. From 1934 until its defeat in World War II in 1945,

Germany was ruled by one of the most repressive and totalitarian regimes that the Western world has ever experienced.

Nazi Education

In 1919, Adolph Hitler's National Socialist party was merely one of many small semifascist groups that had organized in protest against the Versailles Treaty and the Weimar Republic, and it had only seven members. The National Socialists had a confused political ideology. Originally, the party had been associated with certain German workers' groups, and there was a semisocialist overtone in its early political statements. As it sought to rekindle German nationalism, and reunite all Germans into one political force, it came to exalt state power and totalitarian control of all social agencies. Moreover, the party became racist, seeking to eliminate Jewish as well as foreign influences in German affairs.

In 1920, the National Socialist party adopted a platform that called for the complete reconstruction of German life and culture. Among its various planks were several that contained educational recommendations:

1. State schools should be expanded to increase attendance opportunities.
2. Educational goals should be redirected to practical life and should give children a proper conception of the state's role and authority.
3. The state should provide increased public health, education, and physical training opportunities and facilities.
4. Gifted children of poor parents should be educated at state expense.[4]

By 1923, the National Socialists, or Nazi party, had grown to the degree that Hitler joined forces with General Ludendorff and unsuccessfully attempted to seize the Bavarian state government. Hitler was jailed, and, while confined, set down his plan for Germany in *Mein Kampf* (*My Struggle*), published in 1925. *Mein Kampf* listed three major aims of National Socialist education: (1) the fostering of sound, healthy, and pure Germanic racial stock; (2) the development of citizens who were obedient to authority and accepted responsibilities; (3) the dissemination of ordinary and useful culture. Hitler believed that traditional German education had overemphasized intellectual development and stressed too many nonessential details.

[4] George F. Kneller, *The Educational Philosophy of National Socialism* (New Haven: Yale University Press, 1941), p. 23.

Intellectual cultivation should come only after the development of physical strength, character, and responsibility. According to Hitler:

> . . . A man of little scientific education but physically healthy, with a good firm character, imbued with the joy of determination and will power, is more valuable for the national community than a clever weakling.[5]

Hitler's political theory of the *Führer* principle asserted the leadership role of the *Führer,* and the silent unquestioning obedience of the followers was made into an educational doctrine. The school and youth groups were to foster a sense of personal subordination to the common welfare.

It was not until the economic depression of the 1930s hit Germany that the National Socialists began their march to power. In the elections of 1930, they polled more than six million votes. In 1932, the Nazis controlled one-third of the seats in the Reichstag, and President von Hindenburg gave the chancellorship to Hitler. Within a year's time, the Nazi party had achieved monolithic control by abolishing other parties and proclaiming the National Socialist state.

The Nazi government quickly imposed its political philosophy on educational institutions. A decree of September 1933 required the teaching of Nazi theories of race and heredity. The various teacher organizations were abolished, and the National Socialist Association of Teachers, an organization subservient to the party will, was made the sole representative of teachers. When the German invasion of Poland precipitated World War II, the Nazi Association of Teachers established a special war program. Each school week was inaugurated with a war celebration hour in honor of past and current military victories, and the week's instructional program followed the theme of the war hour. In conjunction with military authorities, the association prepared pamphlets designed to cultivate pride in the armed forces. In geography, for example, instruction dealt with military and strategic problems, such as communication lines. The children were taken on marches into the countryside and encouraged to draw simple military maps.

One of the most sorry spectacles of the Nazi period was the politicalization of the universities. In the late nineteenth and early twentieth centuries, German universities were famous for their freedom to teach and to learn. In 1933, about one-fourth of the universities' faculties were dismissed because they were politically or racially unreliable in the eyes of Nazi administrators. Those who remained took public oaths to support National Socialism and Hitler. In 1934, Bernard Rust, a devoted Nazi, was named Reich minister of science,

[5] Adolph Hitler, *Mein Kampf* (Boston: Houghton Mifflin, 1943), p. 408.

education, and culture. Academicians quickly followed the party line. Professor Philipp Lenard of the University of Heidelberg developed what he called German physics on the thesis that all science was racially determined.[6] The curriculum was warped to prove that Germans were racially superior. The universities began to offer such studies as racial thought, inheritance, and legislation. Along with their concentration on race, they offered numerous subjects related to the military, such as war chemistry, geography, economics, science, and mathematics.

Because of their politicalization, the German universities declined intellectually and became mouthpieces for Nazi propaganda. There were a number of reasons for the Nazi misuse of higher education. Hitler was essentially an antiintellectual who disliked scholars and academics. The Nazi regime wanted people who were committed to action programs to accomplish political purposes and had no use for scholars who wanted to pursue truth through objective scholarly methods. After 1933, the Nazi party replaced the university as the avenue to success. Under the Hitler government, the regime controlled faculty appointments and the entry of students into the university. As a result of these policies, faculty and students were often intellectually irresponsible and incompetent.

In a completely totalitarian society such as that of Nazi Germany, informal, or milieu, education takes on added significance. The mass media and informal agencies of education were harnessed to serve party goals. Among these informal educational agencies was the Hitler Youth Organization, headed by Baldur von Schirach, whom Hitler had appointed as "Youth Leader of the German Reich." On December 1, 1936, all non-Nazi youth organizations were abolished, and German youth were expected to join the government-sponsored Hitler Youth Organization, which was to form character by developing self-discipline and physical courage in German youngsters and make a concerted effort to cultivate a sense of racial awareness and pride.

The Hitler Youth Organization was organized into three major divisions: The Hitler *Kinderschaft,* ages six through nine, emphasized physical exercises and activities designed to cultivate toughness, endurance, self-confidence, fighting spirit, and will power. The *Jungvolk*, ages ten through thirteen, continued physical training, introduced simple military tactics and exercises and gave instructions in Nazi racial and political ideology. Anti-Semitism was deliberately encouraged. Between fourteen and eighteen, young German males were members of *Hitlerjugend,* the Hitler Youth proper. During this time, they spent one year in the German countryside in the *Landjahr* pro-

---

[6] George L. Mosse, *Nazi Culture: Intellectual, Cultural and Social Life in the Third Reich* (New York: Grosset and Dunlap, 1968), pp. 201–205.

gram, which was used to improve physical fitness of urban youths. The boys lived in *Landjahr* camps where instruction was given to improve health, provide familiarity with country life, and furnish experience in the corporate life of strong leadership and obedient following.

In 1935, labor service was made compulsory for all Germans between the ages of eighteen and twenty-five. Compulsory labor was to inculcate a communal spirit and a true concept of the dignity of work and was also a prelude to compulsory military training.

The Hitler Youth movement also involved a process of selecting a political elite. Children and youth who demonstrated signs of conformity to the Nazi conception of leadership were chosen for special training in National Political Training Institutes and in Adolf Hitler Schools. This group was to be prepared for positions of leadership in what Hitler conceived to be the thousand-year Reich. Fortunately, Hitler's empire crumbled within twelve years after the National Socialists gained power. The victorious Allied powers—the English, Americans, French, Russians, and others—were finally able to crush the Nazi regime, which had once seemed invincible.

After World War II

After World War II, Germany was a ruined nation. Her major cities had been devastated by Allied bombing, and the last major battles of the war were fought in her streets. When hostilities ended, Germany was divided into four occupation zones, which were assigned to the major Allied powers, the English, French, Americans, and Russians. Toward the end of 1945, the British and American occupational authorities began to reconstruct German administration by establishing state governments, which began to function as the prototype of what would become a West German government. Two major political parties arose, the Social Democrats, a socialist party headed by Kurt Schumacher, and the Christian Democrats, a revival of the old Catholic Center party, which had widespread Protestant support; the latter party was headed by Konrad Adenauer, who became the first chancellor of the new German Federal Republic in 1949. In its zone of occupation in eastern Germany, the Soviet Union proclaimed the Communist-controlled Democratic Republic of Germany.

The most obvious crisis facing the restoration of a functioning educational system in postwar Germany was the destruction of school and university physical facilities. Despite the difficulties caused by a lack of facilities and capable teachers, the schools in the British and American zones were functioning in the first year of occupation. In the zones of the Western powers, a strong effort was made to dismiss the National Socialists from teaching staffs and to eliminate Nazi and military ideas. Textbooks had to be revised in order to eliminate Nazi racial propaganda.

In the German Federal Republic, control of education was returned to each of the ten states and West Berlin. While the federal government established certain general principles, each of the eleven education authorities organized school systems that exhibited differences in curriculum, textbooks, and religious instruction policies. In order to maintain some coordination, the educational ministers of the various states established a permanent secretariat in Bonn, the federal capital, to provide for reciprocity of examination certificates, exchange of students, and other matters affecting interstate cooperation.

In terms of educational institutions, the basic school in the German Federal Republic is the *Grundschule,* a common elementary school that enrolls pupils for either four or six years, depending upon the policies of the particular state. Instruction in the Grundschule is efficient, and high achievement is expected of students. Reading skills and verbal expression are emphasized to cultivate a high level of literacy. Art, music, and physical education are also part of the curriculum. The former emphasis on nationalism has been tempered by the inclusion of international studies.

Upon completing the Grundschule, the students are differentiated into the various secondary institutions. There are still the old gymnasium, which emphasizes Latin and Greek; the Realgymnasium, which emphasizes foreign languages, mathematics, and science and retains Latin but omits Greek; the *Oberrealschule,* which requires two modern languages and gives special emphasis to science and mathematics; and various forms of *Aufbauschulen,* which were established to provide advanced basic education to rural children so that they might also have the opportunity for secondary education. The trend in secondary education has slowly been away from the heavy reliance on classical subjects, and the more modern secondary schools exceed the older classical gymnasium in numbers.

Conclusion

The recovery of both western and eastern Germany after World War II demonstrated German vitality, persistence, and energy. The German Federal Republic developed one of the soundest and most stable financial and industrial systems in the world and once again became a major European power. West Germany gives all the appearances of a progressive and democratic nation. However, there are still fears on the part of Germany's eastern and western neighbors when they recall her expansionist past. The quest for reunification, which began with the Reformation, still remains a basic drive for most Germans since there are today two Germanys, one in the west and one in the east. Like the nation that it serves, German education has also returned to a position of prominence in that it has maintained an exceedingly high literacy rate and prepared workers, technicians, and administrators for life in one of the world's most prosperous nations.

Suggested Readings

Alexander, Thomas. *The Prussian Elementary Schools*. New York: Macmillan, 1919.

Barnard, Henry. *German Educational Reformers*. Hartford, Conn.: Brown, Russell and Gross, 1878.

Bruck, W. F. *Social and Economic History of Germany, 1888–1938*. New York: Oxford University Press, 1938.

DeGarmo, Charles. *Herbart and the Herbartians*. New York: Scribner, 1895.

Dunkel, Harold B. *Herbart and Education*. New York: Random House, 1969.
————. *Herbart and Herbartianism*. Chicago: University of Chicago Press, 1970.

Heiden, Konrad. *A History of National Socialism*. New York: Knopf, 1935.

Herbart, Johann F. *Outlines of Educational Doctrine*. New York: Macmillan, 1901.

Hitler, Adolf. *Mein Kampf*. Boston: Houghton Mifflin, 1943.

Huebener, Theodore. *The Schools of West Germany*. New York: New York University Press, 1962.

Kandel, Isaac L. *The Making of Nazis*. New York: Teachers College, Columbia University, 1934.

Kneller, George F. *The Educational Philosophy of National Socialism*. New Haven, Conn.: Yale University Press, 1941.

Lilge, Frederic. *The Abuse of Learning: The Failure of the German Universities*. New York: Macmillan, 1948.

Mosse, George L. *Nazi Culture: Intellectual, Cultural and Social Life in the Third Reich*. New York: Grosset and Dunlap, 1966.

Pinson, Koppel S. *Modern Germany*. New York: Macmillan, 1954.

Rosinski, Herbert. *The German Army*. New York: Harcourt, Brace, 1940.

Russell, James E. *German Higher Schools: The History, Organization and Methods of Secondary Education in Germany*. London: Longmans, Green, 1907.

Samuel, R. H., and R. Hinton Thomas. *Education and Society in Modern Germany*. London: Routledge and Kegan Paul, 1949.

Shirer, William L. *The Rise and Fall of the Third Reich*. New York: Simon and Schuster, 1960.

Ulich, Robert. *The Education of Nations*. Cambridge, Mass.: Harvard University Press, 1967.

CHAPTER 21

Russian Education

In the nineteenth century, Russian political, social, and educational life was dominated by the absolutism of the czars. The most clearly antiintellectual policies occurred in the reign of Nicholas I (1825–1855), whose "Nicholas System" was intended to stop the growth of Russian liberalism by suppressing people as well as ideas. At the Russian frontiers, books and papers of foreign visitors were carefully examined to ensure that no anticzarist literature was allowed to enter Russia.

Nicholas I conceived of the ideal state as a highly disciplined one in which all subjects recognized obedience to state authority as their paramount duty. Like his predecessors and successors, he depended on the Russian aristocracy and bureaucracy, the army, and the Orthodox Church to sustain the official government policy of "autocracy, Orthodoxy, and nationalism."

According to the principle of autocracy, the czar as head of church and state was responsible only to God. Power and authority flowed from the czar to his ministers and from them to local officials. A vast army of civil servants was required to staff the centralized and hierarchically arranged bureaucracy. Its ranks included government ministers, school inspectors and administrators, police officers, tax collectors, provincial governors, judges, bureau heads, railway employees, postal workers, telegraph operators, and various clerks. Inferior officials had to show both the proper deference to superiors and the appropriate degree of arrogance to inferiors. Although the secondary schools were supposed to produce trained civil servants, most of the bureaucrats were poorly trained individuals, whose promotions came from willingness to conform rather than from administrative expertise. The absolutism that began in the czar's palace permeated the entire system.

To uphold the principle of Orthodoxy, the czar protected the privileged position of the Russian Orthodox Church against rival denominations. Nicholas sought to insure strict doctrinal adherence within the church and tried to convert his non-Orthodox subjects to the church. It was the task of the Procurator of the Holy Synod, the czar's personal representative to the church's governing body, to enforce the emperor's will in religious matters. Instruction in the theological seminaries was to conform to Orthodox interpretations. The village priests and parish schools were to teach love of the czar and discourage dissent among the lower classes.

Nicholas' policy of nationalism called for the creation of loyalty to the czar and his government. The czar believed that a thoroughgoing nationalism would save Russia from what he felt were the pernicious effects of liberalism and radicalism. He wanted the kind of education that would indoctrinate his subjects in the principles of autocracy, Orthodoxy, and nationalism and thereby preserve the political and social status quo.

The symbol of the Nicholas System was the secret police, or the Third Section of the Imperial Chancery, directed from 1826 to 1844 by Count Benckendorff. The Third Section comprised uniformed police and a large cadre of secret agents who harassed and carefully scrutinized the intelligentsia of writers, journalists, and teachers.

Nicholas I attempted to suppress all liberal and socialist sentiments, and he encouraged the growth of conservative and nationalist support of the regime. Count S. S. Uvarov, minister of education from 1833 to 1849, did very little to advance popular education. He believed that Russian education should support the principles of czarist autocracy, Russian Orthodoxy, and nationalism by (1) cultivating pietistical reverence for the czar, (2) encouraging patriotism, and (3) perpetuating the socioeconomic status quo. Members of the lower classes were discouraged, as an official policy, from seeking an advanced education. Conceiving of education as an indoctrination in patriotic submissiveness, Uvarov did not consider it his function as minister of education to improve educational standards since this would have challenged the status quo. During his tenure, educational standards declined, especially in the secondary schools.

Nicholas I inherited what was at best only a very rudimentary set of educational institutions. Catherine II (1762–1796) had founded the first state schools in 1775. Alexander I (1801–1825) had established the outlines of an educational system, consisting of parish and district elementary schools, secondary schools, and universities. Nicholas overturned the School Statute of the more liberal Alexander I who had, at least in theory, permitted schooling for members of all social classes and had provided some scholarships for able but poor students. However, Alexander's statute was never implemented on a large scale and schools and teachers were generally unavailable.

The more reactionary czar Nicholas I promulgated a new School

Statute, in 1828, which clearly defined the different types of educational institutions. Parish schools were for the children of the lowest social classes. District schools were designed for the children of merchants and townspeople. Students from the parish and district schools were ineligible for entry into the secondary schools, which were to prepare upper-class children for civil and military service and instill in them reverence for Russian traditions and institutions.

The universities of Moscow, Harkov, Kazan, St. Petersburg, and Kiev were also brought under strict government scrutiny by Nicholas I, whose minister of education saw that no undesirable political theories were expressed by either students or faculty. Professors were appointed by the Ministry of Education on the basis of their loyalty to the regime. Spies were used to watch students and teachers. Official textbooks condemned liberalism and glorified czarist "autocracy and Orthodoxy." In order to halt dissent from spreading among the intellectuals, Russian students were forbidden to study in foreign universities.

Nicholas' son, Alexander II (1855–1881), was initially somewhat more tolerant than his father. During Alexander's reign, some notable reforms were enacted that permitted a slight thaw in the usual reactionary social and political climate. In 1861, a ukase, or imperial decree, was issued that liberated the more than twenty-three million serfs from bondage on estates owned by aristocrats, changing the serf's status from bond servant to free peasant. The labor supply was increased as many former serfs left the countryside and migrated to cities. Alexander II also introduced important administrative and judicial reforms. In 1864, a new law code based upon English and French practice was promulgated. Reforms were also initiated in local government. In the cities, partially elected municipal councils were created. In rural areas, zemstvos, local governing bodies, were established, which had charge of schools, roads, hospitals, and agricultural improvements within their areas. This limited experience in local government encouraged a number of moderate liberals, known as Constitutional Democrats, to work for constitutional government in Russia. During the period from 1881 to 1917, the zemstvos increased in strength and resisted efforts by Alexander III and Nicholas II to reduce their powers. Actively opposing government intervention in educational policy-making, the zemstvos passed a resolution in 1903 demanding that the government submit all educational matters to them. In 1904, the zemstvos formed the Union of Liberation, which aimed to constitutionalize Russia. Although they made slow progress toward a more liberal and constitutional Russian government, their influence should not be exaggerated. A representative national assembly, or Duma, was not established until after the Revolution of

1904. Even then, the inept czar, Nicholas II, was usually able to subvert it.

Alexander was generally more tolerant in educational matters than either his predecessor, Nicholas I, or his successors, Alexander III (1881–1894) and Nicholas II (1894–1917). The strict censorship that had been imposed on teachers during the reign of Nicholas I was relaxed. The zemstvos improved local elementary education by increasing the number of schools, broadening the curriculum, and improving standards. Secondary education was reorganized on the basis of German models, and universities were given broad powers of self-government.

Disaffection of the Intelligentsia

The intellectuals, or intelligentsia, constituted the basis of opposition to autocratic czarist repression. Many were from the aristocracy and had traveled or been educated abroad. When they returned to Russia, they found the unenlightened social and political conditions intolerable. The intelligentsia became self-appointed critics of the government and tried to stimulate the spirit of reform in what was a generally unresponsive peasantry and working class.

The intelligentsia included students and writers, both male and female, who met secretly to discuss social, political, and philosophical ideas. They ranged across most of the political spectrum from moderate reformers to radicals, anarchists, and nihilists. The left-wing intellectuals attacked basic Russian traditions and believed that the entire sociopolitical structure had to be destroyed. As visible signs of their opposition to the regime, traditions, and status quo, the young men wore long hair, while the women wore theirs short.

In the 1860s, a philosophical posture known as "nihilism" became popular among the disaffected intellectual youth. Rejecting all traditions and conventions, the nihilists claimed to believe in nothing. Nihilism was a protest against a repressive society that stifled personal freedom. At first, the nihilists expressed their feelings in literary form and then adopted terrorist methods as many of them became anarchists.

Mikhail Bakunin (1814–1876) personified the alienated upper-class youths who turned to violent forms of protest. He advocated an uncompromising violence against the established order. As a fanatical anarchist, Bakunin, once an officer in the imperial guard, urged violence, assassinations, riots, and revolution as necessary instruments in achieving human freedom. He claimed that a man could be truly free only in a lawless world where the institutional structures of church, family, and state had been destroyed. Since he was an uncompromising opponent of the czarist regime, Bakunin was imprisoned in Siberia. He escaped and spent his life wandering throughout Europe searching for, and participating in, revolutionary activities.

In contrast to the anarchist Bakunin, the more moderate among the intelligentsia were inspired by the liberal writer and theorist Alexander Herzen (1812–1870). Even though he was a moderate, Herzen's writings were suppressed by the czarist regime, and he left Russia in 1847 to begin a lifelong exile. He settled in London, where he edited a weekly journal, *Kolokol* (*The Bell*), which was smuggled into Russia and widely read. His criticisms of czarist repression and backwardness even reached Czar Alexander, who read *Kolokol*. Herzen did not believe in nihilism, and he rejected the violent terrorism of the anarchists. Adhering to liberalism, he called for the establishment of the basic freedoms of speech, press, and assembly in Russia. Like most liberal humanitarians, Herzen placed great faith in the powers of education to bring about a Russian enlightenment.

Some of the liberal intelligentsia formed discussion groups, where they held dialogues about the meaning of life, politics, and society, believing that if enough discussion were generated, it would spill over into the countryside. Like most talkative liberals, they hoped to find a peaceful solution to their country's pressing social, economic, and political problems. In the meanwhile, Alexander II and his advisers, increasingly fearful of the rising tides of intellectual discontent, turned a deaf ear. The vested interests represented in the civil service, aristocracy, army, and church were not to be moved by dialogues.

Some of the disaffected intellectuals then decided that they would have to do more than discuss Russian problems. Believing that the government might be more responsive to pressures for reform that emanated from the masses of the population, they decided to go to the peasantry and educate them to recognize their oppression. During the 1870s, young men and women gave up their studies to go among the people and educate them to demand reform.

The students who participated in what was called the Narodnik (People's) movement dressed as peasants, lived with them, and tried to blend into village society. Although a few Narodniks were successful, many were arrested and exiled to Siberia. Like many intellectuals who have sought to work among the common people, the Narodniks did not fit in and were resented as troublemakers by the people whom they desired to help. Often the peasants were angered by their denunciations of their "little father," the czar, and turned the Narodniks over to the authorities.

In 1879, some of the young Russians, despondent over their failure in going to the people, turned to violent forms of protest. They organized a movement called the "People's Will," which demanded complete democratization of Russian life. Using assassination, this group started a terrorist campaign against government officials. Hunted by the police, these professional revolutionaries plotted against the government and led agitations and strikes. In 1881, Alexander II, the czar who had initiated some major reforms, was assassinated by terrorists because his reforms had not gone far enough.

Chernyshevsky's What Is to Be Done?

Among the disaffected intellectuals of nineteenth-century Russia was Nicholas Chernyshevsky (1828–1889), a major literary and revolutionary figure who wrote *What Is to Be Done?*, a novel that enjoyed tremendous popularity among Russian students and intelligentsia. Chernyshevsky attended the University of St. Petersburg, taught school, and wrote for the leftist journals. In 1862, he was arrested for writing revolutionary proclamations to the peasantry and was sentenced to imprisonment at hard labor, from which he was not freed until 1883. While in prison he wrote *What Is to Be Done?* This novel explored the character and attitudes of the new generation through a discussion of individual problems in the face of unyielding social institutions, conventions, and pressures. Because of the czarist regime's inefficient censorship, the book's publication was permitted. *What Is to Be Done?* became one of the great books of the Russian radical intelligentsia.

Chernyshevsky's place among the Russian radical movement has been variously interpreted. He has been referred to as a populist, a nihilist, a utopian socialist, a Slavic cultural nationalist, and a materialist. His novel was supposed to have exerted an influence on Lenin, who called Chernyshevsky a vanguard fighter and wrote a manifesto also entitled *"What Is to Be Done?"*

The heroine of Chernyshevsky's novel, Vera Pavlova, overcame the stolidness of her wealthy and conservative upbringing and established a cooperative dressmaking shop, where fifty working-class girls worked. The shop's profits reverted to the employees, who reinvested them in the enterprise. This cooperative establishment was a symbol of both socialism and feminism. The women in the novel were liberated individuals who sought to create a new society based on cooperation.

Chernyshevsky's novel also portrayed what might be interpreted as a generation gap in nineteenth-century czarist Russia. It called for the emancipation of young people to resolve many sociopolitical and institutional problems that their parents had neglected. Chernyshevsky emphasized the need for introspection, self-discipline, and sensitivity.

Although he conceded that formal schools were necessary to teach reading and other basic skills, real education involved the development of sensitivity to moral, social, and political problems. It was more important to convert adults to the new society rather than to reconstruct formal schooling. Vera Pavlova, for example, was able to persuade fifty humble working-class girls who had little formal education to accept a cooperative and socialist pattern of life by appealing to their mutual self-interest.[1]

Chernyshevsky portrayed the new generation of young Russians as simple individuals who would dedicate themselves to single-minded, honest effort and thereby build a new society.

Nineteenth-Century Literature

Russian literature, especially fiction, became a major intellectual force in the nineteenth century. Novelists such as Turgenev, Dostoevsky, and Tolstoy used their artistry to analyze human beings within the context of Russian history and culture. Ivan Turgenev (1818–1883) in *The Diary of a Sportsman* realistically described the life of the peasantry before the emancipation of the serfs. His masterpiece, *Fathers and Sons*, described the generation gap between the old and the young.

Feodor Dostoevsky (1821–1881) used the novel to probe the twists and turns of the human mind. Among his more famous works were *Crime and Punishment, The Brothers Karamazov,* and *The Idiot.* His writings were dominated by the theme of a brooding and mystical Slavic temperament.

Of all the nineteenth-century Russian writers, Count Leo Tolstoy (1828–1910) had the greatest educational impact. Tolstoy held views on art, religion, society, politics, and education. Much of his fiction portrayed individuals who were caught up in crucial historical movements. His greatest novel, *War and Peace,* dealt with Russian life and society during the Napoleonic invasion. A social reformer as well as a novelist, Tolstoy feared that modern civilization was failing because of institutional imperfections. Formal education had been corrupted by institutionalized schooling. Turning to a primitive Christianity, Tolstoy developed a theory of individual and social reform based on the simplification of life. His doctrines were imbued with his belief in the virtues of poverty, humility, peace, and nonviolence. True to his belief in the simple life, Tolstoy saw the Russian peasant as a desirable model for social regeneration.

Tolstoy's zeal for social reform led him from literature to education.

[1] Nicholas G. Chernyshevsky, *What Is to Be Done?* (New York: Vintage Books, 1961), p. 301

He realized that the Russian literati were far removed from the real Russians, the masses of illiterate peasants for whom literature was useless. In 1859, Tolstoy opened a school at Yasnaya Polyana, his estate. As a result of teaching in his own school, he became involved in pedagogical theory and plans for improving Russian national education.

Tolstoy questioned the value of the government's emphasis on industrialization when the masses of people were still illiterate. He proposed the establishment of a Society of National Education to establish schools, prepare instructional materials, train teachers, and disseminate educational ideas. Although he approached government officials, he was not given official encouragement.

To improve his understanding of educational theory and practice, Tolstoy decided to visit the more advanced school systems of Germany, France, and England. In 1860, he made an educational tour of western Europe, visiting schools and speaking with educators. To his dismay, he found that Western education was lifeless and unimaginative. Moreover, he wrote, it ruined innocence. Since it was a form of coercion, it had a harmful effect on the learner. Genuine education had to be based on simple principles so that children and unsophisticated peasants would eagerly and willingly absorb it.[2]

After his tour of western Europe, Tolstoy returned to Russia in 1861 to continue his work in the village school at Yasnaya Polyana. He refused to prescribe a set program of instruction. Among the subjects offered were reading, composition, penmanship, grammar, religion, history, drawing, singing, mathematics, and natural science. Fearing the overcomplication and overinstitutionalization of life, he insisted that the school be a model of simplicity. He wanted it to be flexible, adaptable, and characterized by student freedom. Although the school day was twelve hours long—from nine in the morning until nine in the evening—students came and went as they pleased.

Although government inspectors certainly would have criticized the noise and apparent disorder at Yasnaya Polyana, Tolstoy claimed that such "free order" was necessary to genuine learning. "Free order" frightened the traditionalist because it was such a radical departure from conventional education. Artificial rewards and punishments had no place in Tolstoy's school. He opposed the use of corporal punishment as being inconsiderate and disrespectful toward human nature. He believed that children who were respected as reasonable beings would recognize that order was necessary. He also felt that rigid discipline, lack of freedom and initiative, and a constant demand for silence and obedience had a stupefying effect on children.

Tolstoy felt that children contained within themselves creative pow-

[2] Ernest J. Simmons, *Introduction to Tolstoy's Writings* (Chicago: University of Chicago Press, 1968), p. 92.

ers that should be encouraged. Furthermore, he believed that education should be a morally creative force that would advance the cause of human brotherhood and eliminate everything that isolated individuals from the human family. As a moral enterprise, education should do more than cultivate intellectual or literary skills. It should cultivate the heart, will, and emotions.

Opposing what he regarded as forced education according to prescribed patterns, Tolstoy said that traditional schooling had degenerated into a kind of conditioning that neglected the student's interests and creative powers. It developed hypocrisy, aimlessness, and dullness rather than truth, openness, and originality. Institutionalized formal education, by trying to form individuals into predetermined molds, was a kind of moral tyranny that infringed on the student's right to self-determination.

Tolstoy was not a typical representative of nineteenth-century Russian education. He was an unusual man who tried to establish an education based on the aesthetic mode of experience as it was conceived by the artist. Certain aspects of his theory bore a resemblance to the educational reforms of Pestalozzi and Froebel. It was not Tolstoy's view of education that was to prevail in czarist Russia, however.

Czarist Autocracy

After the assassination of his father Alexander II by a terrorist's bomb, Alexander III ascended the Russian throne in 1881. He had opposed his father's limited reforms and was determined to rule Russia with a firm hand. Alexander chose his former tutor, Constantine Pobedonostsev (1827–1907) as his chief adviser. Pobedonostsev, who was Procurator of the Holy Synod from 1880 to 1904, believed that autocracy was the source of Russian greatness. He opposed representative government on the grounds that it would destroy the paternalistic relationship that existed between the czar and his subjects. Together, the czar and his mentor inaugurated a program of reaction that was like the system employed by Alexander's grandfather, Nicholas I. The regime sought to buttress czarist autocracy by:

1. Repressing all dissent and criticism.
2. Extending the police powers of the central government.
3. Reducing the powers of the local governments.
4. Using the press to propagandize for the regime.

The program of Alexander III was supported by conservatives throughout Russia who had been horrified by the murder of Alexander II. The bureacracy, army, Russian Orthodox Church, nobility, and landed gentry rallied behind their new czar. Many of the peasants also came to his support. Critics of the government were accused of being anti-Russian. The various opponents of the regime—liberals, socialists, and radicals—went underground to await a more favorable time to work openly for the reform of Russia.

Pobedonostsev, the leading spokesman for the regime, had a simple philosophy that asserted that faith was the foundation of Russian society. The czar, he asserted, should have faith in himself as the agent of God, and the people should have faith in their ruler. Pobedonostsev used both informal and formal educational agencies to indoctrinate the people.

Alexander's regime encouraged those propagandists who favored its policies and suppressed its critics by a rigorously imposed censorship. A special committee composed of the Procurator of the Holy Synod and the ministers of interior, justice, and education was empowered to suppress any offending press at its discretion. Newspapers suspected of holding dissenting views were required to submit all copy for censorship. Public libraries were also placed under surveillance by the ministry of education which was to remove unapproved books from circulation.

Among Alexander's supporters were the writers who belonged to the Panslav movement. These nationalist journalists asserted that Russia was divinely ordained to unite all of the Slavic peoples of Europe into a vast empire. The major literary exponent of Panslavism was Nicholas Danilevsky (1822–1885), who wrote *Russia and Europe*. Danilevsky claimed that Slavic civilization was destined to dominate the world. The Russian czar was destined to liberate the Slavic peoples of eastern Europe from Turkish and German domination and give them Russian rule with its Orthodoxy and autocracy. The government also supported such journalistic allies as Michael Katkov, whose *Russian Messenger* and *Moscow News* were among the most influential propaganda vehicles for the regime.

Pobedonostsev believed that schools needed to be brought under greater supervision in order to purge teachers who held antigovernment views. He steadfastly opposed the concept of universal education that was becoming popular in western Europe. Fearing that schools had grown too permissive, he urged that firm discipline be restored. Pobedonostsev wanted to place elementary education under the control of the Orthodox Church. Under his auspices, the number of parish schools increased from 4,500 in 1882 to 32,000 in 1894. These parish schools were usually inferior institutions that offered only a limited primary education. Their curriculum concentrated on patriotic indoctrination, the singing of religious hymns, and the rudiments of reading.

Pobedonostsev was assisted in implementing his educational policies by Count Ivan Delyanov (1818–1897), who sought to preserve the secondary schools as upper-class institutions. He ordered the investigation of all applicants for admission to secondary schools so that no lower-class children would be admitted. Tuition fees were increased as a further means of discouraging lower-class children from trying to rise above their social class.

The policies of Alexander III continued the tradition of czarist autocracy that had been established by his predecessors. The czarist regime sought to reinforce its policies of autocracy, Orthodoxy, and nationalism. The schools, the press, and the pulpit were enlisted to propagandize for the regime. Although Alexander sought to leave his heir a Russia in which autocracy was firmly entrenched, the repressed forces of change were destined to erupt.

The Fall of Czarist Russia

From 1881 on, the official policy of the czarist regime was reactionary and autocratic. Both Alexander III and his successor Nicholas II were unenlightened rulers. There was, however, a fundamental difference in their characters. Alexander III had been a strong and vigorous person, whereas his son Nicholas II was weak and vacillating. The Fundamental Laws of the Russian Empire still asserted that "To the Emperor of all the Russias belongs supreme autocratic power. Submission to His power, not only from fear, but as a matter of conscience, is commanded by God Himself." As supreme autocrat of Russia, the emperor was the ultimate arbiter of law and supreme defender of Orthodoxy. Starting in 1904, a series of events occurred that seriously weakened the position of Nicholas II, who was destined to be the last of the czars. In the Russo-Japanese War (1904–1905), the Russian army and navy suffered a humiliating defeat. The homefront seethed with discontent as students, workers, intellectuals, and even the middle class protested the government's repressive policies and inefficient conduct of the war.

It was the events of "Bloody Sunday," January 25, 1905, that led to an open revolt against the czarist government. Father George Gapon, an Orthodox priest, had attempted to lead a massive peaceful demonstration to present a petition to the czar. As the assembled workers in Gapon's demonstration reached the square before the Winter Palace, they were fired upon by troops. Five hundred demonstrators were killed, and the estimates of wounded reached three thousand. In protest, widespread general strikes occurred. Even the moderates turned against the czar. Nicholas II, realizing the gravity of events, issued a manifesto on October 30 that granted freedom of person, conscience, speech, and assembly and the right to form unions. The October Manifesto also provided for a representative government vested in an elected Duma, or assembly. In the first elections, the Constitutional Democrats received a majority. Although they were moderates, the czar regarded them with suspicion and dissolved the Duma.

Diplomatically, Russia, along with France and England, was a member of the Triple Alliance and considered herself the defender of Slavic interests against Austria and Germany. When World War I came in 1914, Russia found herself at war with the Germans and Austrians. The Russian armies were handicapped by an inefficient defense ministry. The crushing defeats of the war and the ineptness of Nicholas II and his ministers produced a crisis during the period from 1914 through 1916. In 1917, the czar was forced to abdicate, and a provisional government was established. In July 1917, a coalition government headed by Alexander Kerensky took power. It was overthrown by Lenin's Bolsheviks in October 1917, and a Soviet government was established that imposed a Communist dictatorship on Russia.

The Bolsheviks seized power at a time when the nation was disintegrating. The effects of war and political instability had demoralized the people, 75 percent of whom were illiterate. Economic life was at a standstill. The Bolsheviks had inherited a legacy of cultural, economic, and political backwardness. Lenin decided to take ruthless measures to modernize Russia and move it into the twentieth century.

Soviet Russia

Karl Marx, believing that communism would first come to industrialized western Europe, had dismissed agrarian and peasant Russia as a possible location of proletarian revolt. In fact, he had feared that reactionary Russia might seek to crush such revolts when they occurred in other Western nations. Since he had written about education in only very general terms, Marx was not particularly useful to the Bolsheviks in terms of specifying particular educational policies once power had been seized.

Nikolai Lenin (1870–1924), who had directed the Bolshevik seizure of power, had a pronounced influence on the course of Soviet social, political, economic, and educational policies. Lenin saw the school as an ideological weapon in the arsenal of the dictatorship of the proletariat that could be used to assist in the destruction of the bourgeoisie. However, most of Lenin's energies were directed to fighting the White armies in the Civil War (1917–1921) and to restoring Soviet productivity by temporarily permitting a slight resurgence of capitalism in the New Economic Policy (1921–1928). Lenin died in 1924 in the midst of the latter program.

The educational system that the Bolsheviks acquired from the czarist

Romanov regime had served "autocracy, Orthodoxy, and nationality" rather than the interests of workers and peasants. The Russian reverses in World War I had wrought havoc on schools as well as all other areas of Russian life. During the best days of the old regime, only about 20 percent of school age children were in elementary schools, and probably no more than 700,000 had been enrolled in secondary schools.[3] In 1919, the Communist Party Congress recommended the establishment of coeducational working-class schools, which were to emphasize practical and socially productive labor. Instruction was to be given in the regional language, and the schools were to be free of any religious influence.

Lenin saw education as a necessary instrument in achieving the economic modernization of the Soviet Union. Higher literacy rates could be used to increase industrial and agricultural productivity. He asserted that schools could be potent weapons in securing a one-party state.

For the new Communist regime, education had three major purposes: (1) cultivation of literacy; (2) development of allegiance to socially productive labor; and (3) undermining the values, traditions, and way of life associated with czarist Russia. In 1921, a concerted drive began to separate church and school. Religious instruction was prohibited, and religious literature was banned. Church schools, seminaries, and monasteries were closed. New textbooks were openly antagonistic to religion. The Communist youth organization, Komsomol, sponsored antireligious plays, demonstrations, and exhibitions. Teachers were warned that they had to abandon either their religion or their profession.

Some of the Communist officials also sought to weaken the authority of the family. In the early years, some extreme Bolsheviks wanted children removed from the home and reared in special schools. However, neither Lenin nor his wife, Krupskaya, who took a special interest in education, supported this plan. There were some cases of children denouncing their parents to authorities for antistate activity.

Anatoli Lunacharski (1875–1933) was appointed commissar of enlightenment by Lenin and given the task of creating a new Soviet socialist culture. Lunacharski introduced a unified Worker's School that covered the entire course of education. He opposed the inherited system of differentiated schools that divided students on the basis of socioeconomic class. The new Worker's School reflected the Soviet philosophy of a classless society in which every child would have an identical education and an opportunity for higher education. Children would be provided with food and, when necessary, shoes and clothing. It was during his administration that certain aspects of American progressive

[3] Edward A. Ross, *The Russian Soviet Republic* (New York: Century, 1923), pp. 370–373.

education were introduced into the Soviet Union. In order to create a collectivist pedagogy, Soviet educators devised the "brigade" method, in which a number of students were given a collective assignment and collective responsibility for its completion. Such cooperative methods were popular because the Soviet educators felt that they developed collective attitudes, destroyed old class divisions, and could be related directly to work goals.

During the romantic stage of Communist education, as Lunacharski's administration was often called, grades and entrance examinations were abolished as residues of the old pre-Communist mentality. In place of grades, various substitutes were tried, such as workbooks, collective diaries, reports, and teachers' observations. Corporal punishment was also abolished.

Lunacharski and the Russian educators of the 1920s borrowed extensively from non-Russian theorists, such as Montessori, Kerschensteiner, Dewey, Kilpatrick, and Thorndike. Anna L. Strong, among the first foreigners to observe Russian schools, noted that "every new book by Dewey is seized and eagerly translated into Russian."[4] The Russians supplied, of course, their own Marxist-Leninist interpretations.

The Russian school of the 1920s was permissive. Some schools were controlled by student committees. In some elementary schools, the pupils had a voice equal to that of their teachers. George S. Counts, an early commentator on Soviet education, reported that "Book learning was discredited; Communist youth leaders spied on teachers; examinations and graded efforts were labeled the marks of bourgeois reaction and were abolished."[5]

During the 1920s, Soviet educators advanced pedology as a scientific approach to education. The pedologists attempted to apply biology, physiology, and psychology to the study of children's behavior and learning. Asserting that the individual's behavior was determined by heredity and social forces, the pedologists claimed that people could be changed by a process of environmental alteration, although nothing could be done about heredity.

Polytechnical education became a key aspect of Soviet schooling because of its stress on work and the desire to develop a functional, classless, society. Through polytechnical education, the student was to be introduced to an active and practical application of science to agriculture and industry.

During the early years of Communist rule in the Soviet Union, the party came to exercise control over education by appointing its members to key administrative positions. Once this was accomplished, the

[4] George Z. F. Bereday, William W. Brickman, and Gerald H. Read, *The Changing Soviet School* (Boston: Houghton Mifflin, 1960), p. 64.
[5] George S. Counts, *The Challenge of Soviet Education* (New York: McGraw-Hill, 1956), p. 84.

loyal Communist administrators could then develop party-dominated teachers' and students' organizations and slowly remove older, non-Communist teachers as more reliable new teachers were prepared along party lines. In the universities, those suspected of anticommunism were systematically purged and replaced by Marxists. Positions in philosophy were filled by reliable Marxist-Leninists.

The Soviet government, recognizing that formal schooling would be inadequate to adapt the Russian population to a Communist way of life, organized a number of youth movements to indoctrinate the new generation in the principles of the new society. The Komsomol (Union of Communist Youth) was founded for youths between the ages of fourteen and twenty-three. The Young Pioneers enlisted children between the ages of ten and sixteen, and the Little Octobrists those between eight and ten. These organizations indoctrinated children and youth in the Communist ideology and served as centers of party activities in the schools. Under their auspices, Soviet youth embarked on political activities and joined adult party members as working cadres in agriculture and industry.

By 1928, signs of a reaction against the early stage of educational experimentation began to appear as teachers and parents voiced complaints against undisciplined students. Higher schools complained of the inferior preparation of students admitted from lower schools. Those in the Soviet hierarchy who were interested in greater scientific and economic achievements began to feel that the progressive schools of the Lunacharski regime had produced students who lacked a solid grounding in the fundamental skills and subjects.

Stalin and Education

After Lenin's death in 1924, Joseph Stalin (1879–1953), who was secretary of the Communist party, consolidated his position, purged his opposition, and forced his rival, Leon Trotsky, into exile. Stalin introduced the Five-Year Plan in 1928 as a step in the industrialization of the Soviet Union. The plan set a new order of priorities for Soviet education since industrialization would require technicians, managers, and skilled workers. The school could best achieve this end by concentrating on basic skills, science, and discipline, for technicians and engineers would need a firm foundation in the basic and applied sciences.

The student-oriented school of the 1920s was abandoned in this drive to train scientists, technicians, and skilled workers, and the school again became an authoritarian institution. Even the idea that Soviet youth should spend some time as working cadres in agriculture and industry was abandoned. In 1937, the party ordered school administrators, teachers, and youth organizations to concentrate their efforts on formal schooling. Youth organizations had to receive prior approval of the commissar of people's education and the school principal before embarking on activities and programs. Political activities were curtailed, and scholarship was emphasized.

A fixed number of instructional hours were required in basic subjects. Lectures, recitations, and verbal methods replaced the project and brigade methods. In 1927, entrance examinations were reestablished for college admission. In 1932, efforts were made to give teachers increased authority by restoring the use of grades. Projects fell into complete disfavor as the subject matter curriculum was reinstalled. Systematic teacher-directed learning was encouraged. In 1935, regulations governing the length of the school year, the number and duration of daily lessons, and examinations were established.

In the rising nationalism of the 1930s, the theme of Stalin as the personification of the "great man" theory had replaced the earlier emphasis on the corporate or collective hero. The dictator's influence was manifested throughout Soviet life in what Khrushchev later condemned as the "cult of personality." By 1934, Stalin's major rivals had all been purged or were in exile.

The Soviet Union, like Nazi Germany, was a totalitarian state in which the mass media and other informal educational agencies were used to advance party purposes. In 1932, the Culture and Propaganda Department of the Central Committee of the Communist party was given authority to control Soviet cultural life. Newspapers, literature, art, radio, motion pictures, and schools came under party control.

The policies of Stalinist industrialization had an impact on educational theory as well as practice. V. N. Shulgin, Director of the Institute of Marxist-Leninist Pedagogy, asserted that the formal school was destined to wither away. Since the school was only one of many educational agencies, he claimed that informal education had a greater effect than formal schooling. Shulgin, however, had misread Stalin's intention of strengthening both state power and formal schooling. The party journal *Bolshevik* attacked Shulgin's educational theory as dangerous nonsense and said the state was a necessary instrument for the purpose of crushing class enemies.

Stalin's commissar of education was Andrei Bubnov, an old Bolshevik who had been active in revolutionary activity in the czarist period. Bubnov was not a professional educator, but Stalin regarded him as a faithful disciple. With the return of the subject matter curriculum to primacy, textbooks assumed a greater significance, and Bubnov sought to have textbooks written that would emphasize loyalty to the regime —that is, he wanted to "stabilize" textbooks according to Stalinist policies. He felt that the books in history and the social sciences were in particular need of careful scrutiny.

In the area of history, Stalin himself intervened. He wanted Russian nationalism again asserted. Historians were told to portray the facts dealing with basic political events, such as wars, revolutions, and popular movements, and not just the class struggle. New text-books emphasized the historical role of the Russian people and lead-ers. Military heroes of the Napoleonic wars, such as Mikhail Kutuzov and Alexander Suvorov, were resurrected to instill nationalistic pride in the young. Czar Peter the Great was rehabilitated as a progressive statesmen. A Soviet historian has explained this shift in historical writing:

> By the mid-1930's the ideological positions of the bourgeois his-torical writing had been essentially undermined. A considerable portion of the bourgeois historians in the U.S.S.R. had adopted Marxist-Leninist theory. At the same time it was found that the substantial theoretical work done on the Marxist-Leninist concept had been conducted . . . in isolation from concrete investigations. This sometimes led to a certain amount of abstractness, to the re-duction of history to sociological explanations beneath which one felt a lack of any sound foundation of systematized facts.[6]

In 1941, Hitler's armies began Operation Barbarossa, which was designed to crush Soviet Russia in a quick campaign. Hitler's ambi-tious plan was predicated on the rapid collapse of the Red army and the Soviet regime. Disregarding the caution of his generals, Hitler ordered an all-out frontal attack on the Soviet Union and made the same mistake that Napoleon had made in 1812. At first the Russian armies suffered massive losses and retreated far into the Soviet Union; then their resistance hardened, and the German drive was stalemated. The German occupation forces introduced a brutal, repressive policy in the captured Russian areas and failed to capitalize on the discon-tent of Ukrainians and Byelorussians with the Soviet regime.

Meanwhile, in order to solidify Russian opposition to the Nazi in-vasion, Stalin appealed to Russian nationalism in the fight against the German conquerors. Calling upon Russians to fight for Mother Russia, Stalin invoked the names of medieval Orthodox saints and czarist generals. Thus, he used the army and the church, the two strongest links with the nation's past, rather than the party, to moti-vate Russian resistance. The official antireligious program was ended. In 1943, Stalin officially received the Patriarch Sergei, head of the Russian Orthodox Church. By 1944, the German armies were in full retreat from Soviet soil, and the Red armies had entered Poland and the Balkan countries. As they pushed the Germans out of eastern Europe, the Soviet armies set the stage for what would be an extension of Russian power into the small nations of Poland, Czechoslovakia, Bulgaria, Rumania, and Hungary.

[6] L. V. Cherepnin, "Fifty Years of Soviet Historical Science and Some Results of the Study of the Feudal Epoch in Russian History," *Soviet Studies in History*, VII (Summer 1968), 5.

Stalinist Ideology in the Postwar Era

After World War II, Stalinist ideological, cultural, and educational policy became an assertion of a vigorous Great Russian nationalism and a glorification of Stalin as the national hero. From the end of the war in 1945 until Stalin's death in 1953, the regime continuously intervened in Russian cultural and intellectual life. The first phase of this intervention was inaugurated by A. A. Zhdanov (1896–1948), a member of the Politburo who had played a considerable role in the reaffirmation of Russian nationalism in the war. Zhdanov had been instrumental in creating a uniform Central Administration for Propaganda and Agitation in 1938, in abolishing free tuition in secondary schools in 1940, and in reintroducing graduation examinations in 1944.

In 1946, Zhdanov announced to the Central Committee that the time had come to demonstrate the superiority of Soviet socialism in cultural affairs. He also ordered Russian writers to take the cultural offensive by producing a genuine socialist literature. First, however, Stalin and Zhdanov began a purge to purify Soviet culture of those Western bourgeois elements that had entered Soviet life during the war years. Certain leading Soviet writers were criticized, such as the poetess A. Akhmatova for having drawn an inaccurate picture of Soviet life, the philosopher F. F. Alexandrov for lack of energy in expounding materialist philosophy, and the economist Eugene Varga for failure to assert that the collapse of the United States economy was imminent.[7] In 1948, Zhdanov accused Russian musicians, including Shostakovich, of failing to incorporate "socialist realism" in their compositions.

In 1948, Soviet historians were criticized for overemphasizing the foreign elements in Russian history and failing to give sufficient notice to the achievements of heroic Russians. In 1948, the historian N. Rubinstein, author of *History of Russian Historiography,* was forced to recant publicly before his fellow historians for his formalism and objectivism.

In the biological sciences, Zhdanov officially supported the theories of T. D. Lysenko, who had asserted that it was possible to change the heredity of plants. According to Lysenko, wheat could be changed into rye by controlled experimentation with heredity. Psychologists and physiologists were also advised to adhere to Stalinism in their scientific work. The regime praised I. P. Pavlov (1849–1936) as an outstanding example of a Marxist scientist. Pavlov had asserted that all psychological functions were basically mechanical processes.[8]

[7] Georg von Rauch, *A History of Soviet Russia* (New York: Praeger, 1957), pp. 400–406.
[8] *Ibid.,* p. 403.

Through the efforts of Zhdanov, Russian intellectual and cultural life became isolated from communication with the West. Soviet scientists and scholars were forced to follow the dictates of socialist realism as interpreted by Stalin and Zhdanov. As a result, a chauvinistic interpretation was stamped on literature, art, history, and even science.

The degree to which the regime involved itself in distorting scholarly research was shown in the summer of 1950 when Stalin wrote his famous "Letters on Linguistics," which asserted that language is not the concern of particular classes but of the whole people. According to Stalin, language is not limited to particular historical periods but transcends time. When several languages clash, they do not merge into a new language, but the strongest one prevails. Stalin asserted that the Russian language had always been the victorious language.[9]

Stalin did not enter into the discussion of language because he was a disinterested student of linguistics. He had political purposes. Within the Soviet Union, he was interested in pressing Great Russian supremacy over the other nationalities, such as the Ukrainians and Byelorussians. Further, he wanted Russian to emerge as the language of his new empire in eastern Europe—that is, the official Communist language of all the Soviet peoples and the eastern European satellites.

Zhdanov was an advocate of strong measures in the cold war against the Western powers. He believed that it was necessary to use military force in Berlin and also to crush Tito's independent course in Yugoslavia. He died in 1948 in the midst of debates on the further course of Soviet policy. Stalin did not relax his stringent intervention in Soviet cultural life, however. In 1953, he accused a number of doctors of plotting the assassination of Soviet leaders. They were also accused of murdering Zhdanov. There were strong anti-Semitic overtones in the Stalinist attacks. The Soviet Union seemed on the verge of a new purge when Stalin died on March 5, 1953.

Khrushchev's Policies

After Stalin's death, there was serious rivalry for power among his former associates, Beria, Malenkov, Khrushchev, and Bulganin. By 1956, Khrushchev was clearly ascendant, and it was he who demolished the myth of Stalin's heroism. At the Twentieth Party Congress in 1956, Khrushchev attacked the Stalinist cult of personality and detailed Stalin's crimes, accusing him of being arrogant, reckless, greedy, and a violent terrorist. Further, Khrushchev charged that he had been incompetent on many occasions and had jeopardized the security of the Soviet Union.

In 1958, Khrushchev discussed Soviet education in an address, "On

9 *Ibid.*, p. 405.

Strengthening the Ties of the Schools with Life." He warned that the intense academic pressures of Soviet education were overtaxing the health of children and proposed that Soviet education return to its identification with the working class by stressing work training on farms and in factories. He seemed to be proposing a return to the ideas of polytechnical education that had been advanced in the late 1920s. He recommended that Soviet youth be drawn into socially useful work as part of their education and induction into a working-class society. Despite some movements in the direction of Khrushchev's recommendations, Soviet education has generally retained its strong orientation to subject matter disciplines, especially in mathematics and science.

Soviet Educational Structures

Preschool education is an important part of the Soviet school system. Before the Revolution, it had been primarily a private, religious, or charitable undertaking with only about 4,000 children in attendance. By 1958, 2,280,000 children were attending preschool institutions. Soviet preschool education is neither free, compulsory, nor available to all. There are two major preschool institutions: the nursery for the very young, and the kindergarten for older children. Children may enter nurseries at the age of six months. The nurseries are generally adjuncts to factories and industries where the children's parents are employed. Every industry and factory must provide nurseries for their employees' children. Hours in the nurseries are convenient to the parents' needs, and often children are cared for around the clock. Nursery educators provide parental consultation and try to educate parents in child care.

Russian school staffs include teachers, dieticians, doctors, and nurses. This is especially true in nursery schools, where greater emphasis is placed on the physical well-being of the child than on specific intellectual or skill-learning objectives. Considerable time is devoted to medical hygiene.

At age three, Soviet children may enter the kindergarten, which is a voluntary institution operated by local authorities. The school day for the kindergarten child often extends to nine to ten hours. The nursery's concern for physical health continues in the kindergarten where emphasis is given to the child's health, exercise, and diet. The children are made health conscious and trained in elementary health knowledge and hygienic habits. The kindergarten curriculum is more methodological than the nursery school program. The more formal kindergarten instruction centers on art, drawing, music, singing, games, vocabulary, story-telling, counting, reading, and foreign language.

Soviet preschool education is not only convenient for working parents but also enables the state to influence the child's value formation in his most impressionable years. Social, moral, aesthetic, and political values are inculcated at a stage when the child is most receptive.

Before 1958, the basic Soviet educational institutions were the Schools of General Education, of which there were three types: the four-year, or primary, schools, enrolling students from ages seven to eleven; the seven-year, or incomplete secondary, schools, from ages seven to fourteen; and ten-year, or complete secondary, schools, enrolling students from ages seven to seventeen. The essential difference in these various schools was based on age and grade level rather than on curriculum.

In the four-year schools, usually located in remote or rural areas, students learned basic reading, writing, mathematics, and languages. The seven-year schools, also located in rural areas, were considered to be terminal institutions. The most complete form of general education was offered by the ten-year school, a comprehensive and coeducational institution whose curriculum was rigidly structured, with students attending classes for up to thirty-two hours per week. A Certificate of Maturity was awarded at the conclusion of the ten-year school program, which enabled a student to seek admission to an institution of higher learning.

As a result of educational reforms in 1958, the four-, seven-, and ten-year schools were generally replaced by the eight-year school, which serves as the basic Soviet school where most of the people are educated. The eight-year school is divided into two stages: elementary, comprising the first four grades; and secondary, grades five through eight. Children are taught by generalists in the elementary grades and by subject matter specialists at the secondary level. The eight-year school is coeducational and comprehensive.

The curriculum of the eight-year school is essentially oriented to subject matter, with the number of subjects increasing with each higher grade. Emphasis is placed on mathematics and the sciences. As a result of Khrushchev's desire to provide work experience for Soviet youth so that they could appreciate the proletarian basis of their society, the eight-year school has included work-training experiences.

Unlike the nursery and kindergarten, the eight-year school is free and compulsory. There are fees, however, for books, materials, and uniforms. The government provides some assistance for children from poorer families. Compulsory schooling terminates with the eight-year school, when the student may: (1) enter general polytechnical secondary school for three years of study and practical work experience; (2) take an entrance examination and seek to qualify for admission to a semiprofessional school; (3) enter a rural or urban vocational-technical school for a one- to three-year course; or (4) begin work in industry or agriculture.

The Soviets have also expanded higher education. In 1914, there were only 105 institutions of higher learning in Russia. In 1959, the number of such institutions had increased to more than 700. Only about 55 percent of the students enrolled in higher educational institutes attend classes on a full-time basis. About one-third of those continuing their education are enrolled in correspondence courses. There are 40 universities in the Soviet Union, which enroll more than a quarter of a million students.[10] Russian universities are highly specialized and adhere to Marxist theory and practices. Students enrolled in practical and applied studies greatly outnumber those in the liberal arts or humanities. The university is only one form of higher education in the Soviet Union. Technical, agricultural, medical, pedagogic, law, art, and physical education institutes are included in the higher education system.

Conclusion

The foregoing account of Russian education is, of course, by no means a thoroughgoing analysis but rather a historical overview of some of the major events and personalities that shaped Russian culture and education. A large but backward nation only fifty years ago, the Soviet Union is today one of the major powers of the world. In that same half century, it has developed an extensive educational system that has achieved virtually universal literacy in a nation that had once been 75 percent illiterate. It has also made tremendous scientific progress. Unfortunately, Soviet progress has been costly in terms of human life and freedom.

The concluding chapters of this book will deal with educational developments in the United States during the nineteenth and twentieth centuries. Perhaps it is a fitting conclusion to treat American education after having dealt with Soviet education. Since the United States and the Soviet Union have been adversaries for more than two decades, a book dealing with Western education should conclude with a treatment of these major rivals.

[10] N. Grant, *Soviet Education* (Baltimore: Penguin, 1964), pp. 108–113.

Suggested Readings

Alston, Patrick L. *Education and the State in Tsarist Russia*. Stanford: Stanford University Press, 1969.

Bereday, George, William Brickman, and Gerald Read (eds.), *The Changing Soviet School*. Boston: Houghton Mifflin, 1960.

Cherepnin, L. V. "Fifty Years of Soviet Historical Science and Some Results of the Study of the Feudal Epoch in Russian History," *Soviet Studies in History*, VII (Summer 1968), 3–31.

Counts, George S. *The Challenge of Soviet Education*. New York: McGraw-Hill, 1957.

————. *Khrushchev and the Central Committee Speak on Education*. Philadelphia: University of Pennsylvania Press, 1959.

————. "The Creation of the New Soviet Man," *School and Society*, XCV (November 25, 1967), 438–444.

Dorotich, D. "Turning Point in the Soviet School: The Seventeenth Party Congress and the Teaching of History," *History of Education Quarterly*, VII (Fall 1967), 295–311.

Fainsod, Merle. *How Russia is Ruled*. Cambridge, Mass.: Harvard University Press, 1965.

Grant, Nigel. *Soviet Education*. Baltimore: Penguin, 1964.

Hans, Nicholas. *History of Russian Educational Policy*. New York: Russell and Russell, 1964.

————. *The Russian Tradition in Education*. London: Routledge and Kegan Paul, 1963.

Hare, Richard. *Pioneers of Russian Social Thought*. New York: Vintage Books, 1964.

Johnson, William H. E. *Russia's Educational Heritage*. New York: Octagon Books, 1969.

Levin, Deana. *Soviet Education Today*. New York: John De Graff, 1959.

Lyashchenko, Peter I. *History of the National Economy of Russia*. New York: Macmillan, 1949.

Miliukov, Paul. *Russia and Its Crisis*. New York: Collier Books, 1962.

von Rauch, Georg. *A History of Soviet Russia*. Peter and Annette Jacobsohn (trs.). New York: Praeger, 1963.

Rogger, Hans. *National Consciousness in Eighteenth Century Russia*. Cambridge, Mass.: Harvard University Press, 1960.

Ross, Edward A. *The Russian Soviet Republic*. New York: Century, 1923.

Simmons, Ernest J. *Introduction to Tolstoy's Writing*. Chicago: University of Chicago Press, 1968.

————. *Leo Tolstoy*. New York: Vintage Books, 1960.

U.S. Department of Health, Education and Welfare. *Education in the USSR*. Washington, D.C.: U.S. Government Printing Office, 1960.

————. *Soviet Education Programs*. Washington, D.C.: U.S. Government Printing Office, 1960.

CHAPTER 22

Nineteenth-Century American Education

In the nineteenth century, the western frontiers of the United States moved toward the Pacific. Successive waves of immigrants brought with them a variety of ethnic customs and traditions. In the course of this country's development into an industrial nation, much of this European inheritance was transformed into a new cultural heritage, a transformation that had a twofold impact on American education: (1) denominational religious control over schools was gradually replaced by state and local government control, and (2) inherited social class distinctions were swept away by the equalitarianism of the democratic frontier.

In the first half of the nineteenth century, the United States was profoundly affected by an enthusiasm for social reform predicated on the belief that both man and society could be improved. A plethora of reformist proposals for temperance, abolitionism, women's rights, utopian socialism, penal improvement, and popular education swept the nation. Although much of the reforming zeal was dissipated when the reformers' theories were actually applied, the popular system of common schools, or public education, that developed in this period remained as a significant American achievement.

There was initial disagreement as to the most effective means of securing popular education—or at least basic literacy. Although some experiments with mass education were initiated, they were later discarded. The English Sunday School was introduced to the United States to cultivate basic literacy and morality among working-class children, who attended the school on the one day of the week when factories were idle. A charitable institution, the Sunday School was privately financed by well-intentioned philanthropists. Because of its obvious limitations, the Sunday School experiment failed as a major educational institution. The monitorial method of mass education, based upon the experiments of the Englishmen Lancaster and Bell, was also introduced. As explained in Chapter 18, this system was designed to achieve basic literacy by having a master teacher train a number of student teachers—or monitors—who then trained other students as monitors. Although it enjoyed brief popularity in the larger eastern cities of Philadelphia and New York, monitorialism, too, proved inadequate as a method of popular education. While these various experiments failed to achieve their goal, they stimulated the American common school movement by creating a demand for universal public education.

Arguments for Universal Education

The proponents of universal education had a variety of motives, foremost of which was political enlightenment. They believed that the security and maintenance of republican institutions required an educated, literate citizenry—that is, an electorate capable of decision-making—and a competent civil service. As was true in other nations, nationalism was a potent force in stimulating the proponents of universal education, who thought of common schooling as an instrument for integrating diverse ethnic and religious groups into a national identity. The rising business and laboring classes wanted a more utilitarian education to prepare competent businessmen and trained workmen. Many Americans also viewed education as a means of social and economic advancement.

Nevertheless, there was also strong opposition to popular education. Tax-conscious property owners resisted the idea, claiming that it was unjust to tax one man to educate another's child. Other opponents construed popular education as a plot to secure the dominance of one political party over another. Advocates of private religious schools feared that public schools would be irreligious institutions. Foreign language groups feared that a common school would eradicate distinctive ethnic customs and languages.

The Common School

The proponents of a mass system of popular education came to support the "common school" concept as the preferred instrument of elementary education. The word "common" expressed the concept of a community institution based on shared ideas, experiences, beliefs, aspirations, and values.

There were many notable advocates of the common school cause. Such politicians as Horace Mann, Henry Barnard, James G. Carter, Ninian Edwards, Robert Dale Owen, and Thaddeus Stevens pleaded for the passage of common school legislation. The American Lyceum movement, organized in 1826, popularized the idea of common schools. Such educational journals as William Russell's *American Journal of Education*, Henry Barnard's *Connecticut Common School Journal*, and Horace Mann's *Common School Journal* editorialized for the enactment of common school laws by the various state legislatures. These educational journals were also significant as a means of keeping Americans informed of European educational theories and practices. Both Barnard and Mann were familiar with Pestalozzian education and popularized it in their respective journals.

Although most Americans disliked Prussian militarism, many who had visited Europe were impressed by the smoothly functioning Prussian elementary school system. Prussia had included aspects of Pestalozzianism in its schools and established uniform standards, specialized teacher training institutions, and general taxation for school support. Emulating Victor Cousin's report on Prussian schools to the French government, Calvin Stowe undertook a similar overseas mission and reported to the Ohio legislature.

Horace Mann

Horace Mann (1796–1859) was prominent among those who secured the establishment of the common school in the United States. Born in Massachusetts, Mann was reared as a Calvinist but later became a Unitarian. He was educated as a lawyer, graduated from Brown University, and, in 1827, elected to the Massachusetts legislature, where he supported school reform. In 1838, he was named secretary of the Massachusetts Board of Education. His *Annual Reports* and editorship of the *Common School Journal* furthered the movement toward public education in Massachusetts. When he retired from the secretaryship in 1849, Mann was elected to Congress; later he became president of Antioch College.

An understanding of Mann's leadership in education can be gained by examining his educational philosophy.[1] Like many nineteenth-century New England intellectuals, he believed that man could use his reason to achieve perfection. Mann used his political acumen to win support for the common school. Although liberal theologically and socially, he was enough of a consensus politician to agree to the teaching of a "common Christianity" in the Massachusetts common schools. His compromise appeased the Protestant establishment sufficiently to win their support for public education. He convinced hesitant Protestant ministers that the common school would cultivate a common Christian morality, interpreted as a nondenominational Protestantism.

[1] Frank C. Foster, "Horace Mann as Philosopher," *Educational Theory*, X (January 1960), 9–25.

He also believed in the stewardship theory of property, which held that wealthy men, as stewards or guardians, should use their money for the public good. He therefore persuaded the rising class of American industrialists and businessmen that they had an obligation to support common school legislation.[2]

Like many New England intellectuals, Mann was influenced by Emersonian transcendentalism, which asserted that man could attain communion with the Universal Mind, or Oversoul, through intuition, introspection, and detachment from materialism. Transcendentalism gave education a moral significance, and Mann regarded schools as agencies for creating a purer personal and social morality. He also believed that public common schools would contribute to a popular civic awareness and sense of political responsibility. An intimate relationship existed between republican self-government and universal education. Political liberties would remain secure only as citizens made intelligent decisions. Mann asserted that the common school, as a center of civic education, would be a training ground for responsible citizenship and public service.

Although he recognized the injustices of early capitalism, Mann believed that social reform could come within the existent economic framework. In urging the propertied classes to support common school education, Mann bluntly told them that it was in their own self-interest to do so. Property rights could be best protected in a society in which the masses were educated to respect property and encouraged to acquire it. As Mann put it:

Does any possessor of wealth, or leisure, or learning ask, "What interest have I in education of the multitude?" I reply, you have at least this interest, that, unless their minds are enlightened by knowledge and controlled by virtuous principle, there is not, between their appetites and all you hold dear upon earth, so much the defense of a spider's web. Without a sense of the inviolability of property, your deeds are but wastepaper. Without a sense of the sacredness of person and life, you are only a watch-dog whose baying is to be silenced, that your house may be more securely entered, plundered. Even a guilty few can destroy the peace of the virtuous many. One incendiary can burn faster than a thousand industrious workers can build;—and this is true of social rights as of material edifices.[3]

Mann believed that common schools should be supported by the state, controlled by the public, and open equally to all. They should be so excellent that parents would prefer to enroll their children in them rather than private schools. The common school would assimilate

[2] Merle Curti, *The Social Ideas of American Educators* (New York: Littlefield, Adams, 1959), pp. 101–138.
[3] Horace Mann, *Lectures and Annual Reports on Education* (Cambridge, Mass.: Cornhill Press, 1867), pp. 197–198.

immigrants and foreign language groups into a unified American nation. As an institution responsible to the whole community, common schools should be governed by elected school boards.

Mann's conception of popular education was like that of European liberals. It was to be an institution that would emphasize respect for property, contribute to mobility, and cultivate a sense of law and order. There was an element of frontier American egalitarianism in Mann's model of the common school, however. It was to serve all children as it welded commonly shared values.

Henry Barnard

A contemporary of Horace Mann, Henry Barnard (1811–1900) was secretary of the State Board of Commissioners of Common Schools in Connecticut. He also served as state commissioner of public schools in Rhode Island (1845–1849), chancellor of the University of Wisconsin (1858–1860), and United States commissioner of education (1867–1870).

Barnard was more conservative socially, politically, and philosophically than Mann. Like that of Mann, Barnard's life coincided with the growth of American capitalism and industrialization. With urbanization, there was an attendant increase of tenements, slum conditions, child labor, and economic class conflicts.[4] As a supporter of laissez-faire economic theory, Barnard felt that some social dislocations were inevitable. Like the European liberals, he believed that natural laws of supply and demand operated economically and that individual competition best insured social progress. He further believed that American education should reinforce the principles of economic individualism. Since American factories and mills needed trained and docile workers, Barnard proposed a functional curriculum based on his conception of economic realities. He argued that educated men would be more productive workers than ignorant ones. Barnard also believed that the common school should advance American nationalism through civic education that stressed love of the national heritage and heroes.

Barnard wrote copiously about school priorities. Although reading, writing, and arithmetic were necessary, the proper aims of education, he said, meant more than the mere attainment of basic skills; they should also include the promotion of good health and cultivation of proper values.

In Barnard's *First Annual Report* of 1839, he advised Connecticut teachers on subjects ranging from writing to religion.[5] Since reading, writing, and arithmetic were basic to later schooling, he said, the

---

[4] Curti, *op. cit.*, pp. 139–168.
[5] John S. Brubacher's *Henry Barnard on Education* (New York: McGraw-Hill, 1931) is a skillful editing of Barnard's annual reports.

primary branches of learning should be stressed. Spelling should be correlated with reading and writing. The practical uses of arithmetic should be emphasized. The English language, combining spelling, reading, speaking, grammar, and composition, was to be the primary subject in the common district school. Like Mann, Barnard urged more adequate teacher education, establishment of normal schools, and increased financial compensation for teachers.

Enactment of Common School Legislation

According to the Tenth Amendment of the United States Constitution, education was among the powers reserved to each state in the Union. Since education was not conceived of as a federal or national prerogative, the events connected with enacting common school legislation varied from state to state. This decentralization of education, based on state authority, sharply contrasted with the educational systems of most continental European nations, where the right to control and administer education was vested in the national government. Even within a particular state, there were variations from local district to local district as to the degree of support of, and quality of instruction provided by, the schools that were established.

Massachusetts, a leader in the common school movement, served as a model for the other New England and the Midwestern states. As early as 1827, Massachusetts had made tax support of schools compulsory. The movement to enact common school legislation was more gradual in the Middle Atlantic states. With the exception of North Carolina, common school legislation was generally neglected in the Southern states until after the Civil War.

The process by which a state adopted legislation providing for compulsory common school education went through four major phases:

1. The state enacted legislation that permitted school districts to operate as legal taxing and administrative bodies if the majority of the district's residents agreed.
2. The state then encouraged the formation of school districts by granting monies from its general school fund to those districts that voted to support common schools; at this stage, the formation of districts was still optional. The state's school fund was derived from the sale of public land, tax collections, lotteries, or distribution of federal revenues.
3. The formation of school districts became compulsory, but tax support was usually inadequate for providing elementary education for all children resident in the school district. Districts were forced to collect fees through the rate bill, a tuition payment.
4. Finally, the state legislature required compulsory and completely

tax-supported public education. With the discontinuance of the rate bill, elementary education became available to all children resident in the school district.

Common school education became the foundation of the American public school system. Taxation for public school support was enacted into law by the various state legislatures. Upon this basis, public school education was later extended to include secondary and higher education.

Secondary Education

Although publicly supported and controlled elementary schools had been established in most of the states by the time of the Civil War, the public secondary school did not emerge until the latter half of the nineteenth century. Its appearance completed a sequential, integrated public school system. American youngsters could proceed from the kindergarten, through the common elementary school, to the high school, and eventually complete their education in a state college or university.

Concept of the Educational Ladder

Theoretically, the concept of the American educational ladder refers to a single, articulated, and sequential school system, open to all regardless of socioeconomic class or religious affiliation. The ladder concept was the educational counterpart of the equality of opportunity associated with Jacksonianism. In contrast to European dual educational systems, which differentiated secondary students into separate educational tracks, the American system was supposed to be a unified one.

The progress of the educational ladder concept in American education was tied directly to the evolution of the secondary school, which itself experienced three stages of institutional growth: (1) the colonial Latin grammar school, (2) the late eighteenth- and early nineteenth-century academy, and (3) the late nineteenth- and twentieth-century public high school.

Decline of the Latin Grammar School

The colonial Latin grammar school, an upper-class preparatory school, was attended by those destined to attend the colonial colleges of Harvard, Yale, and William and Mary. The Latin grammar school had a narrow curriculum based upon ancient Greek and Latin writings.

Even before the American Revolution, Benjamin Franklin and other critics of the Latin grammar school objected to its narrow classical curriculum. Franklin's proposal of 1749 for an English academy in Philadelphia would have offered a more realistic curriculum. Since the Latin grammar school did not satisfy practical needs, private venture schools offering a variety of subjects and skills, such as modern languages, navigation, bookkeeping, and surveying, appeared in commercial centers like New York, Philadelphia, and Charleston.

After the Revolution, the Latin grammar school fell into disfavor. A more utilitarian kind of secondary education was needed to prepare students for citizenship and industrial vocations. As the Latin grammar school declined, a new secondary school, the academy, emerged.

As a popular institution resulting from spontaneous but unorganized demands, the academy lacked a well-defined design.[6] Theodore Sizer, an eminent historian of the academy, has referred to it as a social institution that exemplified the optimistic American enthusiasm of the heady, but unrealistic, decades from the Revolution to the Civil War.[7] By 1855, 263,096 students were enrolled in 6,185 academies, a manifestation of its great popularity. Secondary education, exemplified by the academy, offered an extremely individualistic approach to educational organization, control, and curriculum.

The academy incorporated features of both the Latin grammar school and the private venture school. The Latin grammar school, primarily a college preparatory school, offered Greek and Latin classics, whereas the private venture school offered accounting, bookkeeping, navigation, modern languages, surveying, and other practical subjects. As an ill-defined synthesis of these two institutions, the academy offered both the classical college preparatory curriculum and practical subjects. The needs of a rising middle class of businessmen, professionals, and entrepreneurs, were met by the academies.

Academy Curricula and Control

The academy's curriculum attempted to satisfy three major needs: (1) the rise of a more direct democracy attendant on the Jacksonian extension of suffrage made it necessary to extend civic education to more people; (2) commercial and industrial expansion created a demand for people skilled in navigation, accounting, and modern languages; (3) an increase in the number of colleges created a demand for more schools.[8] The courses offered were organized into three major

[6] Theodore R. Sizer, *The Age of the Academies* (New York: Bureau of Publications, Teachers College, Columbia University, 1964), p. 12.
[7] *Ibid.*, p. 1.
[8] William M. French, *American Secondary Education* (New York: Odyssey, 1957), p. 58.

curricula: the college preparatory classical course, the terminal English course, and the normal course for teacher education. There were also military academies, which were especially popular in the South. Within the general framework of these major curricula, a number of hybrid programs appeared, such as classical-English, English-scientific, commercial-English, and normal-English. The academies offered courses on a wide variety of subjects, including classics, Latin, Greek, English, oratory, composition, rhetoric, literature, French, Spanish, Portuguese, German, trigonometry, bookkeeping, accounting, surveying, geography, United States and general history, logic, moral philosophy, astronomy, chemistry, drawing, religion, natural philosophy, geometry, algebra, needlework, phrenology, optics, geology, biology, botany, domestic science, and agriculture.

The quality of instruction offered by the academies varied considerably. Some instructors were competent; others were ill-prepared and interested only in a quick tuition fee. Based on the psychology of mental discipline and the acquisition of factual information, the common methods of teaching were drill, textbook memorization, recitation, and repetition. Among the many weaknesses found in the academy were a chaotic proliferation of courses, disorganized courses, and numerous short courses taught for only a few weeks. There was no uniform accreditation system.

Most academies were private or semipublic schools, with control vested in boards of independent, self-perpetuating trustees. Although some academies received local or state subsidies, the trustees usually sustained the initial expenses of building the academy, hiring the staff, and attracting students. Student tuition fees formed the bulk of support.

The academy period coincided with a period of intense religious revivalism during which religious denominations proliferated and sought to be perpetuated through education. Methodists, Episcopalians, Baptists, Roman Catholics, Presbyterians, Congregationalists, and other denominations founded academies to offer religious, social, and vocational education. Some academies were downward extensions of state colleges and universities. Since many colleges chartered by state legislatures had no ready supply of adequately prepared students, colleges often established secondary schools to prepare students in the literary skills and classical languages needed for college entrance.

As an educational institution, the academy reflected the nineteenth-century American sociocultural and political milieu. The Jacksonian exaltation of the common man, removal of property requirements for suffrage, and frontier individualism found an educational corollary in the academy, whose open enrollment policy and nonstructured curriculum reflected "free enterprise," Jacksonian laissez-faire and economic individualism. As a laissez-faire educational institution, the academy extended the spirit of the small entrepreneur into formal education.

The early decades of the nineteenth century also revealed a great faith in the possibility of securing social reform through educational efforts. Reform movements, ranging from temperance to Owenism, relied on education as a means of gradually securing the desired reforms. This climate of reformation was stimulated by the increased educational opportunities provided by the academy. The American Civil War, however, eroded this naive optimism of the first half of the nineteenth century. A more realistic and concerted effort was made in the second half of the century to replace the unwieldy academy with a more stable secondary institution, the public high school.

In the 1870s and 1880s, academies declined, and public high schools increased. During this same period, the United States was changing from a rural to an urban society. Because of a larger taxation base, urban populations could support extensive public secondary school systems. When individual economic entrepreneurship was replaced by the corporate economy, the entrepreneur's educational counterpart, the academy, became obsolete. The emerging public high school was better designed to satisfy the rising expectations of increasing city populations and the demands of corporate industry.

Rise of the High School

Although a small number of high schools had existed in the United States since the English Classical School of Boston was founded in 1821, the high school was not firmly established as the dominant American secondary educational institution until the second half of the nineteenth century. In the 1880s, the public high school eclipsed the academy as the major secondary school. The United States commissioner of education reported in 1889–1890 that 2,526 public high schools enrolled 202,063 students. In comparison, 94,391 students were enrolled in 1,632 private secondary schools and academies.[9]

The transformation of the United States from an agrarian to an urban and industrial society stimulated the rise of the public high school. In rural America, farming was a family enterprise in which children shared the work of adults. For example, the farm child was expected to help with chores, milk cows, and assist with harvesting. An industrialized society required more highly trained persons with increased vocational competence. The complexities of city life made the participation of youth in socioeconomic life increasingly indirect. Thus the school began to act as an intermediary between the worlds

[9] Edward Krug, *The Shaping of the American High School* (New York: Harper and Row, 1964), p. 5.

of the child and the adult. The high school, in particular, served to introduce adolescents to their adult roles.

The transformation from a rural to an urban society was also accompanied by an increase in information. The basic literacy provided by the common elementary school was no longer adequate to prepare a person for intelligent participation in industrial society. The high school attempted to provide increased educational experience to enable youth to assimilate and use the expanding areas of knowledge.

As an upward extension of the educational ladder, the high school could not proceed until elementary school development was well advanced. The high school movement received additional impetus from a growing popular sensitivity to the needs of children and youth. Child labor legislation, by removing adolescents from factories, made them available for school. Compulsory attendance laws were enacted to reduce juvenile delinquency and produce more worthy citizens by increasing educational opportunities.

In many respects, the late nineteenth-century high school movement was a continuation of the earlier common school movement, which had established the principle of state responsibility for tax-supported elementary education. In the closing decades of the nineteenth century, a concerted effort was made to extend public education to the secondary level. The decision of Justice Thomas C. Cooley of the Michigan State Supreme Court in the Kalamazoo case of 1874 was one of several precedents that extended the principle of public tax support to the high school. The group of taxpayers of the Kalamazoo school district who had initiated the suit to prevent the levying of a tax for high school support argued that its college preparatory curriculum did not merit public taxation.

Justice Cooley, basing his decision on the right of equality of educational opportunity, upheld the right of the Kalamazoo school district to tax for support of the high school. Since the state already maintained public elementary schools and colleges, Cooley stated that it would be inconsistent for the state to fail to provide the means of moving from elementary to higher education. The state was obligated to provide basic elementary education and was also responsible for maintaining equality of educational opportunity. According to Cooley, the school board had the right to levy taxes for high school support in order to facilitate the movement from elementary school to college.

Cooley's decision encouraged state legislatures to enact laws first permitting, and then compelling, local boards to establish high schools. When the high school became the dominant institution of secondary education, it was possible for a student to attend an articulated sequence of publicly supported and controlled institutions beginning with kindergarten, extending to elementary school, through high school, and reaching the university.

The early history of the American high school was a confusing one. While some educators defined it as a college-preparatory institution, others felt that it should be a "people's college" offering manual, industrial, commercial, and vocational programs. At first, the high school appeared to be repeating the history of the academy. A multiplicity of ill-defined curricula arose, often within the same school, where could be found such programs as ancient classical, business commercial, shorter commercial, English terminal, English science, and scientific.

In 1892, the National Education Association established the Committee of Ten to standardize the high school curriculum. This committee, headed by Charles W. Eliot, president of Harvard University, included William T. Harris, the United States commissioner of education among its members. Eliot, an important teacher in higher education, extended his interests to elementary and secondary education and sought to make the school's program more efficient. He guided the committee's decision toward two major recommendations: (1) an earlier introduction of several subjects in the upper elementary grades, and (2) no differentiation in the treatment of subjects for college preparatory and terminal students.[10] The Committee of Ten recommended eight years of elementary and four years of secondary education. Four separate curricula were recommended for the high school: classical, Latin-scientific, modern language, and English. Each curriculum included a foreign language, mathematics, English, science, and history. The modern language curriculum permitted the substitution of modern languages for Latin and Greek, and the Latin-scientific curriculum emphasized mathematics and science.

Subjects considered appropriate to high school study were classical and modern foreign languages, mathematics, natural and physical sciences, and history. High school students were to study a small number of subjects for longer periods of time. Every high school subject was to be taught in the same way to every student regardless of his future career.

Although the committee stated that the high school did not exist exclusively for college preparation, its report stressed college preparatory subjects. Basing its curricular recommendations on the psychology of mental discipline, the committee contended that these subjects could be used by both terminal and college preparatory students to train their powers of observation, memory, expression, and reasoning.[11]

[10] *Report of the Committee on Secondary School Studies* (Washington, D.C.: Government Printing Office, 1893), p. 17.
[11] French, *op. cit.*, pp. 113–114.

Higher Education

The colleges established in the English-speaking colonies of North America followed the patterns of the dominant English universities, Oxford and Cambridge. Attended by sons of wealthy families, the English universities emphasized liberal and professional studies. In addition to educating the scholar, professional, and theologian, the English universities sought to cultivate well-rounded "gentlemen." Early American higher education, following English antecedents, educated the elite classes rather than the common people. The American college of the colonial era had inherited, via the English experience, the basic structure of western European higher education, which had originated in the medieval universities of Paris, Salerno, and Bologna. The essential curriculum was the liberal arts: grammar, rhetoric, logic, music, astronomy, geometry, and mathematics.

Latin had been the language of instruction in the medieval universities, and the Renaissance of the fourteenth and fifteenth centuries reemphasized Latin and Greek as the languages of the educated man. The element of religion emerged with the Protestant Reformation, as the contending denominations used higher education to fix doctrinal commitment and train an educated ministry. Colonial higher education was thus derived from: (1) the structures of the medieval university, (2) classical Renaissance humanism, and (3) the zeal of the Protestant Reformation.

The Massachusetts Puritans, motivated by Calvinism, believed that an educated ministry was needed to establish Christianity in the wilderness. On October 28, 1636, the Massachusetts General Court created Harvard College. Since its primary function was to educate ministers, the college emphasized the ancient languages—Hebrew, Greek, and Latin—needed for scriptural scholarship. The entire program of studies rested on the foundation of Calvinist theology. After Cotton Mather had persuaded Elihu Yale to provide the initial endowment, orthodox Congregationalists established Yale in 1701 to preserve established religious doctrines.

The plantation-owning Southern gentlemen sent their sons to England for liberal and professional studies. In 1693, however, Virginia received a royal charter that established the College of William and Mary. Princeton was chartered in 1746 in New Jersey as a Presbyterian institution of higher education. King's College, destined to become Columbia, was chartered in 1754 to serve New York's Anglicans. The University of Pennsylvania was chartered in 1779. By the time of the Revolution, Dartmouth in New Hampshire, Brown in Rhode Island, and Rutgers in New Jersey had been established as institutions of higher learning.

Enrollments in the colonial colleges were small. Although the clientele came from the economically and socially favored classes, financial support was meager, and the quest for funds always a problem. Complaints about food, lodging, and quality of instruction were heard from students despite the authoritarianism of the institutions. The colonial college curriculum resembled the following:

First Year: Latin, Greek, logic, Hebrew, and rhetoric
Second Year: Greek, Hebrew, logic, and natural philosophy
Third Year: Natural philosophy, metaphysics, and moral philosophy
Fourth Year: Mathematics and review in Latin, Greek, logic and natural philosophy[12]

Although Washington, Jefferson, and Madison urged the establishment of a national university under federal auspices in the Constitutional Convention, the proposal was defeated. President Washington's first inaugural address again urged that one be established. Jefferson, too, as president, unsuccessfully recommended a national university. Although a national university was not established in the early national period, many colleges were founded. In addition to private colleges, numerous state colleges were chartered in the West and South. New denominational colleges were founded on the frontier to train an educated ministry.

The Dartmouth College case of 1819 established a precedent that guaranteed the independence of the private college from state control. After the state legislature of New Hampshire had taken control of Dartmouth College and established a new institution called the University of New Hampshire, Daniel Webster argued for the upholding of the original charter before the United States Supreme Court. Webster won a decision that affirmed the original charter. Chief Justice John Marshall, basing his decision on the contract clause of the federal constitution, held that the original charter granted by King George III was contractual and could not be impaired. The college was restored to the board of trustees and returned to its earlier status as a private educational institution.

The Dartmouth College decision ended state efforts to transform private educational institutions into state-controlled institutions and protected the continued existence of the independent privately controlled college. The Dartmouth College case strongly sanctioned the system of higher education in the United States, which produced both a private and a state-supported system of colleges.

[12] Frederick Rudolph, *The American College and University: A History* (New York: Knopf, 1962), pp. 25–26.

State, Denominational, and Land-Grant Colleges

Encouraged by a federal land-grant policy, new state colleges and universities were established in the early nineteenth century. Ohio was the first to benefit from this policy, which gave two townships for the establishment of a state university to each state entering the Union. The Ohio Enabling Act, which provided land grants for higher education, established a precedent followed as other states entered the Union.

Many of the early state colleges were located in inaccessible small rural towns, because college location was often determined by political expediency. Since college preparatory schools were usually lacking, many colleges had to maintain their own secondary departments. Usually, after a brief burst of enthusiasm, relationships between the legislatures and the state colleges were poor. Libraries, staffs, and facilities were usually inadequate.

Religious denominations also established private institutions of higher education in the first half of the nineteenth century, in the wave of religious revivalism discussed earlier in this chapter. Established to educate the denominations' ministers and build religious commitment among their members, these colleges also offered liberal arts and practical subjects. The denominational college movement was related to the parallel academy movement in secondary education. Thus, Presbyterians, Congregationalists, Roman Catholics, Methodists, Lutherans, Christian Disciples, Baptists, Episcopalians, Quakers, Mormons, and other denominations dotted the American landscape with numerous small liberal arts colleges.[13]

By the mid-nineteenth century, the federal government had established a number of specialized institutions of higher education whose programs were directed to specific educational objectives rather than to general higher education. The military academies at West Point and Annapolis are examples. In 1856, Columbia Institute for the Deaf, later named Gallaudet College, was established. After the Civil War, Howard University was established to educate the freed men.

A movement for the land-grant college and university culminating in the Morrill Act of 1862 was a phase of American educational history that demonstrated the interaction of social, economic, and political forces upon education. During the first half of the nineteenth century, classical and professional curricula dominated colleges, and agricultural and industrial instruction and research were neglected.

[13] For a discussion of denominational colleges, see Allan O. Pfinster, "A Century of the Church-Related College," in William Brickman and Stanley Lehrer (eds.), *A Century of Higher Education: Classical Citadel to Collegiate Colossus* (New York: Society for the Advancement of Education, 1962).

In the early 1850s, Jonathan Baldwin Turner proposed that industrial colleges be established with funds from federal land grants, believing that such institutions would contribute to agricultural and industrial programs.[14] Following the precedents of the earlier general-purpose land grants to the states, Justin S. Morrill, a Vermont congressman, sponsored a land-grant act to encourage agricultural and mechanical instruction. The Morrill Act was designed to encourage the development of practical instruction in agriculture and industry at the college level.

Although President Buchanan, a strict constitutional interpreter, vetoed the act, it was signed by the more liberal President Abraham Lincoln in 1862. The Morrill Act granted each state 30,000 acres of public land for each senator and representative in Congress, based on the apportionment of 1860.[15] The income from this land grant was to support at least one college devoted to agricultural and mechanical instruction. In 1890, the second Morrill Act provided direct grants of $15,000, to be increased annually to a maximum of $25,000, to support land-grant colleges and universities. This act also created similar institutions for Negroes in states that prohibited their enrollment in existing land-grant institutions. The federal government specifically required that land-grant colleges provide instruction in military training as well as agricultural and mechanical subjects. The United States, emergent as a world power, needed more trained military officers than could be supplied by the military academies and came to rely more on the Reserve Officers' Training Corps.

The Morrill Acts were essentially responses to the rapid developments in industry and agriculture in the second half of the nineteenth century. For farmers and laborers, the land-grant college extended economic opportunity and reflected the democratic, egalitarian, and populist trends in the nation. The industrial college concept was an agrarian reaction against the classical domination of higher education. The equalization of educational opportunity provided by the land-grant college reflected populist demands for the democratization of American economic and political life. Although populism was a last major agrarian assertion against the growing urbanization of the United States, business and industrial interests, otherwise opponents of agrarian radicalism, supported the land-grant college as an invaluable instrument in industrializing America. In spite of this cooperation, the agricultural interests dominated at first. Land-grant colleges were established in rural areas, and strong pressures were exerted on them to develop a "science of agriculture."

[14] Allan Nevins, *The State Universities and Democracy* (Urbana: University of Illinois Press, 1962), p. 14.
[15] Benjamin F. Andrews, *The Land Grant of 1862 and the Land-Grant College* (Washington, D.C.: Government Printing Office, 1918), pp. 7–8.

Since the passage of the first Morrill Act over a hundred years ago, land-grant institutions have been established throughout the United States. Examples of such universities are Maine, founded in 1865; Illinois and West Virginia, 1867; California, 1868; Nebraska, 1869; Ohio State, 1870; and Arkansas, 1871. Among the agricultural and mechanical colleges are Purdue University, established in 1869; the Agricultural and Mechanical College of Texas, 1871; and the Alaska Agricultural College and School of Mines, 1922. Seventeen Southern states established land-grant colleges for Negroes under the provisions of the second Morrill Act of 1890.

The history of higher education in the United States is a record of American pragmatism, both in meeting the requirements of a changing society and in modifying European concepts to fit American needs. For example, the American university resulted from the imposition of the German graduate school upon the four-year English undergraduate college. In the period between the Civil War and World War I, American higher education was influenced by the nineteenth-century German university, which emphasized *Lehrfreiheit und Lernfreiheit,* freedom to teach and freedom to learn. Such universities as Berlin, Halle, Göttingen, Bonn, and Munich emphasized scholarly research. Using the seminar, laboratory, and lecture, the graduate faculty, holders of the doctorate of philosophy, guided research. In the late nineteenth century, many American professors completed their education with residence in a German university and, upon returning to the United States, sought to shape American higher education in the German pattern. For example, Daniel Coit Gilman of Johns Hopkins and Charles W. Eliot of Harvard sought to develop their institutions into centers of graduate study and research. Johns Hopkins University, founded in Baltimore in 1876, became the American prototype of the German university. Here instruction took the form of lectures to large groups and seminars in which a professor and a small number of graduate students pursued rigorous study and research. The Hopkins methods were emulated by the graduate schools of Harvard, Yale, Columbia, Princeton, and Chicago. Abraham Flexner, a noted student of higher education, urged scholars to: (1) conserve and interpret knowledge and ideas, (2) search for truth, and (3) prepare students to carry on this research.[16] The German emphasis on scholarship and research dominated the American university as the graduate faculty sought to pursue truth and advance knowledge.

[16] Abraham Flexner, *Universities: American, English, German* (New York: Oxford University Press, 1930), pp. 73–74.

Teacher Education

With the institutional growth of American education and the wide-spread acceptance of public support and control of schools, a parallel interest developed in teacher education since the success of the ladder concept depended on an available supply of qualified teachers. Mann and Barnard had urged the establishment of institutions for teacher education. The development of normal schools and teachers' colleges and the discipline of professional education were integral phases in the history of American teacher education.

During the colonial period, teachers varied greatly in personal and educational qualifications. Those in the lower schools were often poorly educated with only rudimentary knowledge of reading, writing, and arithmetic. Some teachers were bond servants; others were students of the ministry or the law who used teaching as a means of support until they could enter these professions. Teacher certification varied from colony to colony. In New England, school committees certified the teacher with the approval of the town minister. In the parochial schools of the middle colonies, the society or church supporting the school approved the teacher's appointment. In the southern colonies, the tutor was selected by the family that employed him. Generally speaking, certification of the elementary teacher was based first on the candidate's religious and political orthodoxy and then on his skill in teaching reading, writing, arithmetic, and religion. The Latin grammar master, who needed a knowledge of Latin and Greek, was usually a college graduate. As a respected member of colonial society, he had a higher social status than the elementary teacher.

During the nineteenth century, American elementary education gained impetus from the common school movement. The leaders of the movement realized that the success of public education would depend upon qualified teachers. Among those advocating professional teacher education was Samuel Hall, a Congregational minister who conducted a private academy. His *Lectures to School-Masters on Teaching* (1833) revealed the plight of common school education in early nineteenth-century New England.[17] Many communities were unwilling to support schools adequately. Moreover, political and religious divisions in the school districts weakened community commitment to popular education. Finally, serious deficiencies existed in teacher qualifications. Hall argued that institutions should be established to educate teachers in the basic skills, literature, teaching method, educational philosophy, and school government.

[17] Samuel Hall, *Lectures to School-Masters on Teaching* (Boston: Carter, Hendee, 1833), pp. 20–21.

One of the major proponents of teacher education was James G. Carter, a Massachusetts legislator who urged establishment of normal schools in Massachusetts and introduced the legislation creating the State Board of Education, of which Horace Mann was the first secretary in 1837. Influenced by Carter and Mann, Massachusetts led in establishing normal schools, and its early ones offered a curriculum consisting of reading, writing, grammar, arithmetic, geography, spelling, composition, vocal music, drawing, physiology, algebra, philosophy, methodology, and scriptural reading.

Other states followed the Massachusetts pattern of normal school teacher education. The New York legislature authorized a normal school at Albany for the "instruction and practice of teachers of common schools." David Perkins Page, head of the school, wrote *Theory and Practice of Teaching or the Motives and Methods of Good School-Keeping* (1847), a standard work in teacher education. Stressing practice teaching in a demonstration school, Page believed that teachers needed experience under classroom conditions. Henry Barnard's *Normal Schools, and Other Institutions, Agencies, and Means Designed for the Professional Education of Teachers* (1851) compiled a literature on teacher education.

The Midwestern and Western states followed the East in establishing normal schools. By 1875, normal schools existed throughout the United States. The curriculum, which was usually completed in two years, consisted of a review of the basic common school subjects, lectures on school-keeping, and practice teaching in a model school under faculty direction. Normal schools initiated the idea of professional teacher preparation and were transitional institutions that eventually became teachers' colleges.

After the Civil War, colleges and universities gradually recognized teacher education. The emergence of the high school as a public secondary school contributed to this belated recognition. Increasing high school enrollments at the turn of the century created a demand for qualified secondary school teachers that was met in two ways: (1) normal schools evolved into four-year degree-granting colleges; and (2) established colleges and universities added departments or colleges of education. The acceptance of pedagogy as a subject of study frequently precipitated academic warfare as some of the traditionalists opposed the new discipline. The University of Iowa established the first permanent chair of pedagogy in 1873, followed by Wisconsin University in 1879, and Indiana and Cornell in 1886. In 1892, Teachers College became a part of Columbia University. By 1900, many colleges and universities were offering programs in teacher education.

Meanwhile, normal schools were developing into teachers' colleges. A large number of them made the transition in the first half of the twentieth century. This transition generally followed a pattern of (1) raising entrance requirements to include high school graduation, (2) adding liberal arts to the courses in professional education, (3) lengthening the program from two to four years, (4) including work in educational theory, (5) receiving degree-granting power, and (6) improving faculties. After World War II, many teachers' colleges became state colleges and universities that granted degrees in the liberal arts, sciences, and other areas as well as in professional education.

In 1890, the superintendent of schools in New York, Andrew Draper, argued for the professionalization of teaching. In outlining a program of professional preparation that included educational psychology, philosophy of education, history of education, and instructional methodology, Draper said:

> . . . a teaching profession cannot be established on a basis which only covers the work of the common schools. The mere knowledge that is to be conveyed to the child is not all that is required on the part of the teacher. A teaching profession will be controlled by the same inexorable laws as hedge about the other professions. In advance of professional training there must be a scholarship foundation, adequate in extent, and sufficiently well laid to place individual teachers, not a few, but all of them, on an equal footing, and in comfortable relations with the ministers and physicians, and architects and engineers, and which will make sure that the mental equipment of the collective body is at no disadvantage in comparison with that of the entire body of persons composing the other professions.[18]

As a result of the work of Draper and others, a body of professional literature emerged. The Herbartian movement, led by Frank and Charles McMurry, Charles De Garmo, C. C. Van Liew, and Elmer Brown, introduced the concepts of apperception, correlation, concentration, cultural epochs, and interest into educational literature. The Herbartians enriched the curriculum to include literature, history, and nature study. The National Herbartian Society, organized in 1892, sought to advance the study of education. In the scientific movement in education, the development of statistical methods for measurement and testing was aided by E. L. Thorndike's work, *An Introduction to the Theory of Mental and Social Measurements* (1904). J. M. Rice also contributed to the study of scientific measurement with tests designed to study spelling achievement.

[18] Andrew S. Draper, *A Teaching Profession: An Address Before the Massachusetts State Teachers' Association, at Worcester, Massachusetts,* November 28, 1890 (Albany, N.Y.: Weed, Parsons, 1890), p. 10.

Conclusion

During the nineteenth century, education in the United States assumed its essential structure. First, the common school was established as the basic institution of elementary education. Secondary education was much slower in its movement to the public realm. For a major part of the nineteenth century, the private academy dominated secondary education. Near the end of the century, it was replaced by a public institution, the high school. The early state colleges established after the Revolution were evidence of the public interest in higher education. After the Civil War, the Morrill Act provided a major impetus to the growth of state higher education.

American education reflected many of the trends that had affected European education in the nineteenth century. Politically, the century was dominated by liberal forces in France, England, and the United States. Popular education was a reflection of liberal attitudes that encouraged an educated citizenry. The century was also a period of intensive industrialization on both sides of the Atlantic, and the elaboration of secondary and higher educational institutions was a response to the need for more highly trained and sophisticated technicians and professionals.

Although it has been exaggerated by most American educational historians, the basic contrast between the American theory of the educational ladder and the dual system of European education must be made. It should be pointed out, however, that much of the equality of educational opportunity that American educators found in their system was theoretical rather than concrete reality.

If the nineteenth century was a time for the establishment of American educational institutions, then the twentieth century was a period of elaboration and refinement of these institutions. Chapter 23 will deal with the further development of American education in the twentieth century.

Suggested Readings

Allen, Hollis P. *The Federal Government and Education*. New York: McGraw-Hill, 1950.

Andrews, Benjamin F. *The Land Grant of 1862 and the Land-Grant College*. Washington, D.C.: Government Printing Office, 1918, No. 13.

Axt, Richard G. *The Federal Government and Financing Higher Education*. New York: Columbia University Press, 1952.

Bailyn, Bernard. *Education in the Forming of American Society.* New York: Random House, 1960.

Barnard, Henry. *Normal Schools, and Other Institutions, Agencies, and Means Designed for the Professional Education of Teachers.* Hartford, Conn.: Case, Tiffany, 1851.

Borrowman, Merle L. *Teacher Education in America: A Documentary History.* New York: Teachers College Press, Columbia University, 1965.

Brickman, William F., and Stanley Lehrar (eds.). *A Center of Higher Education: Classical Citadel to Collegiate Colossus.* New York: Society for the Advancement of Education, 1962.

Brubacher, John S. *Henry Barnard on Education.* New York: McGraw-Hill, 1931.

Brunner, Henry S. *Land-Grant Colleges and Universities, 1862–1962.* Washington, D.C.: Government Printing Office, 1962.

Burton, Warren. *The District School As It Was.* Boston: Lee and Shepard, 1897.

Butts, R. Freeman. *The College Charts Its Course: Historical Conceptions and Current Proposals.* New York: McGraw-Hill, 1939.

————. *The American Tradition in Religion and Education.* Boston: Beacon Press, 1960.

Cremin, Lawrence. *The American Common School.* New York: Teachers College, Columbia University, 1951.

Cubberley, Ellwood P. *Readings in Public Education in the United States.* Boston: Houghton Mifflin, 1934.

————. *Public Education in the United States.* Boston: Houghton Mifflin, 1947.

Curti, Merle. *The Social Ideas of American Educators.* New York: Littlefield, Adams, 1959.

Danforth, Eddy, Jr. *College for our Land and Time: The Land Grant Idea in American Education.* New York: Harper, 1956.

Draper, Andrew S. *A Teaching Profession: An Address Before the Massachusetts State Teachers' Association, at Worcester, Massachusetts, November 28, 1890.* Albany, N.Y.: Weed, Parsons, 1890.

Flexner, Abraham. *Universities: American English German.* New York: Oxford University Press, 1930.

French, William M. *American Secondary Education.* New York: Odyssey, 1957.

Gutek, Gerald. *An Historical Introduction to American Education.* New York: Crowell, 1970.

Hall, Samuel. *Lectures to School-Masters, on Teaching.* Boston: Carter, Hendee, 1833.

Harper, Charles R. *A Century of Public Teacher Education.* Washington, D.C.: National Education Association, 1939.

Katz, Michael B. *The Irony of Early School Reform: Educational Innovation in Mid-Nineteenth Century Massachusetts.* Cambridge, Mass.: Harvard University Press, 1968.

Nevins, Allan. *The State Universities and Democracy.* Urbana: University of Illinois Press, 1962.

Page, David P. *Theory and Practice of Teaching or The Motives and Methods of Good School-Keeping.* New York: A. S. Barnes, 1885.

Report of the Committee of Ten on Secondary School Studies. Bureau of Education Bulletin No. 205. Washington, D.C.: Government Printing Office, 1893.

Ross, Earle D. *Democracy's College: The Land Grant Movement in the Formative Stage.* Ames: Iowa State College Press, 1942.

Rudolph, Frederick. *The American College and University: A History.* New York: Knopf, 1962.

Sizer, Theodore R. *The Age of the Academies.* New York: Bureau of Publications, Teachers College, Columbia University, 1962.

Tewksbury, Donald G. *The Founding of American Colleges and Universities Before the Civil War.* New York: Bureau of Publications, Teachers College, Columbia University, 1932.

Thwing, Charles F. *A History of Higher Education in America.* New York: Appleton, 1906.

CHAPTER 23

Twentieth-Century American Education

By the end of the nineteenth century, the basic institutional patterns of American education had been established. The twentieth century was a time when these institutions were further developed and elaborated. Once the foundations had been laid, the task was to improve the quality of instruction and interinstitutional articulation. During the twentieth century, the major trends in American education were: (1) John Dewey's development of experimentalist educational philosophy; (2) the rise of progressive education; (3) the acceptance of the high school as the major institution of secondary education; (4) the quantitative and qualitative extension of higher education; (5) a further development of teacher education; (6) a movement to achieve racially integrated schools in an integrated society. These major trends will be treated in this chapter.

John Dewey's Experimentalism

John Dewey (1859–1952) exercised tremendous influence on the development of twentieth-century American educational theory. A keen observer, critic, and theorist of American society, Dewey was trained in formal philosophy and devoted his efforts to elaborating a philosophy of education. A prolific author, he wrote *The School and Society* (1898), which recounted his educational practices at the Laboratory School of the University of Chicago. His *How We Think* (1910) stressed problem-solving as the method of complete inquiry. *Individualism Old and New* (1929) investigated recent American social change. *Art as Experience* (1934) treated the aesthetic dimension. Dewey's major statement of educational theory was *Democracy and Education* (1916).

As a graduate student in philosophy at Johns Hopkins University, Dewey studied with Hegelian idealists, who dominated the philosophy departments of American universities at the end of the nineteenth century. Darwinism, however, was more significant than Hegelianism to Dewey. Darwin's evolutionary theory had postulated an environment in which organisms must adapt to survive. For Dewey, the terms "organism" and "environment" were crucial to educational philosophy. The organism, a living creature possessing a set of impulses or drives designed to maintain its life, lives in an environment that both threatens and nourishes its ongoing existence.

According to Dewey, the human organism encounters problematic situations that threaten its ongoing existence. The successful person solves these problems that block activity. Man's interaction with his environment constitutes experience, and each successive problem-solving episode builds a transactional network between the individual and his environment. Man lives in a social as well as a physical environment and forms life-promoting groups. Such human association enriches experience by providing opportunities for increased human interaction where individual experiences grow more complex and hence provide greater opportunities for growth. Human intelligence is the sum total of this shared experience.

Dewey felt that all human association is educative. To ensure cultural continuity, the social group uses education to transmit group experience from the mature members of society to the immature. To put it another way, education is a form of cultural imposition. Occurring at a particular time and place, group experience is imposed upon the children of the cultural group. Without this necessary transmission, each generation would revert to savagery. Formal education is the deliberate process of introducing the young to their culture by providing the tools needed for participation and communication in group life.

Dewey regarded formal education as a selective process. Culture includes the entire experience of the human race. While parts of this experience are valuable, other aspects are detrimental to human growth and association. The school, the specialized social agency for enculturating the young, has a threefold function: to simplify, purify, and balance the cultural heritage that it transmits to the immature members of society. To simplify, the school selects parts of the culture and classifies them into units appropriate to the learner's maturity and readiness. To purify, the school emphasizes those parts of the cultural heritage that have greatest social value and eliminates those judged to be socially detrimental. To balance, the school integrates the selected, simplified, and purified experiences into a harmonious whole that will produce integrated individuals within an integrated environment. In Deweyite terms, the school is a simplified, purified, and balanced environment in which children encounter and solve problems that add to this experience.

Dewey believed that the scientific method, broadly conceived, is man's most accurate and efficient means of directing the process of change. His "complete act of thought," or problem-solving method, involves five steps:

1. Perplexity, confusion, and doubt caused by involvement in a situation whose full character is undetermined. In this first phase, the person's activity is blocked by his uncertainty about the nature of the obstacle blocking the experiential course of events.
2. A conjectural anticipation that involves a tentative interpretation of the given elements of the problematic situation and attributes to them a tendency to effect certain consequences. In other words, the learner defines the problems and locates the difficulty.
3. A careful survey including an examination, inspection, exploration, and analysis of all pertinent data that define and clarify the problem. This phase involves a consideration and investigation of the skills and knowledge that will aid in solving the problem.
4. An elaboration of tentative hypotheses that might solve the problem.
5. Testing the projected hypothesis to secure the desired result. If the problem is solved, then the learner resumes activity until he encounters another problem.[1]

Dewey's "complete act of thought" became the basis of the activity method of learning (or inquiry approach) in which students solve problems based on their interests and needs by using scientific procedure. As a result of learning this process, the child is expected to transfer it to situations in and out of school.

Problem-solving requires internal self-discipline rather than the type of external coercion often administered by teachers in traditional schools in the belief that the child will eventually internalize it. Dewey disagreed with the traditionalists and asserted that discipline comes from the problem itself and is internal to the requirements of the task posed by the problem. Instead of applying external coercion, the teacher should guide the learner in solving problems.

As the student uses the scientific method, the cooperative experience of working with others in associated problem-solving groups enriches his experience. As part of the group, he learns to cooperate with others and to discuss, deliberate, and act. Dewey's method of education stresses the cooperative act, based on shared experience and the use of democratic practices.

For Dewey, the end of education is simply growth, which leads to the direction and control of subsequent experience. Growth involves the ability to relate experiences and to use them. Learning by experi-

[1] John Dewey, *Democracy and Education* (New York: Macmillan, 1964), p. 150.

ence through problem-solving means that education, like life, is a process that involves the continuous reconstruction of experience.

From 1896 to 1903, Dewey directed the University of Chicago Laboratory School, where the chief object was to create a free and informal learning community in which each student was a participant. The emphasis in the school was upon practical and constructive activities that appealed "to the child's social sense and to his regard for thorough and honest work."[2]

In 1903, Dewey left the Chicago Laboratory School to return to his work in philosophy and education. As a philosophy professor at Columbia University, he continued to elaborate his experimentalism, a philosophy that influenced American education and contributed to the "new education" of the twentieth century.

Dewey was familiar with the educational reforms of the nineteenth-century Swiss educator Pestalozzi, and some interesting similarities existed in their educational philosophies. For example, both urged that learning originate in the learner's immediate experience. Pestalozzi stressed that instruction begin in the child's home and proceed from the immediate to the more distant environment. Dewey recommended the maintenance of an "experiential continuum" in which the learner's past experience should be drawn upon in his present situation. Pestalozzi's students at Stans, Burgdorf, and Yverdon engaged in social activities, as did Dewey's students at the Chicago Laboratory School. Although Dewey's pragmatic educational philosophy differed from Pestalozzi's obscure romantic naturalism, both educators emphasized the learner's interests, needs, and experiences.

Dewey was also familiar with the educational theory of Herbert Spencer, the English Social Darwinist. While he could agree with Spencer's stress on science and useful activities, Dewey could not accept Spencer's idealization of a rugged individualism based on the survival of the fittest. Dewey's emphasis on cooperative social activities was the educational counterpart of his reformed Darwinism, which envisioned a sharing and cooperative society.

The Progressive Movement in American Education

While Dewey's pragmatic philosophy contributed to American educational progressivism, the two movements were not entirely synonymous. Experimentalism was a systematic educational theory based on philosophical premises. Although progressive education might have embraced experimentalism, it was a broad and amorphous movement extending back to the late eighteenth- and early nineteenth-century

[2] K. C. Mayhew and A. C. Edwards, *The Dewey School* (New York: Appleton-Century, 1936), p. 32.

naturalistic educators Rousseau, Pestalozzi, and Froebel, who developed educational theories that opposed traditional school practice. The eighteenth-century Enlightenment and nineteenth-century social reformism contributed the concept of "progress," by which man, using reason and science, could shape his environment. Educational reformers claimed that a natural educational methodology could free man by advancing him along the path to a better world.

It should be noted that the American progressive educators prescribed many of the same reforms for twentieth-century schools that Pestalozzi had advocated in the nineteenth century. Both believed that direct experience in the immediate environment was the proper beginning of instruction. They agreed that traditional schools had overemphasized the child's intellectual development and had neglected the cultivation of his physical and emotional well-being.

In the United States, the early twentieth century has been referred to as the era of the "progressive movement," when political reformers fought against corruption, decay, and monopoly. Robert LaFollette, Woodrow Wilson, and Theodore Roosevelt expressed the progressive political philosophy. Jane Addams, Lincoln Steffens, and Oliver Wendell Holmes, Jr., applied progressive ideas to social work, journalism, and law, respectively. The progressive era in education came in the 1920s and 1930s, lagging behind political progressivism by a decade.

Progressive education was a reaction against conventional schooling's prescribed curriculum with its emphasis on basic skills, books, examinations, and discipline. Although they were often merely reacting against traditional school practices, the progressives also developed their own educational philosophy and methodology. They established a number of private schools where they fostered a more permissive attitude to the child and encouraged activities to stimulate his creativity.

Although the American progressive educators were devoted to the cause of liberalizing education, they were not a monolithic group. Some progressives drew their inspiration from European reformers such as Pestalozzi, Froebel, and Montessori. Others were simply interested in creating a school that would follow the child's interests and needs. Some progressives were influenced by Freud, who had warned against repressing the child's instincts. Stanwood Cobb brought progressive educators together in the Progressive Education Association in 1918, and the Association began to publish a journal called *Progressive Education* in 1924, which disseminated the views of its members. Among the major principles of progressive educators were the following:

1. Encouragement of child freedom.
2. Creation of a new school which would contribute to the development of the whole child and not merely his intellect.

3. The use of activities designed to give the child a direct experience with his world.
4. Cooperation between the school and the child's home.

The progressives believed that educational objectives were not to be specified in advance but should originate in the learner's own interests and needs. They felt that learning is a cooperative activity which is to be shared by students, teachers, and members of the community. Progressive educators generally have rejected classroom competition as unhealthy for the learner's social and psychological growth and believe that students learn best by cooperating and sharing their ideas and experiences. In the progressive classroom, the teacher is to direct activities rather than act as a disciplinarian.

William Heard Kilpatrick

One of the great popularizers of Dewey's experimentalism was William Heard Kilpatrick. Born in rural Georgia in 1871, Kilpatrick taught in country schools and at Mercer College, where he rejected traditional education as characterized by a devitalized, bookish approach to knowledge. Centered in the past, bookish education was a mechanical affair imposed upon the child by an external authority. Kilpatrick accepted Dewey's pragmatism as a theoretical rationale to support his belief that education should arise from the learner's interests and needs.

As professor of education at Teachers College of Columbia University, Kilpatrick developed the project method, which elaborated Dewey's conception of scientific method. Basing his method on activities designed to elicit the learner's effort, Kilpatrick distinguished four classes of projects:

1. The constructive or creative project, in which students formulate a plan or design that they later concretize.
2. The appreciation project, whose purpose is the enjoyment of an aesthetic experience such as reading, art appreciation, or music.
3. The problem project, which involves the solving of an intellectual difficulty.
4. The drill project, which involves the learning of a specific skill such as swimming, typing, or writing.[3]

Kilpatrick's lectures at Teachers College attracted large numbers of students, many of whom became educational leaders and advocates of the project method. During the 1920s and 1930s, the method was very

[3] William H. Kilpatrick, "The Project Method," *Teachers College Record* 19 (September 1918), 319–335.

popular among progressive educators who wanted students to participate actively in learning. The group of students working on a project
was considered to be a kind of embryonic democratic society. If they
learned to use the scientific method in solving the group problem, it
was believed that the method could be employed in solving social,
political, and economic problems.

Progressivism: Child-Centered or Socially Centered?

Although Kilpatrick was concerned with both the individual child
and social problems, many progressive educators focused exclusively
on the child. During the depression of the 1930s, this child-centered
orientation was challenged by George S. Counts, who, in *Dare the
School Build a New Social Order?* (1932), urged progressive educators
to work for social reform through the schools.[4] Although the conflict
between the child-centered and the socially oriented factions weakened
progressivism, many of the pedagogical innovations suggested by progressive educators became school practices. After World War II, the
Progressive Education Association disbanded as a formal organization.

Among the critics of progressivism was a group of prominent educators, such as William Chandler Bagley and Isaac Kandel, who were
termed "essentialists." They believed that the most efficient means of
cultivating an intelligent citizenry was through systematic training in
what they deemed the essential subjects and skills: reading, writing,
arithmetic, history, English, and foreign languages. They emphasized
hard work and discipline and saw the school's function to be the transmission of the cultural heritage. They also opposed using the schools
as an instrument for effecting particular programs of social reform,
believing that it would politicize the school and lead to the indoctrination of students.

In the 1950s and early 1960s, Arthur Bestor, in *Educational Wastelands* (1953) and *The Restoration of Learning* (1955), attacked what
he saw as the "educational establishment." Bestor urged a return to
basic education grounded on subject matter. Max Rafferty, in *Suffer
Little Children* (1962), accused progressive educators of weakening
educational standards.

In progressive education, as in any reform movement, there were
extremists whose excesses did not represent the mainstream of the
movement. Reform movements sometimes attract adherents who do
not understand the meaning and program of the movement. Progressive education never dominated American public education. While
some public schools included problem-solving and projects in their programs, their curriculum continued to stress subjects and skills. The

---

[4] George S. Counts, *Dare the School Build a New Social Order?* (New York:
John Day, 1932).

leading progressive schools were private ones.

John Dewey, William H. Kilpatrick, and George S. Counts contributed to the formulation of an educational philosophy based upon the scientific method. The progressives sought to integrate theory and practice and recognized that the school was intimately related to society and that education was therefore a social enterprise. Just as the socially oriented progressives of the 1930s had urged the school to encourage social, economic, and political reform to aid in overcoming economic depression, educational leaders of the 1960s saw the school as an instrument of social and racial integration.

Progressive educators contributed to an enlightened conception of the child. Psychological principles were used to construct method. The stress on problem-solving activities encouraged a functional concept of knowledge as a working instrument by which man could direct the process of change and reshape the environment according to his own designs.

The High School

The high school had become the dominant institution of American secondary education in the years from 1880 to 1920, a period that coincided with the transition of the United States from an agricultural and rural to an urbanized and technological society. During this period, the high school had been primarily a college preparatory institution that placed curricular emphasis on Latin, modern foreign languages, mathematics, science, English, and history. This role of the high school was challenged, however, by those who advocated a more immediately vocational terminal institution, a "people's college." G. Stanley Hall, for example, led a small group of educators who sought to extend the "child study" movement to adolescence. They wanted the high school to respond to the interests and needs of adolescents. David Snedden and others proposed that "social efficiency" be used as criterion for the secondary school curriculum, according to which the inclusion of any subject matter could be justified only if it prepared the student as a citizen, earner, parent, and consumer.

In 1918, the National Education Association's Commission on the Reorganization of Secondary Education issued its "Cardinal Principles of Secondary Education," which listed seven goals of secondary education:

1. The providing of health instruction and the organizing of physical activities to promote hygienic habits.
2. The continued development of fundamental processes such as reading, writing, arithmetic, and communication skills.
3. The cultivation of attitudes that would make the individual a

worthy family member. For example, the social studies were to stress the home as the fundamental social institution; literature was to idealize the home; music and art were to result in a more aesthetic home life. Girls were to receive instruction in home economics and boys in the skills necessary to maintain their future households.

4. Vocational education to aid the individual in supporting himself and his family. This involved an assessment of the pupil's aptitudes, some study of various occupations, and the use of vocational guidance to help determine his career choice.

5. Civic education to encourage intelligent participation in public affairs. The social studies—history, geography, civics, and economics—were to stress good citizenship.

6. The use of leisure for recreation that enriched and enlarged the student's personality.

7. Emphasis on moral qualities that contributed to ethical character, personal responsibility and initiative, and the spirit of community service.

The commission's report recommended close cooperation and articulation between elementary, secondary, and higher educational institutions. It also emphasized the socially integrative function of the high school and recommended that a comprehensive school be developed as a desirable model for American secondary education. Theoretically, the comprehensive high school was to bring students of various socioeconomic classes together in a common educational environment, regardless of their future careers.

Although high school attendance had increased from 110,227 students in 1880 to 2,382,542 in 1920, George S. Counts concluded that the high school was a selective institution that served the upper socioeconomic classes.[5] He found that a close relationship existed between parental occupation and school attendance. More children of native-born parents attended than of immigrant parents. William M. French in *American Secondary Education* attributed the selective character of the high school to three factors: (1) immigrants from southern and eastern Europe lacked a tradition of secondary education; (2) hidden costs in the form of books, supplies, transportation, lunches, and clothing discouraged attendance; (3) rural districts often lacked the economic base to establish high schools.[6]

By 1930, the American high school had undergone a rapid democratization as it began to enroll adolescents from diverse socioeconomic

[5] George S. Counts, *The Selective Character of American Secondary Education* (Chicago: University of Chicago Press, 1922), p. 152.
[6] William M. French, *American Secondary Education* (New York: Odyssey Press, 1957), pp. 101–102.

backgrounds and to offer a wide range of curricula. The increase in public high school enrollments from 4,427,000 in 1930 to 12,310,000 in 1967 is an indication of its subsequent growth.

As the transitional institution between the elementary school and the college, the high school has been subjected to the demands of various special-interest groups. During World War I, for example, patriotic groups eliminated German as a foreign language from the curriculum. Physical education programs were also accelerated to improve the fitness of potential inductees into the armed services. In 1917, Congress enacted the Smith-Hughes Vocational Education Act to provide federal funds to states offering vocational studies. After World War II, high school curriculum-makers, concerned with an increase in juvenile delinquency, introduced programs designed to contribute to social adjustment. The Soviet space achievements of the 1950s, especially the launching of Sputnik, induced a critical deluge from commentators who found the high school program to be "watered-down" and pedagogically soft.

The Conant Reports

In 1958, James B. Conant, a former president of Harvard University, examined secondary education in *The American High School Today*.[7] In distinguishing between comprehensive and specialized high schools, Conant found that the former educated all adolescents in a given district, and the latter offered specialized vocational or academic curricula to selected students.

Conant examined the comprehensive high school and was generally satisfied with its condition. More than half its students were terminal ones who completed their formal education at graduation. College preparatory students were enrolled in appropriate subject matter curricula. Conant called the comprehensive high school an agency of social integration that developed democratic attitudes among students of different intellectual abilities and social backgrounds. He saw the comprehensive high school fulfilling three major functions: (1) providing general education for adolescents; (2) providing elective programs for terminal students; and (3) offering excellent college preparatory programs. Although he believed the comprehensive high school was fulfilling these functions adequately, Conant offered a number of recommendations for improving secondary education. He recommended counseling programs to aid students in electing courses based on their interests, aptitudes, and achievement. Individualized instruction and ability groupings were also recommended.

Conant further recommended a core curriculum of general education

7 James B. Conant, *The American High School Today* (New York: McGraw-Hill, 1959).

to be required of all students, consisting of four years of English, three or four years of social studies, and at least one year of mathematics and science. General education was to occupy half the student's time, with the remainder devoted to elective courses. School administrators were urged to assess community employment needs and introduce diversified vocational education programs to develop marketing skills in agriculture, trade, and industry. Conant's *The American High School Today* was a reasoned assessment of American secondary education. Written during a time of intense criticism, he presented a dispassionate and documented survey that supported the concept of the comprehensive high school and offered recommendations designed to improve it.

In *Slums and Suburbs* (1961), Conant examined contemporary problems of American education and found that metropolitan areas exhibited striking contrasts between impoverished slums and wealthy suburbs.[8] While suburban high schools emphasized academic preparation for college admission, economically deprived slum high schools, often in black ghettos, offered inadequate vocational programs. Only in moderately sized cities and consolidated rural districts did the genuinely comprehensive high school remain, where all tracks and curricula were within one school, bringing students together in the same educational environment. With the decline of the comprehensive high school in metropolitan areas, the populations of particular high schools were based largely on socioeconomic class. The integrative function of the high school was jeopardized, and the concept of the educational ladder was in danger of being replaced by a dual educational system with separate tracks for the upper and lower classes. Such a bifurcation could divide American society into two radically separated groups without a core of common values. In many large cities, socioeconomic segregation was directly related to de facto racial segregation, which further aggravated the situation.

Higher Education

The two major developments in American higher education in the twentieth century were the rapid increase in enrollment and the extensive expansion of the curriculum. Although college enrollments grew throughout the late nineteenth and early twentieth centuries, the greatest increase came after World War II. The curriculum expanded to include more professional, specialized, and technical courses. The twentieth-century university frequently offers courses ranging from business administration, nuclear physics, and hotel and restaurant management to the traditional liberal arts and sciences.

Robert Hutchins' *The Higher Learning in America* (1936), in attack-

[8] James B. Conant, *Slums and Suburbs* (New York: McGraw-Hill, 1961).

ing what he considered the confusion of American higher education, charged that the modern university had degenerated into a "service station" by catering to vocationalism and money-making.[9] Hutchins charged that overspecialization had decreased communication in the university. Antiintellectualism, based on crass utilitarianism, had replaced the theoretical and speculative inquiry that Hutchins believed essential to the cultivation of man's rationality. He argued for a university whose sole purpose was to pursue truth. In contrast, Hutchins' critics have argued that his conception of higher learning isolated the university from important social issues and conflicts. They held that the university should educate individuals in the specialized technologies needed in a scientific age.

Clark Kerr, a former president of the University of California, wrote that the American university had experienced two great transformations: the first at the close of the nineteenth century, when the land-grant movement and German intellectualism produced profound alterations, and the second after World War II, when the university began to educate masses of students and to engage in federally sponsored research.[10] President Kerr described the University of California as a "multiversity"—an institution with an operating budget of almost half a billion dollars, employing over 40,000 persons, operating in over one hundred locations, conducting projects in more than fifty foreign nations, offering 10,000 courses, and envisioning a future enrollment of 100,000 students. Such an institution was no longer a single community of scholars but rather a collection of communities united only by a common name and governing board. In coining the term "multiversity," Kerr wrote:

> The multiversity is an inconsistent institution. It is not one community but several—the community of the undergraduate and the community of the graduate; the community of the humanist, the community of the social scientist, and the community of the scientist; the communities of the professional schools; the community of all the nonacademic personnel; the community of the administrators.[11]

Kerr found several competitors for power in the multiversity:

1. Students, who demanded a greater voice in university affairs
2. The faculty, which possessed some authority over admissions, curricula, examinations, degree-granting, appointments, and academic freedom

[9] Robert M. Hutchins, *The Higher Learning in America* (New Haven, Conn.: Yale University Press, 1936).
[10] Clark Kerr, *The Uses of the University* (Cambridge, Mass.: Harvard University Press, 1963), pp. 86–87.
[11] *Ibid.*, pp. 18–19.

3. Public authorities, such as boards of trustees, state departments of finance, governors, and legislatures
4. Pressure groups, such as agricultural organizations, trade unions, business organizations, and the mass media
5. The university administration itself

Problems of Higher Education

Twentieth-century higher education in the United States has experienced a rapid increase in the numbers of students attending colleges and universities, as is demonstrated by the following statistics: in 1947, 2,238,226 students were enrolled in institutions of higher education; in 1957, 3,036,938; and in 1967, 6,348,000.[12] These increased enrollments severely tested higher education. Expenditures for construction, additional faculty, library expansion, and other college and university needs had to be increased to maintain educational opportunities. To allocate their resources efficiently, some states used expert planning to avoid duplication of facilities. Some states created extensive junior college systems to educate the increasing student population.

The historic decentralization of American higher education produced variations in size, organization, programs, faculties, and standards among the 1,300 degree-granting schools, colleges, and universities. Although most states have attempted to coordinate their higher educational resources, a number of problems complicated such planning. Large population movements, for example, changed educational needs. Although the United States was once a rural nation, its population today is concentrated mostly in large cities and their surrounding metropolitan areas. The original state colleges and universities were located in small towns, some distance from large cities.

The universities established extension branches to provide urban populations with opportunities for higher education. Existing private and denominational colleges and universities, which had often been the only institutions that served the higher educational needs in cities, continued to function in the private sector. Many state governments cooperated with their colleges and universities to devise master plans for future development. For example, California in 1959 established the Coordinating Council for Higher Education to advise the governing boards of the institutions and state officials on financing, functional differentiation, desirable changes in higher education programs, and planning for orderly growth and for the location of new facilities and programs.

[12] From Bureau of the Census estimates cited in B. J. Chandler, Daniel Powell, and William R. Hazard, *Education and the New Teacher* (New York: Dodd, Mead, 1971), p. 54.

California developed a state system of public higher education composed of junior colleges, state colleges, and the University of California.
The junior colleges offered vocational, technical, and arts courses and
also two-year programs of regular undergraduate instruction that
would enable the students to transfer to higher institutions. The state
colleges provided both undergraduate instruction and graduate instruction and awarded the master's degree in the liberal arts and sciences,
applied fields, education, and the professions. Although it also provides
instruction in the liberal arts and sciences, teaching, and the professions, only the University of California offers courses in law, medicine,
dentistry, veterinary medicine, and architecture, and it has sole authority to award the doctorate except in certain areas where a joint
degree is awarded with the state colleges. While California led in developing a master plan to coordinate higher education, other states
also established formal coordinating agencies, such as Texas in 1950,
Indiana in 1951, Wisconsin and Texas in 1955, and Utah in 1959.

Junior Colleges

A number of states have developed extensive junior, or community,
colleges, the most recent institution to appear in American higher
education. In the period from 1850 to 1920, several university presi-
dents such as Henry A. Tappan of Michigan, William W. Follwell of
Minnesota, William Rainey Harper of Chicago, and David Starr Jordan
of Stanford argued that the first two years of undergraduate instruction
should be offered in institutions other than universities so that their
faculties could concentrate on graduate instruction and research. For
example, President Harper of the University of Chicago in 1892 separated the first and last two years of instruction at his institution into
an "academic college" and a "university college." In 1896, these titles
were changed to "junior college" and "senior college." Harper regarded
the junior college as an extension of high school.[13]

The first American junior college was established in 1901 in Joliet,
Illinois, and following this example, others appeared throughout the
nation. From 1920 through 1970, the number of junior colleges steadily increased, but this growth did not free the university from providing basic undergraduate instruction as had been anticipated by Harper
and Jordan. Because of financial pressures, some four-year colleges
reduced their programs to two years during the depression of the 1930s.
Some technical high schools and institutions became junior colleges.
In 1922, 207 junior colleges enrolled 16,000 students. Although the
number of junior colleges had increased to 575 in 1939, the greatest
growth came after World War II. In 1950, the more than 600 two-year

[13] James W. Thornton, *The Community Junior College* (New York: Wiley,
1966), pp. 46–48.

colleges enrolled approximately 466,000 students. As of 1971, 960 junior and community colleges had been established with a total enrollment that exceeds 1,500,000 students.[14]

The contemporary American junior college, or community college, is a multifunctional institution providing the first two years of collegiate studies, upon completion of which students may transfer to four-year institutions. Moreover, it has responded to the need for technically trained subprofessionals. It enables students living at home and working part-time to receive a relatively inexpensive education. It also provides vocational and liberal arts courses for adults. As a community college, it serves as a cultural, educational, and civic center for the people in the community that it serves.

In many of the states that established master plans for higher education, the junior college has become a crucial component of the state educational system. By providing the first two years of education for students who later transfer to four-year colleges, it has alleviated some of the pressures of massive enrollment that have taxed four-year colleges and it has also provided instruction for many students who might have otherwise been denied the opportunity to attend college.

Student Unrest

During the 1960s, American colleges and universities were faced with problems of student unrest, which took the form of strikes, sit-ins, boycotts, and seizures of facilities. The forerunner of these various student movements occurred in 1965 at the Berkeley campus of the University of California. Some students there disputed with university officials over campus political activity and questioned the educational adequacy of the university. Some commentators on student unrest have interpreted such demonstrations as that of Berkeley as a sign of the alienation of youth. President Kerr of the University of California described student anxieties in the large university:

> The multiversity is a confusing place for the student. He has problems of establishing his identity and a sense of security within it. But it offers him a vast range of choices, enough literally to stagger the mind. In this range of choices he encounters the opportunities and the dilemmas of freedom. The casualty rate is high. The walking wounded are many. Lernfreiheit—the freedom of the student to pick and choose, to stay or move on—is triumphant.[15]

In *Education at Berkeley*, the Select Committee on Education of the University of California's Academic Senate reported that student unrest was a great national and international phenomenon that had

[14] Chandler, *et al., op. cit.*, p. 237.
[15] Kerr, *op. cit.*, p. 42.

reached crisis proportions. Although social, political, and cultural alterations had an impact on education, student discontent was also caused by the rapid growth of the student population, changes in social roles and expectations, and the changing temperament of a new generation of students. All of the major elements composing a university —teachers, students, knowledge, and society—were in an unprecedented state of change. The report stated that the modern university faced the very difficult task of preserving academic freedom while being open to change. To combat the students' sense of impersonality and alienation, the Select Committee recommended an increase of seminars and tutorials and of student participation in academic policy-making. Although some students criticized the university for overemphasizing research, the committee said that the close interpenetration of teaching and research created a sense of integration, unity, and coherence.[16]

Contemporary Teacher Education

American teacher education programs assumed definite patterns in the twentieth century. Increased public high school enrollments created a demand for more qualified secondary teachers. The child study movement, the work of G. Stanley Hall, and the progressive education movement contributed insights into the preparation of qualified elementary school teachers. While twentieth-century teacher education had improved over that of the nineteenth century, tremendous variations still existed in the teacher education programs and in the certification requirements of the different states.

Teacher education programs were generally organized into four major phases:

1. General education courses
2. Depth courses in which prospective secondary school teachers specialized in an academic subject, such as English or history, and elementary school teachers studied the subjects and skills of the elementary school
3. Professional education courses in the historical, philosophical, or sociological foundations of education, educational psychology, and teaching methods
4. Laboratory experiences with children and youth culminating in supervised student teaching

Evolving from the early nineteenth-century normal schools, teacher education had emerged slowly and it was not always carefully

16 Charles Muscatine *et al., Education at Berkeley: Report of the Select Committee on Education* (Berkeley: University of California Printing Department, 1966), pp. 3–4.

planned. In addition, the more than 1,100 colleges and universities providing teacher education had their own particular programs.

Teacher education reflected the requirements for teacher certification. In the eighteenth century, religious and political conformity rather than pedagogical competence was the usual requirement for teaching. As public education developed in the nineteenth century, government agencies began to control teacher certification—the granting of a license to prospective teachers attesting to some degree of competency. Districts, towns, townships, and counties were all licensing teachers, and a variety of teacher certificates existed. Some of the licensing agencies administered examinations to determine teaching competency, but, generally, normal school graduates were certified without examination. Applicants for teaching positions without educational preparation or experience were usually certificated upon successful completion of an examination.

Near the end of the nineteenth century, state superintendents or state boards of education began to certify teachers. Certification meant that the teacher possessed a license, a valid certificate, to teach. Statewide certification was a more uniform procedure than that of the numerous local districts. However, each state established its own regulations governing the issuing of certificates and the qualifications needed to obtain them. State certification had a very important impact on teacher education, since it established educational standards and shaped programs of teacher preparation.

The requirement that the teacher possess a bachelor's degree appeared late in the nineteenth century when, in 1896, Utah became the first state to require a degree for high school teaching. By 1920, ten states had such a requirement. In 1950, all states required a college degree as a standard qualification for secondary school teachers.[17]

State patterns for teacher certification are exceedingly complex, with little uniformity from state to state. Variations exist as to the nature of professional preparation, the kinds of certificates granted, and the duration of their validity. Despite these variations, the following are common:

1. Centralization of certification authority in state departments of education
2. Issuance of certificates for definite subjects or specified grade levels
3. A minimum requirement of a bachelor's degree for certification
4. Requirement of specific courses in professional education and in the academic subject matter.

[17] Walter K. Beggs, *The Education of Teachers* (New York: Center for Applied Research in Education, 1965), pp. 50–51.

To introduce some professional uniformity into teacher certification, the National Education Association established the Commission on Teacher Education and Professional Standards (TEPS Commission) in 1946 to conduct a continuous examination of the selection, recruitment, preparation, certification, and in-service training of teachers, and the advancement of educational standards. The National Council for Accreditation of Teacher Education (NCATE) was established in 1952 to accredit the teacher education programs offered by colleges and universities. Proponents of NCATE view the council as a means of providing national standards for teacher education that would induce the states to license automatically all graduates who have successfully completed the accredited programs.

The Great Debate of the 1950s

During the 1950s, a great debate was waged that focused public attention on American education. Like other major developments in American education, such as the evolution of the common school and the high school, the debate of the 1950s related to major social, political, economic, and international trends. The Soviet successes in space, particularly the orbiting of Sputnik, precipitated a critical examination of the quality of American education. Admiral Hyman G. Rickover in a comparison of European and American education found American education inadequate. He and others alleged that the public schools failed to identify academically talented students and to provide challenges for them.[18] He urged an emphasis on mathematics and science to meet the Soviet challenge and to improve the academic quality of American education.

In the period after World War II, profound social and economic changes were occurring in American life. Some critics accused progressive educators of weakening the intellectual content of American schools. The educational debate of the 1950s also involved a series of charges and countercharges in the continuing feud between liberal arts and education professors. Historically, the liberal arts conception of teacher education had dominated college teacher preparation and exerted considerable influence over the preparation of secondary school teachers. This tradition often conceived of education as the transmission of knowledge and intellectual discipline. In contrast, professional education originated in normal schools and the teachers' colleges. The professional educators who emphasized child study strongly influenced elementary school teaching and also affected secondary education by stressing adolescent development. American teacher preparation was an often uneasy merger of these traditions.

[18] Hyman G. Rickover, *Education and Freedom* (New York: Dutton, 1959).

After the Supreme Court outlawed school racial segregation based on law in *Brown v. the Board of Education of Topeka* in 1954, equality of educational opportunity for blacks and other minority groups became a nationwide concern. In the 1960s, attention was focused on improving the conditions of the culturally disadvantaged in both urban and rural areas. Civil rights leaders and others demanded a reassessment of the school and its program.

The late 1950s and the 1960s have been referred to as a period of "revolution in American education." In assessing American education, Francis Keppel, U.S. Commissioner of Education, spoke of two revolutions in American education: the quantitative and the qualitative. The quantitative revolution ensured every American child an education. It began in the common elementary school, reached upward to the high school, and was being extended to higher education. According to Keppel, the second revolution involved improving the quality of education for all Americans.[19]

After World War II, American education faced acute quantitative and qualitative challenges. In the early 1950s, the entry of the wartime babies into the schools created unprecedented population pressures on the educational system. With a serious shortage of teachers and classrooms, schools resorted to double sessions in emergency facilities. To cope with the emergency, more buildings, classrooms, and teachers were made available. Near the end of the 1950s, the emphasis shifted to problems of providing quality education. Educators began to develop new programs to improve instruction and to devise new patterns of school organization. Instructional media and technology were used for educational purposes. Such private foundations as the Fund for the Advancement of Education and the Carnegie Corporation encouraged research and experimentation in teacher education. The federal government supported projects to improve instruction in the arts, languages, composition, social studies, and vocational studies. The National Science Foundation encouraged experimentation to develop new mathematical, biological, and physical science curricula.

Federal Aid to Education

In the late 1950s, Congress became favorable to increased federal support for education. The National Defense Education Act, passed in 1958 and extended in 1964, was designed to improve education in science, foreign languages, and mathematics. The Act supported guidance, counseling, and testing programs and vocational education; it also provided funds for research, student loans, and graduate fellow-

[19] Francis Keppel, *The Necessary Revolution in American Education* (New York: Harper & Row, 1966), p. 1.

ships. In order to keep teachers aware of recent developments in education, the Act provided funds for summer institutes that were held at colleges and universities. This legislation aided all levels of education.

President Kennedy, in 1962, advised Congress of the advances that had been made in discovering and transmitting knowledge. Asserting that the nation needed to improve the quality of its education, he urged that teacher education institutions be given federal aid to examine and improve their programs. President Kennedy saw the teaching profession as the crucial component in providing quality education:

> . . . the key to educational quality is the teaching profession. About 1 out of every 5 of the nearly 1,600,000 teachers in our elementary and secondary schools fails to meet full certification standards for teaching or has not completed 4 years of college work. Our immediate concern should be to afford them every possible opportunity to improve their professional skills and their command of the subjects they teach.[20]

Although the National Defense Education Act was an extensive commitment of federal support for education, many observers believed that higher education remained a critical area. President Kennedy, in 1963, spoke of the problems facing higher education:

> Now a veritable tidal wave of students is advancing inexorably on our institutions of higher education, where the annual costs per student are several times as high as the cost of a high school education, and where these costs must be borne in large part by the student or his parents. Five years ago the graduating class of the secondary schools was 1.5 million; five years from now it will be 2.5 million. The future of these young people and the Nation rests in large part on their access to college and graduate education. For this country reserves its highest honors for only one kind of aristocracy—that which the Founding Fathers called "an aristocracy of achievement arising out of a democracy of opportunity."[21]

Kennedy's efforts to enlist federal assistance for higher education could draw upon a large body of precedents. The Morrill Acts of 1862 and 1890 had granted land to establish agricultural and mechanical colleges. During the depression of the 1930s, universities had benefited from New Deal programs such as the Works Progress Administration, the National Youth Administration, and the Civilian Conservation Corps. During World War II, they had participated in

[20] John F. Kennedy, *Message from the President of the United States Relative to an Educational Program* (H.R. Document No. 330, Feb. 6, 1962), p. 5.

[21] John F. Kennedy, *Message from the President of the United States Relative to a Proposed Program for Education* (H.R. Document No. 54, Jan. 29, 1963), p. 5.

the Engineering, Science, and Management War Training program. The Servicemen's Readjustment Act, or GI Bill, passed in 1944, had provided higher education for 7,800,000 returning veterans at a cost of $14.5 billion.[22]

Drawing upon the precedents of earlier aid to higher education, President Kennedy's request in 1963 urged both the quantitative and qualitative improvement of education. The phrase "a democracy of opportunity" demonstrated his desire to make higher learning available to more students as the Morrill Act had done almost a hundred years earlier. The term "an aristocracy of achievement" reflected a determination to maintain the quality of American higher education. Under President Kennedy's auspices, the National Education Improvement Act of 1963, an omnibus bill, was introduced to provide general aid to education. The Act sought to extend NDEA student loans, liberalize the repayment plan, and increase graduate fellowships. It proposed loans to public and private nonprofit institutions to construct facilities, build or expand libraries, and develop centers to improve instruction in modern foreign languages. Although it was not passed in its entirety, several sections of the National Education Improvement Act were enacted separately. For example, The Higher Education Facilities Act of 1963 granted funds to construct academic facilities in colleges and universities. The Higher Education Act of 1965, enacted during President Lyndon Johnson's administration, authorized federal money for: community service and continuing education programs; college library assistance, training, and research; programs for improving the academic quality of developing colleges; aid to qualified but financially needy high school graduates.

The federal programs for higher education were based on broad social, political, and economic needs. The international tensions produced by the Cold War contributed to a realization that scientific research was related to the national interest and to the military potential of the United States. American universities provided experts who established educational programs in developing nations. Scholarly research contributed to economic expansion, achievements in medicine, and improved social conditions. Certain federal assistance programs to higher education, such as the educational opportunity grants, formed part of Johnson's "war on poverty" program.

Although Kennedy encouraged general aid-to-education legislation, it was not enacted until 1965, when President Johnson proposed aid to elementary, secondary, and higher education, both public and private. The passage of the Johnson legislation revealed a change in congressional attitudes to school assistance. In the past, Congress had been inclined to enact specific programs rather than general aid legis-

[22] Sidney W. Tiedt, *The Role of the Federal Government in Education* (New York: Oxford University Press, 1966), p. 25.

lation. The more successful bills were those designed to improve specific instruction, such as vocational education under the Smith-Hughes Law or mathematics and science under the National Defense Education Act. Representing the first general aid legislation approved for elementary and secondary schools, the Elementary and Secondary Education Act of 1965 was designed to assist in school construction and develop special programs for educationally deprived children. The Act supported a five-year program to make books and printed materials available to school children. Title III of the Act provided for the establishment of model schools, pilot programs, and community centers to aid local school efforts in providing adult education, guidance and counseling, remedial instruction, special services, improved academic programs, and health programs. The Act stressed the improvement of educational research, dissemination of information to teachers and teacher-training institutions, and establishment of regional educational laboratories.

In the 1960s, the federal government financed educational research and development on a scale unprecedented in American history. The long debate between proponents and opponents of federal aid to education subsided. The Act of 1965 indicated that Congress had determined to assist American education. Presidential addresses and congressional legislation demonstrated federal concern for the quantity and quality of American education. Federal legislation had shifted from specific aid or emergency programs to general aid to all levels of education.

Black Education

After the post-Civil War Reconstruction period ended in 1877, the leading Negro spokesman was an Alabama educator, Booker T. Washington (1856–1915), president of Tuskegee Institute. Concerned with educating Negroes in the vocations and trades, Washington urged them to avoid politics. In the 1880s and 1890s, a concerted effort was made to disenfranchise blacks and exclude them from participating in Southern politics. Urging caution and patience, Washington advised Negroes to avoid moving too quickly into professional and political life. The Negro, Washington advised, needed to establish a solid economic base as a skilled worker and craftsman.

Washington worked energetically to make Tuskegee Institute into a respected educational institution and sought to promote amicable relations between whites and blacks in the South. His autobiography, *Up from Slavery* (1901), recounted his career and the difficult early history of Tuskegee.[23]

[23] Booker T. Washington, *Up from Slavery* (New York: Doubleday, 1938).

Washington's social theory was revealed by the address he delivered at the Atlanta Cotton States Exposition in 1895, where he urged blacks to cultivate friendly relations with Southern whites. He regretted that some blacks believed that political participation was more important than owning property or acquiring skills and recommended that blacks seek advancement through agriculture, mechanics, commerce, and domestic service. Washington further believed that blacks should stay in the South and work out their destiny in cooperation with the white community:

> As we have proved our loyalty to you in the past, in nursing your children, watching by the sick bed of your mothers and fathers, and often following them with tear-dimmed eyes to their graves, as in the future, in our humble way, we shall stand by you with a devotion that no foreigner can approach, ready to lay down our lives, if need be, in defense of yours, interlacing our industrial, commercial, civil, and religious lives with yours in a way that shall make the interests of both races one. In all things that are purely social we can be as separate as the fingers yet one as the hand in all things essential to mutual progress.[24]

Washington regarded industrial and academic training as complementary subjects and manual work as a source of uplifting moral power. Tuskegee's educational program therefore stressed the dignity of labor and the vocational crafts and trades. Washington's educational theory resembled that of Pestalozzi, who had also tried to combine useful work and practical skills with academic subjects. Moreover, both Washington and Pestalozzi preferred the practical to the academic.

In assessing the influence of Booker T. Washington on racial relations, it must be remembered that he labored at a time when few white or Northern voices would have aided him, should he have worked for racial equality. Washington's attitude was an uneasy compromise that permitted the Negro a breathing space on the way "up from slavery."

During the 1950s and 1960s, when strong efforts were being made to achieve political, social, and economic equality for blacks, Booker T. Washington was discredited among activists. Perhaps, however, a reinterpretation of Washington's social, political, economic, and educational ideas is needed. In some ways, he anticipated black capitalism by urging that blacks create a solid economic base.

Although the ideas Washington advanced in his Atlanta speech may have been accepted by some, the noted historian W. E. B. Du Bois (1868–1963) became a leading critic of Washington's rationale for black social progress. Du Bois found Washington's position to be paradoxical:

[24] Booker T. Washington, *Selected Speeches of Booker T. Washington* (New York: Doubleday, Doran, 1932), p. 34.

. . . is it possible, and probable, that nine millions of men can make effective progress in economic lines if they are deprived of political rights, made a servile caste, and allowed only the most meagre chance for developing their exceptional men? If history and reason give any distinct answer to these questions, it is an emphatic NO.[25]

Du Bois said that Washington was trying to make Negro artisans into businessmen and property owners, but that he neglected to defend their right to exercise political power. Further, Du Bois accused Washington of counseling "a silent submission to civic inferiority such as is bound to sap the manhood of any race in the long run." Du Bois became one of the leaders in the Niagara movement, which was organized in 1905 to advance racial equality, freedom of speech, abolition of racial distinctions, and equal educational opportunity.

A number of violent race riots occurred in the United States in the early twentieth century. From 1880 through 1920, more than 3,000 lynchings occurred, of which 70 percent of the victims were black. In 1910, the National Association for the Advancement of Colored People was organized under the leadership of Moorfield Storey, a constitutional lawyer, and Du Bois. The NAACP rejected submissiveness and advocated: (1) strict enforcement of the civil rights provisions of the Fourteenth Amendment; (2) equal educational opportunities for all people in all states and a public school expenditure that was equal for black and white children; and (3) the right of the blacks to vote on the same basis as other citizens, as provided by the Fifteenth Amendment.

The NAACP advanced the arguments for racial equality through the courts. Under the leadership of, first, Storey, and then Thurgood Marshall, legal arguments were made against segregation. The Supreme Court declared in *Brown* v. *the Board of Education of Topeka*, in 1954, that racial segregation in schools was unconstitutional. This decision overturned the *Plessy* v. *Ferguson* decision of 1896 that had upheld the legality of separate schools for white and Negro children as a legitimate exercise of states' rights. In rendering the decision of the Court in the Brown case, Chief Justice Warren stated:

Segregation of white and colored children in public schools has a detrimental effect upon the colored children. The impact is greater when it has the sanction of the law; for the policy of separating the races is usually interpreted as denoting the inferiority of the Negro group. A sense of inferiority affects the motivation of a child to learn. Segregation with the sanction of law, therefore, has a tendency to retard the education and mental development of Negro children and to deprive them of some of the benefits they would receive in a racially integrated school system.[26]

25 W. E. Burghardt Du Bois, *The Souls of Black Folks: Essays and Sketches* (Chicago: A. C. McClurg, 1903), pp. 51–52.
26 *Brown* v. *the Board of Education of Topeka,* 347 U.S. 483 (1954).

The Southern states tried to evade the Court's decision. In 1957, after Governor Faubus of Arkansas tried to block integration of the Little Rock schools, President Eisenhower issued an executive order authorizing the use of federal troops to integrate them. In 1962, Governor Barnett of Mississippi attempted to halt the enrollment of James Meredith, a Negro, in the University of Mississippi. Governor Barnett claimed to base his act of interposition on the Tenth Amendment of the Constitution, alleging that the interests of order and safety required him to "interpose and invoke the police powers of the state." President Kennedy ordered federal troops to end the violence in Oxford, Mississippi, and secure Meredith's admission.

At first, observers believed that the decision affected only de jure segregation, that is, a separation of the races enforced by law, as in the Southern states prior to 1954. In contrast, de facto segregation refers to racial separation, whether accidental or deliberate, that exists without legal sanction, as is seen in the residential patterns of many large Northern cities.

After the initial struggles for integration in the public schools of the South had occurred, the movement for integrated education was extended to the large Northern cities, such as Chicago, New York, Philadelphia, and Los Angeles, that had experienced a tremendous growth of black population. In these urban centers, the integration of blacks was complicated by socioeconomic as well as racial factors. Because of racial prejudice and the consequent lack of opportunity for education and social mobility, the blacks suffered economically and were often confined to lower-class status.

The large Northern city was a complex of residential areas, most of which were populated by people of similar economic, ethnic, and often racial backgrounds. Because of inherited residential patterns and increased racial tensions, some areas were either all black or all white, and genuinely integrated residential sections were rare. The Negro population was confined to the center city, where dwellings were deteriorating. As the black ghetto grew, the white population moved out of the center to the fringes of the city or to suburban areas. Examples of this racial movement occurred in Chicago, New York, and Los Angeles.

The school had been the center of racial segregation in the South. As a result of the Court's decision, it became the focal point of the movement for racial equality. Civil rights leaders saw education as a means of social, political, and economic mobility and as an instrument for creating an integrated community. The notion that the public school could continue to serve as an integrating agency was complicated, however, by the fact that schools are usually located in the residential area of the children who attend them. Therefore, since there were very few genuinely integrated neighborhoods in the large Northern communities, neighborhood school enrollment tended to be either all white or all black. Civil rights leaders attacked this arrangement as de facto segregation and urged that it be remedied.

In the 1960s, large-scale protests occurred against this Northern de facto segregation. Some civil rights groups turned to more direct action, such as nonviolent demonstrations and school boycotts. The civil rights groups urged the creation of genuinely integrated schools, charging that the quality of education in inner-city areas was inferior to that of other areas because of financial and teacher shortages. Some suggested busing students from one attendance area to another. Others recommended remapping school districts to embrace both black and white residential areas.

The problem of achieving genuine racial integration and equality of educational opportunity was a complex one. Irrational and emotional groups urged nondemocratic solutions to the problem. The Ku Klux Klan, the White Citizens' Council, and black nationalists advocated segregation. Other groups, such as the Southern Christian Leadership Conference, the National Association for the Advancement of Colored People, and the Urban League, regarded school integration as part of a much larger problem involving economic, social, and political integration.

Educators of the 1950s and 1960s coined a new term, the "culturally disadvantaged." In 1964, the Johnson administration launched a "war on poverty" to eradicate the economic blight and cultural disadvantagement resulting from poverty. Although blacks have often been victims, this problem was not solely a racial one. Unemployment of undereducated and immobile whites was a problem in certain rural areas. Poverty was particularly acute in Appalachia and in the urban slums populated by Negroes, Puerto Ricans, and other minority groups. Although the education of the culturally disadvantaged had long been neglected, the federal government and local communities launched concerted programs to improve their educational possibilities. Retraining programs sought to train adults in employable skills. With a growing insight into the psychological and educational effects of cultural deprivation, educators prepared new instructional materials and methods for disadvantaged children. New teacher education programs were introduced to prepare teachers to cope with the challenge of the inner-city school. An important phase of the "war on poverty" was the fostering of favorable predispositions to school. In particular, the federally financed "Project Head Start" offered preschool experiences for the culturally deprived youngster that would be conducive to later schooling.

Conclusion

American education was elaborated and extended during the twentieth century. The rise of the high school and the extension of colleges and universities throughout the country attested to a general quantitative expansion of educational facilities. At mid-century, however, a growing uneasiness developed among professional educators and the public. It was discovered that the common school concept of Mann, Barnard, and others was still a distant dream for vast numbers of disadvantaged whites and blacks. The most unsettling phenomenon was the fact that as the United States had become an urban nation, its cities had developed with little or no planning. The warnings of ecologists and sociologists had been ignored. The rapid rise of the city had by the 1960s caused its rapid decay. The plight of urban society was also the plight of urban education. Decaying ghettos had decaying schools.

Throughout the 1960s, what sociologists called the generation gap seemed to grow more acute. College students in particular grew more restive, and many resorted to demonstrations that often became violent. There was much debate waged about the need to commit universities to specific social action programs and about the dangers of politicizing institutions of higher learning. Clearly, what Francis Keppel has referred to as the "qualitative revolution" was not going to be an easy one. It was a revolution that went to the very heart of both American life and education.

Suggested Readings

Allen, Hollis P. *The Federal Government and Education.* New York: McGraw-Hill, 1950.

Anderson, Robert H. *Teaching in a World of Change.* New York: Harcourt, Brace, 1966.

Axt, Richard G. *The Federal Government and Financing Higher Education.* New York: Columbia University Press, 1952.

Babbidge, Homer D., and Robert M. Rosenzweig. *The Federal Interest in Higher Education.* New York: Columbia University Press, 1962.

Beggs, Walter K. *The Education of Teachers.* New York: Center for Applied Research in Education, 1965.

Bestor, Arthur E. *Educational Wastelands.* Urbana: University of Illinois Press, 1953.

Bowers, C. A. *The Progressive Educator and the Depression: The Radical Years.* New York: Random House, 1969.

Brown, Hugh S., and Lewis B. Mayhew. *American Higher Education.* New York: Center for Applied Research in Education, 1965.

Brickman, William F., and Stanley Lehrer (eds.). *A Century of Higher Edu-*

cation: Classical Citadel to Collegiate Colossus. New York: Society for the Advancement of Education, 1962.

Brubacher, John S., and Rudy Willis. Higher Education in Transition: An American History: 1636–1956. New York: Harper, 1958.

Brunner, Henry S. Land-Grant Colleges and Universities, 1862–1962. Washington, D.C.: Government Printing Office, 1962.

Bullock, Henry A. A History of Negro Education in the South. Cambridge, Mass.: Harvard University Press, 1967.

Butts, R. Freeman. The College Charts Its Course: Historical Conceptions and Current Proposals. New York: McGraw-Hill, 1939.

Clift, Virgil A., Archibald Anderson, H. Gordon Hullfish (eds.). Negro Education in America. New York: Harper, 1962.

Commission on Reorganization of Secondary Education. Cardinal Principles of Secondary Education. Bulletin No. 35. Washington, D.C.: U.S. Bureau of Education, 1918.

Conant, James B. Slums and Suburbs. New York: McGraw-Hill, 1961.

————. The American High School Today. New York: McGraw-Hill, 1959.

————. The Education of American Teachers. New York: McGraw-Hill, 1963.

————. The Revolutionary Transformation of the American High School. Cambridge, Mass.: Harvard University Press, 1959.

Counts, George S. Dare the School Build a New Social Order? New York: John Day, 1932.

————. Secondary Education and Industrialism. Cambridge, Mass.: Harvard University Press, 1929.

————. The Selective Character of American Secondary Education. Chicago: University of Chicago Press, 1922.

————. The Social Foundations of Education. New York: Scribner, 1934.

Cremin, Lawrence A. The Transformation of the School. New York: Knopf, 1962.

Danforth, Eddy, Jr. College for Our Land and Time: The Land Grant Idea in American Education. New York: Harper, 1956.

Davis, Calvin O. A History of the North Central Association of Colleges and Secondary Schools. Ann Arbor, Mich.: The North Central Association of Colleges and Secondary Schools, 1945.

Dewey, John. Democracy and Education. New York: Macmillan, 1964.

————. Experience and Education. New York: Macmillan, 1938.

Du Bois, W. E. Burghardt. The Souls of Black Folks: Essays and Sketches. Chicago: McClurg, 1903.

Edwards, Newton, and Herman G. Richey. The School in the American Social Order. Boston: Houghton Mifflin, 1963.

Flexner, Abraham. Universities: American English German. New York: Oxford University Press, 1968.

French, William M. American Secondary Education. New York: Odyssey Press, 1957.

Fretwell, Elbert K., Jr. Founding Public Junior Colleges. New York: Bureau of Publications, Teachers College, Columbia University, 1954.

Gross, Ronald, and Judith Murphy (eds.). The Revolution in the Schools. New York: Harcourt, Brace, 1964.

Gutek, Gerald L. The Educational Theory of George S. Counts. Columbus: University of Ohio Press, 1970.

Hofstadter, Richard, and C. DeWitt Hardy. The Development and Scope of Higher Education in the United States. New York: Columbia University Press, 1952.

Keppel, Francis. *The Necessary Revolution in American Education.* New York: Harper & Row, 1966.

Kerr, Clark. *The Uses of the University.* Cambridge, Mass.: Harvard University Press, 1963.

Kilpatrick, William H. *Education and the Social Crisis.* New York: Liveright, 1932.

———. "The Project Method," *Teachers College Record,* 19, No. 4 (September 1918), 319–335.

Kimball, Solon T., and James E. McClellan, Jr. *Education and the New America.* New York: Random House, 1966.

Krug, Edward A. *The Shaping of the American High School.* New York: Harper & Row, 1964.

Mayhew, K. C., and A. C. Edwards. *The Dewey School.* New York: Atherton, 1965.

McConnell, T. R. *A General Pattern for American Public Higher Education.* New York: McGraw-Hill, 1962.

Medsker, Leland L. *The Junior College: Progress and Prospect.* New York: McGraw-Hill, 1960.

Meyer, Adolphe E. *The Development of Education in the Twentieth Century.* Englewood Cliffs, N.J.: Prentice-Hall, 1949.

Muscatine, Charles, *et al. Education at Berkeley: Report of the Select Committee on Education.* Berkeley: University of California Printing Department, 1966.

National Commission on Teacher Education and Professional Standards. *Changes in Teacher Education: An Appraisal.* Washington: National Education Association, 1964.

National Education Association. *Report of the Committee of Ten on Secondary School Studies.* New York: American Book Co., 1894.

Nevins, Allan. *The State Universities and Democracy.* Urbana: University of Illinois Press, 1962.

O'Hara, William T. (ed.). *John F. Kennedy on Education.* New York: Teachers College Press, Columbia University, 1966.

Rafferty, Max. *What They Are Doing to Your Children.* New York: New American Library, 1963.

Rickover, H. G. *Education and Freedom.* New York: Dutton, 1959.

Ross, Earle D. *Democracy's College: The Land Grant Movement in the Formative Stage.* Ames: Iowa State College Press, 1942.

Rudolph, Frederick. *The American College and University: A History.* New York: Knopf, 1962.

Sizer, Theodore R. *The Age of the Academies.* New York: Bureau of Publications, Teachers College, Columbia University, 1964.

Smith, Elmer R. (ed.). *Teacher Education: A Reappraisal: Report of a Conference Sponsored by the Fund for the Advancement of Education.* New York: Harper & Row, 1962.

Tewksbury, Donald G. *The Founding of American Colleges and Universities Before the Civil War.* New York: Bureau of Publications, Teachers College, Columbia University, 1932.

Thornton, James W. *The Community Junior College.* New York: Wiley, 1966.

Tiedt, Sidney W. *The Role of the Federal Government in Education.* New York: Oxford University Press, 1966.

Washington, Booker T. *The Future of the American Negro.* Boston: Small Maynard, 1900.

———. *Working with the Hands.* New York: Doubleday, Page, 1904.

Washington, E. Davidson (ed.). *Selected Speeches of Booker T. Washington*. New York: Doubleday, Doran, 1932.

Welter, Rush. *Popular Education and Democratic Thought in America*. New York: Columbia University Press, 1962.

Wirth, Arthur G. *John Dewey as Educator: His Design for Work in Education* (1894–1904). New York: Wiley, 1966.

CHAPTER 24

Twentieth-Century Educational Trends

Of all the chapters in a book of history, the last is the most difficult to write. Although the historian may believe that he has discovered discernible trends in the past, the tendencies of his own age often escape him. Trapped in the immediacies of the present, he often lacks the psychic distance that is so necessary in establishing a perspective into the human situation. Often the issues that seem so relevant on the surface lose their importance over time. This is not to suggest that the writing of educational history, or any other kind of historical work, can ever be completely detached from contemporary concerns. The historian's views of relevance, importance, and meaning are always conditioned by his present situation and conditions. Nevertheless, it seems that he best performs his professional function when he interprets past events for his own generation. Each generation is part of a historical continuum. Yet, though it shares this common human experience linking it to the past, each generation is unique and must therefore reinterpret and reappropriate its heritage. The preceding chapters were intended to identify the major historical trends and personalities that shaped the Western educational experience. Since each chapter has its own conclusion, this last one will not restate those conclusions but rather identify certain contemporary trends that are significant to education.

Although contemporary developments in education are most properly the concerns of the educational philosopher and sociologist, several trends in present-day education that are of particular interest to the educational historian will be discussed briefly. The thrust of modernization, the problems of the generation gap and student unrest, and the changing criteria of educational authority are three that are of significance for education.

Modernization

In *The Dynamics of Modernization,* C. E. Black has used comparative history to analyze the modernizing process in what are considered
to be the "advanced" nations. Social scientists have defined modernization in various ways. Black describes it as

> the process by which historically evolved institutions are adapted to
> the rapidly changing functions that reflect the unprecedented in-
> crease in man's knowledge, permitting control over his environment,
> that accompanied the scientific revolution.[1]

The modernization process originated in Europe in the scientific
and industrial revolutions of the eighteenth and nineteenth centuries.
Modernization manifests itself by such observable factors as the development of a technological society, a trend toward urbanization, an
industrial rather than an agricultural economy, an extension of literacy, a rise of mass communications systems, and the development
of scientific, managerial, and technological elites. It is dependent upon
mass production and mass consumption. The modernizing process also
profoundly affects the culture and mode of life in a society and erodes
many of its traditional values. The conflicts between modernity and
tradition frequently produce social, political, intellectual, and ethical
tensions.[2] The new leadership groups displace older ruling classes. For
example, the Industrial Revolution created a strong middle class that
eventually replaced the older landed aristocracy as a ruling group.

During the nineteenth and early twentieth centuries, the Western
colonial powers introduced features of modernization into their Asian
and African colonies, and as they have gained their independence
since World War II, these emergent Asian and African nations, as well
as those of Latin America, have sought further modernization. Their
governments and modernizing elites have become aware, however, of
the need to distinguish between Westernization and modernization.
After having experienced the exploitation of a colonial past, these nations prefer to modernize according to their own cultural design.

Modernization does not, of course, occur in a cultural vacuum. To
be viable, it should be adapted to reflect the particular cultural heritage
and conditions of the society in which the process occurs. The scientific
and technological forces necessary for modernization can serve a
variety of social, political, and economic purposes. Ideological premises

[1] C. E. Black, *The Dynamics of Modernization: A Study in Comparative History* (New York: Harper & Row, 1966), pp. 6–7.
[2] For an analysis of the educational implications of the rise of technological
society, see Gerald L. Gutek, *The Educational Theory of George S. Counts*
(Columbus: Ohio State University Press, 1970).

and political programs can give direction to the aims, contours, and means of modernization.

Since modernization has profound effects upon human purposes and destiny, the twentieth century has seen the rise of socioeconomic, political, and educational planning. Both governments and private corporations have sought to direct the course of change through social planning. The Soviet Union, for example, has undergone rapid modernization within less than sixty years, by means of various five-year plans that transformed the country from an agricultural to an industrialized nation. Although limited by scarce economic resources, the government of India also inaugurated a series of five-year plans that have sought to secure national modernization. The Western democracies, although they have also relied on planning agencies, have permitted a greater number of social variables to operate than have the totalitarian nations.

The key role played by modern business in using technology to achieve mass production, distribution, and consumption has had international implications. Mass communications and rapid transportation systems have reduced distances and fostered an interchange of peoples and ideas. In many respects, the global systems of commerce and communication are potent agencies of informal education that have brought about social change on a scale that rivals that of formal education.

The educational implications of modernization are of great magnitude. As has been indicated throughout this book, education involves a process of coming to grips with both the cultural heritage and the processes of change. Man is always what he has been, and change always arises from existing conditions. As a means of socializing immature individuals and bringing them into cultural participation, education must use the thought and value systems of the cultural inheritance. If it is to be a relevant and useful instrument, education must both encourage and discipline the human potentiality for change. The very difficult task of educational theory remains that of formulating viable programs that incorporate both tradition and change.[3]

Modernization requires cadres of trained scientists, technicians, engineers, social scientists, and educators. The advance of literacy has accompanied modernization. The requirements of basic literacy, expert skill, and knowledge that accompany modernization have extended formal education so that more individuals have increased educational opportunities. The socioeconomic planning that is so necessary to modernization also has an educational component known as development education. After World War II, international and comparative

[3] For a comparative discussion of tradition and change in education, see Andreas M. Kazamias and Byron G. Massialas, *Tradition and Change in Education* (Englewood Cliffs, N.J.: Prentice-Hall, 1965).

education took on an added dimension as teams of educational experts from the more modern nations were invited to assist in educational planning and development in the less advanced countries.[4] The thrust of modernization is a major phenomenon of the twentieth century that has global significance for both society and education.

The Generation Gap

In the 1960s, there was considerable discussion of the generation gap between the old and the young. In the popular media and some professional circles, it was a simplistic conception used to create stereotypes in which individuals under the age of thirty were depicted as being open to social and political change while members of the older generation were resistant to such change. Although such stereotypes were the products of overgeneralization, most observers agreed that large numbers of articulate young people were questioning, challenging, and rejecting established values. It should be noted, however, that there were individuals over thirty who questioned established cultural and institutional patterns and younger persons who supported the status quo.

Although various theories have been put forth to explain the generation gap, attention might be focused on the effects that technological society has had upon Western conceptions of childhood and adolescence. The Industrial Revolution and the rise of technological civilization reduced the hours of labor needed to produce commodities. As the amount of labor time decreased and surplus wealth accumulated, greater expenditures could be directed to social services and to education. In primitive preindustrial societies, the period of childhood was very short, and the young person entered adult society and occupations upon reaching puberty. In contrast, the years of childhood have been extended in technological societies, which have recognized the time between puberty and adulthood as adolescence, a special period of human development.[5] As indicated in the discussion of modernization, science and technology are intricate instruments that require the expenditure of a great deal of time, effort, and study for their mastery. Modern societies have therefore had to extend the years of

---

[4] The educational aspects of development are treated in Don Adams and Robert M. Bjork, *Education in Developing Areas* (New York: David Mc-Kay, 1969), and C. E. Beeby, *The Quality of Education in Developing Countries* (Cambridge, Mass.: Harvard University Press, 1968).

[5] See chapter 3, "Educational and Social Change," in Carlton E. Beck, Normand R. Bernier, James B. MacDonald, Thomas Walton, and Jack C. Willers, *Education For Relevance: The Schools and Social Change* (Boston: Houghton Mifflin, 1968), pp. 57–77, for a discussion of education in primitive and technological societies.

formal education and create advanced educational institutions to prepare scientists, technicians, engineers, and managerial personnel for
their socioeconomic roles. For a growing number of persons, this extension of formal education has deferred entry into occupations until
they reach their late twenties or early thirties.

In Western and other modern societies, the youth who are engaged
in advanced preparation have formed a special cultural subgroup,
which is characterized by its own modes of speech, dress, behavior,
and values. This group, often the student population, is prone to reject
the cultural patterns and preferences of the older working population
and also those of their own age group who are in unskilled or semi-
skilled labor. In the 1960s, this large group of young people began to
feel the urgency of social problems and demand their immediate
solution.

Student Unrest

In the 1960s, student unrest was evident throughout the world. Student dissent and demonstrations took place in such varied political and
cultural areas as the United States, the western European nations, the
eastern European communist bloc countries, and emergent African
and Asian nations. Although student protests were, on the whole, an
expression of antipathy toward established political, social, and educational institutions, the immediate issues that precipitated them varied.
In Czechoslovakia, the students supported the short-lived Communist
reform government of Alexander Dubcek and its program of increased
personal, political, aesthetic, and educational liberties. It is interesting
to note that the students identified with Czechoslovakia's democratic
heritage from the years between the world wars. In their demonstrations, pictures of such historic democratic leaders as Tomáš Masaryk
and Eduard Beneš were prominently displayed. When Soviet and other
Warsaw-bloc nations intervened to crush the Czechoslovak liberalization in August 1968, the Dubcek government was deposed and the
student movement forced to go underground.

In France and Germany, radical factions of militant students took
to the streets on several occasions in an attempt to initiate a social
revolution, but the protest movements generally failed to receive popular support. In 1967, some French students attempted unsuccessfully
to bring down the Gaullist government. The radical western European
student movements were often associated with a vague strain of revolutionary anarchism that tended to alienate workers and others who
might have sympathized with students in the past.

In China, the government of Mao Tse-tung used students as instruments in what was labeled the "Great Proletarian Cultural Revolution."

The students received support from Mao's faction in the Chinese Communist party and from the army. The ostensible purpose of the cultural revolution as announced in the *Liberation Army Daily* of April 18, 1966, was to: (1) create new socialist and proletarian works and models; (2) emancipate the mind by overcoming superstitions; (3) encourage revolutionary, militant, and mass criticism of literature and art; and (4) use Mao Tse-tung's ideology to reeducate writers and artists.[6] The real purpose, however, was to eliminate Mao's political rivals and destroy the residues of custom and tradition that persisted after the Communist seizure of power in 1949.

In its early stages, the Maoist supporters encouraged the Hung Wei Ping, or Red Guards, an organization of adolescents ranging in age from twelve to eighteen, to effect the proposed cultural revolution. In 1966, the number of Red Guards was reported to be eleven million.[7] These militant students carried with them *Quotations from Chairman Mao*, a digest of the Chinese leader's thoughts, which was to inspire them as they reeducated Chinese adults. It is interesting to observe that the Chinese youth movement was quite different from that of other nations. While most European and American student movements generally opposed the political establishment, the Chinese Red Guards acted as an arm of the established Maoist faction in harassing political opponents within the Communist party and government apparatus. Once the Red Guards had served the political purposes of the Maoist regime, the movement fell into disfavor and was discarded.

The motivations of protesting university students in India were different from those of their Chinese or Western counterparts. Underlying student discontent was the massive unemployment that extended even to technicians and engineers. Higher education, which was patterned after the English model, had been the avenue to success in India. The educational system was excessively theoretical, abstract, and verbal and was directed to the passing of examinations. The major objective of the Indian student movement was to seek the expansion of higher educational facilities so that more places might be available within the colleges and universities. There was also a reaction against the external examination system. Indian students often became involved in the political controversy between those who advocated Hindi as a national language and the language of university instruction and those who advocated the continued use of English and regional languages.

A striking change occurred in the attitudes of college students in the United States between the decade of the 1950s and that of the 1960s. In the 1950s, the atmosphere at most American colleges and universities was decidedly nonactivist and nonpolitical. While some students

[6] Chiu-sam Tsang, *Society, Schools and Progress in China* (Oxford, England: Pergamon Press, 1968), p. 239.
[7] *Ibid.*, pp. 242–243.

participated in traditional American political movements such as the Young Republicans and Young Democrats, political activity was a minor part of university life and occurred within established procedures. Although the alleged antisubversive investigations of Senator Joseph McCarthy was one factor that tended to reduce political activism on American university campuses in the 1950s, probably the most important influence was the students' general attitude. After World War II, the American university was attended by large numbers of former servicemen who were older than the typical college student and often married. These former servicemen, subsidized by the GI Bill, were strongly oriented toward definite career goals and determined to receive their degrees as quickly as possible. The industry of the wartime veterans helped to create a mood that encouraged the diligent, though often narrow, pursuit of serious study.

In the 1960s, the mood changed, and students became politically active, voicing their criticisms of established American institutions and processes. Originally, much student activism was directed to the support of the civil rights movement. By the mid-1960s, the focus of student protest centered on the continued American involvement in the Vietnamese war. Political activists organized a movement in support of the unsuccessful presidential campaign of Senator Eugene McCarthy in 1968. When four students were killed by National Guard troops in the aftermath of a student demonstration at Kent State University in Ohio, a large-scale student protest developed, which resulted in a major student strike in the spring of 1970.

Student activism in the United States has produced a number of militant organizations such as the Students for a Democratic Society (SDS), a small group that has demanded radical social, economic, political, and educational changes. Blacks attending American colleges and universities have demanded an increase in the number of black students admitted to higher education and the creation of black studies, or African-American cultural studies, as a part of the curriculum.

The student activism of the late 1960s produced a crisis in American higher education. Unlike some of their European, Asian, and Latin-American counterparts, colleges and universities in the United States have sought to maintain a certain distance from direct involvement in political action, claiming that scholarly research and scientific investigation proceed more objectively and efficiently in an open environment that is free from particular political, ideological, or programmatic commitments. Those who argue for the maintenance of this objectivity assert that colleges and universities are delicate institutions that can perform their social and intellectual functions only within an environment that permits a variety of interests, pursuits, and investigations. They contend that the binding of the university to particular political programs and platforms can destroy academic freedom and ultimately the university. In contrast, those who want colleges and universities to become more politically and socially committed assert that they cannot be genuinely objective institutions and that claims to objectivity are, in reality, rationalizations for the perpetuation of the status quo. By failing to identify with and encourage specific action programs, these critics charge, American colleges and universities have grown increasingly irrelevant as educational institutions.

Authority in Education

Since the time of Plato's *Republic,* both educational theories and concrete educational systems have dealt with the issue of appropriateness in education. Plato, for example, discussed the patricular kind of education that was appropriate to a class society divided into philosopher kings, military defenders, and the working masses. In the early United States, the usually democratically inclined Thomas Jefferson spoke of an education appropriate to an aristocracy of intellect. Authoritarian churches, institutions, and states have also developed educational schemes in which schools offer education based on appropriateness to particular groups or classes. Conceptions of education resting on doctrines of appropriateness are usually based on a hierarchical organization of society in which socioeconomic and political authority is also hierarchically arranged. In the nineteenth century, the rise of the concept of equality of educational opportunity associated with the common school in the United States and the social welfare state in Europe introduced the mass systems of relatively uniform education. Although equality of educational opportunity was in many instances more of a political slogan than a pedagogical reality, the concept of a uniform system of relatively equal education attracted popular support, especially among those who would benefit from the socioeconomic mobility that it promised and often actually produced.

While Plato, Jefferson, and other educational theorists were able to state the questions of appropriateness and equality of education in relatively clear terms, the rise of modern technological society has complicated the issue. Dependent for its operations on mass production and consumption, mass industrialized society requires skilled scientific, technological, and managerial elites. Since these elites perform highly specialized roles, their formal education reflects this specialization. Even Soviet education, which publicly asserts the dogma of working-class equality, educates these technological elites in specialized institutions. As the process of modernization and industrialization becomes increasingly global, the older theological or hereditary elites are likely to be displaced in Asia and Africa.

In formal education, in particular, the conflict between those who conceive of the school as being selective and those who see it as a comprehensive social agency remains a crucial issue. In fact, many educators continually try to effect an uneasy compromise in which the school serves both selective and comprehensive purposes. The arguments for the maintenance of the comprehensive high school in the United States and the attacks on streaming in Engish education are only two instances where the issue of appropriateness and equality of education come to focus in the school situation. The rise of the twentieth-century technological elites, however, has had consequences for general education that transcend the immediate questions of comprehensive schools, streaming, and grouping. General education has been defined in various ways, but Broudy's definition of it as "that education which presumably every man *as man* should have" has become increasingly relevant.[8]

Since the rise of the national school system in the late eighteenth and early nineteenth centuries, nation-states have conceived of general education as designed to instill a sense of national identification in the individual. Curricula designed for this purpose have usually consisted of the study of the language, literature, history, government, and traditions of the particular nation.

In the English and American laissez-faire liberal tradition of the early nineteenth century, freedom from government intervention was recognized as an important prerequisite of individual liberty. This tradition originated as a middle-class reaction against the absolutist state or church and against the divine-right-of-kings theory of political authority. The welfare-state conception of modern liberalism and socialism asserted the state's obligation to protect the rights and opportunities of all individuals, especially members of oppressed groups. In the nineteenth century, the working classes benefited most from the extension of government into social, economic, and educational affairs. In the twentieth century, government intervention has benefited minority groups, such as Negroes in the United States and untouchables in India. Nash has pointed out that in complex societies individual freedom becomes increasingly dependent on the state's willingness to intervene to establish the social, economic, educational, and cultural conditions that contribute to the full development of the citizen.[9]

In contrast to the laissez-faire state, some nation-states, as history has recorded, have initiated police state systems of thought control in an attempt to exercise complete control over the lives of their citizens.

[8] Harry S. Broudy, *Building a Philosophy of Education* (Englewood Cliffs, N.J.: Prentice-Hall, 1962), p. 292.
[9] Paul Nash, *Authority and Freedom in Education* (New York: Wiley, 1966), p. 67. Nash's book is particularly recommended as a philosophical discussion of the question of the legitimacy of authority in education.

Ancient Sparta was an example. Napoleonic France was an early prototype of the modern state that has sought to enact literary and educational censorship and control. The secret police of czarist Russia harassed intellectuals in the nineteenth century, and repressive Soviet regimes have sought to exercise thought control in the twentieth century. Perhaps the most infamous exercise in totalitarian repression was that of Nazi Germany, which sought to crush intellectual, artistic, and academic freedom in the 1930s and 1940s. In writing about the state and academic freedom, Nash states:

> Man needs to be able to enjoy complete freedom of thought on all subjects, no matter how heretical, embarrassing, unfashionable, or dangerous; he needs to be free to publish his ideas without fear of persecution from government or vested interests. The State must work both to protect him from such threats to his freedom and to create an atmosphere in which his intellect will thrive.[10]

While the curriculum of general education has sought to build an identification with the nation-state, there are educators who minimize cultural differences among men. Asserting that the powers of human reason transcend climatic variations, national boundaries, and geographic and linguistic barriers, those who base their conceptions on Aristotelian, Thomistic, and classical realist premises assert that general education is primarily designed to cultivate man's intellectual powers. According to Robert M. Hutchins:

> Education implies teaching. Teaching implies knowledge. Knowledge is truth. The truth is everywhere the same. Hence education should be everywhere the same.[11]

Educators of a pragmatic, experimentalist, and often progressive persuasion have usually rejected both the national and the exclusively intellectual variants of general education. Such individuals as John Dewey and William Heard Kilpatrick emphasized a process-oriented education that conceived learning to be the mastery of the problem-solving technique according to the scientific method. They believed this mode of inquiry to be equally useful to all men. Dewey and Kilpatrick also asserted that scientific inquiry, as a commonly shared, open, and public means of verification, proceeded most humanely and adequately in a democratic environment open to the testing of belief, value, and experience. Although process-oriented education has enjoyed great popularity among American educational theorists, its influence has begun to wane as demands are made for more subjective, aesthetic, and often mystical modes of inquiry.

[10] *Ibid.*, pp. 71–72.
[11] Robert Maynard Hutchins, *The Higher Learning in America* (New Haven, Conn.: Yale University Press, 1962), p. 66.

Recently—especially during the 1960s—educators have shown a renewed interest in subjective and private modes of inquiry. A number of books have appeared on existentialism in education.[12] It is interesting to observe that some of these works were written by former Deweyites who have deserted the view that the scientific method presents an exclusive avenue to truth. In contrast, they have asserted the importance of the individual's own appropriation of knowledge. This has often taken the argument that a greater freedom of choice should be available to the individual student. In some ways, the rejection of Dewey's experimentalism is also a rejection of the significance that he gave to group processes in education.

The demands for greater freedom of choice for the learner have also brought about a renewal of interest in mystical and aesthetic modes of knowing. While this development has focused attention on the arts, poetry, drama, literature, and the film as educational vehicles, it has also raised fears that a new dogmatism based on irrationalism may be coming onto the scene.

Conclusion

The purpose of this concluding chapter was to comment on three of the major trends that are having a significant impact on education. Modernization, the alienation of youth, and the issues raised by changing conceptions of authority are, however, only three of the many developments that are affecting contemporary education. It will be the task of future historians to comment on the significance of such other developments as the impact of the revolution of rising expectations; the emergence of the Asian, African, and Latin-American "third world"; the revolution in educational innovation, methodology, and media; the impact of ecumenism on age-old religious tensions; the women's liberation movement; and the growing awareness of the ecological dimension of life. It is hoped that the preceding pages, which attempted to trace the course of educational history from the ancient Greek and Roman civilizations to present-day technological mass society, will illuminate some of the persistent themes and basic issues that are a part of the Western educational experience.

[12] For examples of existentialist philosophizing about education, see George F. Kneller, *Existentialism and Education* (New York: Wiley, 1966), and Van Cleve Morris, *Existentialism in Education* (New York: Harper & Row, 1966).

Suggested Readings

Adams, Don, and Robert M. Bjork. *Education in Developing Areas.* New York: David McKay, 1969.

Beck, Carlton E., Normand R. Bernier, James B. MacDonald, Thomas Walton, and Jack C. Willers. *Education for Relevance: The Schools and Social Change.* Boston: Houghton Mifflin, 1968.

Beeby, C. E. *The Quality of Education in Developing Countries.* Cambridge, Mass.: Harvard University Press, 1966.

Black, E. E. *The Dynamics of Modernization: A Study in Comparative History.* New York: Harper & Row, 1966.

Broudy, Harry S. *Building a Philosophy of Education.* Englewood Cliffs, N.J.: Prentice-Hall, 1962.

Erikson, Erik H. *Youth: Change and Challenge.* New York: Basic Books, 1961.

Greene, Maxine. *Existential Encounters for Teachers.* New York: Random House, 1967.

Gutek, Gerald. *The Educational Theory of George S. Counts.* Columbus: Ohio State University Press, 1970.

Heilbroner, Robert L. *The Great Ascent: The Struggle for Economic Development in Our Time.* New York: Harper & Row, 1963.

Hutchins, Robert M. *The Higher Learning in America.* New Haven: Yale University Press, 1962.

Katz, Joseph. *The Student Activists: Rights, Needs, and Powers of Undergraduates.* Stanford, Calif.: Institute for the Study of Human Problems, 1967.

Kazamias, Andreas M., and Byron G. Massialas. *Tradition and Change in Education.* Englewood Cliffs, N.J.: Prentice-Hall, 1965.

Keniston, Kenneth. *Young Radicals.* New York: Harcourt, Brace, 1968.

Kennan, George. *Democracy and the Student Left.* Boston: Atlantic–Little, Brown, 1969.

Kneller, George F. *Existentialism and Education.* New York: Wiley, 1966.

Michael, Donald N. *The Next Generation.* New York: Random House, 1963.

Morris, Van Cleve. *Existentialism in Education.* New York: Harper & Row, 1966.

Nash, Paul. *Authority and Freedom in Education.* New York: Wiley, 1966.

Tsang, Chiu-Sam. *Society, Schools and Progress in China.* Oxford, England: Pergamon Press, 1968.

Index

ABOUT THE AUTHOR

Gerald Lee Gutek, Professor of Educational Leadership and Policy Studies, as well as Professor of History at Loyola University, Chicago, received his B.A., M.A., and Ph.D. from the University of Illinois. He has since served as Chairperson of the Department of Foundations of Education and as Dean of the School of Education at Loyola. Dr. Gutek writes in the areas of the history of education, the philosophy of education, and comparative education.